INTELLECTUAL MANHOOD

INTELLECTUAL MANHOOD

University, Self, and Society in
the Antebellum South

TIMOTHY J. WILLIAMS

The University of North Carolina Press
Chapel Hill

Cover illustration: Marshals, 1855. North Carolina Collection
Photographic Archives, The Wilson Library,
University of North Carolina at Chapel Hill

Complete cataloging information can be obtained at the
Library of Congress Catalog website.

ISBN 978-1-4696-1839-5 (pbk.: alk. paper)

ISBN 978-1-4696-1840-1 (ebook)

In loving memory of my parents,
Harold E. Williams Jr.
and
Evelyn N. Williams

Towards the attainment of mental superiority
during your collegiate course, you have made some
advance. Other, and still greater advances remain hereafter
to be made. You may now be youth of promise; but you must
long, and diligently trim the midnight lamp, before you will
arrive to the stature of intellectual manhood.
—Eliphalet Nott, president of Union College, 1814

Towards the attainment of mental superiority during our
collegiate course we have made some advance. Other and still
great advances remain hereafter to be done. We may now be
youth of promise, but we must long exercise the most indefatigable
industry before we arrive at intellectual manhood.
—Charles Wilson Harris Alexander,
University of North Carolina student, 1827

Contents

Figures

Acknowledgments

I first discovered the richness of antebellum collegians' intellectual world in several big, dusty volumes of literary society minute books in the Z. Smith Reynold's Library at Wake Forest University. As an undergraduate history major, I had no idea that these sources, and hundreds more just like them, would become the focus of my early career. But they did, and I must first thank the scholars at Wake Forest University who shaped my own pursuit of "intellectual manhood," especially Simone Caron, Susan Z. Rupp, Robert Beachy, and William S. Hamilton. At the University of North Carolina, many scholars provided invaluable support. I cannot imagine a greater mentor than Harry L. Watson, who not only helped me shape, ground, and complete this book, but also provided steady encouragement during many of the most difficult moments of my life. Donald Mathews, John Kasson, James Leloudis, Heather Williams, Kathleen DuVal, Jacquelyn Hall, Mike Green, and Theda Perdue also helped me imagine this book's possibilities and offered invaluable comments at critical junctures. Alfred Brophy of UNC's School of Law provided insight into antebellum literary addresses, sent copies of addresses, and read several chapter drafts. Finally, Erika Lindemann offered tremendous guidance and support. Her years of work on antebellum student writing, which are abundantly manifest in two rich collections in *Documenting the American South*, have been invaluable. I owe her thanks for source references, research tips, interpretations, and deep insight into James Dusenbery and his family. All of what we know about Dusenbery comes from her efforts, and *Intellectual Manhood* is richer because of her.

The research and writing of this book was funded in part by the Spencer Foundation, as well as the Institute for Southern Studies at the University of South Carolina. I am also grateful for the support of several other institutions. At the University of North Carolina, grants from the Center for the Study of the American South and History Department provided early research funding. The staff at the Southern Historical Collection—especially Laura Clark Brown and Matthew Turi—offered research leads and made "the Southern" a second home. Clark Tew provided assistance with the

Dialectic Society records. I must also thank the staff at the North Carolina Collection, Special Collections Library at Duke University, North Carolina State Archives, Wake Forest University Archives, and South Caroliniana Library.

As any historian knows, support from within the wider profession is essential. I am grateful to the members of the St. George Tucker Society, who honored me with a rigorous and helpful discussion of this work. I have also benefited significantly from comments and suggestions from many scholars, whose work I greatly admire: Mary Kelley, Jennifer Green, Stephen Berry, Anya Jabour, Lorri Glover, Craig Friend, Wayne Urban, Roger Geiger, and Amy Wells-Dolan. In addition, Peter Carmichael has been a great friend during the entire process of writing this book; he provided helpful feedback, sage professional advice, and meaningful encouragement. I also owe John Mayfield special thanks. He scrupulously read a draft of this book and offered astute comments and ample encouragement that have sustained me through the daunting writing and rewriting process. His many clever phrases and ideas have enhanced this book greatly.

As I prepared this book for publication, I enjoyed support from many other colleagues. Alex Oberle made the map of UNC graduates. At the Institute for Southern Studies I had the honor of working with and learning from Walter Edgar, Mark Smith, David Moltke-Hansen, Bob Ellis, Tara Powell, Mindi Spencer, Madeline Wood, and Evan Kutzler. At Appalachian State University, I received crucial support from Michael Mayfield, Sheryl Mohn, and Sonya Long. I am also grateful to the staff at the University of North Carolina Press, particularly Chuck Grench, Lucas Church, and Paul Betz. The press secured two of the most careful and conscientious readers I could have imagined—Steven Stowe and Nicholas Syrett—whose suggestions for revision undoubtedly strengthened this book; I thank them for their kind and helpful criticisms. Finally, Eric Shramm's careful editing and incisive comments greatly improved the book, and any errors in the following pages are my own.

Because this book has followed me through so many years and so many different places, I must acknowledge my historian friends from UNC and beyond: Elizabeth Smith, Tom Goldstein, Christina Snyder, Patrick O'Neil, Nancy Schoonmaker, David Silkenat, Dwana Waugh, Jacqueline Whitt, Ben Wise, James Broomall, Diana D'Amico, Christina Davis, John Hale, Camille Walsh, Michael Hevel, Julie Mujic, and Kanisorn Wongsrichanalai. Each of these scholars not only helped shape my work but also lightened the load with good conversation and friendship.

I must also thank my family and friends beyond academia: Andrew Williams, Margaret Williams, John and Louise Mundy, J. P. Mundy, Meg McKee, Janice McKee, and Stephanie Pavlis. Their love and support never cease to inspire and humble me. Most of all, I owe infinite thanks to Dean Mundy, whose love, enthusiasm, confidence, humor, and patience have sustained me through the entire process of researching and writing this book. He is also an amazingly gifted scholar and writer. He read every word I have written on this subject, and at every stage of the process tried to convince me that everything would turn out just fine. I cannot imagine having written this book without him.

My parents, Harold and Evelyn Williams, did not live to see this book in print. Just two weeks after I submitted the first draft for review, my mother died; eight months after that, my father died. They both suffered from cancer. In the last week of my father's life, as I was caring for him at our home in Virginia, Dad called me to his bed at three in the morning, agitated with what the hospice nurses called "terminal anxiety." As I prepared his medicine, he softly said, "I'm sorry for interrupting your book." Before remembering that I was in the midst of revising this book for publication, I replied, "What book?" I assured Dad that he did not interrupt a thing, that both he and Mom only made it possible. I am forever grateful for the lifetime of love and encouragement they provided me. From them I inherited the inner strength to finish what I started. I dedicate this book to their memory, with the belief that they know that I did it.

Author's Note

In order not to encumber the reading of this book, I have retained the original spelling in manuscript sources without using [*sic*] except in rare cases where misunderstanding is possible or where editors of published or unpublished transcriptions have included it. Doing so maintains the authenticity of students' intellectual lives and abilities and reminds us that poor spelling has always frustrated professors.

INTELLECTUAL MANHOOD

Introduction

This is a book about the intellectual culture of men's higher education at the University of North Carolina, which opened its doors to students in 1795 before any other public college or university in the United States. This is not, however, an institutional history. Rather, it provides a deep look into intellectual life—into the transmission, reproduction, and consumption of knowledge about self and society—and its role in creating a distinctively bourgeois culture in antebellum North Carolina. Most standard narratives of American higher education depict antebellum southern colleges as crucibles of an elite regional identity, where young men learned to be gentlemen and southerners above all else. Accordingly, historians have painted a fairly bleak picture of intellectual life on southern college campuses. Echoing the oft-repeated sentiments of the great American intellectual Henry Adams— "Strictly, the Southerner had no mind; he had temperament"[1]—these narratives portray southern students not as intellectual agents, but as brash and unthinking rabble-rousers, whose collegiate shenanigans uniquely derived from a ruggedly individualistic and honor-bound southern culture. Even more problematically, some historians have offered these arguments as proof of inevitable sectional conflict and civil war.[2]

Intellectual Manhood challenges these narratives and reveals that students cared about these matters far less than historians have claimed. As agents in their own education, students created a world of intentional intellectualism that favored bourgeois values and both national and regional belonging. Misbehavior may have impeded education at times, but this was not a regional peculiarity. Tensions between mind and temperament, which Henry Adams associated with his southern classmates at Harvard, emanated instead from a much broader process of maturation that occurred among collegians throughout the United States whenever young men attempted to leave boyhood. This intellectual culture did not displace the cultures of gentility and honor commonly associated with the South but mingled with them, shaping students' development as men.

Understanding the educational experiences of southern collegians—placing students at the center of their education—is significant in and of itself for our understanding of higher education in the Old South, as well as for understanding power, culture, class, sectionalism, intellectual life, and identity formation generally. More than any other group, college alumni became leaders within their communities, states, and the nation. They entered learned professions such as law, medicine, ministry, and education that aligned squarely with the social middle class, but they also remained deeply connected to the elite planter class. In these capacities, they wielded great power in shaping southern society. Most recently, collegians have been the subject of important works on southern men's history.[3] Far less studied, however, are the intellectual structures that gave meaning to young men's lives.[4] Higher education provides the ideal setting for such an investigation, for within colleges and universities young men had at their disposal myriad intellectual resources for both intellectualism and contemplation.[5]

This book makes three major claims about southern students' higher education that offer new perspectives on southern intellectual culture broadly. The first of these is that the transition from boyhood to manhood, not regional identity, was students' most pressing concern. For nineteenth-century students, manhood was defined in contrast to boyhood, not womanhood; it meant being an adult.[6] Not quite boys and not yet men, collegians were youths. Their experiences at college, as well as the way they understood their education, were defined by a constant tug of war between boyhood and manhood. Certain tensions emanated from this stage of life that were inherent in the boyhood-manhood dichotomy: mind versus temperament, impulse versus restraint, and dependence versus independence. These tensions were perfectly ordinary developmental struggles of upper- and middle-class southern whites; sometimes they hindered education but other times they opened up creative opportunities for young men to fashion adult selves.[7] The second claim is that this pervasive focus on maturation made the individual self the primary focus among students. Questions of how the self was defined, composed, articulated, and empowered therefore framed not only young men's maturation but also the content and exercises of university life and learning. The third claim is that this focus on self was consistent with middle-class or bourgeois culture developing in the United States in the antebellum period. In this book, I use the terms "bourgeois" and "middle class" in a cultural rather than economic sense to define individuals who were deeply committed to the idea of self-improvement, or, as Rodney Hessinger has put it, "those aspiring people who sought to improve themselves and those around them."[8] In common with the broader American bourgeoisie, North Carolina students learned industry, self-discipline, restraint (physical, emotional, and social), respectability, merit, professional success, and ambition.

The University of North Carolina presents a unique view of the role of colleges in the proliferation of bourgeois values within the South. Between 1795 and 1861, young men came from within North Carolina as well as from Virginia, Tennessee, Alabama, Mississippi, South Carolina, Louisiana, Georgia, Florida, Texas, Kentucky, Arkansas, Iowa, Connecticut, Maryland, Missouri, and New York to receive an education at the United States' first public university. By the Civil War, 1,683 young men had been graduated from the university; hundreds more had attended without receiving a diploma. The university became one of the largest universities in the nation, enrolling as many as four hundred students by 1860.[9] As the University of North Carolina grew in the antebellum period, so did its class base. Many students were sons of planters, but others were sons of professionals—merchants, grocers, teachers, ministers, and professors who only aspired to elite status.[10] Thus, the traditional designation of southern colleges as "elite"—as the exclusive domain of great planters and different from middle-class institutions—simply is inaccurate. Rather, students belonged to what I call an "educated class," which drew from both the upper and middle strata of southern society and united under similar cultural values and practices that defined the national bourgeoisie.[11]

This argument places higher education more prominently in the literature about the South's *embourgeoisement* during the antebellum period and thus further elaborates on transformations of the region in the era of the market revolution.[12] According to Jonathan Daniel Wells, a coherent and vibrant middle class emerged during the antebellum period as a result of financial, linguistic, and ideological connections between regions, especially through education.[13] Jennifer Green has explored these educational connections within southern military academies, arguing that these institutions promoted social mobility while colleges "benefited primarily the elite." Where military schools promoted bourgeois professionalism, self-restraint, and industry, she argues, colleges fostered rugged independence and rowdiness.[14] Within the larger body of literature on the antebellum South, how-

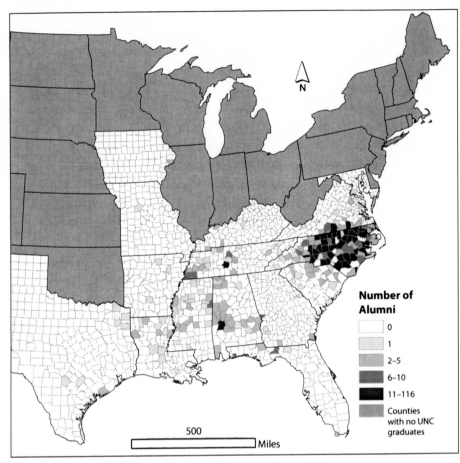

Number of
Alumni

	0
	1
	2–5
	6–10
	11–116
	Counties with no UNC graduates

500 Miles

State Origins of UNC Alumni, 1795–1861

ever, the lines between bourgeois and elite southerners seem more porous.[15] In his study of Virginia colleges in the Civil War era, Peter Carmichael argues that Virginia college students "were not a bunch of provincial sons of slave holders whose view of the world never extended beyond the Blue Ridge Mountains. Instead, they craved bourgeois respectability, hungered for professional success, followed personal ambition, and desired material trappings of a middleclass lifestyle."[16] Stephen Berry's work on young southern men in the same period, some of whom attended college, reveals a similar picture of the striving, ambitious, and literary southern male.[17] In this book, I argue that education was a process that allowed for considerable cultural permeability within the South's educated class. I explore how these cultural and class connections were forged in college, paying particular attention to student engagement with bourgeois values and their practices of self-improvement, as well as how those values mingled with traditional values of the southern elite, such as honor.

On account of especially rich sources from the 1840s and 1850s, several students appear consistently throughout this book, whose stories help to paint this picture. Feel the growing pains of William Sidney Mullins, the son of a Fayetteville, North Carolina, grocer and a pious Methodist mother, whose inherited wealth allowed the family to live quite well. Enjoy the clever antics and quixotic escapades of James Dusenbery, the eldest son of a successful planter, tanner, and merchant from Lexington, North Carolina, who owned at least twenty-three slaves and a large eight-room house neighboring local physicians and planters. Enter the world of Walter Lenoir, the dutiful but easily discouraged son of one of western North Carolina's most elite families, with large landholdings and many slaves. Follow the diligent studies of the aspiring lawyer Thomas Miles Garrett, an orphan from Bertie County, North Carolina, who was the legal ward of his brother and financially dependent on a maternal uncle. Meet young men such as William Bagley, the seventeen-year-old son of a Williamston, North Carolina, merchant, D. W. Bagley; Ruffin Tomlinson from the farming community of Johnston County, North Carolina, not far from the university; and Joseph John Summerell from Halifax County. All of these young men attended local academies for boys prior to matriculating at North Carolina. For most of them, their college writing comprises the only records of their lives.[18]

One important way in which students such as these framed their cultural values was in terms of gender, and this book pays particular attention to students' emerging ideas about manhood, which they viewed as male adulthood. Because this is a history of intellectual life, students' *ideas* about manhood take precedence. The masculine ideals southern students admired, as well as the ways in which they pursued them, especially resembled those values of "restrained manhood" expounded by many bourgeois Americans. According to the historian Amy Greenberg, restrained men valued sobriety and discipline, they abided by the so-called "protestant work ethic," and they believed in honoring chastity and "true womanhood."[19] At the University of North Carolina, these values and practices of restrained manhood also bore a southern accent. Restrained manhood complemented the idea of the southern gentleman, whose judgment and propriety brought public esteem and validation, and whose honor was predicated on his self-control.[20] Although ideals did not always match reality, and collegians could be quite juvenile and dangerously violent, these behaviors reflected the lingering influence of boyhood, not regionally specific masculine values. Thus, when college students and faculty wrote about going to college to become men, they specifically meant cutting off ties to boyhood through education.[21] This involved empowering young men to elevate mind over temperament, restraint over impulse, and independence over dependence. When they did this, they arrived at one of the most important goals of higher education: "intellectual manhood."

Defining Intellectual Manhood

Intellectual manhood provides a unique framework within which to understand southern collegians, but also power, class, and culture in the antebellum South. Widely used in the nineteenth century, the term indicated mental maturity and distinguished men from boys. It existed alongside other attributes of male maturity such as moral manhood, physical manhood, and social manhood. Educated men were supposed to possess each of these traits, but intellectual manhood was the most important goal of higher education. According to one 1853 textbook, education alone marked "the difference between being a child and ascending from that state to intellectual manhood."[22] Intellectual manhood was the culmination of a long process. In his textbook *Formation of a Manly Character* (1854), George Peck defined intellectual manhood as knowing one's self, controlling one's mind, acting wisely, and speaking intelligently.[23] Intellectual manhood, thus, was almost prerequisite for other manly attributes, for it was difficult to attain moral manhood or social manhood without mastering and expressing oneself in these ways. On campuses across the country, college presidents and students alike used the term. As this book's epigraph reveals, the president of Union College, Eliphalet Nott, invoked intellectual manhood in an 1814 address to graduating seniors, and the North Carolina student Charles Alexander repeated his injunction in the halls of North Carolina's Dialectic Society thirteen years later (albeit without crediting his source). Intellectual manhood reached farther south, too, into the rough hinterlands of the Old Southwest, where the Baptist minister T. G. Keen urged students in Alabama "to put forth the energies of intellectual manhood."[24] The term also appeared in popular culture. William Gilmore Simms, perhaps one of the nineteenth century's most popular writers, idealized intellectual manhood in two novels, *Beauchampe* (1842) and *Charlemont* (1856). "There is a sort of moral roughening which boys should be made to endure from the beginning, if the hope is ever entertained, to mature their minds to intellectual manhood," he wrote in *Charlemont*.[25] More ordinary writers also employed the term. Writing in his diary in 1848, the twenty-five-year-old Georgian Henry Craft contrasted "the high purposes & grand obtainments of most exalted intellectual manhood" with "the merest toy which amuses the youngest child."[26] In all, intellectual manhood was almost ubiquitous in antebellum American culture. It differentiated the boy from the man and thus accomplished the main goal of higher education.

The pursuit of intellectual manhood related to the transition from boyhood to manhood, but it also anticipated the "boundaries of power" separating men and women.[27] Although women could possess intellectual manhood, men considered it a male virtue possessed by a female. In 1822, a writer for Boston's *Atheneum* admitted that only exceptional women could possess the mental maturity of an adult male. "But perhaps the rarest example of intellectual manhood is Catherine the Second, Empress of Russia," he wrote. "She indeed seems to have very little woman in her nature." This comment reflects the educational thought of antebellum America, which held that male education always anticipated men's movement beyond the household, into new towns, cities, or territories, but female education was never viewed as a means to move beyond the home, her intended "sphere."[28] Thus, while female education included many of the same subjects as male education, and although female intellectual culture inspired self-fashioning, promoted ambition, and elevated heroism, young men typically did not see these similarities in the ways that historians do. In 1852, a contributor to the *North Carolina University Magazine* wrote, "We too commonly lose sight of the self-evident proposition, that the same education, the same amount of intellectual training bestowed upon boys and girls, must be acting upon very different 'raw material.'"[29]

Intellectual manhood took on added meaning as a racial and class construction in the slave South. In *Slavery: Its Origin, Nature, and History* (1861), Thornton Stringfellow compared white and black males, arguing that the African was no less male than the white man but only lacked intellectual manhood. "The age of twenty-one, which gives bodily maturity to both races," wrote Stringfellow, "develops moral and intellectual manhood in the white race, while the African remains, at the end of that time, a mere child in intellectual and moral development, perfectly incapable of performing the great function of social life."[30] Espousing a similar sentiment, one

North Carolina student wrote, "We should endeavor to elevate ourselves as much as possible from the brute & in order to do this we must be educated."[31] Intellectual manhood elevated educated men not only above racial inferiors but also class inferiors, and students often blended race and class arguments. According to historian Harry L. Watson, some southern intellectuals feared that the "common folk" might be degraded to the status of slave without education.[32] In summarizing Eliphalet Nott's call to intellectual manhood, for example, Charles Alexander explained, "The mere idea of our having been at college acquires for us considerable influence among the common people. They look to us and imitate as much as possible our every action." Another student wrote, "More will be expected and required from you by your country, your parents, and your God than from the uneducated vulgard."[33] Thus, the more grown up a young man became, the closer he approached intellectual manhood, and the more he ascended the South's class and racial hierarchy. Motivated by this concern for mental improvement, social mobility, and superiority, students pursued intellectual manhood.

The all-male context for students' pursuit of intellectual manhood is also significant. The vast scholarship on southern honor reminds us that men's gendered power in the South ultimately came from within all-male peer groups.[34] As the historian Edward Baptist explains, one of the enduring contributions of the work on southern honor has been to remind us that "access to women was not the sole factor that shaped competitions for male power."[35] In her study of civic fraternal orders in Virginia, for instance, historian Ami Pflugrad-Jackish finds that fraternity men established "a civic brotherhood . . . that marginalized the role of women in the public sphere and bolstered the respectability of every white man regardless of his class status."[36] For the subjects of this study, college was a microcosm of the fraternal public life in which they would live and lead, valorizing those in possession of intellectual manhood while marginalizing those who lacked it. Accordingly, common folk, women, and slaves appear largely as symbolic others in student writing, and rarely as individual agents or even individuated persons.[37]

These are the broad outlines of the intellectual manhood ideal to which young men aspired in the antebellum period. The idea of intellectual manhood was so much a part of educational culture that, even if all students did not use the term in private writing, they would have understood its import. An expression of restrained manhood, intellectual manhood reflected many values of the American bourgeoisie, including restraint, perseverance, industry, and self-improvement. Formal and informal university life catered to these goals in its pedagogy and curriculum. Intellectual manhood also complemented certain regional values. The process of achieving intellectual manhood, for instance, required mastery of the self—complete control over one's mental and moral development. Too, a man who possessed intellectual manhood brought honor to himself and to his community.[38] In these ways, the idea of intellectual manhood buttressed the South's racial, social, and gendered hierarchies but also resonated with attitudes about the self—its development and its significance—that defined antebellum American intellectual culture.

Excavating Intellectual Manhood

Placing southern collegians at the center of the educational process and retracing their pursuit of intellectual manhood reveals new aspects of male maturation, as well as manhood in the antebellum South. In particular, it brings the life of the mind explicitly into the picture of young manhood. The conventional treatment of male maturation, especially in the South, has almost entirely neglected intellectual life. In his path-breaking *Southern Honor*, Bertram Wyatt-Brown argues, for instance, that southern males' "entry into young manhood took more social forms" than for northern youth.[39] This perspective remains central in much of the literature on southern collegians. Lorri Glover's chapter on college education in *Southern Sons*, for instance, deals with the "(mis)behavior" of southern collegians; in her interpretation, education was a matter of social performance, or playing the part of a gentleman. Similarly, Robert F. Pace's study of antebellum collegians explains that southern colleges were "halls of honor," where collegians' preoccupation with reputation trumped academic integrity and intellectualism.[40] It is a contention of this book, however, that men embodied, at times, competing masculinities that could both be restrained and rugged, competitive and cooperative, and they often tried to work these things out in their minds, on paper, and within communities. But restraint was always the goal because men were supposed to embody restraint. These struggles of male youth defined in many ways their experiences within higher education and their pursuit of intellectual manhood.

A growing literature on men's inner emotional lives has opened pathways to understanding how young men understood and grappled with social expectations for adulthood. Anya Jabour, for example, has argued that historians have emphasized "public rituals of power" over men's "private displays of emotion," and missed ways in which various styles of masculinity coexisted within southern male culture.[41] Similarly, Stephen Berry has revealed an emotionally charged, often conflicted world of coming of age in which young men struggled to understand, define, and tame their deepest desires, their ambitions for love and glory. In particular, Berry suggests that ambition was "a constituent element of the antebellum male life" that must certainly have come from within higher education.[42] *Intellectual Manhood* takes this proposition seriously and offers a deeper look at the intellectual construction of the male self, particularly ambition, or what I consider belief in the self's heroic potential. Specifically, I view ambition not as an essential or inherent element of male life but as a product of intellectual life transmitted and explored largely through education.

This task requires approaching southern men's history from the perspective of intellectual life and asking how young men, collectively and individually, read, wrote, spoke, and imagined their way to adulthood.[43] This approach has proven especially fruitful in the field of women's history, illuminating how education fueled women's ambitions and empowered them socially and politically.[44] Like these scholars, I draw on methods used in the history of the book, especially reader response and reception theories of literary studies.[45] From this perspective, students' borrowing records, library catalogs, as well as letters, diaries, essays, orations, and published literary magazines, reveal a vibrant literary culture at the center of student life. Young men read aloud, borrowed books, and gave advice to one another about reading. In literary societies, they gathered as "interpretive communities" and engaged in what the historians Mary and Ronald Zboray have termed "literary socialization," acquiring advanced forms of literacy, especially literary taste and genre selection.[46] In private, students integrated what they read into their own lives, usually by writing about what they read in diaries and in letters, which served as a way to imagine and fashion the self.[47] In the words of Michel de Certeau, this was a world of "everyday creativity."[48] Because students integrated what they read into their own lives, we can better understand the role of intellectual life in the lived experiences of both education and maturation.

In order to reconstruct and explain students' intellectual life, I have relied on more than one hundred private manuscript collections of students' letters and diaries, as well as literary society minutes, library catalogs and borrowing records, book marginalia,[49] class compositions, notebooks, speeches, student magazines, and memoirs. Additionally, I have drawn from a rare trove of more than 800 extant addresses and speeches archived by the Dialectic and Philanthropic Societies. Moreover, this is the first study to quantify, classify, and contextualize literary society debate questions. I compiled a database of nearly 4,000 questions debated in both the Dialectic and Philanthropic Society and recorded within twenty-seven manuscript minute books. As much as possible, I tried to situate these debates within a wider context, using samples from other studies as well as my own less comprehensive research into similar societies such as Guilford County, North Carolina's Philomathesian Society, Wake Forest University's Euzelian and Philomathesian Societies, and the Oxford Union Debating Society.[50]

The richness of this source base is due to the printing, communication, and transportation revolutions of the early nineteenth century, which made educational materials easier to obtain.[51] Collegians everywhere experienced a flood of print materials, including fictional works, periodicals, and advice literature, as well as paper and blank books. In this print culture, reading and writing enterprises significantly mediated the formation of adult personas for college youth and served as proxy forms of new relations between private experience and identity occurring elsewhere in the republic, especially self-improvement. Diaries, a major source in this book, capture these moments particularly well. The urgency of self-improvement during youth that the university culture harnessed often encouraged students to turn inward and work on the self.[52] These literary processes were similar to those which Steven Stowe located among elite young women, whose private journalizing created a "narrative of feelings" for coming of age.[53] In making commitments to write in diaries, North Carolina students are representative of young men of a national educated class who had the means and the time to engage in such pursuits.[54]

These sources reveal a great deal of continuity within the intellectual culture of higher education during the antebellum period, and despite the social and political changes of the time, I view this era as defined more by continuity than change.[55] Broadly, these continuities included a persistent emphasis on maturation within university life and learning, a focus on self-improvement, and a uniquely romantic view of the individual self's heroic potential. These cultural phenomena developed in the late eighteenth and early nineteenth century. Evangelicalism, markets, party politics, biography, fiction, and education claimed great significance for the individual self, defining it as something that could be made (and remade) over time and through hard work.[56] Significantly, this work occurred in formal education, but also in informal university life, where young men ascribed to contemporary notions of "self-culture." These features of antebellum intellectual culture reflect what the historian Walter Houghton has termed "the Victorian frame of mind," and I often refer to this culture as Victorian.[57]

A Cultural Profile of Life and Learning at North Carolina

The pages that follow address two fundamental questions: What was educational about higher education at the University of North Carolina? And what was manly about it? Here, education must be construed broadly as a cultural process occurring both within and beyond formal classrooms and spaces.[58] The manliness of this education refers specifically to how education influenced the process of leaving boyhood, which was young men's most pressing concern. The three parts of this book examine the cultural processes by which young men learned to idealize, fashion, and apply intellectual manhood—the ideal goal of their journeys away from boyhood. Individual chapters follow students as they moved between dormitories and lecture halls, debating society halls, libraries, chapels, parlors, and local brothels, creating multiple spaces for learning about self and society at the University of North Carolina.

This was largely a student's world, and so students' voices take precedence here. Nevertheless, in order to understand their world, a few general remarks about the faculty and the cultural life of the institution are necessary. First, the faculty was consistently small. Most southern institutions, including North Carolina, employed between four and six professors, as well as several tutors, who assisted with teaching and supervision. Five professors and two tutors taught and supervised one hundred and sixty-nine students at North Carolina in 1841, for example.[59] Second, the faculty consisted of serious scholars with some advanced education and records of community leadership. University faculty led the region's intellectual life and maintained connections with other educators in North Carolina as well as at other universities. Third, the faculty was religious. All professors belonged to one Christian denomination or another, and some were clergy. They presided over mandatory daily prayers and weekly chapel services, but they did not actively proselytize students. They did, however, offer a view of religion that complemented the mental and moral improvement necessary for cultivating intellectual manhood.

Religion played an important role in the life of the university, particularly by instilling bourgeois individualism and by mitigating tensions of youth culture. Religious life at North Carolina reflected a moderate strand of evangelicalism, best described simply as Protestant Christianity. According to one *North Carolina University Magazine* writer, "The religious character of the institution is evangelical or orthodox."[60] Presbyterians, Methodists, Baptists, and Episcopalians founded churches in Chapel Hill in the early nineteenth century, and students attended these churches regularly.[61] There were always many differences among these denominations, but educated southerners typically fit the mold of a more tempered, Enlightenment-inspired Protestantism. Students were taught to value religious devotion through prayer, scripture, and church attendance. They responded to calls for conversion and worked on moral improvement by creating personal spaces and opportunities for self-reflection and improvement. But they were not so pietistic that they were detached from the world. Thus, religious culture at Chapel Hill was never the revival culture that characterized much of the early evangelical movement in the South.[62] That culture was institutionalized in many of the denominational institutions such as Wake Forest, Trinity (now Duke), Emory, and Mercer, but not at North Carolina, where the faculty promoted morality rooted in Christianity but intended for a secular world.[63]

Students also created an intellectual culture around mental and moral improvement similar to other U.S. colleges and universities. Most significant to students were the university's two student-organized literary societies. Founded immediately after the university opened, the Dialectic and Philanthropic Societies followed a tradition of student literary associations that had begun in the early eighteenth century. Membership was not compulsory, but every student belonged to one society or the other. Students met privately each week in ornate chambers containing extensive and cosmopolitan libraries. They read aloud from the most renowned books, delivered speeches, and debated various social, moral, historical, and political questions. These activities were not only important elements of a manly life but also the means to fashion intellectual manhood through mental and moral improvement.[64] In the late antebellum period, students began to found chapters of national fraternities, which provided additional opportunities for camaraderie and intellectualism, but, as the historian Nicholas Syrett has indicated, these were not as popular in the South as they were in the North. Indeed, North Carolina's fraternities espoused moral, intellectual, and social values so similar to literary societies that they did not replace literary societies until after the Civil War. Consequently, they are not a key focus of this book.[65]

The antebellum collegian's world was largely but not entirely male. Students maintained meaningful relationships with mothers, aunts, sisters, and cousins. They also began new relationships with single young females from their home communities or in Chapel Hill. These relationships made up a vibrant "informal education" and contributed to students' development as adults.[66] In this quasi-homosocial environment, collegians drew from both traditional southern notions of honor and rugged independence and more restrained expressions of manhood such as sobriety, temperance, and chastity, which defined the emerging national bourgeoisie. Nevertheless, because youth were self-focused, students were concerned primarily with their own self-development; meaningful relationships with the opposite sex would come later. Students often stated in letters and diaries that they were reluctant to pursue either courtship or marriage until they became established in a lucrative profession. This mindset influenced the informal curriculum of sex and intimacy at college.

Finally, North Carolina's collegiate culture was distinctively southern in its reliance on enslaved men and women. The slave population in Orange County, North Carolina—the location of the University of North Carolina —was highest in 1830, when slaves numbered 7,339 and whites numbered approximately 15,000.[67] Students rarely brought their own slaves to campus, but slaves' presence on campus was pervasive. Some professors owned slaves, and the university hired slaves from local slaveowners in order to build and maintain campus property. Although slaves likely did not live with students, they typically worked in households or on campus, hauling students' water, building their fires, cooking their food, laundering their clothes, and driving their carriages.[68] Except for occasional references to local or family slaves, slaveholding was not a common topic in student writing and did not figure into the formal curriculum and pedagogy; thus it is not a focus of this study. State and national debates about slavery, however, did influence campus life and learning in several ways, especially in the capstone moral philosophy course and in students' weekly literary society debate exercises. In these contexts, students grappled with the slavery question in both abstract and practical terms, revealing the broader relevance of young men's pursuit of intellectual manhood to public life. Throughout the period under study here, there was no consensus around proslavery ideology, as students continued to question whether slavery crippled or advanced American civilization. Their debates about slavery, like their education more broadly, therefore shed greater light on the South's diverse patterns of thought and sectional consciousness leading up to the Civil War.

From University, to Self, to Society

Part I, "University," excavates the formal structures of university life and the gendered nature of student life, especially its ties to bourgeois attitudes about self-improvement that pervaded Victorian America. Part II, "Self," examines how young men received and appropriated knowledge in informal social and private settings, which often overlapped. The four chapters of Part II pay particular attention to how ideals offered in formal contexts influenced young men's developing intellectual manhood. Part III, "Society," focuses on students' developing attitudes about the role of intellectual manhood within society and consists of one chapter. It is not a study of students within society, which exceeds the limits of this book. Instead, this chapter offers an analysis of students anticipating society and adjusting their self-construction and self-articulation accordingly.

In all, students inhabited and helped to create an intellectual culture at North Carolina in which education framed the creative work of imagining, constructing, and applying intellectual manhood as fundamentally heroic. Indeed, all of higher education, formal and informal, served young men's heroic potential. The end result was the Victorian gentleman who could lead the republic, shape intellectual culture, and guide his family to the benefit of society. As a result, students derived great power and privilege from this education, but they did not always and urgently articulate that sense of power in terms of region, as some scholars have suggested. In other words, antebellum education did not create proto-Confederates. Until the 1850s, this education took on a distinctively American character whereby North Carolinian, American, and southerner were not mutually exclusive identities. Only in the late antebellum period did sectionalism begin to weigh heavily on young men's identities as men. Prior to that period, maturity rather than region was the most salient concern for young North Carolinians.

PART I

UNIVERSITY
Idealizing Intellectual Manhood

The University of North Carolina was chartered in 1789, following a vague state constitutional mandate for at least one university to instill "useful knowledge" in the state's youth.[1] Its founding was part of a national movement to establish new colleges for the new republic.[2] Prior to the Revolutionary War, the northern colonies boasted several colleges—including Harvard and Yale—but the College of William and Mary was the South's only institution of higher education. After the Revolution, North Carolina's leading Federalists envisioned a public university that would mold conscientious citizens.[3] Other states soon followed: Franklin College (now the University of Georgia) and South Carolina College in 1801, and the University of Virginia in 1816. The greatest period of growth in southern higher education began in the 1820s, largely due to the proliferation of denominational colleges and the establishment of public colleges in states formed out of the Old Southwest and Louisiana territories: Tennessee, Alabama, Mississippi, and Louisiana.[4] In all, between 1800 and 1850 the number of colleges in the United States grew from twenty to more than two hundred, and many of them were in the South.

During this time, the University of North Carolina gradually became one of the largest, most active universities in the region, with graduating classes around and sometimes surpassing a hundred students.[5] While political and economic volatility riddled the university in its early years, after the War of 1812 aggressive new leadership and relatively stable state politics allowed the university to flourish, albeit with some occasional financial setbacks.

Although the university was public, by virtue of its establishment by the General Assembly, it was not funded though state appropriations. Instead, funding came from the sale of the state's escheats, but it had little more in state support.[6] Also powering the university's growth and expansion were national industrial developments associated with the so-called market, transportation, and communication revolutions, particularly technological innovations such as steam printing and transportation, which made educational materials easier and cheaper to obtain and created a national mass market for readers.[7] Professors and students at North Carolina did not retreat from national developments, but embraced them as much as their coffers allowed, expanding to meet the state's demands for educated leadership. As was the case elsewhere in the United States, higher education's expansion had deep cultural implications, particularly with regard to extending middle-class, or bourgeois, values throughout the state. At the University of North Carolina students adapted many bourgeois values, especially industry, temperance, self-discipline, and emulation, to their intellectual culture. The pursuit of these values was intertwined with ideals of restrained manhood idealized in the notion of intellectual manhood, which students pursued in formal university settings.

Although significant social and political changes occurred during the antebellum period, the focus here is on the intellectual culture of higher education, which was defined by continuity. First, formal university life—its daily structure, literary societies, pedagogy, and curriculum—consistently catered to students' transition from boyhood to manhood. This process was defined by struggles between impulse and restraint, mind and temperament, and dependence and independence, which were at the core of what young men thought manhood was all about. Sometimes student life, tied as it was to male youth culture, resulted in disorder and chaos, impeding students as they struggled to mature; other times, a more mature, intellectually grounded campus culture directed young men to lead mature lives. The curriculum, pedagogy, and literary societies addressed the tensions and growing pains associated with maturation by emphasizing mental and moral improvement, which was the prevailing educational philosophy of the time.

Second, mental and moral improvement was always a matter of individual self-development, or self-improvement. According to the historian Stephen Greenblatt, the self is "a sense of personal order, a characteristic mode of address to the world, a structure of bounded desires."[8] While the self has always been an implicit focus in the literature on southern manhood, intellectual culture offers new insight into how precisely young men consumed and appropriated *ideas* about selfhood. Formal university life propagated ideas about self-development. The pedagogy and curriculum provided the means to understand, achieve, and express the self's "personal order" by offering opportunities for mental and moral improvement, providing male exemplars of ideal selfhood, and encouraging emulation. Students carried these ideals and practices with them into their literary societies as well. In college, students also learned to articulate the self in letters, diaries, class compositions, and public orations, as well as private expressions of desire and love. This education, especially in the expression of self, was important for young men who would, as members of the educated class and the learned professions, assume leadership positions in families, communities, their state, and the nation.

Third, these pursuits of the mature self, embodied in the pervasive intellectual manhood ideal, were viewed as heroic. In this way, students' efforts were characteristic of a Victorian world in which emulation and hero worship figured prominently. A mix of great anxiety and optimism challenged students along the way, but in learning to think, act, and speak like men, they came to imagine themselves as individuals with great heroic potential. The subjects of a classical education opened young men's minds to the call to greatness by providing male exemplars of the self-fashioned ideal. Even if young men were not called to be great leaders, they learned that education elevated them above others. Thus, a classical education was always part of the web of power and exclusion that distinguished educated men from common whites, free and enslaved blacks, and women of all classes. The symbolic presence of young men's perceived social inferiors gave urgency to the project of maturation, but at college power rested within and emanated from students' more immediate male world.

Intellectual histories seldom treat these subjects from a student perspective, but students were *always* agents in the development of educational culture. The ways students tried to make sense out of formal education and maturation can help us make sense out of it as well, and better understand the cultural work and value of antebellum higher education. Part 1 considers formal sites where both education and the struggles to leave boyhood occurred—the campus, classrooms, recitation halls, and literary societies. These chapters uncover resources and structures of intellectual culture at North Carolina in traditions of student life, the university's intellectual settings and resources, and the pedagogy and curriculum. The three chapters that follow reconstruct this intellectual world and show how it shaped young men's transition from boyhood to manhood and created the perfect ambiance for idealizing and constructing intellectual manhood.

CHAPTER ONE

Going to College

In 1853, the *North Carolina University Magazine* published an account of college life in an article entitled "Musings of a Student." The anonymous author drew particular attention to the figure of the collegian: "Somewhat matured in mind, yet not strong enough to cope with the world, he despises his childhood, and casting off the schoolboy garb, vainly tries to wear the manly robe; yet it must be worn, for College life is so short that ere he is aware of it, he is ushered into the world where, unless it is worn, he must go down before the proud lance of some doughty knight. The object of College life is to learn to be a man, and in no place could it be better learnt."[1] More than a rowdy ne'er-do-well, the antebellum collegian was an agent in his own maturation, struggling to leave behind boyhood in a seemingly epic struggle for survival in a frightening adult world.

In no uncertain terms, these "musings" reveal what countless southerners believed was the purpose of college: becoming a man. Perhaps Harry St. John Dixon of Mississippi put it best when he wrote in his diary, "I will go to college to return a man!"[2] In the antebellum United States, becoming a man meant leaving childhood for adulthood, or "casting off the schoolboy garb," as the *Magazine* author put it. Often, this process involved community testing and community approval, as some scholars have argued, but not always.[3] Deeper emotional and intellectual work fueled the process of maturation, as young men considered the idea of manhood, specifically the intellectual manhood ideal expounded by the educated class. This ideal equated boyhood with temperament and impulsivity, and manhood with mind and restraint. Students had to work hard to leave boyhood.

Several tensions related to youth and maturation influenced the intellectual culture of higher education at North Carolina: boyhood versus manhood, impulse versus restraint, and dependence versus independence. Students relied on several important sources for making the transition from home to college and, ultimately, from boyhood to manhood. First, family relationships remained significant sources of stability for students, who continued to locate their emerging adult identities within their families. These relationships generally helped students in the maturation process, but sometimes presented challenges. Second, students received support from within the college community. Faculty encouraged young men to strive for eminence and distinction. They placed ambition at the center of the educational experience and used emulation and merit to promote studiousness and morality. Third, and most significantly, students helped one another mature into men as they gathered in literary societies, competed for grades and distinctions, and emulated one another. In the process, collegians learned how to speak the language of the emerging American bourgeoisie, who valued restraint, self-discipline, industry, sobriety, and emulation as means to manhood and even to greatness. In order to grasp the importance of this culture to young men's development, it is first necessary to understand how young men and their families prepared for, invested in, and adjusted to college.

Preparing for College

Southern families went great lengths to provide for boys' early education.[4] Sons of planters often trained with private tutors and attended local academies. Largely elite institutions, these schools charged tuition and were not the same as public schools or "common schools," which lacked political support in the region.[5] Private academies flourished in the early nineteenth-century South, and in North Carolina about six new academies were chartered every year between 1800 and 1825. Most of these were day schools, and some were library societies or benevolent societies that operated academies.[6] Generally, academies prepared boys for college entrance exams by offering rudimentary Latin, Greek, arithmetic, natural philosophy, and rhetoric. Students also practiced declamation and oratory within academy debating societies. Sometimes teachers encouraged certain pupils to consider college, but there was never an expectation for higher education. A young man (or his father) might write to college presidents for official catalogues in order to learn about collegiate entrance requirements, curricula, and expenses.[7] If a young man made the choice for college, he could be admitted upon successful completion of an entrance examination, which determined the class a student would enter. Promising but underprepared students might be admitted to the university as "irregular" students who could attend classes in preparation for retaking the entrance exams, but they were not enrolled.[8]

The case of William Bagley illustrates this process. Bagley began to think seriously about college in the summer of 1841, when he was a student at the Williamston Academy (where his father, a merchant, served as board member). He hoped to enter college as soon as possible but received only lukewarm support. His father questioned whether it might not be cheaper and more expedient for his son to continue a program of self-education. "He believes in a man educating himself I suppose," Bagley complained to a friend in 1842. Nevertheless, Bagley's father requested catalogues from colleges, including a university in New York, and young William ultimately decided to try for the University of North Carolina. "With the start I have I can go on & be prepared to enter any class in College, I think, with hard study, but still it will go much harder with me than if I were at some school where I could have the advantages of good society."[9] Bagley took the entrance exams for the University of North Carolina sometime in 1842 but did not fare well; he was admitted as an irregular student, however, and was instructed to study for the entrance exams. During this time, Bagley's friend, Edward Yellowley, a student at the University of North Carolina, helped him prepare. In February 1843, he reported having "read every Latin book this side of College," as well as Greek and arithmetic.[10] He took the entrance exams again in June 1843, "passed on everything he tried for," and was admitted to the sophomore class.[11]

Some families had concerns with sending their sons to college. Given the agrarian nature of the early republic, especially the South, some parents questioned the practical relevance of collegiate education; others questioned its effect on a young man's morals. Harry St. John Dixon all but had to beg his father to go to college. He even wrote an essay on the subject, "Why is it I should not go to college?" In it, the young Mississippian (already quite prone to mischief) promised, "You shall never see me intoxicated, if it is the cup you fear," and this tipped the balance in his favor.[12] An institution's proximity to home, family commitments, and the cost of travel were also considerations. While many southern males went north to attend Harvard and Princeton, most chose to attend a southern college or university. Some southerners may have rejected northern education, desiring a regional education for "southrons," but most southerners attended southern schools for practical reasons more than ideological ones.[13]

There was no stigma attached to not attending a college or university.

Nor was there a stigma attached to trying college and failing. Southern families believed that some children were naturally fit for higher education and others were not. Students who matriculated at the University of North Carolina but who were not graduated often went on to become highly successful planters, statesmen, or professionals. Common in an age with no professional schools, some students who left college went on to study privately for a specific profession. In 1820, one disgruntled North Carolina student wrote to his cousin about his reason for leaving college: "My intention was, when I left Greensville, to have joined college, for the purpose of studying philosophy, & chymistry: but upon inquiry, I found there was no philosophical apparatus & that the chymical laboratory was so very deficient . . . that I declined matriculating, thinking it would be of more utility to me, to study privately."[14] Family duty was the primary reason for either not attending or remaining at college. This was often a financial decision, and young men occasionally left school rather than drain the family coffers.

Paying for College

Tuition and expenses at southern colleges and universities were higher than institutions elsewhere in the country, burdening even students from the wealthiest families.[15] At North Carolina, antebellum students could expect to spend anywhere from $161 to $195 annually (or between roughly $3,500 and $4,300 in 2012) on tuition and related expenses.[16] In 1841, standard annual expenses at North Carolina included: "Tuition, $50; Room (at College), 2; Servant hire, 5; Deposit (for damages), 4; Board for 40 weeks, at $8 to $11 per month, 74 to 102; Bed and Washing 16 to 22; Wood 5; Candles 5." Students had the option of buying their textbooks. According to the University of North Carolina's 1841 *Catalogue*, "The whole series of books, for the four years, may be purchased for $60 or $70. It is desirable that every Student shall retain his Text Books, and take them with him when he leaves College; but as in most instances they are parted with to the succeeding classes, at a reduced price, this item of expense is thereby rendered less burthensome to many."[17] Of course students had additional expenses, and some students would spend more than $300 annually. For example, Henry A. London, one of ten children of a Pittsboro, North Carolina, merchant, spent $144.50 in the fall 1862 term and $205.55 in the spring 1863 term. In addition to the expenses listed in the catalog, London spent money on furnishings for his own room, including rent for a bedstead, mattress, linens, one bureau, bucket, dipper, baskets, and chairs; clothing items such as a cap, coat, and shoes; "treats" such as watermelons, peaches, and apples; stationery items such as books and stamps; literary society dues; social events such as a "possum supper"; and admission to one concert and one fair. He also paid for haircuts, laundry, and dental appointments (he had to have one tooth extracted and five cavities filled in the spring).[18]

Not surprisingly, students' letters home often contained requests for more money. William Bagley wrote to his father at the start of the fall 1843 term: "I shall need some money in order to pay my tuition, boardbill &c., as I have had to pay well for everything I have used since I have been here. My board bill will be from 50 to 60 dollars at the end of the session, & my tuition connected with room rent & servant hire, I understand, will be $31.50 which I have to pay in advance."[19] As the historian Lorri Glover has revealed about southerners in an earlier period, fathers often sought to inculcate values of frugality among sons at college. These lessons continued into the antebellum period, as fathers replied to their ostensibly needy sons with admonitions against overspending.[20] Requests for financial support also reflected the "semi-dependence" that defined the period of youth, when young men strived for independence but depended on parents' financial support.[21] This arrangement frustrated many young men. For example, Walter Lenoir struggled with college expenses and accrued debts in Hillsboro. "It distresses me to think what a drain my education must be upon you at such a time as this," he wrote to his father. "I long for the period to arrive when I shall no longer be a burden to my parents but shall be able to assist and cherish them."[22] Although Walter's immediate solution was to leave college, both his father and David Swain, the university president, convinced him to remain.[23]

Unlike other educational institutions in the region such as military schools, colleges and universities typically did not subsidize students' educations. There were, however, exceptions. The North Carolina General Assembly, for instance, stipulated that native North Carolinians who could not pay for college but demonstrated superior aptitude and morality could attend without charge, but the historical record is not altogether clear on how many of these students there were.[24] Instead, paying for a young man's collegiate education sometimes became a community affair, as extended family members might loan money to young men for college expenses.[25] Financing education through kinship ties, however, placed additional pressure on young men who wished to honor their families.

The experiences of nineteen-year-old Thomas Miles Garrett typify those of young men who saw great value in higher education but were burdened by college expenses. Garrett, whom we have already met, was an orphan with high hopes for greatness, fame, and distinction. After completing the required entrance examinations with flying colors, Garrett entered the sophomore class in 1848. He soon found college expensive and solicited his uncle, Augustus Holley, "for his support in pecuniary matters, which he verry willingly granted me." Still, ends did not seem to meet. "I have come to C. Hill and spent one year, my expenses have been great and I have almost arrived at that period at which I can neither proceed with decency," Garrett wrote in his diary in July 1849. Young men worried about reputation, and not fulfilling a debt hurt Garrett's sense of honor. Making matters worse, Garrett received a letter from his aunt at the end of his first year, explaining that his uncle "had purchased a scholarship in the institution at Boydton VA—Randolph and Macon College—and wished me to [accept] the offer of it with its benefits and emoluments to me." Sad to leave North Carolina, Garrett wrote to his brother to intervene, but to no avail; Garrett's aunt and uncle asked him to take the scholarship at Randolph Macon College. Bound by duty, Garrett felt "constrained to accept the offer." As the days went on, Garrett was increasingly depressed about leaving Chapel Hill, but ultimately his aunt and uncle conceded to his wishes to remain at North Carolina, and he was graduated in 1851 due largely to a long-standing tradition of kin and community aid in planter culture.[26] Students such as Thomas Miles Garrett remind us that many of these students were aspiring members of a broader, educated class who saw college as an opportunity for upward mobility.

In all, the efforts of North Carolina families and their sons to get to college (and remain there) underscore the cultural value that higher education carried as both cultural capital and as an important rite of passage. For many young North Carolinians, this transition truly began when they arrived at the college in Chapel Hill. "Separated from home and friends for perhaps the first time, the student feels those curious emotions that beset one upon entering a new and untried course," wrote one student author of the *North Carolina University Magazine*.[27] For the subjects of this book, travel to the college in Chapel Hill marked the beginning of this journey.

The College in Chapel Hill

In August 1861, Preston H. Sessoms and his brother, John, left their hometown of Colerain in northeastern North Carolina, for Chapel Hill, 140 miles away. Preston was about to begin his first year at the University of North Carolina, and his brother accompanied him on the journey. They took a steamboat from Colerain at "about 11 o'clock" on a Monday night and traveled through the night up the Chowan River toward Virginia. At six the next morning, they disembarked in Franklin, Virginia, and went into the center of the town to catch a train to North Carolina. Unfortunately, their train had derailed, and the two brothers waited approximately five hours to board the train that would take them to Weldon. When then they arrived at Weldon at three in the afternoon, the brothers had missed the chance to change trains and travel to the next station in Raleigh. So they remained in Weldon, "took the cars for Raleigh" the next morning, and then traveled more than one hundred miles until four in the afternoon, when they arrived in Raleigh. There, they transferred cars and departed "as . . . quick as possible for Chapel Hill." Having traveled "as fast as forty miles an hour," they arrived that evening "at seven or eight o'clock."[28]

Preston Sessoms's account reveals that, even within North Carolina, the journey to Chapel Hill was long and arduous. The Sessoms brothers were actually lucky. Living at the end of the era explored in this book, they had the privilege to travel by rail. For most of the antebellum period, however, there was no rail system that could carry a student across the state, and a lack of canals, bridges, and easily navigable waterways made river transportation impossible.[29] Students often traveled with books, clothing, personal items, and occasionally (though rarely) a personal slave. Students were also vulnerable to the elements: rain muddied the roads, causing carriages to get stuck along the way; summer heat and winter cold could make any trip unbearable. Not uncommonly, students became ill en route to college.[30] In any generation, students traveled along uneven dirt roads leading to Chapel Hill, arrived on Franklin Street, the main road through town, and walked northward to campus.

North Carolina's campus spanned nearly one hundred acres, surrounded by village lots to the north and forest everywhere else. It lay between two major roads that connected Chapel Hill to adjacent communities—Franklin Street ran along the east-west axis and Columbia Street along the north-south axis. A stone wall ran along Franklin Street in order to keep out marauding cows and pigs. Beyond the wall, campus grounds accommodated lush trees, ornamental shrubs, flowering and fruit-bearing plants, birds and small game, and natural water sources. Gravel paths extended into town, accentuating the landscape.[31] One student described the campus—or "grove," as it was sometimes called—as "a retreat of the Muses."[32] The university took great care to maintain the campus, relying on slaves as well as employed stewards, landscapers, and groundskeepers. Both enslaved and free blacks were "hired out" for construction of university buildings through the antebellum period.[33] Eight buildings were erected on the campus between 1793 and 1860: Old East (1793) held classrooms and dormitories; South Building (1798) served as the main university building; Person Hall (1797) served as a chapel and gathering hall before 1837, after which it held classrooms; Gerrard Hall (1822) was the university chapel after 1837; Old West (1822) held dormitories; Smith Hall (1851) was home to the university library; and New East (1857–59) and New West (1857–59) held dormitories for members of the Dialectic and Philanthropic Societies, respectively, as well as meeting rooms and libraries.[34]

Students lived either in campus dormitories or in local boarding houses and hotels. There were three dormitory buildings on campus during the antebellum period: East, West, and South buildings. The rooms were about 288 square feet in size and designed to house two students, but as the university grew as many as three or four students shared a room.[35] Dormitory rooms were available only on a first-come, first-serve basis, so students sometimes resorted to rolling dice to determine housing once they arrived on campus.[36] Students often preferred to live among hometown friends, relatives, or fellow literary society members. As a result, the spatial arrangement of dormitories mirrored the east-west axis of North Carolina culture: students from the eastern part of the state tended to stay in East Building and those from the western part of the state in West Building. For students such as James Dusenbery, living among friends was invigorating. He lived on the third floor of West building and boasted, "We are a jovial, roistering company & our determination is to enjoy to the utmost the halcyon days of youth."[37]

Dormitory life was a new experience for many young men, and students sometimes wrote about their roommates.[38] An 1853 number of the *North Carolina University Magazine* poked fun at dormitory life when a contributing author complained about his annoying roommate's constant singing and humming. "The most boring thing in creation is a fiddling, fifing, fluting, singing room-mate," he wrote. "Did you ever have one? Did you ever see one? Did you ever hear one? May you always escape. . . . Look at him. He sings. Now he rolls his eyes towards the Heavens as if he were certain the spheres were going to pitch in and accompany him. . . . I wonder if the boy thinks music a manly and becoming exercise."[39]

Local Boarding houses provided great alternatives for students who desired quieter or roomier lodgings. In 1846, John Osborne Guion decided to move from campus to the village. "I have no room-mate, and I believe it is preferable not to have one, at least to running the risk of getting a bad room-mate," he wrote to his cousin. There were at least eleven boarding houses and two hotels in Chapel Hill by 1819.[40] By far the most popular option in the village was Nancy Hilliard's Eagle Hotel, which stood across Franklin Street, about fifty yards from the closest academic buildings (East and South). Chapel Hill's many hotels and boarding houses also fed students regularly. In the antebellum period, there were no institutions that resembled today's campus dining hall. Early students usually dined at Steward's Hall, which was notorious for its "most intolerable" fare and closed in 1819; thereafter it became a boarding house.[41] The food at hotels and boarding houses did not always meet expectations, either. Nathan Neal complained bedbugs, as well as the food at his boarding house: "Our fair [sic] at the Hotel is pritty [sic] sorry[,] badly cooked and filthy. We have corn pie[,] beef[,] gingercake &c. flies no rarity to be cooked[.] Cups and saucers are not clean[.] Coffee very weak, but I have it very sweet, and get a plenty but not so much as I like."[42]

In these ways, young men quickly learned that the college in Chapel Hill was different from home. If the long, grueling journey did not open their eyes to the unique world that awaited them, the everyday experiences of college culture did. College provided a new social and emotional landscape on which young men's journeys to manhood occurred. Students believed that their actions in college would determine the men they would become. Tensions associated with young men's maturation—impulse and restraint, mind and temperament—significantly influenced the social and emotional experiences of antebellum student life.

Antebellum Student Life: Between Boyhood and Manhood

In 1857, William A. Wooster, an eighteen-year-old freshman from Wilmington, North Carolina, wrote a class essay entitled "home and College Life

A college youth. Ambrotype of James Hilliard Polk, taken while a student
at the University of North Carolina, c. 1859–60. James Hilliard Polk Papers #5259-z,
Southern Historical Collection, Manuscripts Department, Wilson Library,
University of North Carolina at Chapel Hill.

contrasted." Among the many "striking & plainly defined" differences were
those related to growing up. "In College we have not the strong will of the
Father, nor the pleading voice of a mother to check us in our career of sin,"
he wrote. "No kind friend is near to tell us when we err, or to smile approval
when we do well." Students' destinies were "in a measure in our own hands
and 'tis here the great battle of life begins." They needed "moral courage"
at college "more than at any other time of life." While beholden to their
parents by virtue of their age and unmarried status, young men neverthe-

less had control over their own mental and moral development for the first time.[43]

Student life took shape in this environment between boyhood and manhood. In his history of higher education, Burton Bledstein argued that "the idea of young manhood as a sphere all its own" acquired new relevance in the antebellum period, influencing the formal structures and individual experiences of higher education.[44] At North Carolina, as with most other colleges and universities, all students were youth but they ranged widely in age. Freshmen were often as young as fifteen, and many juniors and seniors were in their early twenties.[45] Consequently, they varied greatly in physical development. Some students had barely hit puberty when they began college, and their smooth, beardless faces stood in marked contrast to older classmates, many of whom sported quite respectable beards. Those still in the midst of physical change did not escape the attention of older students. As soon as a freshman saw "a sprout upon his chin," joked one student, he would stand before the mirror and just stare at it for hours.[46] Some younger students' voices had not changed when they matriculated. When they assembled in any of the university's wood-floored and paneled rooms, students' voices must have sounded like the cacophonous timbres of a boys' choir, resonating with high, medium, and low pitches. Students also possessed a striking "diversity of individual character." One student identified four major types of students: the "smart men"; those social climbers, or those who wished to befriend only "the most influential men in college"; the joking, "good-natured fellow"; and the "college bore," who demonstrated "too great a contempt for books."[47] Regardless of their individual characters, however, these youth were all going through the same transition from boyhood to manhood, and college life catered to that maturation process.

The structure of the school day was geared toward disciplining youth. Students awoke at six o'clock each morning to the college bell's predictable and loud toll.[48] They dressed in plain, often homemade clothes, including trousers, a long-sleeved cotton shirt, shoes, and sometimes a jacket, and left their rooms to attend compulsory prayers in Person Hall.[49] The school day's first recitations began at seven o'clock in South Hall, the university's main academic building; afterward, students ate breakfast. Two or three hours of study time followed, though crowds of students commonly gathered "in front of one of the College buildings" to watch dogs fight in the street or to discuss politics.[50] When the bell rang again, students rushed to a second recitation at eleven, followed by dinner (the largest meal of the day) at noon, and then a third recitation. Students were typically free after two in the afternoon, and the bell rang at eight o'clock in the evening, summoning them to their rooms for study and sleep, though playing games of whist, reading novels, and cigar or pipe smoking were quite common as well.[51] This sort of daily routine—at once regimented by university affairs yet filled with free time—set the stage for the emotional transition that occurred at college.

Homesickness often interfered with students' emotional and academic lives. In 1820, one student wrote, "My mind is frequently & imperceptably abstracted from the treatise of the author, by the recollection of my relations, my friends & the pain of my acquaintance in Virginia, from whom, I so reluctantly parted & who are ever present to my mind, during my time of relaxation." He felt confident, however, that his "homesick thoughts are wearing off, & I am in hopes within a few weeks to resume my wonted cheerfulness & be able to devote my attention solely to the acquirement of literary knowledge."[52] Many students were also bored and noted the "*dryness* of the times about Chapel Hill."[53] As Hugh Torrence wrote to a friend from home in 1828, for example, "The times have been very dull indeed since I returned I have no sport at all the only amusement I have when I am not at study, is my flute."[54] And in 1842, James Dusenbery wrote in his diary, "The week has passed away without a single incident occurring to break the dull monotony of College life."[55]

The monotony of college life sometimes bred misbehavior, as it did at other U.S. colleges and universities. Student riots occurred at Yale, Harvard, Virginia, and North Carolina in the early national period, as the sons of Revolutionary-era heroes sought to claim their manly independence.[56] Large-scale riots and rebellions eventually waned, but student letters from the antebellum period also describe campus shenanigans and community violence throughout the country. One antebellum North Carolina student wrote, for instance, that the "dangers to which a young man is exposed during that part of his life which he passes in college, are numerous and difficult to oppose with a firm, unyielding spirit."[57] Another complained, "A sojourn of two years and a half in a place like this [Chapel Hill] is enough to ruin a saint much more a mortal."[58] Students drank, gambled, fought, and pulled pranks on campus. Many students resisted authority and sneered at discipline.[59]

While scholars have attributed young men's misbehavior to a number of factors, including resistance to faculty control, class tensions, and the demands of southern honor, there is little doubt that departure from boyhood was central to all of them.[60] Consider the case of swearing, a vice frequently cited in faculty records, literary society minutes, and student writing. Many students believed the practice had everything to do with immaturity.[61] In 1805, for instance, one student was called by the faculty "to answer for profane swearing in uncommon degree," which the faculty stated was "so nearly connected with dissoluteness of morals in general, and which tends to precipitate corruption of youth."[62] Throughout the antebellum period, students and faculty associated this vice with immaturity. In 1854, an anonymous student critiqued his classmates' speech habits: "Among a large collection of young men and *boys*, where women's radiant countenance is not present to place a bridle upon the tongue, the morality of conversation is very apt to be held in very low estimation—boys are prone to descent to vulgarity."[63] This writer touches on the endemic problem of youth being away from parents and, for the first time, responsible for restraining the impulses of boyhood.

Students associated rowdiness and dissipation with boyhood, not manhood. The editors of the *North Carolina University Magazine* went so far as to argue that pranks were "essentially necessary to the ultimate well being of affairs" at college. "The pent up fires of juvenile fun are bound to come out," they explained, "and if not permitted to escape in broken doses such a quantity of combustibility might be generated as to produce 'somethin' orful [awful]."[64] The problem, however, was that "somethin' orful" usually did come out of even the mildest form of "juvenile fun." Freshmen, in particular, experienced intense alienation and violence in the form of hazing. The most insidious form of hazing in the antebellum period was called "smoking out." This ritual involved closing at least one young man up in a room filled with dozens of lit cigars and leaving him to suffocate. One student recalled the gross details of "smoking" freshmen: "Heard of the Sophs smoking the [freshmen] till they vomited and one of them . . . was very ill which greatly frightened them."[65] Another form of hazing involved included tricking freshmen into donating money for liquor that upperclassmen would purchase and drink for themselves. Called the "Fresh Treat," this ritual not only humiliated younger students and gave older students a sense of superiority, but also reflected an unrestrained campus drinking culture.[66]

Excessive drinking was probably the most prevalent misbehavior on campus, and usually it only reinforced collegians' immaturity.[67] For instance, drinking often led to "spreeing," a common collegiate revelry that typically consisted of minor disturbances but sometimes snowballed into serious violence. This was consistent during the entire antebellum period. In 1818, two students were "called to answer for disorderly conduct" before the faculty in which they drank heavily and "then went out into the Street where they were guilty of great disorder—breaking into a neighborhood kitchen—beating a negro and disturbing the white family." All parties were suspended but ultimately readmitted after formal apology. They had been suspended because they violated Sabbath rules.[68] In 1849, Thomas Miles Garrett remembered a veritable bacchanalia among nearly fifty students who went to the circus in the nearby town of Hillsboro. Students "engaged in drinking and carousing, each endeavouring to outstrip the other in velocity of his inebriation, the height of liquor in his class." Before long, several students appeared "in that state of insensibility that they could not exercize any of their senses." They turned over carriages and broke the wheels of wagons outside the circus. When the evening ended, they stumbled back to campus and loudly rang the college bell, disturbing everyone's sleep. The next day lessons went poorly, at least for Garrett, who professed to be a member of the Sons of Temperance but enjoyed the evening as much as his rowdy classmates.[69]

Fights among students were not uncommon at the antebellum university. In August 1841, a fight broke out between two members of the Philanthropic Society, Joseph M. Bunch of Rutledge, Tennessee, and William D. Rice of Eutaw, Alabama. Allegedly, Bunch had insulted Rice at a Philanthropic Society meeting the night before, and Rice called for a duel. The next day, the young men gathered outside of Nancy Hilliard's hotel to watch the fight, most of them cheering for Rice (because Bunch was very unpopular): "Beat him Rice—Kill the d. . . . .ned rascal." According to Dusenbery, "Bunch sustained the . . . fight for some minutes when he received a blow which made him recoil several feet & fall. As he did so, his eye rested on a pistol he had dropped at the first of the fight, which he seized & fired, not at the man he was fighting, but through mistake, at his brother. The ball merely grazed his hip & passed on without farther injury." The two participants continued to fight "unequally for several minutes," Rice armed with a stick and Bunch with nothing, until President Swain and other professors arrived at the scene and quelled the violence. Both Bunch and Rice were dismissed from the university immediately. In the end, James Dusenbery concluded, "Bunch was a rascal & deserved his beating but it was really a shame to compel him to fight at so great a disadvantage."[70] In many ways this incident calls to mind Henry Adams's famous critique of southerners like Roony Lee, waiting around the corner with a gun to revenge insult.[71] As was typical of campus violence across the country, fights at North Carolina could involve slighted honor and wounded pride. No matter the cause, campus violence influenced students' private, moral, and emotional development. This was particularly true as young men found themselves alone, without the protection of fathers and mothers, to traverse the rocky path from boyhood to manhood.

Restraining College Life

As the foregoing stories of campus misbehavior suggest, young men required formal structures to restrain their boyish impulses. Given the distance from their sons, parents usually were not the most immediate source for restraining students' impulsive, "juvenile fun."[72] Instead, the university maintained strict rules for student comportment. In the antebellum period, the Board of Trustees implemented thirty-five ordinances to ensure students' "moral and religious conduct," including proscriptions against improper public deportment and dress; swearing; possessing "obscene" books or pictures; trespassing; attending or betting on horse races; carrying weapons without permission; possessing or drinking liquor without permission; dueling; and not keeping the Sabbath. Often, fear of being expelled, or even temporarily "rusticated" (sent away from college), forestalled misbehavior, but not always.[73] Tutors—recent North Carolina graduates employed as teachers and dormitory monitors—were charged to "individually and unitedly suppress disorders, not only in their own, but in all the buildings."[74] Because tutors were not much older than students, young men did not hesitate resisting their authority. When this occurred, students customarily appeared before the faculty, who ordered them to apologize to the tutor and then acquitted the culprits.[75]

In addition to regular rules and regulations, a broader culture of religious life on campus enforced restraint and morality. Unlike the many denominational colleges that emerged throughout the South during this period, the University of North Carolina was non-sectarian and espoused a moderate evangelical Protestantism. North Carolina students were required to attend public prayer services in the University Chapel twice daily (in the morning and evening). On Sundays, they were required to attend

Chapel in the mornings and Bible recitations in the afternoons. In these recitations, students answered questions about biblical geography and history, but they did not interpret scripture.[76] Seniors studied under President Swain, a Presbyterian; juniors studied under Elisha Mitchell, a professor of chemistry, geology, and mineralogy who was also a Presbyterian minister; sophomores studied under William Hooper, professor of ancient languages and rhetoric and an Episcopal priest who later joined the Baptist church; and freshmen studied under William Mercer Green, an Episcopal priest.[77] Thus, religious culture on campus blended the beliefs and practices of several Christian denominations. Students could also attend one of the local churches. By the late antebellum period, Chapel Hill boasted Presbyterian, Methodist, Episcopal, and Baptist churches. University faculty played an important role in establishing and governing each of these institutions, and students often sat in their congregations on Sunday mornings. According to Kemp Battle, students "were enjoined to reverence the Sabbath, to use no profane language, not to speak disrespectfully of religion or of any religious denomination."[78]

Clergy-professors sometimes addressed unrestrained student conduct in weekly sermons to students. In 1841, for example, Professor William Mercer Green delivered a sermon to the students on the "utter folly [and] great wickedness of profane swearing." James Dusenbery and William Mullins sat in the congregation that day and shared similar reactions to the sermon. "I head a sermon last Sabbath morning for the first time since leaving home. It was delivered by Prof. Green [and] set forth in glaring colours, the utter folly [and] great wickedness of profane swearing," Dusenbery wrote in his diary. "It is a habit that I have resolved never to indulge, not only for the sufficient reason that it is sinful, but because it is useless, immoral [and] ungentlemanly."[79] Mullins praised it as "an excellent sermon on the vulgar, and disgusting practice of profane swearing." He added to his reaction that the sermon "seemed to have a very beneficial effect on his audience, if their countenances were an index to their feelings." For his part, though, Mullins wrote that he was "thoroughly ashamed of ever having been guilty of so low, and disgraceful a vice." Yet he admitted that despite his own "repugnance to the practice, so strong is the force of habit that I find it impossible to abandon it. . . . It has become so linked to my conversation by long usage, that so far my most strenuous efforts to cease the polluting evil have entirely failed."[80] Swearing violated core evangelical teachings about restrained manhood. Since the late eighteenth century, southern evangelicals played an important role in introducing piety, sobriety, and nonviolent behaviors into white male culture, enhancing the status of the Christian gentlemen as one of exemplary public comportment, including chaste expression.[81] These lessons played a role in religious life on campus, as professors sought to create an environment for restrained manhood.

Significantly, the religious climate at North Carolina was not the revival culture that characterized so much of the southern evangelical experience in the antebellum period. Few revivals, in fact, occurred even within close walking distance to Chapel Hill, and students who wished to attend a revival first had to solicit permission from the university president. Students often derided camp meetings as havens for religious fanaticism.[82] In 1841, Dusenbery and his friends, for example, went to a camp meeting eleven miles away from campus, where they found overwhelming spectacles of wailing, fiery sermons, and racial mixing that did little more than confirm their own status as gentlemen. His summary is worth quoting in detail for its depiction of a religious revival as antithetical to the values of restrained, intellectual manhood:

> On reaching the ground we found ourselves to be the only decently dressed fellows there & consequently the centre of attraction. The people stared at us as we passed along & remarked to each other "Them must be scholars." We got to devilling a little negro & cuffy [a black person] after staring at us for some time turned up his eyes with a most meaning & significant look & says he "You'se scholars." And by the time we had been there 15 minutes young men & maidens, old men & negroes had come to the pretty unanimous conclusion that we *were scholars*. . . . After the night sermon a prayer meeting was held & the ground soon became literally covered with prostrate forms. The pit behind the stand was full with negroes, to overflowing & the funk they raised was tremendous. Every old darkee became suddenly inspired with some divine commission, felt himself a preacher & a host in himself & strove to make himself heard. . . . We looked on in silent wonderment until near midnight & then leading our chargers from the bushes, where they had been feeding upon stake-oats for 16 hours, we charged home-wards at the rate of eight miles per hour.[83]

Because young men went to college to receive an education in manhood that distinguished them from common folk and slaves, the university offered a more restrained, institutionalized, and moderate Protestant experience. This was due, in part, to the faith backgrounds of the antebellum professors, who typically affiliated with one of these Protestant denominations and professed Protestant beliefs aimed at moderating individual behavior and preserving social order.

In addition to creating a restrained religious culture, some faculty members cultivated close relationships and coached them along the path to manhood. Granted, students did not always see eye-to-eye with their superiors—and many actively made fun of faculty—but the professoriate often provided much-needed counseling to young men. Walter Lenoir, for example, met privately with President Swain for encouragement about his future. Other faculty spoke with students in their homes and recommended books. These relationships honored students' growing sense of independence but still provided a sense of parental guidance that many students desired.

More typically, advice to students came in the form of public address. William Hooper, professor of classical languages, delivered many addresses that the students requested to be published. In an 1830 "Discourse on Education," for example, Hooper reminded students that "the chief business of education is, to develope, to cultivate, and to train towards perfection, all the useful and agreeable powers of man," and to do that, students needed to rally "on the side of virtue." Hooper urged students, whom he addressed as "my young friends," to reform their habits and guard against pernicious conduct common to college life. "How must a son," he asked, "who has spent a night in drinking, gaming, or debauchery, dread lest his irregularities should reach the knowledge of his parents"? No student could "rise in the morning with a conscience void of offence" and attain "all the honors that collegiate acquirements can confer," unless he abstained from dissipation.[84] Hooper offered friendly, though grave, advice about the proper conduct of life.[85] The strongest guidance for young men, however, came from classmates.

A "Band of Brothers": Literary Societies

Formal university structures, including faculty supervision and religious culture, helped young men adjust to college life. In the process of preventing and correcting student misbehavior, they created an institutional culture of restraint at the university. Some historians have argued that southern all-male peer groups rendered these efforts ineffective. Lorri Glover has argued, for instance, that the "behaviors that adults found upsetting and defined as arrogance, dissipation, and violence, young men found gratifying and interpreted as pride, independence and the exercise of manly power."[86] But this was more the exception than the norm. Students' experiences within their literary societies reveal, for instance, that southern peer groups did not always work at cross-purposes with university faculty, but in tandem with the shared values of restraint and intellectual manhood. The mission of each literary society, like college life generally, was to turn boys into men. Thus, the historian James McLachlan has appropriately called these societies "colleges within colleges."[87]

The student-organized Dialectic and Philanthropic Societies were the only institutions of student life for most of the antebellum period.[88] These institutions were part of a long intellectual tradition in American colleges and universities, dating back to the colonial period. Indeed, literary societies were established at every new public and private college or university of the early republic. Following this tradition, the University of North Carolina's Di and Phi Societies (as they were commonly called) were intended for and governed by youth.[89] They served students' intellectual needs by providing opportunities to learn parliamentary procedure, acquire oratorical and debating skills, and collect, read, and discuss literature. Societies also provided space for socialization, and many young men made lifelong friends and important professional connections. Moreover, these societies promoted emulation, as students competed with one another for collegiate honors. In the process, literary society members encouraged one another along their journey from boyhood to manhood, emphasizing mind and virtue over passion and vice. In these ways, literary societies fulfilled young men socially, morally, and intellectually.

Literary societies were not the only organizations on campus, but they were by far the most important. In southern colleges such as North Carolina, fraternities first appeared on campus in the 1840s but did not achieve popularity comparable to literary societies until after the Civil War. When fraternities first formed at Chapel Hill, the university quickly forbade them, and many students feared that these secret organizations might undermine friendships forged in literary societies.[90] "I would also caution the new members," one student explained in 1855, "against joining any of the numerous secret clubs which have lately sprung up amongst us for they are calculated not only to destroy that social and pleasant intercourse among the students for which our college has always been noted but they are in direct opposition to the principles of the constitution of the Dialectic Society."[91] Of course, peer admonitions did not keep students from joining fraternities, but literary societies did the major work of the socialization of youth at the antebellum college.[92]

Literary societies provided a unique structure in which this socialization could occur. First, constitutions and bylaws promoted both intellectual work and character formation by regulating student behavior during society meetings. Second, societies elected officers—president, vice president, secretary, critics, and censor morum—to enforce rules and exemplify proper decorum and comportment. For example, the censor morum—named after the censor of the Roman Senate, who censured senators' behavior—"notice[d] every violation of the laws of society that comes under their observation."[93] Finally, each society had a system of fines whereby students paid small amounts of money if they laughed audibly or talked in the hall, picked fights, arrived late, or failed to participate in regular literary exercises. Students at North Carolina were thus not unlike their northern counterparts who, according to the historian James McLachlan, created in literary societies "an extraordinarily intense and unremittent system of education by peers."[94] This structure went largely unchanged during much of the antebellum period and as such underscores several important continuities in young men's transition from boyhood to manhood during that era.

First, maturation was a primary concern in each literary society throughout the antebellum period. Students relied on their own heightened age consciousness to inspire themselves toward intellectual manhood. "Youth is the time to establish those practices which will adhere to us in old age," one student wrote in 1805, "and if we sow the seeds of vice, we cannot expect to reap the fruit of virtue. A man of education but destitute of virtue will never become respectable in the world unless among his equals; whereas a virtuous man will never want respectable friends."[95] Or as another student explained forty-five years later, youth was "pliant," a phase of life in which one's individual nature was in a "state of fluidity and transition." Students needed to cultivate "habits of industry and sobriety and reflection," which alone "determine whether you are to rank among the ornaments of society, or among the grovelling tribes of drones and profligates who counter the earth with an existence alike useless and mischievous."[96]

Second, students explicitly evoked the goal of becoming men when addressing behavioral problems in weekly society meetings during the entire antebellum period. "The Society would rather make men of you, than deprive you of your money," one student argued when discussing a problem with fines for poor attendance at meetings. He urged his fellow members to "come out then and act nobly your part." By encouraging discipline, order, and regularity among fellow members, literary society members believed they were contributing to one another's larger goal of reaching adulthood.[97] In his 1859 inaugural address to the Dialectic Society, Junius Cullen Battle chided his classmates for excessive laughing, which he deemed "more after the manner of schoolboys than of men."[98] The literary societies also prohibited swearing, and students were either ejected from meetings or fined for using profane or "unrestrained use of language."[99] Thus in their regular society addresses, students reinforced gentlemanly rules of conduct and echoed lessons on daily speech habits articulated in sermons about swearing.[100]

Third, young men's peer education in literary societies consistently upheld emerging mainstream, bourgeois values and traditional southern values. Literary societies members, for instance, reinforced bourgeois ideals associated with intellectual manhood such as industry, sobriety, and self-discipline, which were considered absolutely necessary for the vision of a good society and the cultivation of intellectual manhood.[101] Literary society rules and regulations were also compatible with the southern tradition of honor. Joseph John Jackson used an agricultural metaphor in his inaugural address to the Dialectic Society in 1838, for example, to illustrate how the Society's laws and regulations assisted the cultivation of virtue and the pursuit of greatness. Like the farmer who rids his garden of weeds that obstruct a plant's growth, "the laws for our regulation . . . open the path of honor and distinction to our view." Moreover, society culture mandated that each member point out anyone who "is destitute of the 'mens conscia sibi recti,'" or "that independent consciousness of integrity which can characterize the gentleman and man of honor by associating with gentlemen in this hall he too is turned from the contemplation of his kindred earth and his views directed to what is truly honorable and worth contending for."[102]

Finally, this system of peer education consistently relied on and exalted the strong friendships forged in literary societies.[103] Assembling as a "band of brothers," new members of the Dialectic Society pledged to "contract a Friendship" with one another "which shall not be forgotten, when we meet in the serious business of Life."[104] Restraining boyish impulses required the efforts of all society members. "Since we are so constituted, the society being composed of individual members, that we must all 'share in the disgrace and participate in the honor of each member,'" another student explained in 1859, "it becomes a duty which every member not only owes to society but to himself, that he not only act correctly, but also see that the deportment of others is good."[105] Members of each society maintained, moreover, that only friendships rooted in mutual attainment of wisdom and virtue were true. "If you are desirous of living agreeable to your Companions and fellows, can you firmly establish either friendship or esteem without paying any regard to mental acquirements?" asked one member of the Dialectic Society in 1841. No friendship, he went on to argue, was ever permanent or meaningful "whose union & intimacy" was not "formed with a view to our improvement" and a desire to be wise.[106] Moreover, students told one another to beware hasty friendships, which were made superficially and defied "sound policy and rational judgment."[107] Though each literary society had members who did not get along, members regulated as much as possible any rivalries, or at least attempted to enforce codes of conduct that might ameliorate soured friendships.

In these ways, literary society members inspired one another to develop mature virtues including industry, temperance, mutual aid, and sympathy. They relied on many tactics to encourage one another to work hard. They reminded one another of the value of education, obligation to family and to community, and the need for ambition. Most importantly, young men relied on their own age consciousness. As a "band of brothers," literary society members worked to ameliorate many of the new social and emotional issues of youth, which college life brought out in very real terms. Young men who sought to abandon their schoolboy ways and assume intellectual manhood in its place could find in the structure of college life the incentive to do so.

These are the most important structures of student life, and they presented various creative opportunities for young men coming of age. Young men could, for instance, participate in the rowdy youth culture of student life, which existed between boyhood and manhood, but they could also find many opportunities to restrain those impulses within peer-directed literary societies. Indeed, as the historian Jennifer Green has found in military academy life, "no monolithic concept of manhood existed among southern youth of the [antebellum] period."[108] Instead, collegians were presented with many opportunities to create and recreate individual identities— sometimes with help from others, but not always.

William Mullins and College Life

William Sidney Mullins's experiences at college bring into focus the many social and emotional forces of youth that nagged young men after they made the long journey from home to a new and alienating college world. His journey through the first years of college particularly illustrates how the bourgeois culture of university life and traditional elements of southern culture, especially honor, existed alongside one another as part of the creative process of maturation.

Like other southern males who pursued and invested in higher education, Mullins had high hopes and great ambitions. A grocer's son, Mullins wished to become an active member of the region's educated class, specifically a scholar and a renowned lawyer. He attended the Donaldson Academy in Fayetteville, North Carolina, made excellent marks, and showed much promise for success at college. But he did not enjoy much parental support for his higher education. Although his father had encouraged education, his mother, a devout Methodist, was skeptical of the influence of higher education on her son's piety. His mother and father also seemed to have had a strained relationship that affected his emotional life. "Family dissension have embittered all my hours and made that home, which should be a haven of bliss, a scene of torment," he wrote. "It is not a pleasant place." Mullins never suggested any cause for this family strife, though it weighed on him at college.[109]

When Mullins arrived at North Carolina in 1839, both the Dialectic and Philanthropic Societies courted him. He joined the Philanthropic Society and, as a freshman, showed great enthusiasm for schoolwork and sought the approval of prominent members of his literary society. In his sophomore year, however, he befriended "the three most dissipated students in college," Shepard K. Nash, Alfred M. Taylor, and Lucious J. Johnson. Widely known as campus rowdies, they drank, gambled, and swore, and Mullins "unconsciously received a tinge from their character, and . . . became a rowdy." He got drunk every night and kept liquor "habitually in my room."[110] Association with these rowdies tarnished Mullins's reputation among the distinguished members of the Philanthropic Society, especially his childhood classmate William H. Haigh, who criticized Mullins's behavior. Mullins felt betrayed by Haigh's attempt "to excite odium" against him. Falling in with the wrong crowd, Mullins lamented in his diary, was almost the worst thing he could have done so early in his college days.[111] By the beginning of his junior year, however, Mullins's dissipated friends slowly left Chapel Hill. Nash had been expelled, Johnson had been graduated, and Taylor would soon be dismissed for misbehavior. Mullins's junior year, in fact, seemed quite promising until he instigated a campus-wide prank that further diminished his popularity and called into question the very meaning of honor that so many southern men valued.

Mullins felt the full weight of male honor culture in October 1840. He and his friend and fellow member of the Philanthropic Society, James Delk, decided to instigate a hoax—a "sham duel." Their friends made all the arrangements necessary for the staged duel, which promised to be a funny joke until word spread around campus; freshmen in the Dialectic Society reported to be "frightened nearly to death" at the prospect of open violence on campus. Rumors of the "sham duel" culminated in Mullins's and Delk's ultimate admission that it was a ruse. The hoax alienated Mullins from his fellow Phis, who viewed his dishonesty as an affront to their honor and that of the society. His classmates derided him as the "Hero of the Sham Duel," which humiliated Mullins, prompting him to threaten anyone who ridiculed him to a duel. "I wish to have no trouble, but if they force me to an encounter," he confessed in his diary, "I shall not shrink from carrying it to extremes, even if it involves one of their lives. I will endeavour to teach certain individuals that it is not as easy to put down a student, as they may think. That this is their design, I am convinced, and I am forced in self defence, to carry the war into Africa." Indeed, Mullins carried his pistol with him on campus, though he never instigated a duel.[112]

Reflecting on the "sham duel," Mullins wrote that he learned "several important lessons." First, delaying the hoax was "fatal." He and Delk should have met immediately and demonstrated that all the plans were in jest. Second, he was "not sufficiently prudent" in how he handled the instigation of the hoax. Finally, and most importantly, he learned "*never to engage in such an affair again. They can do no good—they* may *do much harm.* Those who are hoaxed are apt to be offended: and those not, raise a laugh that is rather annoying. They do not produce a favourable impression of an individual's steadiness or gravity and are well adapted to diminish respect."[113] In short, Mullins learned about the power of cliques, respect, and honor in youth culture. His humiliation as the "hero of the Sham duel" underscores the seriousness with which young southern men did, in fact, view affairs of honor. These young men could not stomach the notion of staged, nearly

Barnumesque humbugs when it came to duels because, as Kenneth Greenberg has argued, they were supposed to elevate honesty.[114]

To discuss this affair in terms of honor ignores the other side of the equation—the broader values of restrained manhood contained within peer expectations. The affair was not just dishonorable; it was also immature in its unrestraint. As "hero of the Sham" duel, Mullins also learned that the young men he respected, in turn, respected men who were disciplined, temperate, if not sober, industrious, and polite. In order to stake his claim in the educated class, Mullins soon figured out that he had to resist the impulses of youth and withstand the temptations of vice and dissipation. The struggles within this peer culture prompted him to turn inward, temper his boyish impulsivity, and cultivate restrained manhood.

Religion helped to mitigate these tensions and provide a set of ideals that would help him leave the world of his youth and enter the world of intellectual manhood. During his first three years at North Carolina, Mullins had become disaffected with his mother's Methodist faith and sought a religion that worked for him as he pursued intellectual manhood. He disavowed the Methodist church completely and viewed it as an impediment to his intellectual and moral formation. He sneered at the demonstrable lack of education and eloquence among Methodist and Presbyterian preachers. So during his junior and senior years, he began attending the Chapel of the Cross, the newly built Episcopal Church in Chapel Hill, which had been founded and presided over by William Mercer Green. Green's sermons made a lasting impression on Mullins. An ambitious scholar, Mullins desired a faith more suited to his intellect than to his heart and found it in the more restrained Christianity of the Episcopal Church. He prayed to be "speedily converted." And as we shall see in chapter 5, his faith provided the foundation for his self-improvement efforts.[115]

THESE WERE THE MAJOR STRUCTURES that framed students' experiences of college life. When young men arrived at the college in Chapel Hill, they found a new emotional and social landscape. Occupying a space between boyhood and manhood, college life presented both challenges and rewards for young men in pursuit of mental maturity, or intellectual manhood. In a variety of social settings on campus, students confronted head on the tensions of youth—boyhood versus manhood, impulse versus restraint, and dependence versus independence. Although largely left on their own to make sense out of this world, students found external encouragement from parents and faculty, as well as a strong "band of brothers" in literary societies. Together, young Dis and Phis guided one another to distinctions, ameliorated the emotional conflicts of college life, rearticulated core ideals of intellectual manhood, and helped to create a strikingly restrained bourgeois culture on campus. This culture existed alongside the rowdier side of college life often explored in scholarly literature. Peer-education worked for students because it catered to maturation.

As "colleges within colleges," literary societies also served the main goals of higher education: mental and moral improvement. Students consistently reminded one another of the reasons why they came to college in the first place; as William Seawell explained to his Dialectic Society brethren in 1825, "You come here to know how to learn, to implant fixed roots of habitual application which in after life will enable the mind to triump[h] over every foe which besets its wayfaring in the journey of science. It is to trace that course of discipline—to exhibit the features of that regimen which is to assist the growth and give robustness to the mental constitution."[116] The following chapter examines student engagement with the formal pedagogy and curriculum, particularly the focus on restraint over impulse, mind over temperament, and the exaltation of greatness and heroism.

CHAPTER TWO

You Come Here to Know How to Learn
Pedagogy and Curriculum

On Monday, 4 October 1841, Ruffin Tomlinson, a junior at the University of North Carolina, recorded in his diary that he had read "Milton upon education" and praised it as "one of the best pieces in the english language." He copied Milton's definition of "a complete and generous education" into his diary: "that which fits a man to perform justly, skillfully, and magnanimously all the offices both private and public, of peace and war." Tomlinson thought about this definition for some time and then turned to the community of scholars and students around him for their answers to the question, "What is the object of an education?" First, he asked David Swain, the university president, who replied, "The object of an education is to write and to speak." Then he asked the professor of chemistry and geology, Elisha Mitchell, who replied, "To fit a man for after life." Afterward, he asked his friend, William C. Hunt, who replied: "To put a man in the possession of the power to think for himself." Tomlinson finally concluded that the object of education was "to enable a man to discharge the duties of life to the best advantage to himself and his fellow beings."[1]

As these definitions suggest, formal education at antebellum North Carolina was construed broadly as a means for young men to improve themselves for the betterment of society. Educators relied on the centuries-old classical curriculum, a four-year program of studies designed to promote mental and moral improvement. The curriculum was "classical" not so much because it emphasized Greek and Latin, but because its origins dated back to antiquity.[2] Freshmen and sophomores primarily studied Greek and Latin, but also geometry and algebra. Juniors and seniors continued Greek and Latin studies, but also studied additional mathematics and science courses such as natural philosophy, astronomy, chemistry, geology, trigonometry, and fluxions (calculus), plus rhetoric, logic, belles lettres, and sometimes French. In addition, seniors studied moral philosophy, political economy, and constitutional history.[3] The curriculum culminated in public examinations and commencement speeches that showcased not only the knowledge acquired in college but also the ability to express that knowledge in formal speech (see chapter 3).

Although historians of southern higher education have mostly focused on how this classical education taught political leadership and social polish, a closer look at education as a cultural process reveals that this was not merely an "ornamental" education for elite planters.[4] As Jane Turner Censer has argued, "Male education was practical in its results, since it fitted young men for a variety of positions," including those in the most popular alumni professions such as law, medicine, ministry, and education.[5] The classical curriculum was also practical insofar as it aided in the transition from boyhood to manhood; it equipped young men with tools and resources for self-development, or self-improvement. It did so by providing structure for mitigating the tensions explored in chapter 1—boyhood versus manhood, mind versus temperament, impulse versus restraint, and dependence versus independence. This chapter considers both how this education occurred from the student perspective and how it prepared them to enter the broader educated class of southerners.

A comprehensive treatment of the curriculum is impossible here, but when viewed holistically and through the lens of student writing, it is clear that all branches of the curriculum catered to the transition from boyhood to manhood. According to the historian Caroline Winterer, a "classical education" was a "molding process" that "ennobled the self and formed the conscientious citizen."[6] Fostering mental and moral maturity, or intellectual manhood, was central to this curriculum. The pedagogical emphasis on recitation promoted discipline, restraint, competition, and merit, which were key components of this ideal. Individual subjects complemented this process. Dead languages and ancient texts taught these values and, at the same time, introduced young men to ideal models of restrained manhood.[7] Science education expanded on this work. Not only did science and math cultivate demonstrative reasoning skills useful for any number of professions, as well as public life, it also prepared young men for careers in scientific professions and engineering. Significantly, this science education helped to restrain young men's developing ambition by grounding science in core Protestant beliefs about the natural world.[8] The senior-year moral philosophy course taught young men not only how the mind operated, but how it could be improved and why improvement was noble for the self and society.

In the process of this higher education, young men learned restraint, ambition, competitiveness, judgment, and reason, which they blended with traditional southern notions of honor and independence. Meanwhile, they learned to think of both the self and the world in terms of sublimity, grandeur, and greatness. Like the individual self, civilization could be improved under the direction of educated elites in possession of intellectual manhood. These romantic attitudes fueled the process of maturation and characterized intellectual culture beyond the classroom. It is first necessary to understand how pedagogy functioned as a mechanism for fashioning the male self.

Pedagogy and Maturation

Recitation was the primary pedagogy of nineteenth-century education. It emphasized mental and moral improvement and required rote memorization of accepted truths about language and humanity. Professors expected students to recall and paraphrase information from assigned texts, but they were not asked to engage the texts critically.[9] Students were not allowed to bring textbooks or translations of classical texts to class.[10] In recitation rooms, students sat (alphabetically by last name) on wooden benches facing the professor's desk, behind which hung a blackboard. In an 1856 class essay, seventeen-year-old Thomas Mason depicts a professor seated "on a high rostrum, assuming all the dignity of his lofty station" before thirty or forty "young men of all sorts of characters and dispositions."[11] Sometimes professors quizzed students at length, but not always. In 1857, Henry Francis Jones recalled, "Mr. Fetter [professor of Greek] took me up this morning, no more though than I expected. He didn't keep a fellow up more than two minutes."[12] Students usually knew when they might recite, for professors followed the alphabetical order of the seating arrangement when questioning students.[13] But professors were not always so predictable. George Thompson was surprised, for example, when he "was taken up" six times in his geometry class in one week. "I call that getting tolerable high up in the pictures," he joked in his diary.[14] Sometimes misbehavior undermined this pedagogy. According to one student writer, some students were "grave and sober," but others were "all fume and fuss" or simply "trifling beyond all tolerance."[15] Professors usually conducted junior and senior recitations, leaving the underclassmen to tutors, who were often not as prepared as professors to distill a large body of scholarship. Consequently, students often disrespected tutors during recitations. Contemporaries often faulted classical pedagogy for these reasons.[16]

At its best, recitation promoted several core values of the southern bourgeoisie. By ascending the professor's rostrum to explain an abstraction, recall a fact, or translate a passage, a student could demonstrate values of intellectual manhood such as perseverance, diligence, self-discipline, and authority. Recitation, in other words, provided a forum in which young men could perform roles that mimicked their future public duties of commanding authority in a competitive world; it proved that he could compete and win.[17] But these lessons sometimes also touched a raw nerve when it came to the code of southern honor. Structured as it was, recitation threatened to embarrass students, for it required deference to authority and the possibility of revealing ignorance.[18] Although students did not usually write about fear of embarrassment in such abstractions, they did write about how the nineteenth-century classroom's hierarchical spatial arrangement generated anxiety. In September 1857, Henry Francis Jones wrote in his diary, "I have a tremendous hard lesson to get to night. I dread it too. It is a greek lesson."[19] In these ways, recitation catered to both bourgeois values but also threatened male honor.

In addition to recitation, professors also delivered lectures, which modeled reason, eloquence, discipline, and restraint of intellectual manhood. Usually part of science education, lectures supplemented and extended assigned reading. "The object of these lectures is not to exhibit in a popular dress the various subjects noticed in your text books," Professor James Phillips explained to his natural philosophy students.[20] Sometimes professors conducted experiments, which students often anticipated, though they never participated in them. As a result, lectures could become quite boring.[21] William Mullins, for example, noted in his diary "the dryest kind of lecture" on calculus, which was nearly as boring as the ninety-minute chemistry lecture he heard later that year.[22] These shortcomings aside, lectures sought the same end as recitation: mental improvement through the active use of attention, memory, and self-discipline. Students' classroom notes reflect this pedagogy, as well as the hierarchy between professors and students.

Students who took notes during lectures often copied them afterward into readable prose, using published outlines and textbooks to supplement what they heard in class. In 1820, Joseph Hubbard Saunders kept a detailed notebook of Denison Olmstead's chemistry course at North Carolina, which illuminates student engagement. He copied Olmstead's main points, underscored keywords and phrases, and critiqued the conclusions. In a lecture on heat and temperature, for example, Saunders noted that Olmstead argued, "Under ordinary circumstances, therefore, dark, or, black, clothing is [more] suitable for a student in a hot day, than light colored." Supporting this point, Olmstead explained, "That Negroes are more able to bear heat, than white persons, is not to be ascribed entirely to *habit*, for the same holds true when negroes are brought up in cold climates; but it is to ascribe to their black skins; for they are *gainers* by *their radiating surfaces*." Saunders then critiqued Olmstead: "This cause of Prof. Olmstead does not appear very satisfactory to me for, when negroes are exposed to the direct influence of the sun, as in a cornfield, it appears that as their black skin is a very great absorbing surface." Saunders, however, may have misunderstood Olmstead, whose outlines for the course explain, "In Summer light coloured clothing best in the sun—dark coloured in the shade—why negroes bear the heat better than white people."[23] Saunders likely confined his remarks to his private notebook. Thus, while lectures required deference to authority, students might have assumed some intellectual freedom when they took possession of the material in private study.

Students identified study with maturity. It promoted mental discipline and, therefore, promised to turn boys into men. Students cautioned one another against anything that might hinder study—idleness, dissipation, socializing, and extracurricular reading (see chapter 4). In 1822, for example, Dialectic Society president James Dickson recommended to his classmates "unremitted application and persevering assiduity in the prosecution of the studies of your respective classes." Moreover, he cautioned them to beware false assumptions that young men achieved distinction without study. "Let no one pride himself upon the preposition of brilliant talents or eminent abilities, let him not harbour the pleasing but delusive idea that he can make himself master of any branch of literature or science without diligence & industry," he argued.[24] Study also required focus and direction. As Thomas Garrett wrote in his diary, "If a man studies as his inclination leads him without any settled purpose or object, that resolution which is necessary to have to be master of his own powers will be gradually further removed and more difficult to recal[l]."[25] Students consistently promoted these study habits in literary society addresses throughout the antebellum period, arguing that study promised to facilitate intellectual maturation. In the process, they instilled broader values of restrained manhood.[26]

Students' study habits varied. Some students studied their lessons each night, while others gleaned over assigned readings quickly in the morning before breakfast or between recitations. James Hilliard Polk reflected on the best times for study in his diary: "At the still hours of night I can fix my whole mind on my lessons, but in the hustle of day, there are too many objects to engage the attention." So he decided that "night, dark night, when all nature has sunk beneath the hour of sleep, then is the fit time for the student to store his head with the hidden treasures of ancient lore."[27] It also was easier for students who roomed alone to study at night, after their classmates went to bed.[28] Because students could predict when professors would call on them to recite, many of them only studied when they expected to recite. Whenever they chose to study, however, students usually turned to assigned texts, although sometimes textbooks complicated lectures. Reading for his natural philosophy course, for instance, Thomas Garrett complained, "This day has been entirely taken up with the science of Optics in Philosophy, a subject quite interesting indeed; but I would willingly escape from the duty of studying it in the language of the author," which was "obscure" and "unintelligible."[29] Not surprisingly, then, students often studied together. As Henry Francis Jones explained in his diary, "I had mathematics this morning, and I made Jim help me last night for the first time."[30]

In a fictional memoir, Edwin Fuller compared his study habits with those of a close friend. He wrote, "Ned studied to learn all his lesson—to know every part of it; while I often picked over those points on which I thought I should most likely be examined. He studied to master the subject—to become acquainted with a language or to understand a problem; I studied to make a good recitation. He stored up for the future; I looked no farther ahead than the next morning's lecture." Fuller especially remembered studying Homer. "Ned would worry a whole morning over an idiom; and passages that I found no difficulty at all in rendering would afford him an hour's work with lexicon and grammar," he wrote. But Fuller used an annotated edition, "a great friend of the student," and used "its voluminous references" to "cram all that it was probable the professor would touch upon." His recitations, however, were not usually successful. "All the portions I had prepared so carefully were given to others to render or construe," Fuller recalled, "while I would be taken up on some part I had thought too simple for my attention, and would be found woefully ignorant." As a result of his studying, he only made a "brilliant recitation" about twice a month.[31]

Many young men required incentives to study, but a grading system did not exist in the antebellum period. Instead, faculty met at the end of each session, determined each student's class standing, and completed reports, which were later sent to a student's family. In 1835, Charles Pettigrew wrote to his father, "The trustees passed a law that the parents of each student should be informed of the manner he was conducting himself in the institution." But he questioned the effectiveness of this system and explained that it was "very difficult to distinguish between men nearly equal." He also added, "The teacher is biased sometimes in favour of one to the disparagement of another."[32] Nevertheless, Charles conceded that the system worked: "There has been a much greater amount of studying in college since this plan has been adopted."[33] Only very general reports were sent to parents at the end of terms. Tod Caldwell's 1837 report, for example, read that the faculty "have the pleasure to state that your son, is regarded as an excellent scholar, and of exemplary deportment." The faculty also discussed students' individual academic performances in each class and then voted on who deserved a first, second, or third distinction. Students called those who were so distinguished "1st, 2nd and 3rd 'might' men." The faculty announced the recipients of the three highest distinctions annually at commencement and published their names in local newspapers.[34]

Merit-based distinctions produced mixed opinions among students. Although class distinctions promoted industry, merit, emulation, and ambition, sometimes those values clashed with the code of southern honor, as a class set of essays on the topic demonstrates.[35] In 1840, Richmond Pearson wrote, "The hope of reward is the prime mover of every action in life. What, we would ask, incites us to practice the virtues of industry, and frugality in the common affairs of life: but the hope of acquiring that competence which is necessary to its enjoyment?" Not all students agreed, arguing that merit might cause humiliation among peers and a slight to personal honor.[36] In 1842, Edmund Covington complained that his report reflected neither his intellect nor his effort. "I struggled hard to crown the hopes and wishes of my friends at home and to secure the approbation of the faculty here. But what is my reward?" he confided to his diary. The faculty's report diminished his hopes and "blasted" his "innocent and laudable ambition." Worse, it besmirched his reputation. "I have studied mainly for my improvement," he explained. "But a youth of my age and character sets a high value on a reputation for qualities whether of the head or heart. My fellow students know that I have studied—they know my report and altho' they may tell me that the faculty are unjust, they will rejoice at that injustice in secret."[37] For Covington, the system of community validation often discussed in literature on southern men mattered greatly, but it also existed alongside other incentives for success.

In all, classroom pedagogy emphasized disciplining the mind, honing attention, and thinking maturely, which students were supposed to apply to private study. Although not every student studied seriously, academic distinctions provided some incentive to cultivate industry, perseverance, and diligence. Core curricular subjects proposed a rubric for this pursuit by insisting that young men focus on improvement and self-discipline. They also provided ideal models of restrained manhood for students to emulate. This process began with ancient languages and literature.

"At the foundation of all advancement": Ancient Languages and Literature

In 1835, when nineteen-year-old Kenelm Lewis learned that his younger brother had begun studying Latin, he wrote from Chapel Hill, "This may be considered a new era in your life."[38] Indeed, classics had served as a rite of passage from boyhood to manhood for centuries, providing educated elites with tools for self-fashioning and preparing them for leadership.[39] In the antebellum South, like the nation as a whole, Latin and Greek study catered to existing attitudes about gender, especially the notion of men's and women's separate spheres. Boys and young men studied the classics more than girls and young women because of the public roles males were expected to play. According to Elizabeth Fox-Genovese and Eugene Genovese, the classics "never became a part of the ideal of southern womanhood" to the extent that it did the ideal of the southern gentleman, whose refined taste, linguistic polish, and erudition conferred elite social and political authority.[40] Yet antiquity's educational value transcended the southern gentleman ideal of refinement. Learning dead languages sharpened young men's minds and taught not only self-discipline, industry, and perseverance, but human greatness as well as depravity. Finally, the study of antiquity introduced emerging romantic ideas of sublimity, grandeur, and civilization to students' understanding of the world and their place in it. This, in other words, was a thoroughly Victorian education in selfhood.

Most of a young man's higher education concerned antiquity, particularly Latin and Greek language study. University of North Carolina president Joseph Caldwell explained in 1827, for example, "The basis then of a liberal education is correctly laid in a knowledge of language as the essential instrument of thought and reasoning, without which the researches and communications of science could be prosecuted within but very contracted limits."[41] In their first two years, collegians studied Latin and Greek grammar and syntax intensively, using various grammatical primers.[42] Simultaneously, students studied ancient texts concerning government, oratory, philosophy, and aesthetics.[43] They typically began studying easy Latin texts such as Quintus Curtius's history, *Cornelius Nepos*, and progressed through more advanced works, including Cicero's *In Catilinam*, *Philippicae*, *De Officiis*, *De Senectute*, and *De Amicitia*; Horace's *Odes*, *Satires*, and *Art of Poetry*; Virgil's *Georgics* and *Aeneid*; Ovid's *Metamorphoses*; Caesar's *Commentaries*; and Juvenal's *Satires*. Simultaneously, students moved through a Greek-language curriculum that usually began with one of the Greek historian Xenophon's three popular works, *Anabasis*, *Cyropaedia*, or *Memorabilia*, and continued with Demosthenes' orations and Homer's *Iliad*. Upperclassmen also studied Greek histories of Herodotus and Thucydides, and Roman histories such as Tacitus's *Agricola* and *Germania*; they also read Greek tragedies like Sophocles' *Oedipus Rex*.[44]

Believing that philology, the study of language, best promoted mental and moral improvement, professors expected students to translate as many as eighty lines of Greek or Latin text, line by line, and answer questions about vocabulary, grammar, and syntax.[45] Students typically dreaded the tedious memorization and recitation of grammar. When the going got rough, however, some students cheated.[46] Ample English translations circulated in the Dialectic and Philanthropic Society libraries, and some students created crib notes. In 1846, a group of students compiled "The Fresman's Friend," a study guide containing a translation and answers to possible recitation questions for Xenophon's *Memorabilia*.[47] Among the reasons students gave for using translations was that deficiency in Latin and Greek wounded their self-esteem. "In the Junior and Sophomore years I was accustomed to study Greek with the aid of a translation," wrote Walter Lenoir to his father. "This session I determined to study without one. The consequence is, that, while I study the lessons twice as long and learn much more in fact than I did before, my apparent standing is worse."[48]

Facility with dead languages was not students' only concern with Latin and Greek. While few Americans doubted the classics' importance in the eighteenth century—the ancients' concerns about government, law, order, and civility resonated in the emerging republic—later generations were more skeptical. Some Americans argued that antiquity did not prepare young men to lead a world in which technological innovation and commerce played an increasingly important role; others feared ancient mores could undermine Christian values. Periodically, students addressed these issues. "The ancient Greek & Romans were heathens," Wilbur Foster explained in a speech to his classmates. He wondered why "the student is taught to see in them the very personification of intellectual and moral excellence" when the ancients knew nothing of God or the Bible.[49] For another student, Richard Hamlin, the problem was one of utility. "This age of improvement loudly demands a new system of education," explained Richard Hamlin to his classmates in 1858. "It calls for practical knowledge that prepares us for the stormy sea of life." For students who wished to enter a profession or become farmers or planters, what use were ancient authors? These critiques notwithstanding, most classical scholars and students found that classical and Christian morality were compatible; antiquity both supported Christian values and bolstered ideals of restrained manhood. While some colleges decreased classical offerings in the antebellum period, most did not, maintaining that antiquity and Protestant Christianity offered complementary moral lessons for young men.[50]

Specifically, antiquity contained certain motifs that resonated with male youth: mind and temperament, impulse and restraint, boyhood and manhood, depravity and greatness. A careful look at one widely read ancient text—Xenophon's *Memorabilia*—reveals the relevance of classical education to young men's moral development and to the intellectual manhood ideal. Xenophon was one of the most commonly read ancient historians in the early republic. His three major works—*Anabasis*, *Cyropaedia*, and *Memorabilia*—were used regularly at North Carolina throughout the nineteenth century. *Memorabilia* narrates the life and teachings of Socrates, who was prosecuted in 399 BC on charges of undermining Athenian laws and corrupting youth. In *Memorabilia*, Xenophon refutes these charges and praises Socrates' teachings about the role of virtue in creating "perfect men," or those "fit to rule."[51] For young men in pursuit of greatness, this was useful Greek.

Nowhere in *Memorabilia* did Xenophon offer an image of moral improvement as heroic as in the famous parable of Hercules as he matured from boyhood to manhood. The parable goes like this: One day, two women appeared before Hercules—Vice and Virtue—each offering advice on living a great life. Scantily clad and voluptuous, Vice seduced Hercules with "all the sweets of life." Then, Virtue, "fair to see . . . adorned with purity, her eyes with modesty," approached Hercules and said, "I know your parents and I have taken note of your character during the time of your education. Therefore I hope that, if you take the road that leads to me, you will turn out a right good doer of high and noble deeds, and I shall be yet more highly honored and more illustrious for the blessings I bestow." She urged him to worship the gods, cultivate friendships, and perform good deeds. In the end, Virtue won the fight for Hercules' future.[52] According to the historian James McLachlan, this parable of the "Choice of Hercules" was used for centuries to instill morality among young men. Addressing ancient youth, Cicero wrote, for instance, "It is more in accord with nature to emulate the great Hercules and undergo the greatest toil and trouble for the sake of aiding or saving the world, if possible, than to live in seclusion, not only free from all care, but reveling in pleasures and abounding in wealth, while excelling others also in beauty and strength."[53] In his 1850 inaugural address as Dialectic Society president, James Patton, first quoting Horace— "Nil mortalibus arduum est" (Nothing is difficult for mortals)—urged his classmates to emulate Hercules, who dared to lead a virtuous life.[54] The parable related to young collegians, who found themselves on moral *terra incognita* at college, without daily guidance from parents. They knew well the urgency of youth to create a foundation for manhood, and this text conveyed a morality completely compatible with mainstream, middle-class morality, particularly values of perseverance and virtue.

Whether all students derived deep moral lessons from ancient texts is impossible to know, but student writing from literary societies reveals how, at some level, they engaged with these themes. Like *Memorabilia*, Xenophon's widely read *Cyropaedia* was also useful to students. Translated as "The Education of Cyrus," *Cyropaedia* chronicles the development of Cyrus the Great, whose decades-long reign led to unprecedented expansion of Persian civilization. Students studying *Cyropaedia* lauded Cyrus's sobriety and temperance. "Temperance was his [Cyrus's] cardinal virtue, as it was of all his countrymen at the time," explained Elam Alexander in an 1823 address to the Dialectic Society. "It was temperate & hardy Macedonians who achieved the conquest of the degenerate & effeminate Persians. but in turn, they too, with their master, fell a prey to the luxuries & vices of the people whom they conquered such has been the usual order of events. . . . The same order still prevails and prevails universally. Youthful intemperance generally prevents the attainment of any excellence."[55] Significantly, Alexander underscores Cyrus's restraint and applied it to young men's maturation and their developing ambitions. If young men were to leave boyhood, they first had to restrain their passions and elevate mind over temperament.

The tension between impulse and restraint appeared in other curricular texts, including Cicero's two famous philosophical works, *Cato Maior De Senectute* (Cato on Old Age) and *Laelius De Amicitia* (Laelius on Friendship). Written in the final years of his life (45–44 BC), just after the Roman Republic collapsed, these texts taught values of moral improvement and self-fashioning.[56] Set in 150 BC, *De Senectute* consists of lectures that the eighty-four-year-old Cato, a distinguished Roman soldier and censor in the Roman Senate, delivered to two young men. He delineates "the principles and practice of the virtues, which, if cultivated in every period of life, bring forth wonderful fruits at the close of a long and busy career" and at life's end. Specifically, he recommends moderation in diet and sex. Outside the classroom, students appropriated Cicero's moral lessons in their own development.[57] On 21 August 1849, Thomas Miles Garrett read *De Senectute*, praising its "many useful lessons of morality from which both the young and old may profit," which included "temperance, and self-rule, restraint of passion and subjection of the will." In all, he believed that Cicero professed a "purity of morals" that "belongs more properly to the Christian age" than to antiquity. "So high, his philosophy," he concluded, "so sublime his precepts!"[58]

Garrett's reflection reveals a uniquely Victorian perspective on grandeur and sublimity. According to the intellectual historian Walter Houghton, Victorians thought within a framework of "noble emotions" that grew out of early nineteenth-century romanticism. They possessed an enthusiastic outlook on human potential and were captivated by civilization, intellectually, morally, socially, and physically.[59] Antiquity inspired many young men to greatness by allowing them to imagine the grandeur of past civilizations. According to the historian Stephen Berry, ancient texts "functioned as tutorials on the dos and don'ts of civilization building generally" by showing the "heroic character" of past empires.[60] In 1812 one student summarized this outlook when he wrote, "Many generous youths have caught from the perusal of the classic pages that ardor which carried them to the summit of fame."[61]

This outlook is particularly evident in young men's historical thinking. One student's contemplation of classical texts is worth quoting at length for its distinctively Victorian outlook:

It is the profound Greek and Latin scholar who can at pleasure transport himself into Greece with all its refinements, tread the soil of Athens and Sparta and behold the monuments erected to departed greatness, visit the plains of Marathon and witness the glorious struggle and immortal victory of Miltiades, walk in the groves of Academus and listen to the philosophical lectures of a Plato, saunter along the banks of Ilissus and imagine himself charmed with the sweet and melodious strains of Apollo's lyre, enter Rome when at the zenith of her renown and listen to the soul enrapturing eloquence of Cicero and others who graced the Roman Senate, associate himself with the shades of her departed heroes and sages and acquaint himself with the passions and motives, by which, they were actuated in their earthly career. Such advantages as these, give a new tone to the mind, an expansion of thought and a manliness of feeling, which otherwise must have been lost.[62]

By transporting young men to far off lands, ancient texts brought the individual hero to the foreground of students' imaginations, fueling the creative process of maturation.

Antiquity thus promoted emulation, which shaped students' self-fashioning efforts. This relationship between classical heroes and self-identity was embedded in the South's literary and popular culture. In the year that he contemplated going to college, Harry St. John Dixon of Mississippi found inspiration for growing up in the pages of a classical dictionary. "In my C. Dict'y I read an interesting sketch of the great philosopher's life, Aristotle. Oh! I wish I was able to be such a man." A few days later he contemplated other ancient greats: "Who can cast an indifferent eye on Hannibal's career, Caesar's victories, Sylla's [sic] and Marius' struggles, the patriotism of the Gracchi, Cicero, Brutus, Pericles, Socrates, Epaminendas [sic], Lycurgus, and Demosthenes?"[63]

At the University of North Carolina, evidence for student engagement with past heroes is especially evident in literary society debates. Although literary society debates existed primarily to apply a classical education to contemporary concerns, they occasionally involved antiquity. Major figures of antiquity—Coriolanus, Caesar, Hannibal, Cicero, and the Gracchi

—received special scrutiny. For instance, students consistently took up the questions of whether Brutus was justified in murdering Julius Caesar, whether Coriolanus was justified in inciting insurrection in Rome, whether Leonidas was right to sacrifice himself at the Battle of Thermopylae, and whether Cleopatra's death was "the result of true courage or pride."[64] These topics allowed young men to contemplate the human capacity for greatness and baseness, heroism and villainy.[65]

In all, ancient language and literature provided a linguistic foundation for a young man's education and a moral foundation for his character. Although students spent most of their time in language acquisition, this process instilled self-discipline, diligence, and industry, thereby bringing them one step closer to intellectual manhood. Moreover, antiquity was useful as part of a broader "molding process" that accompanied the transition from boyhood to manhood. Students were introduced to moral exemplars in an array of classical texts, whose virtues were rooted in restraint, not impulse, and mind, not temperament. In the process, students also learned to define greatness and heroism as timeless virtues. The scientific curriculum built upon this foundation and grounded it within a restrained Enlightenment style of Christianity.

"The admiration of whatever is great and noble": Mathematics and Science

Mathematics and science are often overlooked or disregarded in the scholarship on antebellum collegiate education, but these subjects served three important purposes. First, they continued the process of mental and moral improvement of youth, providing resources and methods for acquiring intellectual manhood. Second, these subjects prepared young men to enter learned professions of the southern educated class, including medicine, but also surveying and engineering. Third, scientific education grounded young men's pursuit of self in Christian morality, tempering their emerging ambitions.

North Carolina was one of only a handful of southern institutions that maintained a heavy emphasis on antiquity while simultaneously expanding its scientific curriculum.[66] Like Latin and Greek, mathematics fostered mental and moral improvement.[67] "The great utility of the mathematics consists in its tendency to give that equilibrium to the powers of the mind which enables us to reason truly, judge accurately, and decide correctly upon such subjects as fall under our investigation," wrote one student in 1818.[68] Students began with algebra and geometry, continued with trigonometry, and finished with calculus. They read textbooks widely used in the United States, as well as some written by their professors.[69] For example, when Joseph Caldwell served as professor of mathematics in the early nineteenth century, he wrote "A New System of Geometry," which circulated as a manuscript among students until he published it in 1822 as *A Compendious System of Elementary Geometry*. By the 1840s, students also read Charles Davies's *Elements of Geometry and Trigonometry*, which offered a sophisticated course in geometry as preparation for more advanced (and applied) mathematical and scientific instruction.[70]

Math education prepared young men for many positions that would require demonstrative reasoning such as law, medicine, education, and the ministry. In *A New System of Geometry*, Joseph Caldwell explained that the principles of geometry "have a singular power to sway the understanding in its deductions concerning the rules of human conduct."[71] Students spent most of their time studying definitions, axioms, theorems, and proofs. In recitations, they explained solutions to various mathematical problems, such as measuring the distance of celestial objects. Professors' lecture notes suggest that students were expected to draw diagrams on the blackboard, rely on concise language, and draw from their knowledge of mathematical facts to prove their answers.[72]

Science education also offered a practical education for young men and prepared them for futures in engineering, surveying, and the professional military. Science offerings expanded substantially during the antebellum period.[73] According to faculty records from 1846, for example, freshmen were examined in algebra and geometry; sophomores were examined in a range of scientific subjects, including "Natural Philosophy, Analytical Geometry, Navigation, Surveying, Mensuration of Heights and Distances, and Spherical Trigonometry"; juniors were examined in "Differential and Integral Calculus and Astronomy."[74] Both theoretical and practical applications of these subjects were emphasized. In a lecture on plane trigonometry, James Phillips explained, "One of the most familiar and useful applications of plane trigonometry, is to the determination of the heights and distances of remote objects. But, as questions in each of these departments of the science may be indefinitely multiplied, it is intended here only to present such problems as are most likely to occur in practice, and are best calculated to suggest the modes of procedure in other cases." He went on to explain how to use the tools for measurements.[75] This one example sheds light on a broader pattern throughout the United States, including the South, of expanding science to meet the vocational needs of students, as well as the improvement of states. As chapter 7 demonstrates, when it came to current affairs, these were important concerns of antebellum students.

Advanced mathematical and scientific courses also promoted moral improvement and therefore contributed to bourgeois styles of manliness, especially what Peter Carmichael has termed the "Christian gentleman ideal."[76] In 1858 Wilbur Foster, a junior, explained that the natural sciences had certain "moral effects," including "enlarged ideas and more elevated conceptions of the greatness and goodness of God." He explained further, "We are taught to see in these works of a kind and beneficent hand and we are involuntarily to reverence and adore it. Our hearts are purified, our moral nature refined, and our minds exalted. Such are the benefits flowing from the study of the natural sciences."[77] This thinking was common in a pre-Darwinian world. In a study of fifteen American colleges between 1815 and 1860, one historian discovered that "science professors . . . found a religiously inspired moral imperative for the study of science and agreeable to their own thoughts and interests."[78] In many scientific lectures such as these, professors engaged students in what the great intellectual historian Perry Miller has called "science as a form of contemplation," making science suitable for both intellectual and moral improvement and compatible with Protestant Christianity.[79] North Carolina professors such as James Phillips, in fact, embraced religion in scientific education.

Phillips's natural philosophy and astronomy classes exemplify the extent to which antebellum science complemented young men's religious and moral development. For seventeen weeks, juniors studied natural philosophy, a purely theoretical course that emphasized the development, methods, and theories of Newtonian physical sciences ranging from laws of motion and gravity to the properties of solids, liquids, and gases.[80] Phillips explained that the natural world provided the best source for contemplating God's omnipotence: "The contemplation of the works of creation excites the mind to the admiration of whatever is great and noble, accomplishing the object of all study, which is to inspire the love of truth, of wisdom, of beauty, especially of goodness, the highest beauty, and of that supreme and eternal mind which contains all truth and wisdom, all beauty and goodness."[81] Phillips's astronomy course echoed these themes. In this senior-year course, Phillips taught astronomical history, the history of ideas about the earth and its properties (but not a Darwinian history based on evolution), planets' observable properties and their satellites, and various other "heavenly bodies," including comets.[82] His lectures evoked both a spirit of sublimity and a deep reverence of God. For example, a lecture entitled "On the Sun, & zodiacal light" began with James Thomson's "hymn to the sun": "O Sun / Soul of surrounding worlds! in whom best seen / Shines out thy Maker! may I talk of thee. . . ."[83] Another lecture elaborated on these connections between science and divinity: "We may . . . be pardoned if we continue to pursue our path into the depths of space, to contemplate & admire those worlds which are sprinkled in such profusion above us, & which are but the shadows of His power who formed, sustains & governs them."[84]

Astronomy also fueled students' ambition by opening their minds to worlds beyond reach. As James Phillips urged his students, "Exercise your imagination much more than your memor[y]. i.e. read little and think a good deal, see demonstrations or solutions for yourselves, at least try your own power as often as possible; in this way you will find you progress to be both rapid and easy. you will acquire a mathematical spirit, a relish for researches and a facility for discovering and inventing. Try to develop, without assistance of any kind, what you may have read, to deduce corollaries, to make applications and only seek in your text books for a confirmation of the results which you have reached alone. 'Sic itur ad astra.'"[85] Antebellum students had opportunities to observe the heavens at the university's observatory, completed in the 1830s, but lectures were the primary mode of exercising the imagination.

Scientific lectures supporting God's existence, omnipotence, the sublimity of nature, and the heroic potential of scientific enterprise resonated with some students. In 1849, Thomas Miles Garrett recalled in his diary discussing these topics with his friends: "How wonderful is space! how difficult! how impossible to conceive an utter void, where reigns nothing, and is nothing, filling and coextensive with eternity. How numberless the stars! how vast the spaces of their orbits." Nature, in fact, substantiated Garrett's own faith. He continued, "How omnipotent is God! Can any one doubt but that there is a God when he sees all these demonstrations of his will and his power! Oh inconceivable mystery! Better were it that man even in pride should bow in humble and devoted belief, than employ his weak faculty of reason in solving such wonderful works."[86]

Garret's implicit critique of skepticism is noteworthy, for it underscores the limitations of antebellum science education. Professors and students were comfortable examining science so long as it did not call into question God's divinity and biblical authority. Consequently, students did not study emerging ideas about evolution or polygenesis, which were considered too avant-garde. Instead, they favored a more Enlightenment-grounded science of contemplation that located the individual self as powerless in a universe created by an omnipotent creator. They articulated these feelings with romantic language of the time, which was common among bourgeois Americans.

Antebellum science education also framed a progressive historical narrative that complemented the expansionist fervor within Victorian America. In this narrative, knowledge, grounded in virtue, had laid the foundation for Western civilization and could likewise push the boundaries of American civilization. Introductory lectures in each of these subjects faithfully charted the progress of science from ancient Greece to modern Europe. For example, James Phillips began his course in fluxions with ancient mathematics, which afforded "contemplation of the more quiet progress of civilization." Math and science, he argued, were "intimately . . . connected with the advance of the arts, & above all, with the intellectual improvement of our species."[87] Progress and the expansion of civilization were two reasons why educational reformers wished to incorporate more science into antebellum college curricula, and many students at North Carolina also saw value in this pursuit. In 1859, Cicero Croom explained that science, as with history and commerce, was an important element of what Stephen Berry has termed "civilization building."[88]

Thus, as a model of demonstrative reasoning, an investigation of God's greatness, and a catalyst for ambition, antebellum science education continued the "molding process" of antebellum education and prepared students for manhood. As one student remarked, science gave young men confidence "to be sure in all we undertake, to have, at least the law on our side, so as not to struggle in vain against some insuperable difficulty opposed to us by natural causes." At the same time, it was useful. Science illuminated the "easiest, shortest, most economical & most effectual" means to an end, which young men could apply in various public settings as adults.[89] Most importantly, science instruction never challenged core values of Protestant Christianity. As a study of the sublime, it imbued students with reverence for God's omnipotence as revealed through nature, opened doors for students to contemplate their role in the universe, but did not teach emerging scientific thought about evolution and geological time. Mental and moral philosophy complemented this education by focusing on the male self and his duties to others and to God.

Know Thyself: Mental and Moral Philosophy

The course in moral philosophy was a senior-year capstone course taught by the college president that addressed a range of discrete subjects, including (in order of presentation to students) intellectual, or mental, philosophy (how the mind operated); moral philosophy (theoretical and practical ethics); political economy (ethics applied to nation states, commerce, etc.); and U.S. constitutional theory and history (a case study of moral philosophy in practice). These subjects provided a coherent ethical system that addressed all possible theoretical and practical questions regarding men's moral obligations to self and to society. Moral philosophy brought together a variety of subjects, each aimed at teaching students how to lead virtuous private and public lives.[90] The course, therefore, had important implications for men's dependents, including slaves, wives, and children.

Readings in moral philosophy offered a conservative view of humanity in which educated elites were society's natural leaders; they ordered, controlled, and disseminated knowledge and shaped civil society through the exercise of moral leadership. As Frederick Rudolph has explained, "Moral Philosophy encouraged the choice of Hercules; it lacked democratic pretensions; it located virtue and wisdom not in the people but in an educated few [men] fit to be their leaders. And it carried the reassuring message that knowledge could be ordered, unified, and contained." Antebellum moral philosophy was essentially Christian (emphasizing benevolence, veracity, justice, and the golden rule) and republican (emphasizing individual liberty and elevating the common good over self-interest). While the course did not teach men's duties differently or more effectively than Christianity, by virtue of its foundations in science and reason rather than doctrine, professors teaching the course could evade charges of sectarianism.[91]

The course and assigned texts were intended specifically for young men and provided both esoteric and practical guidelines for moral life, emphasizing in particular core values of restrained manhood. These guidelines conformed to expectations that elite young men practice self-control. For example, in an 1835 composition, "On Moral & Intellectual Philosophy," Julian Leach wrote about moral philosophy's unique relevance to young men. "For what is more important to the young who are just entering on the great theatre of life, and proposing to themselves either happiness or greatness, than to have an instructor which will teach them their duty, on what to found their hopes and their great destiny?" he asked. "Are not these the very subjects on which they [young men] are most solicitous of information?" Mental and moral philosophy, he argued, taught young men how to regulate their conduct and their hopes and to perform their moral duties. The overarching idea behind the course, he concluded, was to teach a young man "Gnothi Seauton," to know thyself, or to recognize that one's own soul is "the spring of all action and Governor of volition."[92] Arriving at this level of self-knowledge took hard work and careful attention to each branch of moral education, beginning with the study of the human mind, or mental philosophy.

Mental philosophy was at the root of all moral education, for knowledge of one's own mind allowed an individual to understand the minds of others and, thus, human society. Quoting Alexander Pope's famous *Essay on Man* (ca. 1732), David Swain explained to his students, "The proper study of mankind, is man."[93] The study was premised on Scottish common-sense realism, a school of thought founded by Francis Hutcheson, Thomas Reid, James Beattie, and Dugald Stewart and popularized in the American colonies by John Witherspoon, president of Princeton University. Scottish realism was not an esoteric or metaphysical philosophy, but a systematic approach to mind and matter. Thomas Reid, in particular, argued that there were certain common principles that all men could understand and that the mind was the active agent of all understanding, perceiving, and judging of those principles.[94] All the perceptions of which knowledge consisted, Reid argued, were "a part of the furniture which nature hath given to the human understanding. . . . They are part of our constitution, and all the discoveries of our reason are grounded upon them. They make up what is called *the common sense of mankind*."[95] Behind this process was the theory of faculty psychology, which viewed the human mind as compartmentalized into three discrete powers, or faculties—the rational, emotional, and volitional (that is, reason, passions, and will). Each part of the mind had to be balanced with the other; character was the "controlling" center, or at least reflected "the proper development of 'the whole man.'"[96]

Mental philosophy texts led students through the psychological arguments of Scottish philosophers, modeling their inductive approach to knowledge and applying them to a set of gendered and class ideals about men and moral leadership. Antebellum students primarily studied John Abercrombie's *Inquiries Concerning the Intellectual Powers and the Investigation of Truth* (1830), a synthesis of Thomas Reid and Dugald Stewart's theories about the human mind that was used widely in academies, colleges, and universities in Britain and the United States. The text is principally concerned with helping young men develop what Abercrombie called "personal identity." In so doing, Abercrombie explains the structure of the human mind, the uses of reason to investigate truth and correct impressions of the mind, and finally the importance of mental discipline.[97]

Abercrombie's text presented a rubric for heroic individualism compatible with the great-man archetype to which young men aspired. Because of its relevance to intellectual manhood, Abercrombie's description warrants quoting at length:

> Does a subject occur to him, either in conversation or reflection, in which he feels that his knowledge is deficient, he commences, without delay, an eager pursuit of the necessary information. In prosecuting any inquiry, whether by reading or observation, his attention is acutely alive to the authenticity of facts, the validity of arguments, the accuracy of processes of investigation, principles which are illustrated by the facts and conclusions deduced from them, the character of observers, they style of writers; and thus, all the circumstances which come before him are made acutely and individually the objects of attention and reflection. Such a man acquires a confidence in his own powers and resources to which those are strangers who have not cultivated this kind of mental disciple. The intellectual condition arising out of it is applicable alike to every situation in which a man can be placed, whether the affairs of ordinary life, the pursuits of science, or those higher inquiries and relations which concern him as a moral being.[98]

Great men differed fundamentally from men with "listless" and "torpid" characters on account of their mental strength and ability to cultivate and construct oneself. Julian Leach echoed these sentiments in his 1835 essay, arguing that young men who learned to regulate their minds and morals possessed an "internal secret power," which alone "elevates those who cultivate it." The ideal man stood in stark contrast to boys, who were "naturally prone to excess of every kind." The attentive student of mental philosophy could readily achieve this ideal through strenuous mental exercise.[99]

These are the main ideas of mental philosophy, which formed the first part of the overall moral philosophy course. Moral philosophy built on them and contributed substantially to the broader project of students' moral education. In an 1830 address on education, for example, William Hooper, professor of Latin, explained to North Carolina students, "In proportion, therefore, as the intellect is exalted, and the taste refined, there is need that our moral nature should be confirmed in rectitude, and all our affections enlisted on the side of virtue."[100] Thus, the senior-year moral philosophy course located the center of moral guidance in the individual himself and aimed to teach him to make the "Choice of Hercules" of virtue over vice. During the first third of the nineteenth century, students studied William Paley's *The Principles of Moral and Political Philosophy* (1785), the standard moral philosophy textbook used in American colleges and universities. When other institutions began to replace Paley's text with more modern, American works in the 1830s, the University of North Carolina adopted Francis Wayland's *Elements of Moral Science*, which became the standard moral philosophy text in American colleges and universities in the antebellum period and sold nearly 100,000 copies by 1865.[101]

Significantly, this was a Christian character education that viewed young men primarily as boys, in need of moral guidance. A Baptist minister, professor of mathematics and natural philosophy at Union College, and president of Brown University, Francis Wayland (1796–1865) staunchly advocated educational reform in the United States, particularly a more holistic moral education that balanced modern subjects and evangelicalism. His *Elements of Moral Science* reflects this educational philosophy, and it can be viewed as a handbook outlining young men's duties and obligations to God and to humanity.[102] It deals with both theoretical ethics and with practical ethics, each of which conveyed bourgeois values of evangelicalism, self-fashioning, and benevolence. Young men learned that men's obligations to love God required a "spirit of devotion," prayer, and keeping the Sabbath. In particular, "a devotional spirit" consisted in "making the moral use which is intended, of all the objects of intellection that come within our experience or observation." In other words, everything knowable emanated from—and contained lessons about—God. Because of its connection to religion, moral philosophy related to young men's attitudes about character and reputation. Wayland covered topics such as obligations, oaths, slander, and ridicule. In all, he imbued his reader with mainstream Protestant values and ascribed to them civic importance.

Wayland's moral philosophy also conveyed bourgeois teachings about sex and gender, particularly concerning chastity. Wayland taught that "sexual appetite" was natural but moral philosophy was supposed to ascertain the limits to sexual indulgence. In keeping with Christian ethics, Wayland condemns adultery, polygamy, concubinage, and fornication. He notes, in particular, that "unchaste desire is strongly excited by the imagination," and "the law of chastity forbids all impure thoughts and actions; all unchaste conversation, looks, or gestures; the reading of obscene or lascivious books, and everything which would naturally produce in us a disposition of mind to violate this precept."[103] In addition, Wayland warns young men of the severe punishments that "God has affixed" on those who breach the laws governing sex: "Let the seducer and the profligate remember that each must stand, with his victim and his partner in guilt, before the Judge of quick and dead, where a recompense will be rendered to every man according to his deeds."[104] Appealing to the Christian conscience, Wayland provided a clear ethic for young men as they developed self-consciousness as sexual beings.

This education in sex and gender conformed neatly to bourgeois expectations for restrained manhood and complemented the prevailing ideology of separate spheres in antebellum America.[105] In particular, Wayland's *Elements of Moral Science* taught that sex roles emanated from seemingly natural laws and duties of chastity, informing the "duties which arise from the constitution of the sexes": duties of husbands and wives, parents and children, and single young men and women. "Let it be remembered that a female is a moral and accountable being . . . that she is made to be the center of all that is delightful in the domestic relations; that by her very nature she looks up to man as her protector, and loves to confide in his hands her happiness for life," he wrote. He asked his readers to consider, ultimately, whether there was a greater crime than the violation of a woman's moral nature. Thus, while moral philosophy drew students' attention primarily to the self, there were great implications for this self-focus on others.

These attitudes framed the ideal of the southern belle in particular, which southern intellectuals occasionally took up. Thomas R. Dew, William and Mary's president and professor of moral philosophy, perhaps best underscored the implications on southern women of molding the male self as heroic: "He [a man] is the shield of woman, destined by nature to guard and protect her. Her inferior strength and sedentary habits confine her within the domestic circle; she is kept aloof from the bustle and storm of active life."[106] Students also appropriated these ideas. In 1857, Hugh Brown contemplated his "future prospects" as a man of letters "among pleasant shades and cool fountains" and "with [a] library of well selected books to while away my life in literary ease." He also imagined "some pleasant partner of my joys to pour out my tea and attend to my linen, and other minor domestic arrangements." His wife "would have to be a woman who would know when to hold her tongue, and be contented in her proper sphere."[107] Thus, formal education imparted attitudes about women that buttressed existing power relations among men and women, providing men with a set of attitudes about women that would characterize their interactions with them in other aspects of college life (see chapter 6).[108]

Classical Education and American Slavery

North Carolina's curriculum was not defined by encroaching regionalism in ways that historians have discussed regarding comparable schools, such as South Carolina College.[109] In particular, student writing does not explicitly contain examples of whether or not the curriculum taught lessons in slaveholding or mastery. Ancient authors such as Xenophon and Cicero, indeed, were slaveholders and aristocrats, and prominent southern intellectuals did not hesitate to make those connections in developing proslavery ideology. Yet when students wrote about, discussed, or debated antiquity, they emphasized its relevance for mental improvement and moral improvement. Ancient authors—themselves observers of republican life and leadership— demonstrated above all the importance of virtuous citizenship, which society's uneducated classes might emulate. [110] Thus, although students did not explicitly turn to antiquity to make arguments for or against American slavery, the spirit of classics was always one of exclusivity, calling young men to greatness and distinction.

Nowhere is the question of slavery more present than in the moral philosophy course, particularly Wayland's *Elements of Moral Science*. Wayland's moral philosophy complemented the university's pervasive moral pedagogy, but his antislavery positions fundamentally undermined southern slaveholding. "Every human being is, by his constitution, a separate and distinct and complete system, adapted to all the purposes of self-government and responsible, separately, to God for the manner in which his powers are employed," he wrote. "Slavery violates the personal liberty of man as a *physical, intellectual,* and *moral being.*"[111] He offered several examples. First, he argued that slavery degraded the character of both master and slave, cultivating "pride, anger, cruelty, selfishness and licentiousness" among the former while fostering "lying, deceit, hypocrisy, dishonesty, and a willingness to yield himself up to minister to the appetites of his master" among the latter. Second, slavery impeded progress and harmed national wealth. In this economic argument, he explained that slavery removed any "natural stimulus" to work and also undermined frugality. Finally, he argued that slavery contradicted biblical truths. "The moral precepts of the Bible are diametrically opposed to slavery," he wrote. "They are, Thou shalt love thy neighbor as thyself, and all things whatsoever ye would that men should do unto you, do ye even so unto them."[112] By evoking liberty, capitalism, and Christianity, Wayland aligned himself with prevailing abolitionist ideology. Yet significantly, Wayland never proposed an immediate end to slavery, which was the linchpin of late abolitionist ideology. "Immediate abolition would be the greatest possible injury to the slaves themselves," he argued. "They [slaves] are not competent to self-government."[113] Instead, Wayland enjoined masters to treat their slaves well. Since the system of slavery was wrong, masters were morally obligated to manumit their slaves, but given the legal presence of slavery, slaves were nevertheless morally bound to obey their masters.

Not surprisingly, Wayland's stance on slavery made him persona non grata in most of the South. Rather than follow a growing national trend to adopt the text for the moral philosophy course, many southern college presidents wrote their own textbooks.[114] Alone among southern colleges and universities, the University of North Carolina continued to assign the book into the late antebellum period, demonstrating the varied and unpredictable attitudes about slavery among elite whites in the Upper South.[115] No evidence exists to explain how President Swain taught this part of Wayland at North Carolina, but he likely did not omit it from the course. According to one historian, "It was provided that no portion of the [moral philosophy] text-books should be omitted, 'but the whole carefully recited, subsequently reviewed, and each member of the class separately and rigidly be examined on the entire system.'"[116]

Of course, there were critics of Wayland at the University of North Carolina. Elisha Mitchell, the Presbyterian clergyman and science professor best known for his geological tours of North Carolina, was perhaps Wayland's most vocal detractor. In 1848, he published two aggressively proslavery sermons, "The Other Leaf of the Book of Nature" and the "Word of God," in which he criticizes Wayland's Elements of Moral Science, especially the position that slavery violated the Golden Rule. "The opinion which after a good deal of thought upon the subject I have been led to form, is, that the divine right of kings, the divine right of landholders; the divine right of property in general, the divine right of slaveholders (and by divine right, I mean a right sanctioned by religion natural or revealed), that all these are on the same footing, and must stand or fall together."[117]

Opinions like Mitchell's, while likely shared by students and professors, did not dictate classroom learning. Nor did they inform public discourse in an official university capacity. Antislavery addresses from professors and students were not uncommon at the university, as chapter 7 shows. In fact, public discourse around slavery at antebellum Chapel Hill reflected a moderate intellectual culture, even on the issue of slavery. In formal capacities, for instance, professors forbade students from discussing slavery and partisan topics in public speeches, and speakers from the outside community often did the same. According to Alfred Brophy, even speakers known for virulent proslavery views either excised them or tempered them when speaking at North Carolina.[118]

The curriculum likewise did not offer an official southern catechism regarding disunion, as was the case with moral philosophy instruction at South Carolina College. According to the historian Michael Sugrue, South Carolina's antebellum moral philosophy professor taught his students that educated men had a duty to enslave blacks, that the "right of secession" strengthened, not weakened, the durability of the Union, and that Americans are not "one people."[119] Although comparable moral philosophy notes do not exist for President Swain's moral philosophy course, the continued use of core Revolutionary-era documents suggest continued education in the importance of a durable union. The expectation was that students would study the laws of morality, cultivate conscience, and then influence social policy accordingly. As students turned their attention outward from individual to society, they addressed practical ethical issues relating especially to the operation of government and civil society. At the end of the course, President Swain delivered lectures on the history of constitutional law. According to an 1846 course catalog—the university's first to provide a detailed course description—the president presented "an analytical review, in chronological order, of the MAGNA CHARTA of King John: The Petition of Right; the Charters of Carolina; the Fundamental Constitution (by John Locke); the Habeas Corpus Act; the Bill of Right[s]; the Declaration of Independence; the Articles of Confederation; the Treaty of Peace with Great Britain, and the Constitution of the United States."[120] In these documents, students traced the history of republican government and analyzed it in the context of men's moral obligations. The influence of these ideals, however, is most discernible in student literary society debates on the durability of the United States (see chapter 7).

IN SUM, a classical education provided forums, tools, and models for young men to leave boyhood and to mold themselves into men, conscientious citizens, or even great leaders. The texts students read, the lectures they heard, and the recitations in which they participated not only catered to their maturation but also conveyed bourgeois values such as industry, restraint, self-discipline, competitiveness, and chastity.[121] While the main focus of mental and moral improvement was on youth themselves, this training anticipated future lives as leaders in families and communities. There was always a distinctive exclusivity of southern higher education. Educated men, students believed, "form the taste of their age, and give a decided cast to the religious and political opinions of those among whom they lived." Indeed, they believed that future generations "cry out from the future to the educated of this age, 'Men of learning you are shaping our destiny for us; to you we look for protection.'"[122] For students to meet this call to greatness, however, they first needed to speak like men. Intellectual manhood required articulation, and speech education figured significantly in both formal and informal education.

CHAPTER THREE

Not Merely Thinking,
but Speaking Beings
Speech Education

On 20 May 1818, twenty-seven years before he became the eleventh president of the United States, twenty-three-year-old James Knox Polk stood before his fellow members of the Dialectic Society at the University of North Carolina and delivered a commanding address on eloquence. He urged his classmates to "reflect upon the high ground which you occupy with respect to the world" and to consider "the necessity of cultivating your oratorical powers." As Polk explained to his classmates, "You may be called upon to succeed those who now stand up [as] the representatives of the people, to wield by the thunder of your eloquence the council of a great nation and to retain by your prudent measures that liberty for which our fathers bled."[1]

Polk's speech exemplifies the importance of speech education in the power of intellectual manhood. Born in 1795 to a well-off slaveholding family in Mecklenburg County, North Carolina, Polk had a keen sense of how oratory inspired and sustained the Revolutionary struggle.[2] Polk and his classmates came of age during the golden age of American oratory and lived in what Carolyn Eastman has termed "a nation of speechifiers."[3] Men were expected to demonstrate intellectual manhood in a variety of public and professional settings. Speech was crucial for the success of future politicians, lawyers, judges, educators, clergy, and doctors, as well as any individual who expected to participate in the public affairs of his community.

This chapter considers how speech education occurred in both the formal curriculum and within the student literary societies. Building on the preceding chapter, the primary focus here is on process. First, it explores the formal study of speech in college, and then how young men engaged with it in literary societies. The curriculum delineated an explicitly masculine oratorical ideal rooted at once in classical texts and pedagogies, as well as national and trans-historical republican traditions. Speech education began for freshmen and sophomores with the study and recitation of Greek and Latin texts. Early in their collegiate careers, students studied exemplary orators from within the classical cannon of texts assigned for Latin and Greek language study. English oratory came later, as juniors and seniors studied rhetoric and belles lettres. This course, however, was not a speech practicum; it only taught literary style and inculcated taste. To put these ideals into practice, students turned to their immediate community of peers. In literary societies, students engaged weekly in exercises in declamation and composition, which helped them hone their rhetorical and oratorical skills.

In each of these contexts, speech education served several interrelated goals of higher education. First, it helped young men along the way from boyhood to manhood. Young men engaged in mental and moral improvement as they did in other curricular subjects highlighted in the preceding chapter. When they read about exemplary orators from antiquity, studied great speeches, learned the rules of composition, and performed oratory, they learned to elevate mind over temperament, restraint over impulse, and independence over dependence. To do this, young men engaged in highly effective and substantial community empowered self-fashioning. In literary societies, for example, students employed the strategies of the broader American bourgeoisie, including emulation and self-discipline, and continued to equate both the means and ends of self-improvement with their own heroic potential. Significantly, these literary societies were sources of validation of speech. By learning how to captivate, convince, and perhaps even silence their peers, young men enacted a society in which power emanated from men and for men. The consequence was that young men also learned to use speech to set boundaries around men's sphere and to group others, especially women, children, and common folk, as a community of listeners.[4] Because students drew from popular ideas about speech and mainstream methods to hone their oratorical skills, it is first important to understand the context of the oratorical world they inhabited.

The Antebellum Oratorical Ideal

Public speech had always been a mainstay of American public culture, but cultural developments in the early nineteenth century made it all the more significant. The spread of evangelicalism in the South brought passion and emotion into southern oratory. Emotion-infused speech converted much of the South, including youth, women, and slaves, to such a great extent that it inverted the social fabric of the region and democratized Christianity.[5] This culture of speech only intensified in the antebellum period and helped to define its intellectual culture. Oratory gained increasing importance in the 1820s, during the emergence of the Second Party System of Democrats and Whigs. By the election of 1840, party organization, modern campaigning, and stump speeches reshaped American politics. Southern intellectual and popular culture also required eloquence and oratory. In public spaces such as literary societies, library clubs, lyceums, theaters, churches, schools, markets, and many private spaces such as household parlors that served public functions, speech validated a man's honor and reputation. In so doing, speech had the power to distinguish men from women, adults from children and youth, and masters from slaves.[6]

In American culture, the orator served as a model of virtue, of devotion to the public good, and of power. In popular and political culture, the orator was quintessentially masculine. "O the orator's joys!" Walt Whitman wrote,

> To inflate the chest, to roll the thunder of the voice out
>   from the ribs and throat,
> To make people rage, weep, hate, desire, with yourself,
> To lead America—to quell America with a great tongue.[7]

Whitman was in line with most other American intellectuals who believed that only great men could "quell America" with speech. In fact, so great was the orator's cultural power that many Americans considered him a "superior order of being" because he alone possessed eloquence.[8] "In a republic, popular eloquence is a powerful engine by which the political aspirant works his way to office and distinction," one writer for the *Southern Literary Messenger* wrote in 1842.[9]

Antebellum periodical literature abounds with discourse on exemplary oratory that associated oratory with heroism and male adulthood. Authors usually described eloquence, which Samuel Johnson defined as "speaking with fluency and elegance," as the key to oratorical success.[10] First, an orator's delivery required "energy and elegance" and "force, earnestness and simplicity." According to one author, the exemplary orator required "resolute ambition and a high moral purpose," and a drive for eminence in every action he took and every word he spoke. He was supposed to grapple "with every kind of knowledge," his imagination expands, and his powers of reason are strong. He must speak universally and appeal to the good of all humanity. His ultimate object was "to combat error and falsehood."[11] At the same time, oratory was all about *feeling*. "The qualities, however, which constitute the elements of oratorical excellence, although they cannot be *dissected*, may nevertheless be *felt*."[12] An orator "does with an audience as he pleases," a writer for the *Ladies Repository* wrote in 1852. He "lulls, excites, calms, irritates, enrages" his audience.[13] Thus, oratory was valued as the art of statesmen, clergy, and educators, whose profession required them to inspire people to think, feel, and do good and virtuous deeds.

Eloquence required hard work and diligent attention to self-restraint. Though nineteenth-century educators believed everyone was born with "oratorical genius," few could cultivate it to perfection. Those who did reached political distinction. In James K. Polk's address with which we began, for example, the future U.S. president reminded his fellow classmates, many of whom were discouraged by the prospect of cultivating eloquence, that "poeta nascitur Orator fit" (the poet is born, but the orator is made). The curriculum played an important role in making orators who met the nineteenth-century oratorical ideal of manhood.

Formal Speech Education: Classrooms and Curriculum

Speech education for males began early in life, usually through reading aloud at home. As one historian of southern oratory has explained, speech education was "a natural part of family life."[14] Fathers sometimes read political speeches aloud; children sometimes would read aloud, too, and their fathers and mothers would critique their reading. When a child was old enough to go to a private tutor, boarding school, or private academy, speech education became more formal and more gendered. The standard pedagogy of speech education emphasized oral recitation, speech, and performance. Teachers instructed boys to recite texts aloud, first in English and then in Latin and Greek, which they were supposed to have memorized in advance for class. Young boys were also called on at an early age to declaim famous speeches and receive criticism from a teacher.[15] In college, young men found a similar approach to speech education rooted in oral recitation. For freshmen and sophomores, speech education largely consisted of reciting memorized Greek and Latin prose and poetry, as well as mathematical theorems.[16]

Speech education was central to the classical learning that characterized American higher education between the Revolution and the Civil War.[17] This educational tradition can be traced back to the ancient Greeks and Romans, who viewed rhetorical training as essential for learning how to become active participants in civil society.[18] Humanists of the English Renaissance placed speech at the center of their intellectual communities, and they emphasized, in particular, Ciceronian rhetoric in their conceptualization of leading citizens. This tradition of using speech education to cultivate citizenship continued in English colleges and universities and then was imported to North America during the colonial era, where the first generations of colonial men were trained.[19] According to the historian Lorri Glover, young students of the early national South "typically adopted this passion for oratory, bragging about their successes and going to great lengths to best shortcomings."[20] During the first half of the nineteenth century, American colleges and universities drew from this rich tradition of higher education through rhetorical training and emphasized above all the classical texts that highlighted the importance of speech to citizenship in ancient republics, including the works of Cicero, Quintilian, Homer, and Demosthenes, who made explicit connections between oratory, morality, civic culture, and manhood.[21] Nineteenth-century educators equated good citizenship with rhetorical action.[22]

The formal curriculum presented a literary canon that depicted eloquence as a universal and timeless masculine value. Grecian oratory, for instance, was intended to captivate students' imaginations about oratory's potential to arouse patriotism. Homer's *Iliad*, which sophomores usually studied, taught important lessons about eloquence and manliness. As one writer for the *Southern Literary Messenger* put it in 1840, Homer invested his heroes "with all the charm of eloquence." The correlation between heroism, oratory, and manliness, the writer argued, made "ancient eloquence" worthy of students' attention. In the third book of the *Iliad*, for example, Homer compared Ulysses' and Menelaus's oratory:

When Atreus' son harangued the listening train,
Just was his sense, and his expression plain;
His words succinct yet full, without a fault,
He spoke no more than just the thing he ought
But, when Ulysses rose, in thought profound,
His modest eyes be fixed upon the ground;

As one unskilled or dumb, he seemed to stand,
Nor raised his head, nor stretched his sceptered hand.
But, when he speaks, what elocution flows!
Soft as the fleeces of descending snows,
The copious accents fall, with easy art,
Melting they fall and sink into the heart.
Wondering we hear; and fixed in deep surprise,
Our ears refute the censure of our eyes.[23]

The writer for the *Southern Literary Messenger* used this passage to demonstrate that Homer's poems—both *The Iliad* and *The Odyssey*—were important to study because they emphasized the "fervid eloquence" of heroes such as Ulysses. The "direct tendency" of Grecian oratory "was to awaken in the bosom emotions of the purest patriotism, and thus to prepare the individual for the most brilliant and effective displays of oratory."[24] Because of the correlation between oratory and "republican spirit," heroes such as Menelaus and Ulysses could serve as timeless models of orator heroes for students in every generation.

Roman oratory likewise offered oratorical exemplars and was thus equally represented in the antebellum curriculum. Historians have noted, in particular, the prevalence of Cicero's *De Officiis* in antebellum collegiate curricula, citing especially its utility for training leaders.[25] Students could also derive broader lessons about manhood from this work, for within the text Cicero explicitly linked virility and the spoken word. According to the historian Maud Gleason, Cicero regarded "the orator as a paradigm of masculine deportment." In an age in which the opposite of manhood was boyhood, not womanhood, and intellectual manhood was an important goal of education, Cicero's rhetorical model fit the bill. Cicero did not offer an antithetical effeminate orator to the masculine oratory hero, but a boyish, unrefined model instead. As Gleason argues, Cicero cautioned his readers against "boorish" deportment and delivery, but not delicacy or effeminacy.[26]

Cicero embodied this oratorical ideal in his famous oration *In Catilinam*. As all schoolboys knew, Catiline threatened to overthrow the Roman Republic around 63 BC, and Cicero's case against him was studied for its rhetoric as well as its republican themes. "Who can conceive of any thing more thrilling and overwhelming than his [Cicero's] orations against Cataline [*sic*]?" wrote one contributor to the *Southern Literary Messenger*. According to to this writer, Cicero's manly patriotism vividly portrayed "the patriot orator, sternly bold, from the magnitude of his cause—for the lives of millions depended upon his success—hatred and abhorrence depicted in his face; indignation flashing from his eye—for love of country was his impelling motive; energy and passion in his every action, and the living lava bursting from his lips;—and the victim, shrinking awe-stricken away—his baseness exposed—his treacherous schemes unfolded to public gaze; he flies a blasted and withering thing—a reckless and degraded outlaw."[27] The author went on to liken Cicero's oratory to that of the founding fathers, who were also patriot orators. Eloquence, "the inseparable companion of liberty," would guarantee the success of the American republic if used by patriot orators in the timeless ways that reached back to the early days of Athens, Rome, and the American founding.[28]

Students' classroom exposure to eloquence and oratory was not limited to reading about orators in ancient texts. Early in college, students explored the history of language and rhetoric, as well as grammar, syntax, and vocabulary in their study of classical texts. Juniors and seniors studied rhetoric and composition, which emphasized the history of rhetoric from ancient to modern times as well as the rules of rhetoric. By a student's junior and senior years, application of rhetorical theory to original compositions and orations became the primary focus. Students read and recited from Rev. Hugh T. Blair's *Lectures on Rhetoric and Belles Lettres* (1783), which was standard at antebellum American colleges and universities.[29] *Lectures on Rhetoric and Belles Lettres* connected the classical and humanist traditions of rhetorical training and promoted an eighteenth-century model of speaking that students applied to their nineteenth-century world.[30] Thomas Miles Garrett especially enjoyed the course on rhetoric. "I am very interested in this study which I deem, probably of as much importance as any in the course of instruction," he wrote in his diary in 1849. He believed that Blair's text was "excellent," and he borrowed "Campbell's Philosophy of Rhetoric" from the Philanthropic Society library to "study in conjunction with Blair." If he continued to enjoy rhetoric, he wrote, "I shall read the great text author Quintilian, on this subject, a book probably abounding with soundness of principle, useful and curious knowledge."[31]

While Garrett's remarks reveal that formal speech education focused more on composition than delivery, public performance was not altogether missing from formal university learning. Students, for example, had many opportunities each semester to evaluate oratory on campus. As chapter 1 demonstrated, weekly church services provided opportunities to hear and critique different styles of oratory. When, for instance, a visiting Presbyterian minister delivered a sermon about humility, William Mullins observed the speaker's plain delivery: "The Rev. Mr. Ely preached this morning in the chapel. He is a Presbyterian clergyman from the North and has come to the university as an applicant for the vacant professorship of Modern Languages. His sermon was very plain but contained much useful matter and suggested several points, well worthy an attentive consideration."[32] Mullins preferred emotionally stimulating sermons. When Professor William Mercer Green delivered a sermon in 1840 on the topic "Whoso loveth the world, is not a friend to God," Mullins praised the sermon's logic and rhetoric: "In dividing his sermon, he [Green] showed first, how the spirit of the world is at direct variance with the commands of God, and secondly the superiority of the Heavenly temper." But he also praised Green's moving eloquence: "I was much affected with some of the sermon and felt sensations almost strangers to my breast, since I have been a member of college," Mullins concluded.[33] Responses like these to sermons represent the few written responses to religion in papers from students attending North Carolina before 1861. Significantly, spoken delivery usually trumped content in students' evaluations of sermons. Students who cared about the sermons and wished to write about them in their diaries noted their emotional responses, making connections between speech and feeling.

Non-religious itinerant speakers also visited Chapel Hill, exhibiting a range of oratorical styles. When a temperance speaker visited Chapel Hill in 1851, the faculty suggested that students attend his speech. George N. Thompson described his reaction to the lecture in detail: "Mr White spoke a speech two hours long and it proved quite interesting, his power of riveting the attention of the audience I have never seen equaled. He is very pathetic humorous, and affecting so much so that at one time you will be following him in his lofty flights in regions of heavenly bliss at another time holding your sides with laughter, and your heels together—and again be so affected at some of his stories that you would weep in spite of your exertions to the opposite."[34] Thompson's reaction evokes the popular appeal of speech. As entertainment, a good lecture riveted an audience's attention and appealed to every sort of emotion and thus also carried educational value.

Though most formal speech education occurred during these reading, composing, and listening activities, the curriculum presented limited opportunities for students to practice public speaking. Seniors had to deliver two orations during the academic year—one in the fall and one in the spring during "senior speaking," which occurred just hours before the annual commencement ceremony. Seniors spoke on topics of their own choosing, which ranged from serious orations on the progress of American poetry to light-hearted pieces about college life and women.[35] In addition to the senior speeches in English, the highest-ranking student in the senior class historically delivered a salutatory address in Latin, and the second-ranking senior delivered the valedictory address in English. This system was in place until 1838, after which the top-ranking senior delivered the valedictory, but sometimes as many as eight students at the top of the class cast lots for the honor of giving the Latin salutatory address.[36] These were, in other words, highly coveted speaking positions. Finally, students who earned distinctions engaged in a public debate on a predetermined topic.[37] For these reasons, commencement speeches were highly anticipated, and students' families and friends, as well as townsfolk, assembled on graduation day to watch students come out to their communities as men and as leaders.

Although commencement showcased years of rhetorical training, the formal curriculum provided little in the way of active participation in speech education. Students, therefore, made speech education central to their weekly literary society duties. The Dialectic and Philanthropic Societies reinforced the connection between eloquence and manhood that formal college education proposed and provided opportunities for students to cultivate the skills that would make them men. This hands-on education in speech also helped to mitigate tensions between impulse and restraint that defined the period of youth.

Literary Societies and Performance

In July 1853, William Lafayette Scott, president of the Dialectic Society, offered his classmates some advice about speaking: "We are not merely thinking, but speaking beings," he began. "Here, of course, I allude not to common parlance, but to public speaking. You may not all be called upon to make long and labored speeches—in fact very few of you may—; but there are none of you, if your lives are spared even till the prime of manhood, that will not perhaps find it necessary on some public occasion to arise in an assembly of men and make a few, plain, practical remarks, or suffer your views on some matter."[38] As future leaders, Scott and his classmates knew they needed to hone their public speaking skills, and they turned to their system of peer education in literary societies to meet that goal.

In the Dialectic and Philanthropic Societies, students taught one another how to speak like men, not boys. Three weekly "literary duties" accomplished this task: composition, declamation, and debate. Students believed that these three exercises complemented the twin goals of higher education that developed intellectual manhood: mental and moral improvement. This would serve them well as adults in a range of professional careers, not just in politics and law, but also in medicine, education, and ministry, as well as forums of community leadership. "It is needless to enumerate the advantages of our literary duties," Robert Williams Henry explained to his fellow members in the Dialectic Society in 1835. "Without practice in speaking extemporaneously it is scarcely possible for any of us to acquire that 'copia verborum' which rhetoricians deem of primary importance to all who propose to address either legis[la]tive judicial or popular assemblies."[39] In 1847, another student argued that the "largest portion of the advantages to be acquired by a collegiate course are to be derived from debate, composition and declamation."[40]

In addition to their educational advantages, these three literary exercises catered to the broader maturation process occurring during youth.[41] For example, William Bonner Jr. explained to incoming members of the Dialectic Society in 1858, "You are now entering upon those duties, that will lay the deep and broad foundation for a man, if properly attended to. It is here you form those qualities that will render you useful."[42] These qualities included the ability to convey knowledge, reason, emotion, sympathy, and passion. As did the formal curricular texts, students understood them as timeless qualities that required hard work to develop.

Declamation allowed students to practice eloquence and cultivate intellectual manhood through performance and imitation of historical oratory. Imagination fueled the process. As one student explained in 1826, in declamation "we adopt as it were their [orators'] sentiments & feelings. We imagine ourselves in their situation influenced by the same circumstances, advocating or opposing the same cause, striving for the same end, animated by the same principles. If such be our course we cannot fail to success."[43] This imaginative act of declamation helped students explore their own heroic potential. Students encouraged one another to deliver speeches by ancient orators such as Cicero and Demosthenes; English orators such as Edmund Burke, Richard Brinsley Sheridan, and William Pitt; and Americans such as Patrick Henry. "Let us emulate their powers & endeavour to imitate their perfections," Henry Elliott declared in his 1826 inaugural address to the Dialectic Society. "Let us *dare* to *excel* & success will crown our exertions."[44] This was emulation, that core bourgeois value, at its best. Understanding how students emulated great orators, whose speeches they read and performed, helps paint a broader picture of the intellectual construction of ambition.

Minutes from the literary societies list the speeches that students declaimed only until the early nineteenth century; afterward, membership increased and students ceased recording every minute of the meeting. Nevertheless, the speeches from the early national period are instructive.[45] In 1796, John Taylor "spoke the Speech of Adherbal to the Roman People imploring their Assistance against Jugurtha"; Hinton James "spoke a piece on Genius"; Edwin Osborne "spoke the Speech of [A]Eneas to Queen Dido giving an account of the Sack of Troy."[46] In 1798, James Hall "spoke advice to youth"; Frank Dancy "spoke Cato Soliloquy"; Laurence Dorsey "spoke on Liberty and Slavery"; Benjamin Sherrod "spoke on industry"; John Pettigrew "spoke from Popes Temple of Fame."[47] The Dialectic and Philanthropic libraries held many texts for students' oratorical training, especially anthologies containing speeches for declamation, which students used as models for style and mined for quotations to incorporate in their own oratory.[48] In addition, society libraries held rhetorical textbooks such as Hugh Blair's famous *Lectures on Rhetoric and Belles Lettres* (1783) and J. Mossop's *Elegant Orations, Ancient and Modern* (1788). Early in the university's history, British models were most prevalent, though in the first two decades of the nineteenth century students gradually supplemented their collection of works on rhetoric with American guides. A careful look at a few of these guides reveals how students appropriated knowledge of rhetoric and oratory into their own efforts of fashioning intellectual manhood.

Oratorical guides significantly catered to students' transition from boyhood to manhood. For example, the Dialectic Society's library purchased E. G. Welles's *The Orator's Guide* (1822), which offered instruction in rhetoric, composition, and oratory in order to refine young men's habits and tastes. "One of the most important objects in the education of youth," Welles wrote, "is to engage them very early in life, in such studies, as are calculated to produce a relish for the entertainments of taste."[49] Welles instructed students to form "clear ideas" in compositions, compose frequently, but not carelessly, and read only well-respected authors. In addition, he included in the guide selections of exemplary ancient orations, as well as modern orations of literary personalities such as Byron, Cowper, Milton, and even Eliphalet Nott, president of Union College. Students could use these oratorical selections in their own declamation exercises.

Students also studied the popular American work *The Columbian Orator* (1797) by Caleb Bingham, an antislavery editor from Connecticut and a 1782 graduate of Dartmouth College in Hanover, New Hampshire, where he later became a professor. Bingham's work inspired Americans as different as the escaped slave and abolitionist Frederick Douglass and the future U.S. president Andrew Johnson. Like its British counterparts, *The Columbian Orator* emphasized the power of elocution through examples of ancient and modern master orators such as Cicero and Demosthenes and Englishmen such as Thomas Erskine and William Pitt. But Bingham's textbook also underscored republican ideals of equality and individual liberty. Bingham excerpted speeches of George Washington, Benjamin Franklin, and Jonathan Mason, a Boston Federalist, to illustrate oratory's unique importance to "the sacred cause of freedom" in America.[50] Students did not dismiss this important work on account of its northern antislavery author. Contrary to the findings of Lorri Glover and Wayne Durrill, young men studying and practicing oratory looked beyond regionalism and embraced the broader urgency of American nationalism in the antebellum period.

Consider John Quincy Adams's two-volume *Lectures on Rhetoric and Oratory* (1810), another popular oratorical guide held in the Dialectic Society library. The work comprises more than thirty-six lectures that Adams delivered to Harvard students between 1806 and 1808. These lectures were so popular that students approached Adams before he even completed the series and urged him to publish them. Adams's lectures soon became popular in colleges and universities in other academic communities. The lectures defended the "science of rhetoric" and the "art of oratory," echoing the messages students heard in their composition and rhetoric classes, that ancient eloquence, especially patriotic oratory, should be central to American education. Adams explained that liberty and oratory were mutually dependent. When the Roman Republic declined, so, too, did Roman oratory. "Under governments purely republican, where every citizen has a deep interest in the affairs of the nation," Adams explained, "the voice of eloquence will not be heard in vain." He urged his collegiate audience, therefore, to aspire toward eloquence.[51]

North Carolina students found Adams's *Lectures* useful, informative, and applicable to their higher education and maturation. On 9 May 1844, some members of the Dialectic Society inscribed the following anonymous commendation on the verso of the second volume's final page: "We have read through the two volumes, and have not only derived a great deal of pleasure but also much information. Those who may be inclined to follow us, will do well to remember that . . . they must be content to receive it with its peculiarities of style, manner &c &c." How did they form this opinion? How did students engage with the text? On one level, students read for instruction, and they underscored the rules Adams set forth for correct rhetoric and oratory and marked passages describing the usefulness of oratory for different professions. For instance, when Adams compared a student's pursuit of eloquence to a soldier's fight for victory, and wrote that eloquence "is to give you a clue for the labyrinth of legislation in the public councils; a spear for the conflict of judicial war in the public tribunals; a sword for the field of religious and moral victory in the pulpit," one student wrote in the page's margins, "This is oratory."[52] But not all students agreed. When, for instance, Adams argued that "moral duties were inculcated" in the youth of antiquity "because none but a good man could be an orator," one student reader responded (albeit with fallacious logic) that "Ergo every orator is a good man" was "an absurdity."[53] Students knew from their own experiences listening to classmates deliver addresses in literary societies that not every orator was a good man, and not every good man was an orator. In one instance, for example, where Adams explains that sometimes speakers misapply another speaker's points for their own contradictory arguments, an anonymous student, identified as "Reader," wrote, "Very common to those who know nothing but wish to be thought wise." To which comment another reader of the text responded that it was "common in our society halls."[54]

Additional markings in the text suggest that students followed Adams's thesis relating oratory to bourgeois attitudes about industry, restraint, and sobriety. For example, one student bracketed off this paragraph in its entirety: "He [an orator] must have a soul of fire; and iron application; indefatigable, unremitting assiduity of exercise in writing and composition; unwearied patience to correct and revise; constant reading of the poets, orators, and historians; the practice of declamation; the exercise and improvement of memory; the attentive cultivation of the graces; and a habit of raillery and humor, sharpened by wit, but tempered with the soberest judgment, to point their application."[55] Adams's ideal orator, elevating mind over temperament, possessed the values that saturated formal university life: application, industry, mental and moral improvement, perseverance, judgment, and reason.[56] He possessed intellectual manhood.

By reading works on rhetoric and eloquence and by declaiming exemplary historical orations, students received not only an education in speech but also an education in ambition and self-fashioning. Speech education introduced young men to seemingly perfect, innate, and timeless notions of greatness—grace, eloquence, emotions, passion, and sympathy. If students imagined greatness in others and attempted to imitate it in literary society composition and declamation exercises, then they could move along the path to distinction, success, and ultimately eminence. This is what Henry Chambers told his fellow Dialectic Society members in 1805: "The men so celebrated for their eloquence, did not acquire it in a moment. We then like them must progress to perfection gradually and by incessant exertions."[57] The consensus was that students needed to consider carefully the means by which great historical figures themselves learned to speak like men.

Nearly every expert agreed that Demosthenes was the best example for young men on the make. Demosthenes was antiquity's quintessential oratorical hero because he excelled at self-fashioning. "If you find your utterance bad," William Hill remarked in 1843, "Recollect Demosthenes declaiming on the sea shore with a pebble in his mouth," perfecting the art of speech.[58] Once Demosthenes perfected his speech, he was able to rally the Athenians, among other Greeks, to fight against invading Macedonians in the middle of the fourth century BC. Summarizing this historic act of patriotism, Alfred Merritt explained to his fellow members of the Dialectic Society in 1852 that Demosthenes "roused his fellow citizens by efforts of oratory almost superhuman, and wrought with in them a willingness to cast their lives as sacrifice upon the altar of freedom. His bosom was the home of patriotism. His head was the seat of what may with justice be called a superior intellect. By means of which he was enable[d] to infuse in other those feelings, which made his own heart beat quick and reared his valiant arm."[59] Demosthenes' heroism inspired collegians across the United States.[60] According to the historian Caroline Winterer, by the antebellum period Demosthenes had "emerged as the archetype of the manly, muscular speaker." American orators ideologically diverse as Hugh Legaré, Thomas Pinckney, and Daniel Webster extolled and emulated him. Demosthenes, college students and educators believed, promoted an emotional, simple, balanced, and forceful style of speech that had, by the antebellum period, come to characterize oratorical culture.[61] Demosthenes' popularity was so great, in fact, that University of Georgia students named one of their literary societies the Demosthenian Society and created a society emblem that illustrated Demosthenes declaiming on the seashore.[62]

North Carolina students relied on one another as "living instructors" to achieve this heroic Demosthenian oratorical ideal. The age differences that existed among students made this peer education possible, as older students —usually the officers of each society—hoped to impress upon their younger classmates the importance of eloquence to intellectual manhood. Predictably, younger students sometimes felt intimidated by older classmates and had to be encouraged to speak in societies. In 1858 a senior member of the Dialectic Society explained to his younger classmates, "We know how embarrassing it is to you to attempt to speak. We were once in the same position. But we advice you to begin now."[63] Not all members were so gentle; some laughed at the slightest mispronunciation of words, or nitpicked a speech's content and delivery.

These shortcomings of peer education aside, students took the reins of oratorical training in literary societies.[64] In addition to the society's president, who delivered his advice on how to improve in society exercises in each term, other officers, especially correctors (in the Dialectic Society) and supervisors (in the Philanthropic Society), helped students to improve in composition and declamation.[65] Correctors and supervisors critiqued classmates for hasty writing, improper spelling and punctuation, poor preparation, and lackluster performances. "When the duty [declamation] is to be performed in this hall," one corrector explained in 1851, "some old worn-out, hackneyed speech is selected, the sentiments grunted out and the feeling, pathetic parts are smothered up in a frigid, careless, life-less manner, that would freeze to death an Icelander." Spelling, grammar, and punctuation did not escape the Correctors' scrutiny either. One critic in 1853 was quite specific in his advice to members: "The members seem to be especially deficient in spelling and punctuation and we would recommend Websters Elementary spelling book and Murrays, Smith's, or Bullions English grammar-and also Perkin's Aid to English composition."[66]

Student officers also emphasized the importance of passion and energy —"manly vigours"—to speech and intellectual manhood.[67] "Declamation has dwindled into a dry—monotonous rehearsal," Henry Elliott complained in his 1826 inaugural address as president of the Dialectic Society. "A listless, apathetic indifference is too often the characteristic of the *dull declaimer*."

He urged members to buck up and perform with "that zeal for oratorical excellence" that should lead "aspiring youth with a noble emulation" of greatness. "We cannot collect & express in a clear systematic & lucid manner all of our ideas upon a subject in one sitting," Elliott explained to a Dialectic Society that seemed to him unusually and alarmingly deficient in composition in 1826. "We must meditate & reflect: we must write & revise if we wish to become more than mere scribblers."[68] As they explained how young men should execute their literary society duties, society officers reminded their fellow members that the goal of composition was to demonstrate mental maturity or intellectual manhood. Achieving that goal required diligent practice.

In addition to these qualities, students also emphasized the rhetorical importance of humility and sincerity, indeed the restraint, that defined intellectual manhood. These values underscored an individual's civic virtue, as Thomas Hall explained to the Dialectic Society: "Whenever anyone demeans himself with an air of modesty & reserve that are the constant accompaniments of youthful merit, and becomes celebrated for his singular integrity abilities and patriotism, the people who when left to themselves are never slow in discovery and rewarding true merit, will not suffer his talents to lie dormant for want of proper opportunities to exert them."[69] Significantly, young men's rhetorical self-deprecation differed from that of women, who used rhetorical gestures of modesty and humility to excuse and underplay the significance of their public addresses. Men, however, used these rhetorical gestures to demonstrate deference to the majority and gain greater access to public life. Modesty, in short, was a virtue that would win a man public esteem.[70]

Students practiced deference in speech because it was a republican virtue that indicated speakers emanated from—and were sympathetic to—the concerns of the body politic. This was particularly the case in inaugural addresses of newly elected literary society presidents, who wished to demonstrate authority and deference at once. For example, Virginius H. Ivy of Norfolk, Virginia, began an 1845 valedictory address to the Dialectic Society by introducing himself as "the humble representative of my classmates." Sometimes the gravitas of a particular topic required humble and sensitive introductory remarks. This was the case in 1805, when Daniel Forney, a student in the Dialectic Society, advocated abolition of slavery in an address to his fellow members. "I am deeply impressed with a sense of the high honor confered upon me in being appointed to address you upon this important, this interesting occasion," he began. "I am highly sensible of my inability to discharge of the duty devolved upon me, and sincerely wish some person more adequate than myself had undertaken the task."[71] Similarly, when John Briggs Mebane gave an address about women's education, he began with a humble mark of deference to the audience: "When I look around and behold the countenances of so many turned upon me I shrink with a heart wounded by the keen edge of criticism, and with feelings agitated by my inadequacy to do that justice to the subject."[72]

It is important to read the lessons between the lines of speeches like these, for they call attention to the unique power structure of the fraternal community of listeners young men created in literary societies. This was a speech education, ultimately, for the assertion of authority among peers. According to Kenneth Greenberg, "Orations were expressions of the ego. They were ways of asserting superiority and being honored."[73] Implicit in this deference and humility was the understanding that speakers had to acknowledge the power of their peers as listeners. In literary societies, students enacted a world in which men's independence and power ultimately rested in the hands of an audience of fellow men who also had ambitions for greatness. Thus, the rituals of public speech in literary societies were steeped not only in bourgeois practices of emulation but also in southern traditions of honor and public speech. In each of these contexts, self-restraint—demonstrated through speech and through humility—was perhaps the most significant variable in the equation of male power.

In these ways, by performing speech in literary societies students underscored certain tensions inherent in maturation as well as manhood. Speech was a way for collegians to show one another that they were no longer boys. They demonstrated this by elevating restraint over impulse (in the above case, restraining ambition with humility) and mind over temperament. The other tensions that student performances reveal is that young men were joining a world in which they constantly had to strike a balance between being a leader and a member of a peer community. As Kenneth Greenberg has argued, this struggle defined both southern statesmanship and mastery. Although students rarely, if ever, wrote about oratory in terms of mastery, it is clear that both the emulation and practice of oratory were exercises in asserting intellectual manhood, or mental superiority, among fellows who shared ambition for greatness equally.

IN CLASSROOMS AND IN LITERARY SOCIETIES, students engaged with an oratorical ideal for male adulthood and citizenship. These identities were presented as timeless. Evidence from antiquity, modern Europe, and the contemporary United States demonstrated to students that eloquence was a crucial component of intellectual manhood. Great orators from each of these worlds likewise demonstrated that efforts to cultivate eloquence were heroic. More than any other aspect of formal university life, speech education reinforced the need for emulation. By emulating great men through declamation and composition exercise, students breathed life into education, transforming it into an imaginative process with great meaning for self-development. Young men not only admired heroes of the past but also envisioned themselves as heroes for a future that, given their youth, was both wide open and imminent. Similarly, if young men were to hone their ambition for greatness, then certain middle-class values such as restraint, perseverance, and hard work were absolutely necessary. In emphasizing the importance of honing speech, literary societies created a vibrant world of intentional intellectualism. This was just the world for students to pursue many forms of bourgeois self-fashioning, which is the focus of the following three chapters.

PART II

SELF
Constructing Intellectual Manhood

The object of college was to turn boys into men, and university life catered to this goal by providing students with tools and resources for self-fashioning. In particular, the pervasive spirit of mental and moral improvement, restraint, discipline, and emulation laid the foundation for intellectual manhood. As speech education in literary societies revealed, however, students had to do the lion's share of the work. Consequently, they created a vibrant "informal curriculum" in libraries, literary societies, friendships, and love affairs. Typically, scholars have neglected the educational quality of the informal education, though this is where students' world of intentional intellectualism is most evident. Throughout the antebellum period, their focus remained on the self, particularly its maturation, which involved restraining boyish impulse, elevating mind over temperament, and pursuing intellectual and moral independence. Often, students turned to exercises of "self-development" (or "self-fashioning," or "self-improvement"). These included attention to reading, writing, emulation, hero worship, and Christian devotional life. These acts of self-fashioning were typical of the American bourgeoisie and they defined the "everyday creativity" of antebellum college life.

A significant feature of young men's pursuit of self during the antebellum years was its literary dimension, its connections to a broader American intellectual culture through books. This culture was predicated on a new culture of books and reading tied to the Market Revolution, which led to the greatest proliferation of print Americans had ever known. According to the historian David Reynolds, the number of books printed in the United States between 1820 and 1860 increased by some eight hundred percent, ushering in a revolution in American popular culture.[1] Southern readers, including students, felt the magnitude of this revolution. In the antebellum period, North Carolina literary society libraries grew at unprecedented rates, amassing dozens of new works every year. These libraries were important "institutions of reading,"[2] providing resources, spaces, and opportunities to read, as well as forums for talking and writing *about* reading. In particular, antebellum students engaged in an ongoing discourse about literary genres, which gave voice to their shared anxiety about growing up as well as the southern educated class's expectations for manhood more generally.[3] Moreover, in their literary lives on campus, students created a distinctive self-culture predicated on self-improvement, emulation, and hero worship. Whenever young men read, wrote, and talked about famous men and women, they used literature to construct adult lives, exercising what the historian Scott Casper has called "biographical imagination." Self-culture inspired them to greatness. In various devotional exercises, secular and sacred, students wrote their lives into history as well. Their diaries became records of self-fashioning, shedding light not only on the personal experiences of becoming adults but the social ones as well.

The informal curriculum's literary quality is also evident in students' interactions with women, including their experiences of intimacy, love, courtship, and sex. Even though the university was all male, it was not uncommon for young women from the village to visit campus to attend lectures, prayer and chapel services, and the annual commencement. In these moments, students' social lives with each other and with young women intersected within intellectual culture. In private writing, students contemplated ideal womanhood, desire, love, courtship, and marriage. They wrote love letters and composed and performed ballads and poetry, which they sometimes published in the *North Carolina University Magazine*. Thus, students' experiences with intimacy, love, desire, and courtship fueled their everyday creativity. Significantly, the written records of these experiences underscore the exclusivity of students' all-male culture on campus, as well as how young men came to view themselves as different from and often superior to others, including women.

As we have seen in Part I, tensions between boyhood and manhood were paramount in students' informal curriculum. Their diaries, letters, and commonplace books particularly reflect the familiar tensions between impulse and restraint, mind and temperament, and dependence and independence that characterized college life. The final chapter in Part II shows, for example, how sex and intimacy sometimes got in the way of ideas of self-culture and restrained manhood, but this was part of the process produced by youth, enhanced by college life, and common among college boys at the time as they sought to leave childhood. In order to understand this informal education, we must first turn to the literary culture that gave it meaning.

CHAPTER FOUR

Reading Makes the Man
Books and Literary Socialization

In 1849, nineteen-year-old Thomas Miles Garrett, a junior at the University of North Carolina, wrote a class essay on the topic of Francis Bacon's maxim, "Reading makes a full man, conversation a ready man, and writing an accurate man." He pondered the meaning of the quotation: "Reading makes a full man, but what does reading imply? Does it merely mean that one should pronounce the words and run through the sentences of an author?" No, "one could not be termed a full man who read only with this view," he wrote. Reading involved "employing the attention to discern, reason to apply, and memory to retain what we read." In fact, Garrett concluded, "there is not probably a single instance of the rise of any great man . . . or at least any well ballanced mind" who did not read in this way.[1] Hardly a day went by, in fact, when Garrett did not record in his diary some reference or response to a book. Between June 1849 and November 1850, he read at least fifty-two titles, including Shakespeare's *Hamlet*, Eugene Sue's *The Wandering Jew*, and Hume's six-volume *History of England*.[2] Garrett borrowed these and other titles from the Philanthropic Society's library, which held nearly 5,000 titles at the time. He took pride in his selections and for the most part read slowly and thoroughly, recording in his diary reports and reflections.

Library records, letters, diaries, and speeches from North Carolina students like Thomas Garrett reveal that young men considered reading an important cultural practice and a path to manhood.[3] Reading qualified students "to appear with ease and effect in polite and refined society," where literary taste and erudition legitimated social status, conveyed independence, and conferred honor.[4] Students also believed that reading prepared them for public life, where they would lead their state, communities, and intellectual culture.[5]

Young men engaged in a variety of literary activities as everyday readers, extending their formal education beyond the classroom into the realm of "everyday creativity." They read aloud, borrowed books, advised one another on what, how, even when to read, and thus engaged in what the historians Mary and Ronald Zboray have termed "literary socialization."[6] In the process, they created a variety of "interpretive communities" and reading cultures that catered to the transition from boyhood to manhood.[7] By acquiring advanced literacy skills, they hoped to elevate restraint over impulse and mind over temperament. They also hoped to signal to peers and superiors their emerging intellectual manhood and claim independence through it. They encouraged one another to read serious genres, including history, biography, and philosophy, but not fiction, which some students claimed undermined the values of intellectual manhood. Nevertheless, novels were a mainstay of Victorian American culture, and students created a vibrant extracurricular literary culture for less serious reading. Significantly, this culture actually catered to young men's maturation and education. In order to understand this cultural process, it is first important to understand students as everyday readers.

Everyday Readers:
Social and Private Engagement with Literature

Reading permeated antebellum college life. Beyond study, students read a variety of texts, including letters, newspapers, periodicals, and literary works of every genre. The effects of the second print revolution invigorated reading culture at North Carolina, and students certainly did not want for something to read. In 1853, one student wrote that "incalculable volumes with every kind of preface, introduction, and dedication have been published, and expressed into every portion of this lettered sphere" on account of recent transportation and print innovations.[8] Aside from finding such volumes within the stacks of the university and literary society libraries, students purchased books locally, usually from local printers in Raleigh or a bookstore in nearby Hillsboro. Sometimes students bought books from book peddlers who traveled through Chapel Hill. Finally, students relied on their families and frequently wrote home for textbooks, newspapers, popular magazines, and literature.[9] In 1841, Montezuma Jones thanked his father for having sent "several newspapers," and wrote that he would be "glad to get more of them."[10] In 1858, William Little wrote a letter to his father, inquiring, "Did you bring the book, Don Quixote, from Aunt Mary's? If you did not, and go down there again before I come home, I wish you would get it, as you said it was such a nice copy."[11] Thus, students' reading networks were broad, encompassing local merchants and distant family members.

Students exchanged literature through the mail and incorporated literary excerpts into letters.[12] In correspondence, they described their current reading and offered commentary on literature. Walter Lenoir reported to his father that he had not read much during the academic year, except "Tytler's history (the new edition enlarged)" and "several volumes of light reading and poetry."[13] Jesse Goodwin Ross wrote to his mother, too, after he had "just placed aside a Biography which for hours has enchained my unremitting attention and peculiar interest."[14] Other responses were more specific. In 1845, for example, William Whitfield wrote to his friend Theodore Kingsbury, a North Carolina alumnus, that he had read an unnamed play that Kingsbury had recommended. "I do not like it as well as 'She Stoops to Conquer,'" he wrote, "but notwithstanding if it is well acted, it will appear remarkably well." Writing home about reading also allowed students to redefine their roles as men rather than boys. William Bagley, for instance, took interest in his younger siblings' educations and wrote to them often about the books that he thought were especially valuable. In 1843, he wrote to his sister, "I hope you will have read the life of Washington entirely through by next winter, so you can read it to Bud," their brother.[15] In 1857, John Dudley Tatum encouraged his sister to follow his example: "I am now reading the life of S. G. Goodrich, or Peter Parley as he is otherwise called, it is written by himself and is quite interesting, probably more so to me because I have always been a great admirer of him. I hope that you will not neglect to read his museum as it was a great source of pleasure as well as profit for me."[16] Months later, he wrote again to his sister, who read the books that he had given her. He recommended that she share the books with their brother, Herbert, and discuss them in his absence. He also explained to her that he was "reading the life of Washington by Irving and am very much pleased with it."[17] Literary exercises such as these allowed students to articulate their adult roles in the larger web of family relationships and responsibilities.[18]

This social culture of reading rested on hours of private engagement with literature, where students selected, read, contemplated, and preserved literature. In private journals and diaries, students recorded when they read, how they read, and what they read. Generally, young men read whenever they had the chance: in the morning before class, at night before bed, in between meals, on vacation, and every time in between. Sometimes they spent an entire day reading one book; other times they read for a few hours before bed. Their responses to literature followed or preceded daily reports about the weather, class, and health, and thus varied in length and substance. In 1841, for example, Ruffin Tomlinson reported in his diary, "Rain last night, but a splendid morning this. Read until breakfast. After breakfast recited to Prof Mitchel upon chemistry, in the afternoon upon Bigalow's technology."[19] Other students were less precise. On the day before he turned seventeen in 1863, Henry London simply wrote in his diary, "cloudy & raining. Saw G Burgwin on a drunk at his room. Read and played cards in afternoon."[20] Regardless of their extent, however, students' reader reports suggest an active reading culture on campus.

Edmund Covington's diary illustrates the range of reader responses that appear in antebellum students' private writing. Born in Richmond County, North Carolina, Covington entered the freshman class at North Carolina in 1839 at the age of seventeen and began his diary on his nineteenth birthday, 25 September 1841. A sentimental young man, Covington enjoyed music, romantic poetry, and American literature, and he helped to found the *North Carolina University Magazine* in 1844. His diary itself was a work of literature: "A Literary Miscellany devoted to Extracts, prose and poetry, English and Latin quotations, quaint and pointed remarks, original compositions, strange and whimsical circumstances."[21] In the diary, he also included a brief, one-page "Catalogue of Books Read by ED Covington Commencing Jany 1st 1842" and ending that November. The catalog indicates that Covington read at least twenty different titles, consisting of thirty-one volumes of modern history, biography, plays, and essays, classical literature, contemporary fiction, and current periodical literature.[22]

Covington recorded both general and specific responses to literature. General reports usually included vague references to reading, but sometimes author and title information. "Came to my room at night with a headache—read a few pages of Thompsons Seasons—fine poet—he is the poet of nature and of nature's God," Covington reported in 1842. When he did not have a headache, Covington crafted more critical responses. Responding to *Hamlet* later that year, for example, Covington briefly synopsized the play before evaluating it. "The play is certainly the poet's masterpiece in tragedy," he observed. "But there is so much contradiction such seeming inconsistency in the character of Hamlet (who is supposed to have been meant by the poet as the hero of the drama) that this play has been the subject of much dispute by writers and has not consequently been subjected to the severest critical censure."[23] Supporting this critique, Covington provided a long excerpt from the play (act 1, scene 2). Not all students, of course, went into such great detail in synopsizing and critiquing literature, nor did many of them provide evidence of engagement with critical literary reviews. Nevertheless, Covington's diary contains a range of ways in which many students engaged with literature. This engagement clarifies the important role reading played in young men's experiences of youth, college, and maturation.

In addition to recording explicit reader responses, students kept commonplace books containing quotations or other short literary excerpts. A medieval practice that continued through the nineteenth century, commonplacing involved copying published literature into personal diaries or journals in order to practice penmanship, hone literary taste, and keep memorable pieces of literature.[24] The practice was popular among young Americans especially. At the University of North Carolina many students kept commonplace books in the 1840s. The practice helped students infuse literature into, and make literature out of, their daily lives.[25] It was also an exercise of self-fashioning in which young men could select passages from texts (or entire texts) that they found morally or mentally "improving." William Mullins "commenced . . . a Common Place Book, after the plan of the immortal Locke," and David Barnes devoted several pages of his journal to extracts of classical texts by Pliny, Lucretius, and Horace.[26] In 1842, Joseph Summerell included in his diary "a collection of choice sentimental, descriptive, eloquent and attractive pieces culled from the most approved authors of prose and poetry." Introducing this section of his diary, Summerell explained why commonplacing mattered to him: "It is by looking over these extracts that I expect to derive much pleasure herafter, and aided by local associations I shall be delighted to recall . . . to my mind the recollections of days and hours that I spent here—most happy moments of my life."[27] By selecting and transcribing literature, young men gave greater intellectual meaning to everyday literary experiences. In order to accommodate these literary practices, students turned to their well-stocked libraries.

Institutions of Reading: Literary Society Libraries

Libraries were important sites for young men's informal education. According to the historian Thomas Augst, who has written extensively on the moral development of adolescent clerks in the northeastern United States,

"Catalogue of Books Read by E D Covington Commencing Jany 1ˢᵗ 1842."
Excerpt from the Edmund DeBerry Covington Diary #1506-z, Southern Historical
Collection, Wilson Library, University of North Carolina at Chapel Hill. According to
this list, Edmund Covington read "Irving's Edition of M. M. Davidson's Davidson's P. Rem[ai]
ns"; "Goldsmith's Rome"; "Middleton's Cicero"; "Shakespeare's Plays [listed twice]";
"Sismondi's European Literature"; ". . . Specimens of class. Po'try"; "Scott's Poet.
Works"; "Hume's England Commenced"; "Herber—Pollock and Hemans"; "Milton—
Gray—Beattie—Collins"; "Stewart's Philosophy of the Mind"; "Life of Governor
Morris"; "Montgomery's poems"; "Hallams Middle ages"; "Last of the Mohicans";
"New York Review [listed thrice]"; "Thompson's Seasons"; and "Human Nature."

circulating libraries provided spaces for moral improvement. More than book repositories, libraries allowed young men to enter into the "public life of literature."[28] Middle-class clerks were not singular in their uses of circulating libraries, for this was a defining feature of literary culture in the antebellum United States, including the South. At the University of North Carolina, libraries provided spaces for literary socialization, as they taught one another how to participate in a literary public. This education included lessons in book management and care, reading methods, and genre selection.

Significantly, the University Library was not the primary source of this socialization process. Housed in a small lecture room in South Building, the University Library consisted of only about 1,900 volumes in the antebellum period (mostly textbooks), and students had to pay fifty cents per session to use it.[29] A separate library building was not erected until 1850, when Governor Benjamin Smith donated money for its construction. The resulting Smith Hall was an eighty-four by twenty-five-foot building built in the Greek revival style, with five windows on each side. Two large chandeliers hung from the ceiling; shelves for as many as 12,000 volumes flanked the walls.[30] Students, however, found that the library was not always conducive to reading. When Thomas Garrett went there in 1849, he found that "some gentlemen had the room sounding and reechoing the shrill note of their whistle. This is the kind of disturbance which I can in no wise bear. I could not request them to hush, for this they would deem impolite."[31] Not all students were as lucky as Garrett even to find the library open. Fordyce Hubbard, a professor of Latin who had been in charge of the building through 1868, recalled that "the College Library was never open to the students; on two occasions only, as I remember, consulted by persons from abroad; and almost never . . . used by members of the Faculty."[32] This inaccessibility was common at most college libraries in the South, often due to faculty mistrust of students and fear of their mistreatment of books.[33]

In contrast to the University Library, the Dialectic and Philanthropic Society libraries were easily accessible and expanded during the antebellum period to meet student needs. With the exception of certain "prohibited books," which could not leave the library's antechamber due to their value, members were allowed to borrow books from each society.[34] Each society expanded its library holdings either by purchasing new titles or accepting donations from professors, parents of enrolled students, and alumni.[35] Both libraries grew substantially between 1820 and 1861. The Philanthropic

Society's collection, for example, grew from nineteen titles, consisting of forty-one volumes, in 1797, to 503 titles, consisting of about 1,500 volumes, in 1822. That number doubled by the mid-1830s, when each society library held 3,000 volumes. The libraries continued to grow, each amassing 5,000 books by 1854 and 8,000 books by 1858.[36] By the Civil War, the two libraries combined held as many volumes as any similar college societies in the United States, except at Yale.[37] Early on, the literary societies maintained manuscript inventories of their books. In 1822, the Philanthropic Society published its inventory, distributing two hundred copies among members and within their home communities, and the Dialectic Society followed soon thereafter. As accession of books increased, librarians organized the catalogs more specifically, standardizing cataloging practices. In 1854, a *North Carolina University Magazine* author explained the significance of these catalogs: "No man can read the hundredth part of the books a good library contains; and yet he must have the full benefit of all that is contained by that department to which he would devote his time and talents; else the greatest utility of a large library is lost."[38] Indeed, the library catalogs allowed students to borrow books more easily and regularly.[39] Library catalogs from each society reveal collecting and borrowing patterns similar to other American collegiate literary societies.[40]

Students filled their bookcases with literature they associated with refinement, gentility, and maturity.[41] A student contributor to the *North Carolina University Magazine* explained, "As a man's character may be known from his association, just so we may estimate a man's taste from the books which comprise his library. These are his intimate friends, his daily companions."[42] Unlike the dusty old tomes that filled the University Library's shelves, the literary society libraries boasted newer books "evidently selected with an eye to the finest copies."[43] Students collected works by the ancients as well as the moderns, American authors as well as European authors. The catalogs listed titles in the following subject classifications: biography, geography, history, novels, plays, poetry, politics and political economy, travels and voyages, and theology. There was also a quite large section entitled "Miscellanies" that included epistles, sermons, and science books. Students arranged library bookshelves according to these subjects and then alphabetically by short title within that subject. However, as Ronald J. Zboray found in bookstores in New England, there was a great deal of "permeability between boundaries of different genres," and sometimes book placement was not always clear.[44] In sum, though, students' book col-

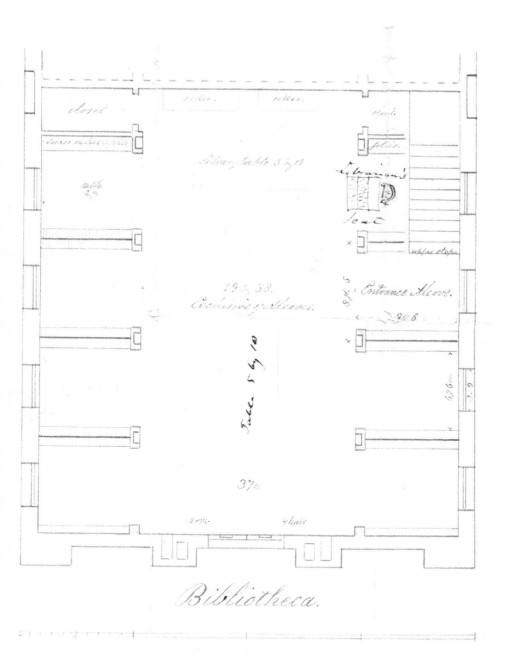

"Bibliotheca," or James Donaldson's architectural plan for the Philanthropic
Society Library in Old East, between 1845 and 1860. North Carolina Collection,
Wilson Library, University of North Carolina at Chapel Hill.

lections resembled those of other national and regional libraries of their kind. They were cosmopolitan in scope, rooted in the liberal arts, and approved by a larger literary community.

Society libraries were more than book repositories; they were centerpieces of student culture.[45] Students held the libraries in high esteem as unique reading institutions associated with their development as educated men. Just one month before graduating, Walter Lenoir wrote to his sister, Sarah, about the Dialectic Society library. "You said rightly that I would miss the Library," he confessed. "Oh! what an inestimable friend is a good library. It fits itself with the nicest discrimination to every mood of our minds. . . . I would shed bitter [tears] if I were cut off forever from the society of such a friend. But do not be alarmed because the Dialectic library is not in the Valley." Though the Lenoirs possessed a family library that could "afford a conciderable amount of literature," Walter could hardly imagine any library that provided so many opportunities for reading as the Dialectic Society's library at the University of North Carolina.[46]

Student borrowing activity varied, though it remained constant and encouraged throughout the university's antebellum history. Between 19 August 1840 and 31 August 1841, for example, Walter Lenoir, surprisingly, only charged four books from the Dialectic Society library, which the librarian recorded as "Curiosities of Literature" (volumes 1–3); "Peter the Great" (volume 1); "Hist U.S."; and "Hist Indian Wars." On the top of the page containing Walter's circulation records, the librarian wrote, "Take more Walter!" In contrast, Lenoir's classmate, William Cowan, charged fifty-five titles between 15 August 1840 and 16 March 1841, including John Todd's *Student's Manual* and unspecified novels by Ann Radcliffe and an unspecified collection of tales by Maria Edgeworth. And according to the same librarian's hasty entries, another classmate, John B. Smith, charged nineteen volumes, ranging from "Shakespeare" to "Life of Van Buren" to "Napoleon."[47]

Literary society libraries were also important social spaces, where students performed and claimed adult identities as readers. Early in the nineteenth century, the libraries were held in the literary societies' meeting rooms, which were located on the third floor of South Building. After 1848, however, when two buildings on campus (East and West Buildings) were expanded to allow for a growing student body, the Dialectic and Philanthropic halls occupied separate spaces. The Dis met on the second floor of Old West and the Phis met on the second floor of Old East. Their libraries were on the third floor of each building.[48] Students retired to these spaces after weekly meetings to peruse the shelves, read at a table or on a sofa, or chat with classmates. On weekends, societies opened their libraries to the public, and townspeople milled around looking at the collections. Occasionally, students brought into the libraries friends or young women whom they wished to impress.[49] Because students wanted others to view them as adults and gentlemen, members of each society competed for the best library. Students often compared the two.[50] In 1849, for example, Thomas Miles Garrett, a member of the Philanthropic Society, examined the Dialectic Society's library in order to see whether it held books that were unavailable to him elsewhere. After spending "a few hours" in the rival library, Garrett boasted, "I found none scarcely except what we have in our library. I think the selection is not superior to that of the Philanthropic, the arrangement not half as good."[51]

Literary society libraries were also important educational spaces, where students relied on their bonds as "brothers" to acquire mature reading habits. As one student wrote, "Libraries are not for ornamental show. Their beauty consists in their utility, and they are to be admired in proportion to the information they contain."[52] Numerous speeches from literary society leaders reveal that young men viewed the chief utility of their libraries as guiding young men toward mental maturity, or intellectual manhood. They taught one another advanced literacy skills in an effort not only to bring esteem and respect to their respective societies, but also to promote mental and moral improvement necessary for antebellum education and private self-fashioning. This process of literary socialization unfolded in several ways, but usually involved common lessons relating books and reading to students' maturation.

Literary society members focused on three general principles about mature engagement with literature: treatment, selection, and reading of books. First, Dis and Phis emphasized proper book handling, equating proper treatment of books with maturity and bourgeois respectability. Because students occasionally lost books (or stole them), ripped pages from them, and wrote in them, each society appointed librarians to enforce rules for the collection, preservation, and borrowing of books, and to levy fines for late, missing, or damaged volumes. Librarians reported to the society presidents, who frequently addressed the society on the state of the library.[53] Students explained that maltreatment of books was ungentlemanly. One student explained that any man "professing to be a gentleman," who tore pages from a book, committed a "great crime." He continued, "Let the next man that puts his fingers upon the leaf of a library book to tear it out remember that he is about to destroy that which he is not, & perhaps never will be able to restore," he warned, "and more, that he is peradventure robbing some dead author of the only monument that was left by him to perpetuate his memory among men."[54] Second, students encouraged reading only useful, or instructive books that befit men.[55] "The studies of youth should be directed so as to bear on the duties and engagements of a mature life," John Madison Stedman told his classmates in 1830, urging them to "furnish" their minds with "suitable books." Students could gather knowledge "from a wide circumference," of diverse authors from their society libraries, but they were to seek only those authors that were suitable and did not have any "manifest tendency to corrupt moral principle and violate taste."[56] Third, students recommended careful reading and admonished desultory reading, which they viewed as a vestige of boyhood. In 1825, for example, Erasmus North explained to his classmates, "A very common rule with respect to the manner in which we ought to read is always to proceed with the greatest care and attention, examining everything as we go & never suffering ourselves to be in a hurry. . . . A most important rule is *read with an active mind*." Moreover, a good reader "will always in the course of reading be drawing reflections; applying them to himself where they can be so applied & be comparing one author with another."[57] Significantly, peer education in reading aimed to restrain boyish impulsivity and therefore complemented formal educational philosophy and pedagogy.

Evidence from diaries reveals that many students incorporated these principles in daily reading habits. For example, when David Alexander Barnes began his journal in February 1840, he transcribed a short paragraph written by Scottish philosopher James Beattie (1735–1803) on attentive reading: "The great art of memory is attention. Without this, one reads, and hears, to no purpose. . . . To read in haste, without reflecting on what we read, may amuse a vacant hour, but will never improve the understanding."[58] Similarly, after William Mullins read some philosophical writing by George Berkeley, he wrote in his journal, "Reading carefully such works [as Berkeley's] trains the mind to habits of thinking in the same perceptive manner [as the author], and leads to the detection of error in writers." Mullins pledged to read "with all the attention that I can possibly give" and to select works that promised to "teach one *how* to think, not *what* to think."[59]

Although conventional prescriptions for young men's reading appealed to many students, these did not take into account students' desires for entertainment, which literary society libraries accommodated in collections of popular literature. Each society collected a variety of magazines. Between 1835 and 1849, the number of titles held in the Dialectic Society library increased from sixteen titles (371 volumes) to forty-nine titles (699 volumes). Important titles included the *Yale Literary Magazine, Dublin University Magazine, Blackwood's Magazine,* the *Ramblers Magazine,* the *Southern Literary Messenger,* the *Southern Quarterly Review, DeBow's Review,* the *Knickerbocker,* and *Harper's New Monthly Magazine.*[60] Students also produced, reproduced, and read serial fiction published in the *North Carolina University Magazine.* Established for one year in 1844 and then launched again in 1852, this publication resembled other literary magazines of the time and contained biography, history, short stories, orations, addresses, lectures, political, philosophical, and scientific essays, serial novels, book reviews, and poetry. Alongside serial stories, too, were shorter stories and tales.[61]

Periodical literature allowed for desultory reading in ways that "approved" literature did not. Students did not have to "study" literary magazines but instead could read quickly and selectively. Moreover, these magazines presented a hodgepodge of ideas, literary styles, and genres. Philosophy and theology were presented beside fiction and poetry, providing a sense of fragmentation not found in curricular texts. According to one historian, popular literary magazines placed a framework around romantic discourse in the first quarter of the nineteenth century.[62] Thus, periodical literature played a role in reorienting young men's reading habits away from traditional modes of reading deeply toward newer modes of reading broadly. Many felt that undisciplined reading would undermine the pursuit of restrained manhood. Nowhere is this tension so pronounced as in literary society discourse about novel reading.

A "Destructive Habit": Novels and Manly Independence

Novels became increasingly popular at North Carolina in the antebellum period. Between 1821 and 1849, the number of volumes of novels held in the Dialectic Society library grew sixfold.[63] In 1845, one student observed, "The whole cry seems now to be for some thing exciting. Consequently novels are all the go."[64] The popularity of novels presented a few problems, not the least of which was forestalling the transition from boyhood to manhood. Writing about the growth of the society libraries, an anonymous author of the *North Carolina University Magazine* equated student tastes with boyhood. "True, we have as yet to satisfy the literary tastes of few except boys," he wrote, "but if we do not soon have men diving to the deepest bottom of our classical and historical lore, it will be our own fault."[65] While young men clearly worried that libraries catered too much to boyhood, students questioned the validity of such arguments. Did novels impede education? Did they undermine the values of intellectual manhood? Did they promote boyish impulsivity at that critical juncture in life when young men required restraint?[66] In regular literary society meetings, student leaders often underscored the hazards of novel reading in an effort to promote mental and moral improvement of youth. They appropriated discourse emanating from deep within American culture and, in the process, conveyed core middle-class ideals about manhood, including restraint, self-discipline, and industry.

In the nineteenth century, young men throughout the United States were instructed to avoid novels at all costs, lest they fall prey to any of the vices long associated with the genre, including idleness, dissipation, frivolity, profligacy, and licentiousness.[67] Students studying Francis Wayland's *Elements of Moral Science*, for example, learned about the moral hazards of novel reading: "No one is corrupt in action, until he has become corrupt in imagination. And on the other hand he who has filled his imagination with conceptions of vice, and who loves to feast his depraved moral appetite with imaginary scenes of impurity needs but opportunity to become openly abandoned."[68] Students found similar attitudes in popular advice manuals held in their own society libraries, including John Todd's *Student's Manual* (1835).[69] A Congregationalist minister who traveled throughout the Northeast in the 1830s, speaking to crowds of college students, Todd warned, "Beware of bad books. The world is flooded with such books. They are permitted to lie in our pathway as part of our moral discipline."[70] Habitual novel reading could cause students to fall behind in their studies and literary society duties, making them lazy and weak thinkers. College life, characterized as it was by constant tensions between boyhood and manhood, impulse and restraint, dependence and independence, particularly exacerbated fears that novels might undermine students' moral development.

Students often echoed the warnings of moralists such as Wayland and Todd. In 1826, Alfred Nicholson told his classmates to avoid novels "as deadly poison."[71] In 1833, William Owen—a novel reader himself—said that novels ought to be "sealed books."[72] In 1845, another student warned his classmates that novels were "always used in depicting some horrible scene or demonstrating the depravities of the human heart."[73] In 1849, Thomas Miles Garrett—also an avid novel reader—admitted, "I know that novel reading is a destructive habit."[74] Finally, in 1853, student reviewers of Charles Astor Bristed's *Five Years in an English University* (1852) remarked that "*no* novels are allowed in the libraries of the [British] debating societies," and should be forbidden in the Di and Phi societies.[75]

Embedded in students' critiques were concerns about age and class that reflect more general expectations for intellectual manhood in the antebellum South. Because students typically read novels quickly and in great number, some students worried that the habit would keep young men in the world of boy culture, which was defined by impulsivity, carelessness, and inattention. "Some admit the necessity of employing every moment in storing away knowledge yet come week after week and load themselves with an armful of Novels, as if they expected to find true wisdom and useful thoughts in these books," one student wrote in 1832.[76] Students believed that novels undermined mental and moral improvement and impeded the attainment of intellectual manhood. Similarly, students worried that novel readers did not employ industry, self-discipline, and restraint—important values of the American bourgeoisie that they hoped to acquire. "Novel readers are like gay butterflies that flit from flower to flower," William Owen explained, but the exemplary reader was a "sober reader of works of practical utility," who "resembles the industrious bee that dives into every flower and gathers its stores of honeyed wealth."[77] Students favored the industrious bee because it was stoic, balanced, attentive, and industrious, but not the butterfly, which was the trifling reader, uninterested in serious pursuits.

Although students invoked many popular arguments to curb novel reading on campus, even the strongest critics read novels.[78] At a time when students had few amusements, novels relieved boredom. Indeed, many students could have argued that novel reading was more salubrious than drinking, fighting, gambling, and carousing. Still, some novel readers might have raised some eyebrows. James Dusenbery enjoyed liquor, "bull dances," prostitutes, *and* Dickens novels, as Michael O'Brien has pointed out, and his classmate, Joseph Summerell, neglected (required) chapel services on account of "being so much interested in a Novel."[79] Fictional works that students read, however, would not have been characterized as "bad books" even in the antebellum era. For instance, society libraries did not contain sensational works such as *The Rake*, *The Whip*, *The Flash*, and *The Libertine*, which were popular among urban youth and noted for their salacious plots and depraved characters. Nor did students write about reading them.[80] The problem, then, was not so much with novels as it was with novel reading and its perceived threat to maturation.

Thus, North Carolina students may have repeated warnings that novels were destructive, but they did not "passively [endorse] the hierarchy of reading matter delineated by social experts," as the historian Elisabeth Nichols has argued about female readers of the same era. In college, young men learned to make their own judgments about texts based on their knowledge of what was most and least appropriate.[81] In other words, they desired to move out of intellectual semi-dependence toward intellectual independence. This is exactly what the editors of the *North Carolina University Magazine* did when they reviewed Donald Grant Mitchell's newly published *The Reveries of a Bachelor: or, A Book of the Heart* (1853). "We admire independence," they wrote. "We wish every man to read and think for himself." They recommended Mitchell's novel not "upon the ground of its learning," but "for its virtuous and elevating character." They wrote, "We love the *book* for we are conscious that if we did not get up from its perusal a wiser, we did a better man." In other words, reading a novel (or at least this novel) could complement students' maturation, and the reviewers especially commended the novel's "scenes of boyhood and youth."[82] These editors raised an important point for young men wishing to become intellectually independent: students could read novels so long as they judged them wisely and fairly.

Intellectual independence in reading also was tied to concerns with honor that are typically associated with "southern manhood." For instance, Thomas Miles Garrett criticized attempts to regulate young men's reading habits. In 1850, he attended Sunday services at the Chapel of the Cross, the local Episcopal church, where he heard a sermon in which the minister "condemned many things," including novel reading. Garrett, however, insisted that if any reader approached a book uncritically, then he hardly ought to read at all. "I would call him a base coward who would fear to read a book," he wrote. "He is a silly body who can be affected by any thing which he knows to [be] imaginary and fictitious. . . . Is he one who reads a book to believe it and for no other purpose, without criticizeing one line or one opinion," Garrett wondered. Such a reader as that, he concluded, "is unworthy to touch such a sacred thing as a book."[83] It was difficult for

Garrett not to associate such supervision with dishonor. If the point of an education was to develop the ability to think for oneself, and if that was a defining feature of educated manhood, then too much reading advice threatened a young man's pride and wounded his honor.

Students' concerns about genre reflect their deeper anxieties about the transition from boyhood to manhood, or from boyish dependence to manly independence, as well as the blending of mainstream bourgeois and traditional southern values in antebellum educational culture. As students, young men remained dependent on the authority of educators and texts for guidance on how to think, act, and feel. Many young men appropriated conventional wisdom about reading and literature in literary society addresses in order to complement the process of higher education. Yet at the same time, college life afforded them considerable autonomy over their lives and encouraged intellectual independence, especially in literary societies. In the Di and Phi libraries, students freely selected books, categorized and cataloged them, borrowed them, and read them. So students were pulled in two different directions: they could bow to the authority of countless sources of reading advice or they could assert their manly independence and read as they liked, confident that they had imbibed the ideals handed down to them through formal education. Attitudes about the destructive influence of novels on maturation and individual identity, however, did not always dictate young men's personal reading lives, nor did they forestall their attempts at self-improvement. In fact, students often turned to novels to understand many themes offered in the curriculum and exalted by Victorian Americans: greatness, heroism, and individual identity. In the process, students used reading as a means to imagine and fashion the self.

Reading and Self-Imagining

Artifacts of students' reading lives reveal that young men viewed literature through the lens of their own development. Many students who took up novel reading in college, for instance, found that fiction did not undermine education; it fueled the broader process of self-imagining occurring during youth. These sources also reveal that young men read novels from a romantic perspective established in formal settings. They read to understand the heroic potential of individuals and civilizations, to transport themselves to faraway lands, where they might contemplate the grandeur and sublimity of human nature.

In this regard, students' reading culture was not unlike American literary culture generally. As soon-to-be adult members of the educated class, members of the Dialectic and Philanthropic Societies stocked their shelves with more European (especially British) works than American, though the number of American works increased over the years. Students' favorite literature comprised many of the novels we call classics today, including works by Sir Walter Scott, Maria Edgeworth, Henry Fielding, James Fenimore Cooper, Washington Irving, William Gilmore Simms, Charles Dickens, and Eugene Sue. Some of the most popular titles included Thomas Moore's *Lalla Rookh*, Sir Walter Scott's *Rob-Roy*, *Ivanhoe*, and the *Talisman*, and Charles Dickens's *David Copperfield*. They also read countless other novels, tales, and romances that were popular in the nineteenth century but have long since been forgotten.[84]

James Dusenbery's commonplace book exemplifies how fictional literature (especially novels, poetry, and plays) accompanied young men on their journey to manhood, enhancing their experiences of college life and fueling the creative process of maturation. Most of what we know about Dusenbery comes from only a few documents from his student days in Chapel Hill, especially the diary he kept between 1841 and 1842, his senior year at the University of North Carolina. A cardboard and leather volume measuring eight by nine and a quarter inches, the diary spans more than 141 pages in three distinct sections: a commonplace book, "Liber carminum et fragmentorum" (a book of songs and excerpts); a journal, or "Record of my Senior Year at the University of Nca"; and a brief letterbook of correspondence with "Mary S.," whom he courted casually that year (see chapter 6). He noted in his diary having read six novels during his senior year: Cervantes's *The Life and Exploits of the Ingenious Gentleman Don Quixote de la Mancha*; Dickens's *Oliver Twist* and *The Posthumous Papers of the Pickwick Club*; George Payne Rainsford James's *The Jacquerie; or the Lady and the Page: An Historical Romance*; Scott's *Redgauntlet*; and Samuel Warren's *Ten Thousand a Year*. Poems that Dusenbery copied into his journal extolled chivalry, including "Sally Roy," "Ellen Douglas" of Scott's *Lady of the Lake*, "The Fall of D'Assas," "The Fall of Tecumseh," "Suliote Mother," and "Casabianca."[85] In all, fictional literature helped Dusenbery to contemplate male heroism, especially in the context of romantic love.

Dusenbery spent hours perusing literature for passages that idealized greatness and heroism. For example, his commonplace book opens with "The Knight of the golden crest," a popular song, which tells of a "knight returned to his princely halls, / From the wars of the holy land." When the knight returned he waved a "silken scarf" that she had given him, "which in earlier days she wove, / When he breathed his vows in the twilight shade, / And was blest with her maiden love." Similarly, he also transcribed the poem "Lochinvar," from Sir Walter Scott's *Marmion* (1808), which narrates the story of a knight, "so faithful in love and so dauntless in war," who rushed from the battlefield to his homeland to rescue his "fair Ellen," who, in his absence, had been promised to "a laggard in love, and a dastard in war." Lochinvar arrives on the wedding night to claim his "lost love," who "look'd down to blush, and she look'd up to sigh, / With a smile on her lips and a tear in her eye. / He took her soft hand, ere her mother could bar," and he carries her away from the castle, never to return.[86]

Lochinvar and the knight of the golden crest embodied Dusenbery's own ideals. He frequently described his social life in terms of chivalry and honor, and he fancied himself "the good & gallant knight, Sir James," who promised to "do his devoir" on behalf of "fair & injured damosels." On Easter Sunday in 1842, for instance, he escorted a young woman, Eliza Holt, from church, and later described himself as "the gallant cavalier who rode by Miss—Eliza's palfrey." Similarly, when Dusenbery went out in a thunderstorm to have sex with a local prostitute, Mary, whom he visited frequently, he portrayed himself as a gallant knight: "My journey thither on Friday night was an undertaking worthy of the famous knight of La Mancha." Thus, literature, particularly fiction, allowed Dusenbery to imagine himself as Don Quixote. He created a cavalier identity for himself, which he derived from his private reading.[87] As chapter 6 shows, too, Dusenbery's emerging sexual identity was tied closely to his reading life.

Dusenbery's appropriation of Sir Walter Scott's "Lochinvar" points to that author's significance in student intellectual life generally. Scott's novels were by far the most popular among antebellum students, as they were among American readers in general.[88] At college, students were told that Scott's literary works were exemplary and that "cheap" and "unsubstantial" literature should not be read at its expense.[89] Students borrowed Scott's *Waverley* (1814), *Guy Mannering* (1815), *Rob Roy* (1817), *Ivanhoe* (1819), *Kenilworth* (1821), and *Anne of Geierstein* (1829).[90] For example, between August 1839 and July 1841, William Mullins borrowed from the Philanthropic Society library four volumes of Scott's *Waverly* novels as well as two volumes of *Rob Roy* three times (once a year) and *Kenilworth* once.[91] And when Dusenbery had a moment in his busy senior year to read a novel, he chose Scott's *Redgaunt-*

let, *A Tale of the Eighteenth Century* (1824). Noting the occasion as special, he wrote, "It is so seldom that I read a novel now a days that I must mention my perusal this week of Scotts 'Redgauntlet.'"[92] Many historians have noted that southerners found in Scott's depictions of medieval squirearchy a parallel world. As the historian Christie Anne Farnham has argued, replace serfs with slaves in Scott's work and the outcome is the Old South. Students' reactions to Scott, however, do not explicitly draw on the parallels between a slave society and feudalism. Instead, their responses indicate keen attention to the prevailing themes of their own intellectual culture: greatness of the self and civilization.[93]

Scott's novels provided opportunities for students to contemplate the grandeur and sublimity of humanity in ways very similar to their study of civilization and science in the curriculum. Students especially lauded Scott's depictions of landscape. Thomas Miles Garrett responded to these themes after reading *Anne of Geierstein*, which is set in fifteenth-century Switzerland and centers around the journey of two war exiles and a magical woman, Anne, who helps them on their journey. The book, Garrett wrote in his diary, was the only thing that he could find of "any interest" in July 1849. He was taken, first, by Scott's description of Switzerland, which helped him to imagine a country he had never seen. "There is scarcely any one perhaps who has a correct notion of the scenery in Switzerland," Garrett wrote, "and although I have erred in forming the idea I have from this novel, the delusion is a happy one for while [I] flatter my vanity by supposing myself aright, I enjoy the rapture which either the mountains in reality or dwelling only in the imagination by their grandier, glory are calculated to excite." Garrett viewed the novel and its characters as a means to understand fixed truths of human nature. *Anne of Geierstein*'s male characters, in particular, seemed to Garrett to embody virtues that he and his classmates aspired to achieve as men. He wrote, "How he [Scott] paints the wildness, the courage, the simplicity, the pride, the strength and activity of the swiss." In the character of the protagonists, Arthur and Rudolph, Garrett found a style of masculinity that reflected his and other young men's ideals. "In the intercourse of young Arthur and Rudloph," he wrote, "we see a verry remarkable truth displayed . . . that courage, true and genuine, must ever be respected, by the haughty as well as the humble, the intelligent as well as the ignorant the brave as well as the cowardly, and by the one sex as well as the other." Here, manliness was a result of character and honor, legitimated ultimately by winning the confidence of other men and the affection of a woman.[94]

Scott was not alone among students' favorite authors. Joseph Summerell, for example, enjoyed George Payne Rainsford James's *Jacquerie* (1841) in part because it was "a most exciting tale, & the interest is maintained throughout," but in part for its instructive value on the customs and culture of the French. *Jacquerie*, he wrote in his diary in 1842, was "on the whole [an] admirable production & deserves to be read with attention by every one who wishes to gain a knowledge of the state of France the manners & customs of the people & their depressed condition under the feudal system. It is well written & shows the author well versed in the language of the french & passions of our nature."[95] Novels like *Jacquerie* and *Anne of Geierstein* provided insight into human nature and civil society, and resonated with students' ambitions to cultivate a truly masculine identity—at once heroic and genteel. And, by transporting students from Chapel Hill to Switzerland, France, and, by virtue of the authors' homes, nineteenth-century England, these works likewise broadened the scope of a reader's understanding of the world.

Students encountered similar themes in European literature about North America. This was the case for George Nicholas Thompson, who began keeping a short diary during his sophomore year at the University of North Carolina. A leatherbound volume measuring five by seven and five-eighths inches, Thompson's diary begins on 1 January 1851 and continues through 21 March 1851. During this time, he gravitated toward popular European works such as Scott's *Waverly* novels, Byron's poetical works, Eugene Sue's *The Mysteries of Paris*, Henry Fielding's *Tom Jones*, and British author Charles Augustus Murray's three-volume work on fictional travels in America, *The Prairie-Bird* (1844). Thompson did not limit his fictional reading to European works but also read contemporary American literature. According to his borrowing records, Thompson read "Irivings Works," Bancroft's *History of the United States*, the *Southern Literary Messenger*, and Cooper's *Last of the Mohicans*.

To many antebellum students, American literature reflected the progress of American civilization. This was the period of America's first "literary renaissance," and it created a new and exciting national literary culture. Students frequently borrowed the works of Washington Irving, James Fenimore Cooper, and William Gilmore Simms at the same time they borrowed works by Byron, Scott, and Dickens.[96] American fiction, they believed, was a sign that American civilization was progressing as it expanded. Responding to the works of Irving, Cooper, and Simms in particular, one student remarked in his diary in 1841, "There is poetry in everything connected with republican institutions. . . . American literature is emphatically the polished history of the dawning and progress of American liberty."[97] Moreover, students believed that American novels compared favorably to European novels. "The Indian novels of Cooper—not to speak of his splendid sea novels," one student wrote in 1848, "whose scenes are laid in the awful solitude of the forest, and on the wide and desolate prairie, and whose characters were the wild red men that roamed over them, have as much exciting incident, accurate delineation of character, and more grandeur of scenery, than the best productions of the author of Waverly."[98] Reading American fiction imbued students with a sense of romantic nationalism growing throughout the United States in the 1840s and 1850s and linked them with the broader educated class of Victorian America. This strand of romanticism influenced how young men thought about the region as well.[99]

Some students' responses to fiction suggest that they read novels for moral improvement and were disappointed when they did not find it. In 1841, William Sidney Mullins read one of the most popular books in antebellum America and the first Canadian novel—John Richardson's *Wacousta* (1832). Set in the aftermath of the Seven Years' War, the novel depicts brutal warfare between Native Americans and the British during Pontiac's War (1763). The protagonist is a warrior named Wacousta, an advisor to Pontiac, who believed that a commander of the British army stationed at Fort Detroit had wronged him. The novel traces Wacousta's journey to vindicate his honor by killing each one of the commander's children. The book was very popular in Canada, the United States, and Britain for its depictions of history, landscape, and Native Americans.[100] "I have recently read 'Wacousta. By the Author of Ecarte,' and hasten to give a sketch of the work," Mullins wrote in February 1841. He wrote a detailed response, which reveals that he read for philosophical reflections and moral insights as well as for amusement. "The impressions produced by it on the mind are dark and gloomy in the extreme. Horror succeeds horror until all is involved in indiscriminate gloom and the spirit shudders at the tales' incidents. . . . No great moral truth is illustrated, nor is there an unusual grace or beauty of style. But forcible description, striking incidents, and thrilling scenes do occur in abundance, and emotions of the soul are variously and abundantly exercised. . . . *No man who reads it will forget it,*" Mullins wrote. He clearly enjoyed *Wacousta* as entertainment, though he derived no moral lessons from it. Nevertheless, the exercise in reading and writing about this "dark and gloomy" book entertained Mullins and promoted thinking about what a book ought to do (promote reflection and morality) and how it ought to be written (with strong language and captivating plots).[101]

At the same time as interest in American fiction grew among students, so too did interest in regional fiction, specifically emerging southern fiction from authors such as John Pendleton Kennedy, Augustus Baldwin Longstreet, Thomas Bangs Thorpe, and William Gilmore Simms. William Mullins was very familiar with Simms, a popular southern novelist. He especially appreciated Simms's novels for their insight into human nature. In fact, he complained in his journal that Simms failed, in his opinion, to illuminate the natural humanity of his characters. "In relation to Simms' works however it may justly be remarked that his characters too much resemble each other. . . . This appears to me his great defect: he cannot seize the great principles and components of character and by a proper union of them each time, furnish a new, yet natural character." Believable and "natural" American places, scenes, and characters compelled students to read fiction produced by, about, and for Americans; they expected fiction to enlarge their understanding of humanity beyond their immediate social contexts.

Tied as they were to mainstream American literary trends and practices, students' reading lives were also influenced by encroaching sectionalism in the late antebellum period. Although library records do not indicate that students read antislavery tracts or novels such as Harriet Beecher Stowe's *Uncle Tom's Cabin*, this literature did not escape students' attention. In particular, they critiqued Stowe's popular novel as a symptom of fanaticism. An 1852 volume of the *North Carolina University Magazine*, for instance, ran a mock book advertisement for "'Uncle Ben's Big Pen,' upon the plan of 'Tom's Cabin,'" and "Aunt Kitty's 'Chicken Coop,'" which equate slaves with livestock. The magazine editors' description of the latter serves as a stark reminder of young men's southern context: "Wherein the old speckled hen says she don't care if master and mistress do devour her brood, she intends, nevertheless, to lay, set, hatch, cluck and scratch as long as she lives; for it is her 'natur,' and besides it is her duty to be faithful to the white people. Quite a hen, that, we should say. We hope all the northerners and southerners will supply themselves with the books, as neither of them panders to sectional prejudices."[102] Such writing, though rare in the antebellum period, reinforces the uniquely southern outlook of antebellum student culture and serves as a reminder of the inextricable connection between intellectual manhood and the antebellum South's racial hierarchy.

IN SUM, NORTH CAROLINA students were everyday readers. They carved out time for books and reading, as well as for writing and talking about what and how to read. In literary societies, students created a culture of intentional intellectualism centered on books and literary socialization. They encouraged one another to carefully select and attentively read literature that would move them along the path from boyhood to manhood, reinforcing the formal objectives of college life: mental and moral improvement. But not all of college could always be so serious, and students craved entertaining literature. As print material saturated the South in the antebellum period, students collected more and more periodical and fictional literature. Though some students believed that reading novels gave free rein to boyish impulsivity and temperament, most found that novel reading could be educational. Novel reading could also serve as a conscious act of claiming intellectual independence, which was so important to traditional southern manhood. At the same time, students approached fiction through the lens of the bourgeois values so central to the outlook they developed in formal university life: a focus on the individual self and its heroic potential. As was true with curricular texts, novels became sites for self-imagining and grandiose contemplation. These themes of greatness and heroism are the subject of the following chapter, which examines young men's engagement with biography, as well as their secular and sacred devotional practices common to the self-culture movement that defined bourgeois culture in antebellum America.

CHAPTER FIVE

Encouragement to Excel
Portraiture, Biography, and Self-Culture

The literary acts young men used to shape their collegiate experiences reflected a broader self-culture movement influencing American males' lives, further demonstrating antebellum Chapel Hill's strong connection to mainstream bourgeois culture. The antebellum self-culture movement was a popularized incarnation of nineteenth-century higher education insofar as it taught that individuals could improve their minds and morals through daily literary acts. In 1841 William Channing famously evoked the spirit of self-culture in an address to working-class Bostonians about "the care which every man owes to himself, to the unfolding perfection of his nature." He argued that every person is endowed with the ability to perfect his intellectual, moral, and social self. Men must rely on themselves, on their inward drive for improvement and perfection, to achieve their potential as human beings. "He, therefore who does what he can to unfold all his powers and capacities, especially his nobler ones, so as to become a well proportioned, vigorous, excellent, happy being, practices self culture."[1] This notion of self-culture complemented the educational philosophy of the formal curriculum, namely the importance of mental and moral improvement, and it appealed to young North Carolina students looking to leave boyhood for manhood, restrain their impulses, and lead worthy, even heroic lives. According to one student, self-culture was "the great mistress of knowledge and worth of all true greatness. The great secret of success, the great portal to distinction!"[2]

Self-culture influenced students' lives in numerous ways, but most significantly through their engagement with literature. In literary societies, students created reading cultures that provided countless sources of entertainment but also the resources for self-fashioning. Members collected portraits of successful university alumni whom they hoped to emulate;

recommended and read biographies; and debated the lives and careers of Western civilization's many great men and women. These societies were catalysts for individuals to internalize the process further. When the school day ended, many students retired to their rooms to construct selves in private through journalizing, reading, compiling commonplace books, and following devotional religious practices. In order to understand how young men pursued self-fashioning within this daily intellectual culture, it is first necessary to understand the urgency with which they viewed this undertaking.

Life's Voyage and the Need for Improvement

Young men liked to think of their own lives in terms of a grandiose, romantic epic. The curricular emphasis on ancient and modern exemplars, the emulation of heroic orators, and the reading of novels played a role in creating this distinctively bourgeois, Victorian culture of ambition and heroism on campus. In this world of intentional intellectualism, students learned that they could all play heroic roles in life's drama. Some students viewed life as a battle, echoing the desires of Longfellow's young male protagonist, "In the world's broad field of battle, / In the bivouac of Life, / Be not like dumb, driven cattle! / Be a hero in the strife!"[3] Others imagined themselves as intrepid voyagers. Contemplating the halfway mark of his collegiate career, for example, Walter Lenoir used the image of life's voyage in a letter to his father in 1841. "In two years and a half more, I will be a man," wrote Walter, "about to embark on life's tempestuous ocean, there to sink or swim by my own efforts, and as the Dispenser of fortune may direct, prosperous or opposing winds."[4]

Though young Walter may not have realized it when he wrote to his father, life's voyage was a significant metaphor within antebellum popular culture. The idea of "life's voyage" may have first appeared in the ancient writings of the Roman dramatist Seneca, and it garnered attention from late eighteenth-century writers such as Oliver Goldsmith and inspired British and American romantics in the early nineteenth century.[5] Thomas Cole's popular series of paintings, *The Voyage of Life* (1842), is perhaps the most famous representation of this metaphor in American culture and contains many cultural elements that resonated with young men, especially its keen attention to maturation.

On four separate canvases, the series follows a male voyager through childhood, youth, manhood, and old age. The protagonist, accompanied by his guardian angel, begins his journey through childhood peacefully but bids farewell to his guardian angel in youth. Alone for the first time, the boy must take control of his fate at the boat's helm. Surrounded by "the romantic beauty of youthful imaginings," Cole's voyager looks confidently to a castle in the air, which symbolizes his future eminence and distinction. "The beautiful stream flows for a distance, directly toward the aeriel palace," Cole wrote, "but at length makes a sudden turn and is seen in glimpses beneath the trees, until it last descends with rapid current into a rocky ravine," or the scene of manhood. In manhood, the hero confronts certain "demon forms"— temptations—hovering in the clouds and rocking the boat. Through faith and perseverance, the heroic voyager reaches old age and his guardian spirit returns and lifts him to Heaven. In all, Cole's allegory reflects both the evangelical and romantic spirit of the age: the individual struggled alone, empowered only by his strength of character and God's grace, to weather hostile storms.[6] Understanding how this allegory figured into students' intellectual discourse reveals the influence of broader, bourgeois culture on students' intellectual development and their reasons for pursuing self-culture in their informal educational life on campus, especially in the literary societies.

This allegory inspired many young men because it reflected their anxiety and uncertainty about life after college. In his 1842 valedictory address to the Dialectic Society, William Sidney Mullins used the voyage of life metaphor to encourage, but also to warn, his classmates. "Time in his onward course hath . . . summoned us to a new part in the drama of Life and we must now assume the solemn responsibility of Manhood and meet our fellow men in the great struggle that must seal our destiny," he declared. Young men such as Mullins dreamed of glory but feared an uncertain, even dangerous future. "We cannot but feel a deep anxiety concerning the events of that struggle," he continued, "and our hearts beat wildly as we hear the waves of the sea on which we must so soon embark beating against the shore where we stand."[7] Much of this fear emerged from uncertainty about adulthood: Would business elude them? Would strangers corrupt them? The best way to prepare for these challenges was through self-improvement during youth.

Thomas Cole's *The Voyage of Life: Youth*, 1842.
Oil on canvas, 34 × 194.9 cm (52 ⅞ × 76 ¾ in.).

Thomas Cole's *The Voyage of Life: Manhood*, 1842.
Oil on canvas, 34 × 194.9 cm (52 ⅞ × 76 ¾ in.).

Self-Improvement and the Need for Heroes

Regular addresses from faculty and distinguished alumni underscored self-improvement in the course of life's voyage.[8] One poignant example is William Gaston's 1832 address before the Dialectic and Philanthropic Societies. Gaston was a well-known slaveowner, lawyer, state legislator, and state Supreme Court justice. A father of five children, he was keenly aware of the obstacles of youth and the need for self-improvement, particularly diligence and perseverance in study or "working at manhood," as the historian Steven Stowe has argued.[9] Most of Gaston's speech to North Carolina students deals with these themes, encouraging young men to cultivate healthy, sober, chaste, and pious habits. In the process, he appeals to ambition: "It is, indeed, on those who aspire to eminence, that these injunctions are intended to be pressed with the greatest emphasis, not only because a failure in them would be more disastrous than in others, but because they are exposed to greater and more numerous dangers of error. . . . Happiness as well as greatness, enjoyment as well as renown, have no friends so sure as Integrity, Diligence, and Independence."[10] In a rather Franklinesque way, Gaston urged his audience to consider the importance of hard work over idleness.

Other visiting speakers touched on similar themes. In June 1839, Bedford Brown, who attended the university briefly in 1813 and then went on to become a prominent state legislator, evoked the voyage of life metaphor to appeal to his audience's ambitions. "Buoyant with hope and filled with anticipation, your minds look forward to the journey of life which lays before you, like the adventurous mariner who is eager to embark on the voyage which he is about to undertake." Brown specifically encouraged bourgeois emulation, diligence, and perseverance: "Impelled by a generous emulation, you are prepared to test the strength and efficiency of that intellectual armour, in the various pursuits of life, which you have acquired through a course of years, by diligent toil and study."[11]

Students could find similar messages about improvement along life's voyage in contemporary advice literature, which circulated in literary society libraries. Between 1834, when society records began, and 1848, more than thirty titles relating to young men's behavior, manners, and morals circulated in each library, including popular works such as George Thomas's *Young Man's Guide* and John Todd's *Student's Manual*.[12] These books proved useful to many students who looked to them for advice regarding self-improvement along life's voyage. Ruffin Tomlinson, for example, read and praised Todd's manual because "it gives excellent advice to every young man."[13] This valuable advice dealt primarily with the need for study, introspection, and emulation. In *The Young Man's Counsellor*, for instance, Daniel Wise encouraged young men in their voyage: "Study well the intricacies and dangers of your course, take counsel of experience, let caution be your pilot, and without doubt, you will escape rock, current, eddy and whirlpool, and, with streamered masts and big white sails, float gayly forth to dare and conquer the perils of the sea beyond."[14] Antebellum students also spoke this language. In an 1825 address to his classmates in the Dialectic Society, Elam Alexander used the popular romantic image of life's voyage in a meditation on maturation and manhood. "Before we actually embark in these scenes, or subject ourselves to the toils and buffetings of real life, we may, as mere spectators, if attentive, receive much useful instruction, and many valuable hints from our own observation & the experience of others," he explained. "And by these admonitory examples we may be directed so to shape our course that we shall avoid the dangerous shoals, and whirlpools, & rocks upon which so many thousand have already been destroyed." What young men needed, in other words, were heroes.

In students' words, heroes were great men who achieved distinction "through continual exertion for the development of physical and mental abilities, from youth to old age."[15] A hero's public reputation and private life had to be unimpeachable. This attitude was quintessentially Victorian. As the intellectual historian Walter Houghton writes, "To the Victorians a hero might be a messiah or he might be a revelation of God, but he was certain to be a man of the highest moral stature, and therefore of enormous importance."[16] The figure of the hero reflects a wide appeal of heroism to Victorians in the United States and Great Britain. In popular fiction of the time, Sir Walter Scott brought the hero out of a mysterious feudal past; Lord Byron wrote of Childe Harold, who drew inspiration from a pantheon of ancient and modern greats; and Longfellow offered heroic "footprints on the sands of time" for wayward travelers to contemplate as they pursued greatness and fame.[17] In historical literature, the hero acquired new salience after the Napoleonic Wars. Generations of young Americans scrutinized the famed general (or Corsican usurper, depending on perspective) and drew moral lessons from his rise to and abuse of power. In politics, young men were no less captivated by American heroes, past or present. This was especially true after Andrew Jackson's victory in the Battle of New Orleans at the conclusion of the War of 1812 and his rise to political distinction through his own self-making. Moreover, with the emergence of national political parties and development of new campaign methods, politicians became celebrities—objects of glorification in rallies, songs, and pamphlets.[18]

As we have already seen, the curriculum provided an array of heroes—Hercules and Odysseus in myth, and Alexander, Demosthenes, Socrates, Caesar, and Cicero in literature and history. These were heroes who shaped empires and civilizations. Likewise, modern intellectual giants including, most prominently, Locke, Newton, and Bacon demonstrated how reason and science made heroes. But the curriculum barely scratched the surface of young men's education in greatness. It was in literary societies that students created self-culture around heroic ideals with deep and persistent conviction. "Ask that one of our number who was called by so many freemen to preside over the destinies of the mightiest Republic of earth," John Lindsay Morehead charged his classmates in the Dialectic Society. "Ask him where it was that he obtained the beginnings of that superiority and the first stimulus to that ambition, by which he raised himself to the highest pinnacle of fame and glory. His answer and the answer of all would be 'in the Dialectic Hall.'"[19]

Portraiture and Hero Worship

In 1854, twenty-year-old Evander McIver assumed a second term as president of the Dialectic Society and delivered an inaugural address in which he encouraged his classmates to pursue mental and moral improvement. As he stood before his classmates he pointed to the many portraits that lined his society's hall, including those of William Richardson Davie, the founder of the University of North Carolina; William Hooper, a Baptist minister and president of Wake Forest College; John Owen, a lawyer and the first Whig governor of North Carolina; George Edmund Badger, Yale alumnus, UNC trustee, and U.S. secretary of the navy in 1841; Thomas Ruffin, chief justice of the North Carolina Supreme Court, where he delivered the most draconian proslavery decision in the state's history; James K. Polk, eleventh president of the United States; David Lowry Swain, former North Carolina governor and UNC president; and several others.[20] Referring to these distinguished North Carolinians, McIver asked his classmates whether they needed "any stronger encouragement to excel in mental and moral culture" than that provided by the alumni whose images surrounded them. These were icons of the constructed self and reminders of students' own heroic potential. Quoting from Henry Wadsworth Longfellow's popular "Psalm of Life," McIver explained the profound value of emulation:

Lives of all great men all remind us
We can make our lives sublime
And in dying leave behind us
Foot prints on the sands of time
Foot-prints that perhaps another sailing on life's stormy main
Some forlorn & shipwrecked brother
Seeing may take heart again.[21]

Three years later another student, Leroy McAffee, assumed the presidential chair in the Dialectic Society, and he, too, pointed to the portraits surrounding him and his fellow members. "And why I ask are these portraits suspended upon our walls? Surely they are for some other purpose than simple ornament," he began. "In the language of Cicero, they are here not only for our contemplation but also for us to imitate the immortal prototypes, that by placing them constantly before our view we may strive to mould our feelings and thoughts by reflecting on the character of these illustrious men."[22]

The Dialectic and Philanthropic Societies actively collected portraits during the entire antebellum period. The Philanthropic Society began acquiring portraits in 1818, and the Dialectic Society began its own collection in 1826. Collegiate portrait collections were something of a new practice in the early nineteenth century. William and Mary had collected two portraits in the early eighteenth century, Harvard had acquired six by 1800, and Bowdoin College created a portrait gallery in 1811.[23] The Dialectic and Philanthropic Society portraits were unique insofar as students themselves commissioned the portraits through society resolutions. In 1821, the Philanthropic Society officially resolved to make portrait collection an integral part of their institutional business when a member moved "that it be requested by Society that such regular members as have attained considerable eminence of which Society will be judge, shall furnish Society with their portraits."[24] Indeed, the portraits that students acquired were almost entirely alumni whose path to distinction began in one literary society or the other. The first two portraits that the Phis acquired, for instance, were of Johnston Blakely, an alumnus who served in the War of 1812, and Joseph Caldwell, the first president of the university. Similarly, the Dialectic Society first acquired portraits of William R. Davie and William Hooper. Combined, the two literary societies ultimately acquired twenty-six portraits; all the portraits, save one of Benjamin Franklin, depicted famous university figures. Because of their immense cultural and monetary value, students placed these portraits in expensive frames and protected them from dust and sunlight with green gauze.[25]

While part of having the portraits of famous alumni certainly reflected attempts for society members to boast and glorify themselves through proximity to great men, students also valued portraits as tools for self-fashioning, as guideposts along life's journey from boyhood to manhood. One of the first portraits acquired in the Philanthropic Society was of Benjamin Franklin, whose own self-construction—his great attention to intellectual and moral improvement through industry and perseverance—served as a model for young men throughout the early republic. Indeed, when Evander McIver encouraged his classmates to emulate the characters represented in the portraits around them, he pointed first to Franklin and instructed them to listen to his words. The immense popularity of Franklin's *Autobiography* in the early nineteenth century is well known. The work was particularly suitable for the improvement of youth, and nineteenth-century parents, educators, and students saw it as a road map for character formation. While late eighteenth- and early nineteenth-century readers lauded the work for its portrayal of civic virtue, its "didactic nationalism," Americans began to read the *Autobiography* for insight into character formation in the antebellum period.[26] William Wirt advised H. W. Miller, a student at North Carolina, to read Franklin's works for inspiration: "We cannot all be *Franklins*, it is true; but, by imitating his mental habits and unwearied industry, we may reach eminence we should never otherwise attain. Nor would he have been *the* Franklin he was, if he had permitted himself to be discouraged by the reflection that we cannot all be *Newtons*."[27]

Young men agreed that portraits of great men should promote ambition and serve as tools for emulation. But how did students "read" these values in the portraits around them? Although it is difficult to ascertain precisely how any student viewed these portraits, clues from within southern culture suggest some possibilities. Kenneth Greenberg has argued that the antebellum South was "an essentially masquerade culture," in which facial expressions, gestures, and bodily carriage expressed honor, mastery, and manhood.[28] Young southern males likely excelled at reading faces and bodies. Portraits of famous alumni dealt with this public dimension of southern manhood and depicted subjects in public and professional settings. Moreover, as members of the educated class, they lived in a "culture of refinement" in which public presentation was supposed to reflect inner character; portraits, then, stood as proxy for the inner man.[29] Each society's portrait collection depicted what students could achieve through hard work and perseverance. Three examples from these collections sufficiently underscore the ideals young men sought to emulate and, in turn, the cultural value of portraiture to students' collective self-construction efforts. They also reveal the important social power that young men hoped to cultivate through education and ultimately exercise as adult members of the educated class.

First, portraits conveyed ideals of professionalism and respectability. The Philanthropic Society's portrait of William Miller, North Carolina's governor between 1814 and 1817, depicts a distinguished man with penetrating dark eyes and well-groomed hair. He wears a high collar and formal scarf around his neck, suggesting not only rectitude of stature but character as well. With hands confidently clasped around a chair draped with luxurious fabric, Miller appears serious yet gentle, and his relaxed jaw and composed facial expression convey an air of equanimity. Miller embodies intellectual and professional achievement. In the background stands the state capitol building as it looked before it burned to the ground around 1830.

The viewer easily recognizes Miller's public significance. Miller had matriculated at North Carolina in 1802 and joined the Philanthropic Society. He was never graduated from the university, but he served as a trustee from 1814 until 1825. He had been a member of the North Carolina House of Commons and served as Speaker between 1811 and 1814, when he was elected for a one-year term as governor. When his gubernatorial term ended, Miller went on to practice law and eventually served two terms in the state senate between 1820 and 1822. President John Quincy Adams appointed Miller as chargé d'affaires to Guatemala in 1825, but Miller died en route. The Philanthropic Society acquired a portrait of Miller in May 1846 "as a present from Mr. C.B. Root of Raleigh."[30]

Second, the portrait of David Swain, former North Carolina governor and the university's president from 1835 until 1868, was acquired in 1852, and it depicts a man of letters par excellence. Although many critics among the faculty and trustees disproved of his administration, students admired him and enjoyed his moral philosophy course.[31] In the portrait, Swain sits in a cushioned chair in front of a simple neoclassical column with a rounded

Black and white reproduction of an oil painting of William Miller (1784–1826),
attributed to George Cooke (1793–1849). Oil on canvas, 25 ½ × 30 in.
Photographic Archives, Wilson Library, University of North Carolina at Chapel Hill.

base, standing to the right of a bookcase of large volumes. A dark curtain
drapes over the shelf and column. One volume appears to be withdrawn
from the shelf, as Swain holds it comfortably in his left hand. His right arm
rests against a wooden side table; paper documents are spread across the
table, some of which lie open-faced while others are rolled together neatly.
Leaning slightly to the left and looking forward, Swain is wearing a black

suit jacket with matching pants, a white shirt, and a dark-colored bowtie. His dark, slightly tousled hair and relaxed forehead suggest comfortable belonging in the room; his deep, penetrating eyes and relaxed jaw command deference. This setting befits the professor who read law with seniors from Blackstone's *Commentaries*, taught moral philosophy, and encouraged many students.

Students emulated Swain because they valued the ideals he promoted, particularly his dedication to North Carolina's history and historical documents. Swain, like many other southern intellectuals, regretted that the lives of prominent southerners did not find their way into the annals of history. When he was president of the university, he founded the state's first historical society in order to collect documents related particularly to North Carolina's contribution to the Revolution, espousing a brand of sentimental historicism common to the romantic literary movement. Students followed suit. Some actively participated in finding and collecting historical documents, and others contributed historical pieces to the *North Carolina University Magazine*, chronicling not only the university's contribution to North Carolina's development but the state's contribution to American history as a whole through the great leaders the university produced.

As students collected portraits of famous alumni during the antebellum period, they not only enlarged their imaginations but also constructed historical narratives of North Carolina and the early republic, giving greater meaning to the self as an articulation of regional and national identity. Antebellum students desired to bring North Carolina heroes into the mainstream historical narrative of American civilization. The state's Revolutionary heroes in particular served as inducement for mental and moral improvement among students. "The Period of our revolution was rendered illustrious by a bright galaxy of distinguished patriots. . . . Do we desire to pluck one leaf from the laurels that adorned the brows of our revolutionary ancestors?" asked one student in 1849. "In obedience to the laws of nature their generation has passed away; another and another has succeeded. Surely it is not of paramount importance that we should exert our utmost endeavors to render ourselves competent to perform deeds worthy of the illustrious stock from which we sprung?"[32]

Finally, therefore, the portrait James Knox Polk, eleventh president of the United States, served for many students as an icon of the state and university's historical significance. A thoughtful and serious student, Polk was graduated from the University of North Carolina in 1818 and went on to

Portrait of David Lowry Swain (1801–1868), unsigned, attributed to William Garl Browne (1823–1894). Oil on canvas, 46 × 35 ½ in. Photographic Archives, Wilson Library, University of North Carolina at Chapel Hill.

become a successful lawyer, legislator, and governor; he was elected president in 1844. In May 1847, Polk visited the university and attended the May commencement ceremony. Prior to his visit, the Dialectic Society asked him to sit for a portrait. "I remember with pleasure my association with 'our common and hallowed fraternity—the Dialectic Society,'" Polk replied, "and though nearly twenty nine years have elapsed, since I closed my connection with it, I am deeply sensible of the great value of the institution. . . . Fully appreciating the honour which you have done me, I beg you to assure the Society, that it will give me pleasure to comply with the request . . . and that I can sit for the artist, at any period during the present recess of Congress."[33] Students saw in Polk an example of how one North Carolinian, through intellectual advancement in college, could go on to bring distinction and honor to the Tar Heel State. The Dialectic Society acquired the portrait by the end of that same summer.

It is perhaps the most romantic of the portraits in the society collections. Polk, formally dressed, sits before a large wooden table, looking into the distance but not at the viewer. He holds a large canvas in his hands—perhaps a map or the Constitution. On the table behind him lies all the accouterments of a man of letters—a book, a quill and ink, a candle. A symbol of progress and expansion, Polk exemplified the ways in which North Carolina students, through hard work in the same Dialectic Society that had produced a president, could likewise rise to distinction.

Miller, Swain, and Polk reflect varying degrees of fame and distinction, but each figure embodied characteristics that young men valued as heroic; they served as icons of intellectual manhood. At a time when college credentials did not directly confer professional status, the images of successful men—military professionals, learned men, lawyers, and judges—could be quite powerful. The process of emulation worked, however, because students knew the stories behind the men, whose heroism was a product of their public lives. "Men seize on a few facts, and from them tell you the true greatness of the individual," wrote one student in the *North Carolina University Magazine*. "We must form our estimate of a man's character from his actions. They are a portion of his personal ideality completely indivisible of the whole; a part, however, that must never be abstracted from its concomitants in our estimation of character."[34] Thus, even in a world in which actions spoke like, if not louder than, words, representations had their limits. Writing anonymously in an 1856 issue of the *Southern Literary Messenger*, one author compared portraiture and biography. "Portraits of distinguished men are eloquent in their teachings to posterity," he wrote, but portraiture never could rival biography in its depiction of a hero's true character. "The hero must . . . be exhibited under all the various and dissimilar relations of life." This, then, was the task of biography—the work behind emulation of great men—and the biographer's task was to carry the reader "into intimate personal association with each of its characters."[35] To

Portrait of James Knox Polk, unsigned, attributed to Thomas Sully (1783–1872).
Oil on canvas, 44 x 33 ¾. Photographic Archives, Wilson Library,
University of North Carolina at Chapel Hill.

understand any man's full heroic potential and the universal truths about manhood, young men turned to biography, America's most popular genre. As one North Carolina student put it, the process was at once grand and personal: "In tracing the historic page on which is enrolled the exploits of departed heroes, the mind is filled with that veneration & gratitude which stimulates an ambition for similar renown."[36]

Self-Improvement and Biographical Culture

Reading and discussing biographies were important cultural practices whereby young southern collegians created opportunities for, and engaged in, self-culture. The antebellum period witnessed a dramatic rise in popular biography. As authors of the *Yale Literary Magazine* noted in 1845, biography had become the "rage of the day."[37] Trends in literary society library catalogs at the University of North Carolina demonstrate the genre's wide appeal in the antebellum period. Between 1820 and 1850, the number of biographical volumes held in the Dialectic Society grew threefold, and the number of historical volumes doubled.[38] While this growth does not match the 600 percent increase in novels discussed in the preceding chapter, it does indicate that students craved biography. Indeed, students collected a variety of biographical dictionaries with wide national and global scope, focusing on male as well as female heroes. General works included William Allen's *American Biographical Dictionary*, Alexander Chalmers's *General Biographical Dictionary*, and three volumes cataloged as *Female Biography*. Individual titles ranged across continents as well, including biographies of Queen Elizabeth I, Peter the Great, Pope Leo X, and Napoleon Bonaparte (of which there were at least four).[39] Borrowing records likewise demonstrate students' strong and eclectic biographical interests. In 1832, William H. Owen, one of the Dialectic Society's most vociferous critics of novel reading, borrowed Scott's *The Life of Napoleon Buonaparte*, Franklin's *The Autobiography of Benjamin Franklin*, Mason Locke Weems's *The Life of Benjamin Franklin*, and John Marshall's *The Life of George Washington*. His classmates borrowed biographies of Peter the Great, Mary Queen of Scots, Lafayette, and Wellington.[40] As was the case with novels, students' discourse about biography as a genre sheds light on their cultural value and provides an important foundation for understanding how they used biography in social and private self-fashioning efforts.

Generally, students discussed four major advantages to reading biography. First, reading biographies helped young men move from childhood into intellectual manhood by extending the larger project of mental and moral improvement into the private realm. "If there is any thing, that improves a man," one student explained in 1841, "especially when he is training himself for usefulness in after life, it is reading history and biography."[41] Second, biographies allowed young men to imagine and anticipate adult roles as leaders, particularly the uses of moral improvement. Here, the lives of both heroes and tragic heroes were equally compelling and useful for moral improvement.[42] In an 1846 presidential address to the Dialectic Society, Alexander F. Brevard argued, for instance, that the lives of corrupt men underscored "by what means any one may have been lead to . . . the course of moral degradation, and its ends," and the lives of virtuous men promoted emulation. "They introduce the mind to healthy trains of thought," Brevard explained, "thus affording illustrious examples of virtues to those who may be called to act under similar circumstances."[43] Third, biographies fueled ambition, that hallmark of bourgeois culture. "This is the province of Biography, by clear and faithful delineations of character, by commemorating the deeds of their Country's great names, to arouse in young generations a lofty, and generous ambition to perform services, and to achieve deeds as high and lofty," Jesse Hargrave explained in 1856.[44] Significantly, this call to greatness reveals a fourth advantage of reading biography in youth: the development of American identity, or what Scott Casper has termed "didactic nationalism."[45] In all, biography provided opportunities to further the mental and moral improvement of youth as they transitioned to manhood. Like emulation of men depicted in portraits, biography ignited in young men a fire for ambition, particularly to become great leaders of their communities, state, and nation.

When it came to encouraging emulation of great patriots, students recommended especially the study of Christopher Columbus and George Washington. In 1848, Theodore Kingsbury praised, in particular, Washington Irving's *History of the Life and Voyages of Columbus*. "It is a book which no reader can commence without pursuing its entire contents, and no one can travel over these without being afforded much amusement and solid instruction," he explained. "Whether we consider the dignity and importance of the subject; the great and momentous events of which it treats, the eloquence and beauty of the composition, or the moral grandeur of the sentiments, no critic can fail to bestow on the work his most unqualified commendation."[46] In addition, Kingsbury instructed his classmates to read Marshall's *Life of Washington*. Like Irving's Columbus biography, this book deserved praise not only for its style but also its moral sentiments. In these ways, students explicitly linked reading biography to the construction of both adult and civic identities.

In addition to discussing these themes in genre discourse, trends in student debates reflect the discursive role biography played in students' self-culture. Historical and biographical debate questions nearly quadrupled in the late antebellum period such that by 1860 almost half of the questions students debated were historical (the other half, as I discuss in chapter 7, were current affairs). In the Dialectic Society, the number of historical and biographical questions exceeded the number of current affairs questions in the 1850s. Students debated European subjects more frequently than American subjects, especially Henry VIII, Elizabeth I, Mary Queen of Scotts, Charles I, Oliver Cromwell, Marie Antoinette, Louis XVI, Peter the Great, and Napoleon Bonaparte.[47] Still, as the antebellum period saw increased attention to American history, students contemplated American figures in weekly debates, especially when they considered questions such as "who deserves the greater praise, Columbus for discovering or Washington for defending America."[48] Generally speaking, however, debates focused heavily on European subjects. Young men found that one figure in particular could offer unique lessons for self-construction and heroism: Napoleon Bonaparte.

Napoleon's biographies engaged students intellectually with the very tensions framing their own pursuit of manhood, especially tensions between impulse and restraint and between mind and temperament. "What charm hangs around the memory of Napoleon!" wrote Alexander Justice in 1844. "At the sound of his name every breast heaves, and every heart beats high with motion." Napoleon inspired soldiers who emulated his military feats and Frenchmen who emulated his patriotism. Although Napoleon "has been called too ambitious," Justice wrote, it should be "to his glory, that his ambition was to place his country upon the highest pinnacle of fame, and to raise for himself that monument, which neither the lapse of years, nor the tongue of calumny could destroy."[49] Napoleon exemplified the very éclat which many young men desired. In 1859, for example, Erasmus Scales delivered an oration before the Dialectic Society, which he titled "What is Glory?" In it, he explained that the love of glory was an innate, timeless, and uniquely masculine trait worthy of emulation. "From the time when God impressed upon man his image, and placed him in the garden of Eden to enjoy its fruits, the love of Glory has been an essential quality in his [man's] character." But Napoleon pursued glory too vigorously and, as a result, Scales argued he deprived France of peace and relegated himself to "a half page of general history." Napoleon's character received scrutiny in a range of historical questions relating to his military campaigns and forced exile, especially.[50]

Despite Napoleon's questionable morals and unrestrained ambition, he was a popular exemplar for young American men in search of heroes. In academies and colleges, young men debated Napoleon's character, and public speakers often referenced Napoleon in addresses, warning young men about misguided ambition. Indeed, his example was an important one. William Channing's remarks on Napoleon's life and career—couched in a rather lengthy appraisal of Sir Walter Scott's equally lengthy *The Life of Napoleon Buonaparte: Volume 1* (1827)—illuminate Napoleon's appeal to biographers and young men alike as a model for moral improvement: "We have desired to awaken others and ourselves to a just self-reverence, the free use and expansion of our highest powers, and especially to that moral force, that energy of holy, virtuous purpose, without which we are slaves amidst free institutions. Better gifts than these we cannot supplicate from God; nor can we consecrate our lives to nobler acquisition."[51]

Young men did not limit their education in greatness only to male figures. Yet while students pursued female leaders, they often subsumed gender beneath the mantle of leadership and heroism. Recall that Russia's Catherine the Great was featured in Boston's *Atheneum* as "the rarest example of intellectual manhood" on account of her heroism, not her gender.[52] In literary society debates, England's female queens, for example, were often lionized for their masculine traits; their feminine characteristics were entirely ignored. In his junior oration before the Dialectic Society, for example, William White Harris contemplated whether Mary Queen of Scots was justifiably beheaded (a question that appears often in literary society records). Regardless of unfavorable historical judgment, he argued, Mary's heroism rested in her ability to withstand adversity. "Amidst all the difficulties and trials, which Mary had to overcome," he wrote, "she regulated the affairs of state, and attended to her domestic concerns, as well as could be expected from a mind, as much perplexed and troubled as hers was."[53] Thus, students looked to female biography not as a way to understand female heroes *as women* but as a way to understand them *as heroes*.

In their discourse about female heroes, students reaffirmed but did not challenge the antebellum period's prevailing doctrine of separate spheres. When editors of the *North Carolina University Magazine* included an excerpt from a speech given to the New-York Historical Society entitled "Female Heroism," for example, they excerpted a portion of the speech that extolled Andrew Jackson's widowed mother for raising her son without a father's support. The student editors offered their reaction: Jackson's mother was heroic because she raised a true patriot. In so doing, they reaffirmed notions of separate spheres as well as republican motherhood. But in the remaining pages of the article, Jackson emerged the true hero.[54] Similarly, when William Lord delivered his Senior Oration to the Dialectic Society in 1858 on the topic of heroism, he explained that American history records the heroism of women and cited Pocahontas, who became a hero because she "interposed her own life to save that of the heroic Captain John Smith."[55]

This example points not only to the greater importance of male heroism in young men's minds, but also to the race of heroism. Students, not surprisingly, relied on entirely white heroic models. When they did look to non-whites, particularly Native Americans, they did not challenge existing racial hierarchies but maintained them, as they did with gender lines. Yet one common thread runs throughout much of students' discourse about heroes, whether male or female, Indian or white: heroic qualities were timeless. They included courage, physical and mental strength in the face of adversity, and sound moral judgment. Students extolled these timeless values and integrated them into their expectations for manhood in public literary society discourse. In this way, literary societies provided a characteristically nineteenth-century education in greatness. Students learned to think biographically as they acquired portraits and biographies, and talked and wrote about them in regular society meetings. This cultural work provided a framework around private experiences of self-construction.

"Among the Just Made Perfect": Reading, Writing, and Devotional Life

Zeal for improvement, hope in the future, and belief that life is an epic voyage prompted many conscientious young men to turn inward and contemplate who they were, who they wished to become, and how they could best make the transition from boyhood to manhood. William Mullins, a student from Fayetteville, North Carolina, could have been a poster child for nineteenth-century self-fashioning. As we have already seen, Mullins's emotional life was rough—he confronted struggles with his family at home and faced problems with classmates at college. This grocer's son desired upward mobility and hoped to become a lawyer. In his first two years at college, he began to question his mother's Methodist faith and sought conversion to a more moderate strand of Protestantism in the Episcopal Church. His political outlook was self-consciously Whig. Not only did he support Whig candidates in the 1840 election, but he also adhered to Whig principles of reform and improvement and applied them to his own personal conduct. When he began his journal in 1840, for example, Mullins wrote about the necessity of self-improvement: "He [a young man] should carefully gather from his past history, wisdom for his future conduct. He must ultimately learn the great truth that his purest happiness is connected inseparably with the constant exercise of virtue. . . . To become acquainted with the abundant proofs of these, which are afforded in my own life, is the object of the Journal."[56] Mullins pursued his own heroic potential through both secular and sacred channels. Although not every young man was as dedicated to self-construction as Mullins, his motivations for and approaches to improving himself warrant close analysis.

In particular, writing in a journal allowed Mullins regular opportunities to scrutinize his progress along life's voyage. In this effort, he was not alone. Perhaps Giles Patterson, a student at South Carolina College, put it best when he penned the first line of his diary in 1846: "I was well; I wished to be better; here I am."[57] Although diaries were jumbled with the stuff of daily life—letters, commonplace books, lecture notes, and financial records—they nevertheless fostered reflective exposition. Some diaries were private, but others were not. Edmund Covington nodded to the publicity of his diary, for example, when he inscribed, "Nemo, nisi amicus, legat has literas" (No one, unless he is a friend, may read these pages).[58] Although most diarists preferred privacy, there was always a risk of someone reading it. "These are my private sentiments," Ruffin Tomlinson explained. "I record nothing in th[is] Journal but what comes upon my fundocordis; I have no reason to do otherwise because I intend no person shall ever read what I write though it is not of much importance."[59] As a largely private and emotional literary form, diaries provided outlets for exploring and developing the self.

Within his diary, Mullins loved to write about lives—his life, the lives of his classmates, and the lives of those who peopled his literary imagination. He wrote extensively about each member of his class in order to remember his classmates, but also to learn from their character traits. "The task I undertake shall be *frankly* performed and I will dare to write fully my thoughts," wrote Mullins. "When I have done, I shall recur to these pages with deep solicitude. My opinion of them then, shall likewise be given here, and I will sit in judgment on myself as well as others. I feel that *may* make the exercise I am commencing now, most useful to me through life, and my character *can* now be vastly improved, while my knowledge *must* be . . . increased."[60] Mullins also noted character flaws. In writing about John Davis Hawkins, for example, Mullins wrote, "He loved pleasure, and he pursued it in College, giving to that pursuit the time which of right belonged to self-improvement. Alas. He was not singular in this respect."[61]

Mullins was not alone in taking up his pen to contemplate his classmates' virtues and vices. Edmund Covington wrote a seven-page "chapter" in his journal, "concerning the future destiny of my classmates of the Dialectic Society." He scrutinized their appearance, morals, intellect, and potential for success. He wrote, for instance, that Jonathan H. Clinch "has good sense—lively fancy but will waste his gifts in a career of pleasure. Not good looking at all"; A. G. Foster "affects independence"; Philemon Hawkins was "a fellow of very fine feelings but limited capacity for study." He described some students simply as "rowdy." Covington even included commentary on himself, but written by his friend W. L. Steele: "E. D. Covington—as for him 'nous verrous' [we shall see]—Is a candid—sensible—good-natured-affable-sympathetic-generous—'jeune homme.'"[62]

In addition to his sharp focus on his classmates, Mullins also incorporated in his private scheme for self-construction many lessons from literary societies about reading biography and history. Between August 1839 and July 1841, William Sidney Mullins visited the Philanthropic Society library at least fifty-five times and borrowed 112 titles, or approximately 148 volumes at a rate of about 9 volumes per month. Library records suggest that Mullins favored fiction, including Scott's popular *Waverley* novels, but also read a good bit of periodical literature, philosophy, poetry, and, of course, history and biography. Mullins read historical and biographical works, including titles recorded as vaguely as "Ancient Europe," "Goldsmith," and "Mary of Burgundy," as well as Homer's *Iliad*, Hume's *History of England*, and Cooper's *The History of the Navy of the United States of America*.[63] Always thoughtful and reflective, Mullins recorded his impressions of the works he read, leaving us traces of his experiences with biography, history, and self-fashioning.

Mullins's reflections typically focused on leadership. In 1841, after he read James Mackintosh's *The Life of Sir Thomas More* (1830), Mullins praised the biography and its subject extensively: "If in reviewing the deeds of such nobleness, the spirit glows not with animation, cold and ignoble must it be. I have several times asked myself if the author has not been too enthusiastic in the praise of his subject: if his enthusiasm has not led him to colour too brightly his virtues and entirely neglect his failings. But I have persuaded myself to answer no. It is so pleasant to find all the virtues there blended in one noble picture, that I would fain believe such was the case and continue to emulate the negative dignity of the character which combined them." Further, Mullins enumerated many attributes of More's character: "unceasing industry," honor, honesty, and "love of virtue." These "distinguishing characteristics," Mullins concluded, "points the mind to excellence and glory in any trial. . . . May he [More] be my polar star!"[64] Mullins revealed a similar ambition in a response to a biography of Cardinal Wolsey in Lardner's *Encyclopedia*. "I will . . . aim high; my goal shall be noble, and if I fail to reach it, I shall not be utterly without consolation. As I look back on past years, I shall see what I strove to be and shall stand at least a monument of good intentions," he wrote.[65] In each case, Mullins focused on the lives of two prominent men in King Henry VIII's court who did not compromise their values or dignity according to the king's request. Mullins located his ambition in core bourgeois values such as perseverance, virtue, honor, and honesty, and he related those values to his own heroic potential.

Mullins's engagement with biography was not uncommon. Portraiture, genre discourse, and historical debates facilitated contemplation of public virtues expected of civic leaders in Victorian America, and other students carried these messages with them into private reading experiences. Several years after Mullins was graduated from North Carolina, Thomas Miles Garrett took up his pen to write about biography. "I have thought that it would be a most profitable exercise to write some thing upon the character of each reighn of English History as I read them," he explained. "The character of each reighn may be supposed to have a verry intimate resemblance to the character of the king."[66] He noted manly qualities of leadership (even in England's female monarchs), including action, virtue, genius, and the ability of individuals to preserve liberty and promote civilization. For example, Garrett praised Henry VIII for "direct[ing] the energies of his people to the attainment of real and solid advantages," including "the elevation of the character and condition of the lower class of subjects." He frequently identified Henry's strong leadership with the "advancement in the civilization of the people," and the improvement of "the manners and morals of the people." Likewise, he praised the king's "ambition and ability" to protect England from external threats to English liberty and Mary Tudor's "bigotry," which "impel[led] her as far beyond the bonds of reason and justice as to endeavor to affect what she might term a reformation."[67] While Garrett learned much history from reading authors such as Hume, he derived chiefly moral lessons that spoke to larger issues of leadership and government that interested him. His responses to literature about nearly every English monarch underscore issues of restraint and impulse and of mind and temperament, which students associated with male adulthood. He focused on historical examples of the corruptibility of power, the fragility of public morals, and the need to regulate public morality and protect people from "aristocratic power," luxury, and slavery. Hume's *History of England* thus helped Garrett articulate his own emerging ideas about manly leadership. Garrett's engagement with biography (and history) resembled that of Mullins and other young male readers in the antebellum period.

As useful and entertaining as biography was, however, the genre did not always address impediments to self-construction, particularly moral obstacles that stood in the way of development as a Christian. Between 1840 and 1841, Mullins recorded his bad habits: drinking, swearing, and masturbating. He masturbated regularly, it seems, and he described his habit as a "deadly vice" that he struggled to "shake off." For instance, he sometimes described his habits in terms of pollution and filth. "Vile habits," he wrote, held a "debasing" and "desperate grasp" on his hardened, "polluted heart."[68] Throughout the year he wrote vaguely of a "calamity" and "irremediable sin" that enslaved him to his passions. He viewed these vague vices as stumbling blocks to his maturation. So he prayed often for grace and wrote his prayers in his journal, demonstrating a strong commitment to evangelical moral discipline as a tool for self-formation. In reflecting on the "dissipation and shameful wickedness" of his first two and a half years at college, "the deliberate wickedness, repeated crimes, and knowing refusals to do right," he could not bear to "enumerate the countless daily violations of Gods most holy law." Instead, he wrote a prayer: "Oh! Lord!" he begged, "have mercy on me. Wicked as I have been, I am not too vile for the Saviour's blood to cleanse me, and through the merits of that blood, I implore thee to subdue my heart and transform it. Oh! Holy Spirit, visit me and abide with me continually, and by thy agency, let me be numbered among the just made perfect."[69] For God to subdue his heart, Mullins believed he had to write as if he were in direct dialogue with God. Yet he also believed he needed to do more than pray; he had to restrain his passions through devotional reading of Scripture and church attendance. He had to play an active role in his own moral improvement.

Devotional reading of Scripture was a key religious practice in Mullins's quest for restraint. He set nighttime aside for "solemn reflection" and private religious practices, which included reading the Bible before he "retire[d] to bed." He hoped that this practice would "have a beneficial effect on my conduct, and will give a healthy, religious tone to all my thoughts and feelings." These practices were widespread in the South due to the pervasiveness of evangelical culture, and young men often traced their devotional life in diaries. James Dusenbery kept track of his Bible study: "I read as far as the Psalms last session & intend finishing the old Testament, the present one."[70] Thomas Miles Garrett was less specific but more methodical about tracing his devotional life. Each day he inscribed "P.A." at the beginning of his diary entry to note "Prayers Attended." At nearby Wake Forest College, Benson Cole also combined devotional Bible study and diary writing. "I commenced last session to read the new Testament through, which I did with great ease," he wrote. "Last session I began to commit proverbs to memory by getting two or three verses every time I went to my dinner, supper, or breakfast, I succeeded very well until I became negligent, and failed a time or two, finally quit, the consequence is I have forgotten what I learned."[71] Even though students were required to attend daily prayer services and weekly Bible recitations and worship services, they carved out space for private devotional practices to facilitate self-improvement.[72]

Devotional life seemed to make it easy for Mullins to imagine his quest for restraint in the epic and heroic proportions introduced at the beginning of this chapter, especially "life's battle." When writing about his plans for self-improvement, Mullins described himself as a Christian soldier preparing for battle, "girding on the armour, destined to be my defence and support in life." He promised to "direct every action," first to "the acquirement of an unalterable habit of perseverance" and second "to the habit of close attention." But he did not stop there. He also promised to pursue "sound practical piety" and "adopt" Christianity "as the rule of my life, the charter of my hopes, the god of my life." Christian devotion, he believed, strengthened him to "bid defiance to all opposition."[73] This language calls to mind St. Paul's letter to the Ephesians, with which Mullins would have been very familiar. In his letter, Paul exhorts the Ephesians to "put on the whole armor of God," the "breastplate" of justice, the "helmet of salvation," and the "sword of the spirit." This biblical language seemed to work for Mullins, whose Christian faith empowered him to overcome formidable vices such as drinking, swearing, and his "deadly vice."[74]

Church was another essential element of Mullins's self-improvement plan. He viewed Sunday church services, albeit required, as sources for contemplation and personal growth. In fact, he vowed to make an effort to attend extra Sunday services, usually at the Chapel of the Cross, in order to forward his self-improvement scheme. "For the poor, trembling sinner," he wrote in his diary, "there is no better time to turn from the evil of his way." At church, Mullins "felt sensations almost strangers to my breast, since I have been a member of college." He wished that such feelings "were habitual residents" within him. "And though the immediate effect [of religion] may soon pass off," he was grateful that "its traces remain[ed]" and allowed him "always [to] have a humble and a better heart." Church, in other words, helped Mullins to renew his commitment to suppress his impulses by reminding him of the blessings of a Christian life. He noted in his diary, for example, that he benefited from hearing Professor William Mercer Green deliver a sermon on "the proper means to be pursued by one who desired the conversion of his soul." Green taught that "prayer, diligent perusal of the Bible, and mediation" were the only "means by which an erring sinner might obtain pardon." Mullins must have sat in the pew nodding during the entire sermon.[75]

In many ways, Mullins is representative of other young men of the antebellum era who took up their pens to do the work of growing up. He took to heart many of the lessons about mental and moral improvement that permeated formal and informal life at North Carolina. He recognized that the passionate impulses of youth, sexual or otherwise, did not make the man. Instead, he wanted to strengthen his mind and morals. His system for moral self-formation fit perfectly into the expectations for antebellum self-fashioning—he went to church, read the Bible, prayed, stopped drinking, and maybe even quit his "deadly vice." Moreover, his quest for fame, distinction, and, indeed perfection echoed the pervasive culture of ambition that defines southern manhood in this era. This zeal for improvement, belief in human potential, calculus for self-fashioning, and ambition for fame place Mullins squarely in the nineteenth century's pervasive spirit of self-culture. We will never know whether Mullins reached the heroic potential he imagined for himself. If he continued to write in journals as an adult, we have no record of it. Nevertheless, Mullins's collegiate experiences show the great degree to which the self's heroic potential figured in the University of North Carolina's intellectual culture in the antebellum period. For all those who sneered at college as a hotbed of illicit sex, drinking, and fighting, students like William Mullins reveal that attitudes about self-culture influenced young men's collective and individual pursuits of maturity.

IN ALL, THIS CHAPTER has shown how students appropriated into their world of intentional intellectualism bourgeois practices designed to restrain boyish impulse. They created a literary ambience steeped in popular notions of self-culture that helped them along the path from boyhood to manhood. They relied on several intellectual resources that bourgeois Americans used in self-culture. The Dialectic and Philanthropic Societies each amassed an unprecedented number of biographical works in their libraries, and the number of historical and biographical debate questions likewise grew exponentially during this period. Students also collected portraits of successful university alumni whom they hoped to emulate. Although these various cultural acts did not always or necessarily require picking up a biography or history and reading it, they do signify the importance of what Scott Casper has termed "biographical imagination."[76] In the process, students promoted hero worship and emulation in a way that buttressed their ambitions for greatness. Finally, the case of William Mullins shows how some students personalized this process. In all, these practices point to the important position of the individual self in antebellum student thinking that had bearing on their attitudes about manhood. Through heroic examples, they saw, and actively reflected on, the importance of restraint and the broader characteristics that distinguished men from boys. Significantly, students' ideas about manhood did not exist entirely in a world of all-male ritual, ideals, and discourse. Just as self-culture anticipated the voyage of life beyond college, students' experiences with women anticipated their lives within society. The following chapter turns to those experiences in order to understand the influence of young men's ideas about themselves in how they understood relationships with others.

CHAPTER SIX

What Is Man without Woman?
Courtship, Intimacy, and Sex

Following an unusually warm January day in Chapel Hill, twenty-three-year-old Joseph Summerell retired to his room to write about the day's events. The morning began with a chemistry lecture attended by "all the fair faces that C. Hill can afford to add brilliancy & interest to our studies." Although the University of North Carolina was an all-male institution, young women occasionally attended university events, including lectures. Yet Summerell and his classmates typically did not think beyond themselves when it came to these visits. "Happy is it for us that these ministering angels pay their daily visits to our lectures," Summerell continued, and then wrote the following meditation on women and men:

> What is man without woman? . . . We ought to cherish, honor &
> respect them as being the origin of our existence as sensative be-
> ings. But they are also the best company that we can possibly have
> to cheer us in the eventful journey of life, ministers of comfort in
> sickness & tribulation, and the guardian spirits of our tender affec-
> tions. How strange must be the notion of some men, of remaining in
> single blessedness . . . destitute of all the comforts, the pleasures, and
> delightful interchange of tender love, which in virtuous intelligent
> & sweet-tempered wife is calculated to inspire, & weave around the
> destinies of our existence here below? Who can be ignorant that it
> is mostly to them we owe the subjection of our angry passions & the
> softening our dispositions with the mildness & tenderness. But those
> points need not be insisted on since they must be so evident to every
> man who has the common feelings of our species.[1]

Summerell's remarks underscore the extent to which young women shaped male students' informal curriculum and intellectual culture. First, young women's visits to campus and interactions with students reminded young men that daily life in an all-male college environment was short-lived—that women, ultimately, might join students along "the eventful journey of life." Second, he reveals that most students were not unlike most other American youth, who valued the companionate ideal of marriage and pursued romantic love in order to complete the project of self-formation. According to Karen Lystra, romantic love derived from the idea of individualism, as one single self sought "a single beloved" who best could complete his or her personality.[2] Although most collegians were not ready to begin a serious courtship, let alone marry, they sought social, emotional, and intellectual connections with single young women. In college, young men actively participated in rituals such as visiting, conversation parties, and letter writing. Studies of education and college males do not often include these rituals under the umbrella of education, yet they formed a significant aspect of students' informal education in self and society. In particular, courting rituals, not unlike other elements of the informal curriculum, compelled students to hone self-expression, to master not only the well-known gestures and performances of social ritual, but also its vocabulary, form, and written quality. In the process of learning to express desire and, sometimes, love, young men pursued and extolled ideals of restrained manhood—chastity, sobriety, and restraint. Finally, Summerell's remarks show that these social interactions with young women during college reinforced prevailing ideals of womanhood, particularly attitudes that women were intrinsically "tender," "virtuous," and "sweet-tempered."

The best exemplars of this ideal womanhood were students' mothers and sisters. In elite and middle-class families, mothers tended to children's moral education, inculcating virtue and piety. Their roles as "moral guardians" continued after young men left home for college, when they wrote to sons, urging them to cultivate virtue. While young men's mothers were the paragon of virtue, their sisters bore that potential as well. Young women were thought to be, by nature, moral vessels, and student writing refers to them as "the fair sex" or "the gentle sex."[3] In 1841, for instance, Richard Wilson ruminated about "the influence of woman" in his junior oration. "Earth has not a more angelic vision, than a young girl just drawing into womanhood with all her new blown charms around," he wrote. "An atmosphere of purity is around her." The presence of young women in student life likewise inspired young men's ambitions for greatness, which characterized much of their experiences of higher education and maturation in college. Wilson continued, for example, "It [woman's influence] stirs the warriors soul, and fires the patriot's heart, and where his banner waves its folds are hands to do and souls to dare what woman please command. It lights the statesman's brow and eloquence bursts blazing forth, and kindles in its audience the flame of high resolve or virtuous indignation."[4] In all, the influence of women, young men believed, was crucial to the pursuit of individual identity and the call to greatness. As Stephen Berry has argued, "Men believed that women were supposed to bear witness to male becoming, to cheer men to greatness, and comfort them along the way."[5] These ideals, in turn, shaped not only how young men interacted with women but also how they viewed their future roles as citizens and leaders—power brokers of the society they would inherit after graduation.

As with other aspects of young men's self-development, however, tensions associated with the profound transition from boyhood to manhood occasionally resulted from these interactions and confounded students as they came of age sexually.[6] Young men did not resist talking or writing about desire, nor did they resist having sex. Many students participated in an active sexual culture on campus, fornicating with local women, soliciting sex from prostitutes, and raping slave women. Thus, while many young men sought legitimate ways to deal with their sexual urges by regulating sexual behavior or avoiding it altogether, others sought ways to legitimate sexual behavior that may have transgressed codes for restrained manhood. In these instances, codes of honor and manly independence that historians have associated with "southern manhood" validated behavior that undermined the ideals of restrained manhood which students idealized in more formal settings. Significantly, these tensions were more symptomatic of young college men of the time than of a particular regional disposition, and students wrote about those experiences in ways similar to collegians elsewhere.[7] In order to understand how these tensions influenced young men's informal education, self-development, and self-articulation, it is first important to understand the heterosocial context of campus life.

Meeting and Courting Women in College Life

In the antebellum period, young men believed that marriage was preferable to bachelorhood, but they were in no hurry to begin a serious courtship while in college.[8] They wished first to finish college, secure independence in a profession, and then marry. "I have quit thinking about the girls. I have other fish to fry," wrote one student to his sister. "It is a waste of time for me to think on such subjects. . . . After I graduate, get my profession, and make something to live on, then perhaps I will strike out."[9] Young women preferred it this way as well. According to Anya Jabour, "Although the ostensible goal of entering society was to make a good match, many young women made their debut with a firm resolve to avoid entanglements."[10] So generally young males and females enjoyed courting but put off courtship. When young southerners did pursue courtship, however, they did not do so lightly. Much of this had to do with the public nature of courtship: despite a young couple's desire for privacy and autonomy, family and friends were often involved in affairs of the heart, and young men approached any admission of love cautiously.[11] Young women also required male suitors to pass rigorous tests of fidelity during early stages of flirtation and courtship.[12]

Students often began relationships with young women during vacations. It was not uncommon for sisters and female cousins to introduce young men to their friends. Students attended social engagements within these networks frequently, in fact. Authors writing for the *North Carolina University Magazine*, for instance, poked fun at young men who spent their entire vacations "luxuriating in the so 'soft light' of their lady-loves' eyes," rather than writing essays for publication.[13] When vacations ended, young men would correspond with the young women they had met at home and occasionally return to college with intense feelings for them.

The case of George Thompson, a student from Leasburg, North Carolina, is instructive. In early January 1851, as his cold and snowy winter vacation came to an end, Thompson took an interest in Susan Lindsay, a young woman whom Thompson and his friends admired "for her intelligence & beauty." He visited her frequently and developed feelings for her. "It appears as if I am better satisfied if I am near Miss Sue L.," he wrote in his diary. "I fear I am permitting *her person* to get a too great a stronghold on my affections[.] I must either find out that she *thinks something* of *me*, and let my affections increase, or if not, I must strive to put down the feelings which arise in my heart—for 'Tis the worst of pain / To love and not be loved again.'" Still, he had begun to fall in love with her and told his mother that he might consider courting her.[14] On the day before he departed Leasburg for Chapel Hill, George spent nearly four hours alone with Sue, hoping to ascertain her feelings and express his own. "I did not tell her how I loved and how much I admired her—yet if she only knew, she would through pity if nothing else, reciprocate my *love*," Thompson wrote. He did, however, find the nerve to ask her whether he might correspond with her while he was away at college. She agreed and, in turn, requested a lock of George's hair by which to remember him. The next day, George left Leasburg with fewer hairs on his head but with a smile on his face, and abundant paper for love letters.[15]

At college, George constantly thought about Sue Lindsay. He wrote her letters, sent her books, and even imagined her as he read Charles Augustus Murray's three-volume work on fictional travels in America, *The Prairie-Bird* (1844). In particular, he greatly admired the novel for its exaltation of romantic love between the two main characters—estranged lovers who ultimately return to one another "with hearts full of pure and ardent love." He delighted in the protagonists' reunion at the novel's conclusion: "I saw Reginald Brandon escape all dangers and return safely home, with his hearts only love, the '*Olitapa*' & I saw Ethelston and Lucy again meet, with hearts full of pure and ardent love—I saw them also joined in the holy ties of matrimony, to enjoy, pleasure by day and *happiness* by night—How I would like to take *her* to my bosom, when I so fondly and affectionately adore, if I would imagine that my adoration was reciprocated—as Reginald Brandon Miss Evelyn Ethelston—his faithful friends and kind brother's Sister!!—but I can scarcely ever believe that such will be my doom—as to enjoy the bliss that those two double Brothers did—Miss Susan." Then, quoting Robert Burns's ballad "O Wert Thou in the Cauld Blast" (1800), George finished his reader response and addressed Sue directly:

> Were I monarch of the world
> With thee to reign
> The brightest jewel in my crown
> should be my *queen*!![16]

Throughout the semester, George nurtured the hope that he might court Sue after college. Unfortunately, his collegiate writings end abruptly, and we have no evidence as to whether or not their love matured. Nevertheless, George's story reveals the extent to which romantic developments begun during vacation influenced young men's experiences at college.

College life also provided opportunities for young men to meet and socialize with single young women from Chapel Hill. According to Kemp P. Battle, the university's growth and financial stability in the 1820s and 1830s invigorated town life and brought young men and women closer together. "The ladies arrayed themselves in finer clothes," Battle recalled, "improved their houses with added rooms and with paint, cultivated grass and flowers on their lawns, frequented the University and Society libraries, rode to hear preaching sometimes in the neighborhood churches, especially Mount Carmel, induced services in the University Chapel, prayed fervently but never aloud, at prayer-meetings, and inaugurated reading clubs."[17] Young single women also attended singing and dancing classes, parties, opossum suppers, balls, picnics, and local camp meetings and revivals.[18] Not all students agreed, however, that there were enough young women or that any of them were worth pursuing. Douglas Beatty complained about this dilemma to a friend from his hometown of Mocksville, North Carolina: "It is true that Chapel Hill is rather bad off for pretty girls but as for that it makes but very little difference with me as I never think of girls now the reason for which I suppose is I . . . never see any."[19]

Visiting was a significant social ritual in which young men and women could meet. Visiting often occurred at formal "conversation parties." At these engagements of fifteen or more attendees, some single young men and women played musical instruments for one another while others conversed. On a pleasant fall evening, for example, Walter Lenoir strolled around campus, listening "till bedtime at the students performing on their flutes and violins, and the ladies singing and playing on the piano."[20] Older friends sometimes initiated younger students in these visiting rituals. William Mullins made his "debut in visiting on the Hill" with his friend Richard Pearson, who was "passionately fond of the Ladies."[21] Although the "debut" of a young man like Mullins was not the same as a young woman's "coming out," it was a valuable rite of passage.

There were many places for visiting in Chapel Hill. Nancy Hilliard's Eagle Hotel—just minutes from campus—was an especially popular place for conversation parties and visiting. "Miss Nancy," as she was commonly called, often invited students to "come and see me and set till bedtime."[22] Moreover, Miss Nancy and her friends occasionally tried to make matches between students and single women in the community. Sometimes these women would take students to the homes of young women, as they did when they took Ruffin Tomlinson to visit Martha Johnson and hear her play the piano.[23] Antebellum students also visited eligible young women at professors' homes. Following expectations of elite southern society, all these visits were chaperoned and structured, and they provided lessons in restraint.

Significantly, young women were not passive participants in these visiting rituals, and their wishes and desires set boundaries for young men. According to Anya Jabour, young women embraced the autonomy that came with single life and often resisted relationships that ultimately might limit that autonomy. This resistance occurred during early and advanced stages of courtship, as young women tested and challenged potential suitors.[24] In late January 1842, Joseph Summerell learned this lesson when he paid a visit to the science professor, Dr. Mitchell, in order to borrow ammonia to remove a stain from his pantaloons, but instead he received a short lecture about courting his daughters. Rising with "marked gravity, but a kind of smile," Mitchell asked, "Mr. Summerell, do you know what law I have made with respect to the young men that visit the ladies at my house [?]" Feeling a bit worried at the direction this meeting had taken, Summerell assured Mitchell that he knew the rules. "Well," said Mitchell, "my daughters have a certain course of studies that they must attend to, & I want you when you visit them to leave at the ringing of the 8 oclock bell precisely. I shall be quite glad to see you at any time provided you leave at the hour specified." Summerell was altogether taken aback at this request because he firmly believed that he "had not proved altogether disagreeable to the ladies," who "no doubt have become tired our visits (not mine particularly), & through modesty could not communicate to us what they wished themselves & applied to their father as the most convenient way of getting rid of our attentions." Although visiting Mitchell's house was "one of the principal sources of my pleasure and a means by which I should prepare myself for the company of females in after life," he resolved to visit less frequently on account of Mitchell's admonition.[25]

Not all students' socialization and flirting rituals were so structured. Students frequently assembled serenading parties in which they played various homemade musical instruments and sang for young women in town. According to Kemp P. Battle, young women returned the honor of a serenade "by showers of rose buds."[26] Students also publicized their love (albeit anonymously) in the *North Carolina University Magazine*, which served as an important medium for flirtation. Nearly every issue of the publication contains poetry anonymously dedicated to local women. Titles included "TO MISS.....of O.....";"To Jennie"; "To Mis ***** of C.H."; and "Lines Respectfully to Miss M. E. M. of Pittsboro."[27] One poem, "To Miss—," reveals the poeticism of students' courtship experiences. The author, "Claude," used pastoral images to evoke chivalry and romantic love:

At early dawn, we've often strayed
Along the meadows green,
At summer's eve, beneath the shades,
The lovely flowers to glean.

We've sat beneath the old elm-tree,
Upon our mossy seat;
Those same old tunes so dear to me,
We sang in chorus sweet.

We've chased the golden butterfly
As he skipped from flower to flower,
And plucked the buds to beautify
Thy curls, from hour to hour. . . .[28]

Poems like these were so prevalent, in fact, that readers complained about them, forcing the editors to defend their publication. "If a girl is to be courted," they wrote in 1852, "why not court her through the medium of the press?"[29]

Sending young women poetry in correspondence was also popular, but many students struggled when it came to writing original verse. "I tried to make an Acrostic on Miss Sue Lindsay's name but did not have time enough to do it," George Thompson complained in 1851.[30] Many students therefore relied less on their own poetic talents than on the least likely source to convey their emerging romantic feelings—a local slave named George Moses Horton.

Horton was born in 1797 in Northampton County, North Carolina, to tobacco farmer William Horton. When he was three years old, his master moved his farm west to Chatham County, North Carolina, not far from Chapel Hill. There, he learned the alphabet by piecing together torn pages from an old spelling book; once he became proficient, he learned to read from the New Testament, a Methodist hymnal, and whatever other scraps of text he could find. As a young man, George hired himself out in Chapel Hill and frequently visited the university, where he became known among students for his literary talents. Many North Carolina students bought love poetry from Horton throughout the antebellum period. As Kemp P. Battle recalled, "When his [Horton's] employer was willing to pay fifty cents the poem was generously gushing. Twenty-five cents procured one more luke-warm in passion."[31] William Bagley was one such student who solicited a poem from Horton. In a letter to his sister, Bagley wrote that he intended to send love poetry to a young woman from his hometown, but admitted "it was composed by a black man at my request." He confidentially copied the poem into the letter:

> Magnet of every tuneful bard!
> Ador'd of lovers on the knee,
> Resplendent girl, my true regard
> Yet never has been told to thee.
>
> Why should I hence forbear to sing
> Impell'd, I cannot love deny;
> Let me ascend on pleasure's wing
> Let me display my love or die.
> Imperial nymph! I must be thine,
> And still thy winning form adore,
> My lips would pain pronounce thee mine,
> So should I smile & frown no more.[32]

Unable to express his love himself, Bagley thus turned to a local slave. Significantly, Horton was able to use money from student purchases to his advantage. He eventually published two volumes while enslaved and another after emancipation. He became the first slave to use poetry to challenge the institution of slavery as well as the first African American to publish a book in the South.[33] Still, students like William Bagley hid the authorship from the female recipients of Horton's love poetry, thus claiming the literary labor of a slave as their own.

For many collegians, courting was a literary exercise, involving correspondence with multiple young women at once. For instance, James Hilliard Polk wrote in his diary, "I intend to correspond with three or four girls next session, when I can have time to write but at present it keeps me as busy as the Devil to get my lessons, but next year I will be fairly started & then I will fool some girls to a certainty."[34] Young men viewed correspondence with single young women as part of their education as gentlemen as well as a means for mental and moral improvement. In a *North Carolina University Magazine* article entitled "Female Correspondents," anonymous student authors wrote, "It is both pleasant and useful to correspond with our friends among our own sex; but that deference and regard due to the fairer sex, renders our correspondence with ladies particularly interesting." In writing to females, in love letters or not, young men had to show "strictest regard for propriety" and virtue. Because writing to females required careful attention, some students worried that their letters would turn young women away from them. This was the case for John Jones, who wrote to his cousin about a mutual friend whom he hoped to impress. "I scarcely know what words I shall use best, to assure Miss Catharine that she has no reason to be at all troubled about the little merriment that has passed between us," he wrote. "Indeed cousin Ann if Miss C. knew exactly the manner in which I view the circumstances she would be entirely satisfied—but I fear that if there is any blame it will fall on my poor head—for unpolished in my style of writing, I might have commit[t]ed some error that was calculated to would female delicacy."[35]

Because love letters were particularly serious business, students were careful about sending them. For instance, deciding whether or not to send a love letter to Cornelia Phillips, the daughter of Professor James Phillips, was a matter of great anxiety and deliberation for Ruffin Tomlinson. "Miss Cornelia Phillips is a very fine girl," he wrote. "I am almost in love with her, if she was wealthy I would cou[rt] her. She is the smartest girl I ever was ac[quainted with]." Tomlinson, however, never told Cornelia that he loved—or even admired—her. As his final days in Chapel Hill approached, he wrote Cornelia a letter about his feelings, hoping she would agree to correspond with him, but at the last minute decided not to send it out of fear of mutual embarrassment. Like other young men and women in nineteenth-century America, Tomlinson was cautious about initiating correspondence. "If you feel disposed to correspond with me upon the subject alluded to above I assure you it shall never cause you any uneasiness on my part," he wrote to Cornelia. "Gratify me, Miss Cornelia, in answering this and therein state yur willingness or unwillingness to [comply with my] wish. . . . I cannot but expect that you will treat this letter as its merits deserve in yours to me. Some ladies are willing to make their communications upon paper others again are not. You opinion upon the matter I know not, but I sincerely wish to gain your consent."[36]

Although young men were cautious about discussing potential romances with women or family members, they were fairly open with one another. James Boylan, for instance, had a heartsick friend from home who had fallen in love years earlier, but his love was never returned, leaving him "forlorn and lost." He wrote to Boylan about his heartache fairly often. "Poor boy!" wrote Boylan to his sister, "his letters are fair samples of the varying and complicated emotions of a heart ill at ease—they betray the softening and subduing influence of love, the painful suspence the burning anxiety, the agonizing doubt, the hopeless misery of despair, and even the pangs of jealousy."[37] Sometimes, however, students complained of hearing too much about friends' love interests. "My room mate has just done reading a love letter from his Dulcinea Del Wake Forest Miss Mariott . . . and he pesters me with his love matters and his letters to her are rare specimens of the ludicrous bombast," complained Montezuma Jones to his brother, Calvin. "He has the girl complete in his power, and he has nothing to recommend as I can see except his vivacity and good nature." His roommate had pursued "Miss Mariott" for some time, but he had "been bucked off by her father, who says he is a stranger, will take her to Ala. And leave her and will certainly drink." According to Montezuma, this would have been surprising had his roommate not embarrassed himself in a drunken brawl at a recent family wedding.[38]

Although students' letters to their male friends were more frank than with female correspondents, young men were often careful not to disclose too much information, even among trusted friends. For instance, When William Bagley matriculated at the University of North Carolina in 1842, he pursued love with great interest, often writing to friends and family from home, including his sister Clementia and close friends at the Williamston Academy. In 1845, William had become smitten with a young woman from home, Mary Robertson, and expressed his desire to court her in a numerically coded letter, this time to his friend Moses. When deciphered, the letter betrays the young man's hopes for and anxieties about love: "I will now tell you of the girl of whom I have the highest opinion to wit Miss Mary Robertson and I should like to have your advice in regard to some matters on the subject do you not think I could live happily with her whom I dearly love although she is not worth a cent And you are well acquainted with her and you must let me know in your next what your opinions are of her whether or not you think she would make a fellow the very best wife family poverty and other considerations to the contrary notwithstanding; you must be very honest in your statement and let me have your sentiments on the subject."[39] Although William Bagley was ready to think about love, he was not comfortable expressing those feelings, at least beyond coded messages with his male friend.

The southern culture of honor sometimes influenced how young men expressed desire and intimacy. They cherished confidentiality and viewed any breech of trust as a direct assault against a man's personal honor. In July 1841, Ruffin Tomlinson worried that his friend, "Bridgers," would tell "Miss M. . W. ." that Tomlinson wanted to court her. "I somewhat fear he [Bridgers] will do me more injury than good. He has got sense enough just about to tell Miss M. . W. . that I have a notion to address her—to tell her he is my confidant. He told me that if he liked her he might court her himself, if he should, I mean to challenge him upon the spot and never to go to see her any more. I expect he will bring me back bad news, for if it was good he would not tell me so. He is too envious. He thinks he is one of the greatest men among the ladies now living. He is a vain. . vain. . man[.]"[40] Telling her would have been a breach of confidence on Bridgers's part and an insult to each young man's honor.

Young men did not typically write about sex in correspondence. One exception is a strikingly candid exchange about masturbation between an 1819 graduate of the University of North Carolina, Iveson Brookes, and his son Walker Brookes, a student at Columbian College in the 1850s. Walker wrote candidly about his habit, and his father returned letters chock full of advice from Sylvester Graham's well-known program for preventing masturbation through dietary regulation. Correspondence of this candid nature, however, is rare.[41]

When it came to desire and sex, students usually turned to more private sources such as diaries. For instance, after William Mullins met several young women at a ball, he bragged in his diary, "I flirted with all of them." Similarly, Edmund Covington wrote in his diary, "Saw a young lady this Evening who . . . bowed to me and sweetly smiled and to whom, if I am so fortunate as to—ever become intimately acquainted with her I will show this record."[42] He then added, "Meeting with the ladies always throws me into—*perspiration* which promotes health, so it is no harm to look at them."[43] Diaries provided spaces where young men could explore their desires freely. In these more private spaces, we can see that a less restrained culture of sexuality existed on campus, presenting obstacles to young men's maturation. In order to understand how these cultures emerged from and enhanced the tensions inherent in the transition from boyhood to manhood, it is helpful to examine the reality and fiction of sex among one student's circle of friends.

The Reality and Fiction of Sex:
James Dusenbery's Diary

James Lawrence Dusenbery's experiences at North Carolina in the 1840s illuminate students' developing attitudes about women, courtship, sex, and expression. As we saw in chapter 4, Dusenbery had a vivid imagination and unique literary panache. He read novels that exalted valiant knights and lovely ladies, and he wrote about his senior year as a grand, picaresque adventure worthy of a Tom Jones or Don Quixote. Indeed, the most prevalent theme in Dusenbery's writing is his quest for romantic love and the ideal woman. For instance, he described this quest in a story about his journey to Chapel Hill after the last summer of his college years. Dusenbery was saddened at the thought of leaving his friends and relatives, but especially three women he had visited during the summer. Each of the three women had given him a flower as a token of her affections; he named two of the flowers in their honor, Sarah and Elvira. Along the way to Chapel Hill, the pot holding Sarah and Elvira broke, causing the plants to die. The third plant, "the one with out name," however, "escaped uninjured amid the wreck of the matter." The lone survivor "stands in all the pride of conscious beauty & seems to look down in scorn upon its less fortunate companions." Dusenbery insisted that the death of Sarah and Elvira indicated that only the most "uninjured," or virginal, woman was suitable for marriage. "Neither Sarah or Elvira is ever likely to be mine for weal or woe," he complained. "I have never yet seen a woman who resembles my ideal model of female perfection. . . . Until I find one who can enchain my roving desires & fix them on herself alone, my surviving hydrangea shall remain without a name." Until that time, he promised only to "cherish & guard" the surviving, nameless plant in the place of his "fair incognita."[44]

Not long thereafter, Dusenbery met a "very pretty little country girl," the "loving, languid, black-eyed Mary," or "Mary S.," as he sometimes called her, who might have been the "fair incognita" of his dreams. The exact details of James and Mary's introduction and courtship are unclear, though they must have begun courting one another shortly before James Dusenbery left his Lexington home to begin his senior year at the University of North Carolina. His summertime entries candidly reveal many romantic evenings with Mary. For instance, he wrote about sitting with Mary and how they kissed while the rest of the family slept. To enhance the memory of the kiss, he transcribed the following verses in his diary:

In linked sweetness, long drawn out;
 I thought to myself, if it were not a sin,
  I could teach her the prettiest trick in the world:
For oft as we mingled our legs & our feet
 I felt a pulsation & cannot tell whether
In hers or in mine—but I know it was sweet
 And I think we both felt it & trembled together.

These verses begin with a line from Milton's *L'Allegro* (1631): "And ever against eating cares / Lap me in soft Lydian airs, / Married to immortal verse, / Such as the meeting soul may pierce, / In notes with many a winding bout / Of linked sweetness long drawn out." While Milton's original verses describe the "sweetness" of creating poetry, Dusenbery altered their original meaning by adding lines from Thomas Moore's ballad "Fanny of Timmol" (1812), which describe sexual pleasure. Mary's body pulsated against his; their intertwining legs, feet, and bodies trembled as they kissed. Poetry thus provided a means for Dusenbery to express memories of, and desires for, sexual intimacy.[45]

Courting Mary only heightened the tensions between restraint and impulse occurring during youth. Dusenbery admitted that Mary was "as virtuous & chaste as most girls are," but that he was "unused to restraint" and feared committing "the *unpardonable sin* against love & gallantry": sex outside of marriage.[46] So he vowed to restrain his desires and preserve her virginity. Of course, this did not stop Dusenbery from thinking about sex. Dusenbery's commonplace book abounds with popular poems and folk songs about sex. For instance, the fifth poem Dusenbery transcribed into his diary—Moore's "Fanny Was in the Grove" (1808)—tells the story of Lubin, and his beloved, Fanny, who

wandered beneath the shade;
Her eye was dim'd with a tear;
For ah! The poor little maid,
Was thrilling with love and fear.
Oh! oh! if Lubin would but sue,
oh! oh! what could Fanny do?[47]

Dusenbery's choice in literature is important here. As historians of reading have argued, literary transcriptions often reflect an individual reader's emotional history.[48] Dusenbery seemed to choose poetry that reflected the shared values of nineteenth-century male sporting culture common in the urban northeast and the rugged independence of southern honor culture, each of which prized aggressive male sexuality.

In folk ballads and poetry, Dusenbery found an alternate world in which sex with Mary was possible. Between two entries about Mary from the fall of 1841, Dusenbery copied a song narrated by a male voyeur who observes a "damsel, beautiful & gay," bathing in a river. As the narrator watches from a distance, he "manfully" pulls off his clothes, and jumps into the water after her. The rendezvous ends with sex:

> She gave a shove & down she dove
> He brought her up again,
> He carried her over to the other shore,
> O! then, O! then, O! then.
> > Fol da diddle &&
>
> O God! Said she I am undone,
> Unless you'll marry me,
> Before to-morrow's rising sun
> Shines on me & thee
> > Fol d diddle &&

As the song concludes, the narrator promises that the two will "join our hands in Hymen's bands / Get married, & do it again."[49]

Still, not having sex with Mary made Dusenbery increasingly ambivalent about her. "Though I do not really love her," he admitted, "there's none I would rather be kissing than Mary." Then, Mary sent news that her family might move to Illinois, further frustrating Dusenbery. He rejected the letter: "I shall not answer her letter, that she may think herself neglected & banish all thoughts of me from her memory." Yet the following month he remained eager to see her. "I shall probably see her next vacation," he wrote. "If so I tremble for her virtue."[50] James and Mary continued to court that year, though in Mary's absence, Dusenbery found sex elsewhere, usually among prostitutes.

Sex and Intimacy in a "Wilderness of Sin"

In August 1841, soon after he presumably fell in love with Mary S., James Dusenbery wrote a tale (as he was wont to do) about his best friend and classmate, "Gooly," who decided to visit "harlots" in the woods with some friends one summer night. His companions were "men of valour of the tribe of freshmen," and they took with them "gifts of raiment & precious metal" to bestow upon the women when they arrived. Along the way the students encountered obstacles beyond their imaginations. As they approached, "the very trees cried out" and "put forth their arms to forbid their passage." But Gooly and the "men of might" who accompanied him "were hardened in their hearts & pressed forward to give battle to the giants of the forest." Angry because the impetuous youth refused to heed their warning, the giants "pressed sore upon Gooly & smote him between the eyes & he fell upon his face to the earth." And thus, concluded Dusenbery, were "Gooly & the worshippers of Baal discomfited before the giants of the wilderness of Sin."[51]

The story of Gooly and the men of might probably unfolded much like Dusenbery said it did: late at night on 13 August 1841, John Williamson (Gooly), a small group of freshmen, and possibly James Dusenbery all set out to meet with prostitutes in the woods just beyond the University of North Carolina's campus. Perhaps the students intended to visit "the depot," "the fishery," or "the kingdom." These were places around the university where Dusenbery found prostitutes during his junior and senior years. Or perhaps they sought a notorious "old house in the bushes north of the village," where Peyton Clements lived, a hunter, who "made money . . . through several physically attractive daughters, not common to all comers but living as mistresses with chosen lovers."[52] In any case, the students were on a familiar journey that night, when university tutors (whom Dusenbery personified as trees) heard them slip out of the building, chased after them, and shouted to go no farther. The students ignored the tutors' beckoning and persisted in their flight from campus, though doing so constituted a serious violation of university rules.[53] In the end, the tutors caught up with the incorrigible students and apprehended them—"smote" them, in Dusenbery's language—for having violated university regulations. The next day, after reflecting on all that had happened, Dusenbery sat down at his desk in "No. 23, on the 3rd passage of the West Building," picked up his pen, and composed a mock epic about Gooly's misadventures, which he titled "First Chronicles."[54]

In "First Chronicles," Dusenbery transformed the Hebrew world of ancestral tribes, exodus, disobedience, and chastisement into a collegiate world of sex and sin that he knew very well. References to the Wilderness of Sin appear in the historical books of the Old Testament—Numbers,

Kings, Deuteronomy, and Chronicles—which detail the history of the early Hebrew people, but Dusenbery transformed the biblical Wilderness of Sin into a metaphor—and an obvious pun—about boyish impulse and disobedience.[55] Like the disobedient ancestral tribes of the Old Testament, Dusenbery's younger classmates were chastised for disobedience, subordinated to the will of all-powerful elders, and consequently embarrassed and mocked as boyish by their classmates. More significantly, Dusenbery's "First Chronicles" brings into focus not only young men's interactions with one another in an all-male youth environment but also their social and private sexual lives in that setting. This social world of sex stands in stark contrast to the views about women that Dusenbery betrayed in his writing about courting with Mary.

Incidents of students leaving campus to visit prostitutes were not uncommon in the antebellum period, despite institutional efforts to restrain student behavior. Ruffin Tomlinson noted in his diary when students visited prostitutes three times between October 1841 and February 1842, and William Mullins also referred to classmates' "sexual propensities."[56] The university's disciplinary records also provide many examples of students buying sex from prostitutes, and cases of sexually transmitted diseases such as gonorrhea also suggest that casual sex among shared partners was a reality on campus.[57] In May 1842, Ruffin Tomlinson commented in his diary, "College has never been clear of the clap."[58] In 1855, the university faculty "resolved that when any student shall be known to visit a house of ill fame in the village or neighborhood, the fact shall be promptly communicated to his parent or guardian."[59] Indeed, universities across the early republic often were established away from cities to keep students from debauchery, sexual or otherwise. As Kemp P. Battle wrote, "Some of the Faculty would leave their warm beds and engage in a race after the offenders" who set out on late-night sprees.[60] Faculty did not monitor them as vigilantly as they might have, however. Tutors were appointed to monitor each of the two dormitories, but given that they were recent university graduates and close in age to many collegians, their authority was not taken seriously. Still, as with drinking, rowdiness, and novel reading, students remained on their own to seek legitimate outlets for sexual urges.

For Dusenbery and his friends, prostitutes provided outlets that did not require self-mastery in the way that sex in courtship did. During his senior year, Dusenbery described frequent visits to places where he found illicit sex, but with only vague mentions of the locations and the women in question, whom he referred to as Em, Miss Reddness (or Red), and the "Herring gals." Dusenbery frequently visited two of these women, Red and Em, whose identities are uncertain, and he seemed to have had ongoing and simultaneous sexual relationships with them. "I slept at the 'Kingdom' on Thursday night & did not get back to prayers next morning. Miss Redness was in fine spirits." The next week he counted three visits to the depot, followed by a visit to Red. "On Friday night Em was from home," he wrote, and "Red & I passed a . . . glorious night in her bed."[61]

Not all of Dusenbery's sexual experiences involved prostitutes. In August 1841, Dusenbery recalled a trip to the fishery. Dusenbery left campus with two friends, Joseph Nelms and James Caldwell, to meet several other juniors and seniors, as well as one female friend, at the depot. "Taking Em with us, we struck into the woods & half hour's hard walking brought us to the fishery. . . . The object of the excursion was to have a real, downright bull-dance with the Herring gals & as many others as we could get together at that place." Dusenbery and more than twenty other young men and women "all crowded into the little cabin. . . . Every man stripped to his shirt & trowsers" and danced until midnight, when the cabin became too suffocating to dance any longer. Dusenbery "was so overcome with sleep & lassitude" that he went to bed, but his friends stayed awake and engaged in "mysterious proceedings . . . during the dark hours of that ever memorable night." Though Dusenbery did not describe the events that transpired while he slept, his conclusion, "Let a veil forever cover them," was explanation enough.[62]

This night in the cabin was not an isolated incident. The next month, Dusenbery penned a second chapter to "First Chronicles," in which he exposed the illicit sex that occurred at the house of "a certain blind man whose name was Edward," who had a "daughter, who was a harlot . . . exceeding comely & fair to look upon, insomuch that she filled the whole land with her whoredoms & abominations." This girl had fallen in love with "a young man of renown, whose name was Reuben" (read Dusenbery). "In the beginning of the ninth month, even the month Elul," the story goes, this harlot had sent her sister's son, Levi, to deliver a message to Reuben: "Why tarriest thou Reuben? Why comest thou not unto me? My thoughts wait on thee continually. All the day long, am I disquieted concerning thee & in the night time, sleep cometh not to mine eyes, neither slumber to mine eyelids, because of thee. Return thou then unto me, O Reuben." So Reuben got together his friends Rufus, "the mighty songster," and "Gabriel, who bloweth the trumpet," and took "a full measure of wine" for the harlot's father, and "came to the house of Edward" where "they found there two of the damsels"; but the third, intended for Gabriel, was ill, and Gabriel "threw himself on the ground & grieved sore." When Edward's daughter saw Reuben, "she ran & met him & fell upon his neck & kissed him." Reuben "embraced her & comforted her all night long." Likewise, Rufus spent the night with the other woman, or, in Dusenbery's language: "He prevailed with her & solaced himself in her arms all the night long. She was unto him as the loving hind & the pleasing roe; her breasts did satisfy him at all times & he was ravished always with her love."[63]

The male privilege and aggressive sexuality that young men lauded occasionally led to rape. In 1840, for example, a formidable group of sophomore "rowdies" organized a club and initiated a month-long series of pranks, or sprees. The "Soph Rebellion," as students came to call it, consisted of stealing professors' horses, removing their tails and painting them, pouring oil over the chapel pulpit, and smearing the building with paint. The rebellious lot then "blackened themselves" and went to a local "negro house," where they "seized Suky Mayhs, a common negro prostitute, tore off her clothes, and painted her naked body!!!" In other words, students assaulted, and perhaps raped, a local slave woman. Their behavior provoked "universal indignation among the Gentlemen of the College" as well as the faculty; the culprits were ultimately expelled from the university.[64] It is likely that some of the "prostitutes" whom students mentioned in their diaries were enslaved women, though students were usually silent on the matter. Despite the condemnation of the students' behavior, these examples demonstrate that casual—even coercive sex—was often excused among male youth because the women with whom they were having sex were either lower-class whites or slaves.

Students' experiences in the "wilderness of sin" reflect the influence of class and race in male thinking about sexuality. Broadly, these relationships could be understood as educational insofar as they provided practice in sexual intimacy before marriage without violating elite sexual mores calling for restraint in relationships with "virtuous" women. Dusenbery and his friends may have found in prostitution an opportunity for what C. Dallett Hemphill calls an "apprenticeship in the sex . . . young men anticipated in marriage."[65] In New York City, the prostitute Helen Jewett sustained relationships with middle-class men—they wrote love letters and play-acted courtship.[66] These relationships were bound by racial as well as class lines.

Extant records do not indicate that students sustained sexual relationships with black women as they seemed to have had with lower-class white prostitutes. Activities in the wilderness of sin instead reinforced male sexual privilege and southern notions of caste and class. Moreover, they legitimated notions that elite white women were "passionless," but that lower-class whites and black women, on account of their innate lack of virtue, were fair game for sexual exploitation.[67] Young men relied on claims about women's virtue based on class and race, to legitimate their sexual behavior. Community approval of this behavior, in turn, validated young men's claims to honor and manly independence.

Young men's informal education in sex and intimacy was deeply influenced by a powerful sexual double standard that defined nineteenth-century elite and middle-class culture in the North and the South. This culture, as Patricia Cline Cohen has argued, "was steeped in the conviction that chaste and respectable women experienced negligible sexual desire and could easily become victims of lustful men. Rarely was male sexual interest itself called into question or rendered problematic."[68] This was a learned behavior. Dusenbery's experiences with Mary S. and in the wilderness of sin, particularly the bragging tone that comes to the surface in his creative exposition about Gooly and the mighty freshmen, show that the southern code of honor sanctioned, even applauded, promiscuity. This conviction shaped young southern collegians' developing attitudes about both masculinity and femininity. Moreover, faculty members, tutors, and parents often turned a blind eye to young men's aggressive sexuality, only inveighing against transgressions when made public. This pattern reflects experiences throughout the early and antebellum republic, when single young men, middle class and elite, left home to make their own manhood.[69] At the same time, a growing insistence on young men's character development, their private and public exercise of virtue, required an altogether different behavior (and an altogether different education) than that found in the wilderness of sin. In public and private experiences of courtship, the ideas of chastity—both male and female—demanded that young men articulate a more refined character. These two contradictory cultures frustrated Dusenbery in his relationship with Mary. Thus, young southern men's emerging sexuality hung in the balance between impulse and restraint, and they had to find legitimate outlets for their sexual urges in keeping with each moral code.

STUDENTS' EXPERIENCES WITH ROMANTIC LOVE, courtship, and intimacy at college provided a powerful informal curriculum in which young men learned how to think about and interact with women. On the one hand, many students sought prostitution as well as casual, and sometimes coercive, sex. On the other hand, many of those same students who visited brothels on the weekends engaged in formal courtship rituals within a more restrained, bourgeois culture of respectability. In visiting parties, balls, and formal courtship, students had to exercise restraint.

Significantly, these worlds of impulse and restraint coexisted in students' informal curriculum at college. Indeed, education happened whenever students faced this tension—when they faced the "Choice of Hercules" of virtue over vice. Ultimately, this education reaffirmed prevailing attitudes about gender roles and separate spheres, and it maintained class- and race-based hierarchies by favoring white men's sexual prerogatives above all else. As with other facets of their education, therefore, the antebellum students' experiences of love, courtship, and sex had direct relevance to women of their social standing, as well as lower-class white and enslaved women. Students' attitudes about women developed as they sustained long-held relationships with mothers, sisters, and girlfriends, and as they pursued new relationships with girlfriends at college. In college, students learned to live as men in a gendered culture influenced at once by traditional southern notions of honor and rugged independence, and more restrained, bourgeois expressions of manhood such as sobriety, temperance, and chastity.

PART III

SOCIETY
Applying Intellectual Manhood

Parts I and II have demonstrated the importance of the individual self in young men's maturation and education. The formal curriculum provided the resources, tools, and ideals for idealizing and constructing intellectual manhood. In the informal curriculum, students used these resources to shape and make sense out of everything from growing up to reading to sex. In the process, young men created visions of male selfhood that were inextricable from the power of intellectual manhood. In college, however, students did not know exactly what roles they would play in life's drama; all they knew was that education endowed them with the potential to play a fundamentally heroic role. Part III, therefore, brings the ideals of intellectual manhood and the exercises of self-culture together as it explores young men's weekly literary society debate exercises. The premise is that student debates can reveal the broad public significance young men ascribed to intellectual manhood. Specifically, this chapter addresses the public questions that students believed awaited them as adult members of the educated class. Often cited as the most important aspect of higher education, debate allowed students to try on their education and create a cultural space in which boyhood was a shadow.

Throughout the first two parts of this book, certain continuities in the intellectual culture of higher education placed southern higher education squarely in the context of a growing Victorian, bourgeois culture in the United States. This culture elevated a restrained style of manhood characterized as intellectual manhood, which synthesized the traditional southern gentry's man of reason, oratory, and performance with the emerging bourgeois man of sobriety, industry, and piety. The hope was to become the Victorian gentleman who could lead the republic, intellectual culture, and family to the benefit of society. In so doing, he would reach the heights of fame along life's unpredictable and dangerous journey. Moreover, their visions of power emanated from assumptions that intellectual manhood distinguished males as adult—superior to dependents, including children, women, common folk, and both free and enslaved blacks. As was true throughout formal and informal college life, these dependents were largely symbolic in the collegians' world.

Students' weekly debate exercises reveal how these features of intellectual culture came together. Held in closed sessions, literary society debates oriented young men's attention to their own group of peers and elevated the opinions of a distinctly male community. As studies in southern honor have revealed, these communities were the ultimate source of validation of intellectual manhood. Thus, individual debates did not have an immediate effect on others. This is not to say, however, that the skills and opinions formed in debate did not matter in the lives of others. Ultimately, they would. As adult members of the educated class, college alumni occupied professional and public positions of authority in which the skills of debate, and the opinions formed in debate, could silence or empower others.

While students' debates certainly were unique in their college context—safe from university oversight and public censorship—they were part and parcel of the performative life of men within the broader southern educated class. Indeed, students themselves viewed their societies as microcosms of a wider world of politics and power. In 1799, one student urged his fellow members of the Dialectic Society to "cultivate and exercise in miniature the principles & actions which will be so necessary when we enter the expanded stage of action." And in 1827, another student echoed that invocation, calling the Dialectic Society a "world in miniature." Thus, when students engaged in weekly debates, they performed the roles of intellectual manhood in ways that were unmatched by any other college experience. In debate, therefore, knowledge, restraint, independence, self-confidence, and heroic vision came together in rich educational experiences, as students performed intellectual manhood within a community of peers.

Although this book has largely examined cultural continuities of intellectual life, great political and social changes did occur, calling to question the meaning and extent of American democracy, the merits of modernizing social and economic structures, and the role and future of slavery within the nation. Although some historians have argued that regionalism was the strongest force acting on young men's education and maturation at college in the early nineteenth century, intellectual culture paints a different picture. As young North Carolinians grappled with change, they did not automatically or blindly embrace regional arguments. Their debates instead remind us of the diverse patterns of southern intellectual life and culture in the antebellum era, as well as the absolute unpredictability of disunion and civil war. Indeed, regionalism did not begin to influence young men's experiences of education and maturation until the very end of the 1850s. At that time, the weight of sectional conflict, the urgency of the proslavery argument, and the faint cries for secession slowly began to erode a long-standing antebellum consensus that students went to college to learn to become American men. The best gauge for the influence of these changes on the intellectual culture of higher education, and, by extension, young men's identity formation, is how students debated them in their literary societies.

CHAPTER SEVEN

The Outward Thrust of Male Higher Education
Debating Every Great Public Question

On 5 June 1844, James Biddle Shepard, the North Carolina state representative from Wake County, former state senator, and 1834 graduate of the University of North Carolina, delivered a commencement address before his alma mater's two literary societies. After encouraging his audience in their educational pursuits, he drew their attention to oratory: "In this country, gentlemen, popular eloquence is the most powerful of all arts. Here the people make and repeal their own laws at their own pleasure. . . . Every great public question, whether of war or of peace, whether of internal or external policy, is fully discussed in their presence. . . . How important, then, is it that the orator should have truth and justice on his side!"[1] No one attending Shepard's speech would have doubted the significance of debating "every great public question" to the pursuit of intellectual manhood.[2] Students believed that debate, like the formal curriculum, "strengthen[ed] the reasoning powers and extend[ed] the empire of research."[3] Students also believed that debate prepared them for public life in politics, law, ministry, medicine, business, and commerce. Even students who became farmers or planters learned through debate to think on their feet and have confidence in their convictions.[4] So what were these great public questions to which Sheppard referred? How did young men define those questions and prepare for them in college? And what relevance did that preparation have to southern public life?

In debate, young men defined discursively what Stephanie McCurry terms "boundaries of power," delineating men's expected roles in terms of gender, class, and race.[5] Because these debates served a powerful function both in young men's education and in their future participation in public life, this chapter first explains the form, process, and history of debates. Be-

173

tween 1795 and 1861, students debated questions related to current affairs; philosophy and morality; government and political economy; history and biography; and education, arts, and sciences. Most questions that students debated related to current affairs. Four issues most vividly highlight how young men learned to enact public roles, as well as define and set power boundaries: reform in antebellum North Carolina; women's rights; Indian removal; and slavery. Each of these issues was rooted in the dramatic transformations of the U.S. economy and political culture in the wake of the "market revolution" following the War of 1812, and each topic tested the limits of young men's commitments to progress and democracy.

These topics were particularly relevant in North Carolina during the entire period under study and point to its unique position within the South. Known as the "Rip Van Winkle state," North Carolina lagged behind the rest of the country in its material and economic development. Equating material progress to moral progress, young men consistently pursued questions about internal improvements and political reform in their literary societies because they considered modernizing and democratizing public life for white men of utmost importance. However, they struggled with that impulse when it came to women, Indians, and slaves, though they did not entirely reject it. Instead, they grappled with the paradoxical embrace of freedom, progress, and slavery—what Eugene D. Genovese termed "the slaveholders' dilemma."[6]

Here, change over time within student intellectual culture is most discernible. Before the 1830s, North Carolina students generally opposed slavery, but after Nat Turner's 1831 rebellion and the subsequent rise of abolitionism, they increasingly expressed proslavery beliefs, though even those attitudes did not go unchallenged. Debates about these topics demonstrate one way in which antebellum students learned to deploy the language of racial, cultural, and gender differences to wield great power over others. Most importantly, these debates bring into focus the intellectual process by which students developed identities that became distinctively southern in terms of slavery and race. The chapter, therefore, concludes with a discussion of the effects of regionalism on student debates. Even as students felt the increasing pressure of sectionalism in the late antebellum period, there was no consensus that regional identity should ever trump American identity. For us to understand the relationships between self and society that students explored in debates, we must first understand how debating occurred in literary societies.

Literary Society Debating

Members of the Dialectic and Philanthropic Societies followed similar debate procedures as literary societies in colleges and universities throughout the early republic and across the Atlantic.[7] Debates were held only among members of one society, usually on Friday evenings between seven and ten o'clock, as part of the society's "regular business."[8] A week in advance of a debate, society presidents announced a query and appointed one principal debater and two assistants for each side.[9] Debates always proceeded in the style of English-language forensic disputation, whereby two opposing debaters answered a single open-ended question such as "Does civilization increase happiness?" or "Should a college be located in a city or in the country?"[10] This debate style imitated the public arena ("forensic" derives from the Latin noun "forum," meaning public assembly or affairs), and it was the common legal and legislative style of debate.[11] Forensic debates were highly structured and followed a predictable pattern. First, principal debaters on each side delivered speeches prepared in advance. Second, assistant debaters continued the debate and then opened the question to the floor. Finally, the society president recapitulated the arguments, the society voted *viva voce*, and the secretary recorded the resolution as either "affirmative" or "negative" in the minutes. Sometimes, though rarely, secretaries noted the length of a debate, or the level of excitement (or boredom), but they never recorded points raised or contested during debate proceedings.

Ideally, forensic debating honed important skills of intellectual manhood such as self-discipline, attention, rhetoric, and oratory. Principal and assistant debaters were supposed to prepare for debates by reading books on the subject, writing their addresses, and circulating drafts in advance. Debaters must have circulated drafts of their speeches among the opposing team prior to debates because many speeches from one side of a debate contain exact quotations from speeches from the other.[12] Not all students, of course, were so diligent. In 1851, George Thompson debated the question "Does the Theatre have an immoral tendency," but he wrote in his journal that day that he "did not make much of a speech."[13] Some students merely disliked debating. "Land, how the Society bothers me very much indeed, and I heartily wish I had not ever seen it," James Hilliard Polk complained in 1859. "To debate is entirely contrary to my principles and having to be fined every other Friday night is rather too expensive, and to make a fool of myself is not what I intend to do if I can avoid it."[14] Many students like

Polk would rather have paid a fine than participate in debates.[15] Neverthe-less, the debates themselves offer a unique portrait of students' intellectual world and the broad relevance of intellectual manhood to North Carolina and the South.

Across the board, literary society debate questions fall into five major categories: current affairs; philosophy and morality; government and po-litical economy; history and biography; and education, arts, and sciences.[16] First, questions about current affairs were the most debated category over-all. Thirty-seven percent of nearly 4,000 debates held in the Dialectic and Philanthropic Societies between 1795 and 1861 fit into this category. These were debates about current political and legal questions discussed at the national, state, and local level, American foreign relations, and also ethical problems that emerged in light of current events in the United States and abroad. Of all the debates in the current affairs category (1,421), 70 percent addressed national affairs, 20 percent addressed North Carolina affairs, and 10 percent addressed global affairs.

Second to current affairs, questions about philosophy and morality made up 22 percent of debates. These questions addressed three types of philo-sophical inquiry commonly categorized in the nineteenth century as men-tal, natural, and moral philosophy. Questions in this category dealt with theology, the meaning of life, the origins and happiness of man, art and nature, right versus wrong, and conduct of life. Here, students often con-sidered questions that related to the transition from youth to manhood, particularly tensions between impulse and restraint and between maturity and immaturity that characterized their formal education and self-culture. For instance, students selected questions that dealt with young men's im-mediate concerns about college life, youth, and conduct of life, including questions about "Debauchery or Drunkenness," dancing, theatre, and other social customs.[17] Moreover, they anticipated their future professional and public lives, asking questions about selecting the "most useful" professions or about ethical conduct in professional life.[18]

Third, government and political economy questions made up 17 percent of debates. These questions dealt largely with the "nature of civil govern-ment and the perfect right of individuals," "republican principles," the "sta-bility of government," and the "preservation of liberty."[19] Students were interested especially in types of government; taxes; public office; agricul-ture versus commerce; and representation, or theories and ethics related to representation. Questions about government and questions about current affairs tended to overlap.

Fourth, modern and ancient historical and biographical questions also made up 17 percent of debates. Forty-four percent of these debates concerned Europe, 28 percent focused on America, and another 28 percent dealt with ancient Greece and Rome as well as general historical inquiries. Finally, questions within the education, arts, and sciences category were the least debated, only 7 percent of debates. Questions in this category examined knowledge, learning, and literature; the collegiate classical curriculum, especially ancient versus modern languages and literature; and student life, faculty governance, and discipline at the University of North Carolina.

Questions that North Carolina students debated did not differ substantially from questions entertained in similar societies throughout the United States and even Great Britain, suggesting a common source for inquiry.[20] No study has traced debates to a common source, but debate questions seem to have been passed down from generation to generation. Extant records from an unknown Greensboro, North Carolina, debating club, the Philomathean Society, reveal that boys debated many of the same questions as collegians. Between 1840 and 1849, members of the Philomathean society debated questions related to education, philosophy, current affairs, government, and history. As was the case with college literary societies, the Philomatheans debated more current affairs questions than any other category of questions; historical questions were a close second.[21]

Neither society formally imposed restrictions on questions. This was not always the case at other colleges, especially the denominational colleges. At Wake Forest College, founded in 1834 by the Baptist State Convention of North Carolina, the Euzelian and Philomathesian literary societies forbade debates on religious topics.[22] There were no such restrictions at North Carolina or other comparable state colleges in the United States. Nevertheless, neither the Dialectic nor the Philanthropic Society debated religious questions that would have undermined Protestant Christianity. Similarly, students did not ban discussion of party politics outright, but they tended to shy away from discussing specific partisan positions or candidates. And while they generally approached public questions from either Whig or Democratic perspectives (or sometimes both), students rarely debated parties *per se*. In 1852, the Dialectic Society debated whether students should even study politics, let alone discuss them in literary societies.[23] In fact, students frequently admonished one another in society addresses for displaying too much "party spirit," causing factions to form among students who otherwise considered themselves a "band of brothers."

Every generation of students looked to debates to understand their obligations to self and to society, but student interest in modes of understanding those obligations changed dramatically between 1795 and 1861. Around 1820, questions about current affairs replaced philosophy and morality questions as the most debated. At the same time, historical questions gained a certain cachet, and by the 1850s they nearly surpassed the number of current affairs questions. This sustained emphasis of current affairs demonstrates that, among antebellum students, learning to decide "every great public question" mattered more than learning for learning's sake. Several factors account for this paradigm shift. First, fewer philosophical questions reflect a simultaneous decline of the Enlightenment in American culture and stagnation of collegiate classical curricula. More simply, students sought a more modern, more relevant mode of investigating the world around them. Second, the rise of the Second Party System and practical politics in the 1820s came to replace policy making directed by theory about republican government.

Most significantly, these epistemic shifts were rooted in print and communication developments that led to greater availability of print material in rural areas, including the Dialectic and Philanthropic Society libraries. Major national and regional periodicals provided sources for debate, including *Blackwood's Edinburgh Magazine*, the *North American Review*, *DeBow's Review*, and the *Southern Literary Messenger*, to name only a few titles.[24] Moreover, students read local newspapers such as the Hillsboro *Recorder* and the Raleigh *Register*, the most widespread newspaper in the state, which they could obtain locally within the village. The editors of the *Register* maintained a close relationship with the university between 1795 and 1861. Their office printed addresses for the literary societies, provided books, and, in the late antebellum period, printed the students' literary magazine. The *Register* followed national politics closely and espoused nationalist ideologies in every current debate save for abolition.[25] While debate records do not suggest a direct correlation between articles printed in the *Register* or any other news source, they do suggest a correlation between increased availability of news sources and interest in current affairs. Thus, as students generated debate queries and crafted arguments, they relied on the resources available to them in their informal curriculum, particularly in their literary society libraries.

Current affairs debates, more than any other category, illuminate how young men created opportunities to apply education to society. Among these questions, four topics merit close attention: internal improvements, women's rights, federal removal policy, and slavery. In debating each of these current affairs topics, young men reproduced prevailing ideologies about gender, race, and belonging. Through debate they not only learned to become citizens and leaders of North Carolina, the South, and the United States, but also to define the parameters of belonging for others.

Reform and Improvement in North Carolina

Debates about North Carolina current affairs enabled young men to use their higher education to the benefit of the state as a whole. As mentioned earlier, North Carolina lagged behind the nation in terms of economic and technological development to such an extent that it became known as the "Rip Van Winkle state." The soil was poor; crops could not make it to market due to a lack of roads and canals; and the people were poorly educated. Traveling throughout the state, Frederick Law Olmstead noted, "North Carolina has a proverbial reputation for the ignorance and torpidity of her people; being, in this respect, at the head of the Slave States."[26] Moreover, the population's growth rate collapsed on account of large-scale emigration to the western frontier, as men hoping to strike it rich through cotton and land speculation (or both) left North Carolina for states like Alabama and Mississippi. At the same time as North Carolina's infrastructure and economy stagnated, calls for a more democratic government echoed in the state's legislative halls. There were three major sources of discontent with the government. First, eastern North Carolina was disproportionately represented in the legislature, as only a few new counties had been established west of Raleigh between 1800 and 1834. Second, white male participation in state government remained significantly limited. At the same time as surrounding states allowed unlimited white male suffrage, North Carolina's constitution maintained that only landholders of fifty acres or more could vote for senator. Moreover, governors and sheriffs could not be popularly elected at all. Third, North Carolina's penal codes remained arcane and enforced only haphazardly at local levels.

Political attempts to ameliorate these grave conditions were few and far between. Only a small handful of reformers—many of whom were North Carolina graduates—began to champion statewide internal improvements in the 1820s. Some reformers such as North Carolina alumnus Archibald Debow Murphey focused attention on improving transportation, including building railroads, roads, and canals, so that North Carolina could participate more fully in the growing national market economy. Others such as Calvin Henderson Wiley, one of the region's most vocal champions of common schools, promoted literacy and education in the state. Finally, university president David Swain was an important advocate for governmental reform. Between 1800 and 1834 there were several calls for a constitutional convention, which finally was held in 1835, expanding representation and voting, though not completely. Another convention would bring universal white male suffrage in 1850. Debates about North Carolina's advancement, then, were perennial questions and had an impact on every generation of students in the antebellum period.

Internal improvements and government reform consumed much student attention. In an 1832 address to his fellow members of the Dialectic Society, nineteen-year-old Jonathan Lindsay Hargrave explained that North Carolina's needs were urgent, and he called on his classmates to consider their "duties as citizens of North Carolina": "She [North Carolina] appeals to us, in the lamentations of her ruined farmers, and the houseless poor, and weeps tears of blood while she points us to the sturdy yeomanry of the country, gathering up the wrecks of their broken fortunes, and with slow & sorrowful steps directing their course to the far west." To Hargrave, the mandate was clear: North Carolina's "rising generation" had a duty to solve the state's greatest problems. Literary society debates about North Carolina's current affairs allowed antebellum students such an opportunity to think through ways to promote the state's "physical and political advancement."[27]

The rising generation's concerns for North Carolina's advancement pivoted around issues of modernization, especially penal reform. Approximately 51 percent of Dialectic Society debates about North Carolina's current affairs dealt with improving the state's penal code. A duplication of the harsh, often torturous system of punishment imported from English common law during the colonial period, North Carolina's antebellum penal system allowed for the branding of women, imprisonment of debtors, and execution of individuals for dueling, theft, horse stealing, and forgery, among other crimes. These capital offenses met with the worst punishment: execution by hanging, torture, whipping, and life imprisonment. There had long been public concern over the harsh penal codes in the state as well as legislative agitation for a state penitentiary. Archibald Murphey had first recommended that the legislature establish a penitentiary, though the bill was rejected by a popular referendum in 1846 and never passed before the Civil War.[28] North Carolina's literary societies questioned whether individuals should be imprisoned for debt or hanged for stealing horses, but the most prevalent question was whether North Carolina should erect a penitentiary for reforming criminals.[29] Nevertheless, students participated in ongoing debates to reform the penal system because they believed doing so advanced the common good and promised to modernize North Carolina's criminal justice system.

The second most important problem facing North Carolina in the antebellum period, according to students' debate questions, was constitutional reform. About one-quarter of the questions students posed about North Carolina current affairs consisted of questions about North Carolina's 1776 constitution. Students first entertained these questions in the early 1820s, when movement for a constitutional convention first occurred, and again in the 1830s when another convention was called.[30] In these debates we see the clearest evidence that students from the western part of the state— the Dis—expressed Whig principles and those from the eastern part of the state—the Phis—expressed Democratic principles. Nearly every time the Dis debated whether or not a constitutional convention ought to be held, whether voting should be opened to all white men rather than just free-holders, and whether the governor ought to be popularly elected, they favored reform. On the other hand, each time those issues arose in the Philanthropic Society, the Phis tended to favor the status quo, exhibiting the most resistance to democratization.[31]

Not all students favored democratization, particularly eastern North Carolinians, who tended to join the Philanthropic Society. Eastern North Carolina had been home to many of the state's wealthiest planters as well as the seat of power until the 1835 Constitutional Convention, when additional counties were created in the western part of the state to balance representation in the General Assembly. At the height of national and state discussions about constitutional reform, members of the Philanthropic Society demonstrated significant, though by no means total, resistance to democratizing state representation. Between 1795 and 1834, the Phis tended to favor more exclusive government in which the state legislature voted for governor; they also resolved against allowing non-Christians to hold office. Only once did the society resolve that the "privilege of voting" not be "confined to freeholders." Moreover, they backed resolutions in formal debate that a constitutional convention should not be called in North Carolina, and that "the basis of representation" should not be changed.[32] In contrast, the Dis tended to favor calling a constitutional convention, splitting western counties for additional representation, and even moving the state capital from Raleigh.[33]

This regional disparity was also evident in each society's debates about internal improvements. In 1828, the president of the university, Joseph Caldwell, published a series of articles, *The Numbers of Carlton*, in which he extolled the power of railroads and proposed that the state government build a railroad from Beaufort through New Bern and Raleigh. He hoped this railroad would channel trade and improve the state's lagging economy.[34] Each society debated whether or not North Carolina should establish a central railroad system. Interestingly, not all Democratic-leaning Phis rejected antebellum reform, and not all Dis embraced it. The Phis often supported the establishment of common schools in North Carolina along with the Dialectic Society.[35]

Overall, students debated issues that got to the heart of what defined citizenship, what defined leadership, and how they, as educated North Carolinians, would shape the broader political culture of the era. Questions of inclusion and exclusion, no doubt, were central concerns here. As students looked for opportunities to exercise civic virtue in "every great public question," they also confronted the glaring contradictions in their commitment to progress and democracy. How did they reconcile their belief in republican virtue, liberty, reform, and material progress in a state and nation that denied women's political rights, removed its native inhabitants from their ancestral lands, and condoned enslavement? Literary society debating provided a means by which young men could address each of these questions and explore the most significant tensions of their time. In the process, young men defined and set parameters around republican citizenship and belonging in ways that confirmed, rather than challenged, prevailing attitudes about gender, culture, and race. No evidence suggests an immediate effect of these debates on others. Nevertheless, these debates would shape the adult perspectives of generations of future lawyers, physicians, clergy, and statesmen, indeed the entire educated class, who would set the parameters of belonging for many in antebellum North Carolina, including especially women, Native Americans, and slaves.

Debating Women

On 18 October 1820, the members of the Philanthropic Society were supposed to debate the question "Should a woman be punished as a murderer by the use of improper means [to] destroy her unborn child?" At no prior time in either the Dialectic or Philanthropic Society's histories had students entertained a question about abortion, though the topic, as worded, resonated with the perennial issue of penal reform in North Carolina. Yet when the Phis convened the day's meeting, Alexander Sims introduced a motion to "dispense with said query" because the topic was "not very becoming and perhaps less improving and more over in a manner calculated to produce levity and disorder in the Hall." In its place, Sims returned to the Society's Enlightenment roots and proposed the less controversial and frequently debated question "Is most happiness to be enjoyed in a state of nature or civilization." The motion passed, and neither the Phis nor the Dis ever considered publicly the question of abortion in weekly debate exercises. But how did this question differ from other questions about crime and punishment? How might a debate about abortion produce levity? Were young men concerned that the discussion might become uncomfortably graphic? On one hand, students' last-minute dismissal of the abortion question reflects the expectation of propriety when it came to the South's educated class. On the other hand, the silence on this issue underscores a broader pattern of excluding women in the process of defining and gendering the public sphere.

As the dismissal of the abortion question illustrates, literary society debates could have significant bearing on the lives of women. Often they took the form of moral philosophical questions about young men's private duties as husbands and fathers. Recall that Francis Wayland's *The Elements of Moral Science* provided a coherent, biblically grounded moral system governing gendered roles within the household, especially the duties of marriage. Occasionally these topics entered literary society discourse, as students explored issues such as bachelorhood, marriage, divorce, and polygamy. In 1805, the Dis resolved that polygamy was not "justifiable"; in 1807, that "divorces [were] morally or politically admittable on any occasion"; in

1835, that "marriages contribute[d] to the happiness of life"; in 1824, that a man should never "marry for money"; and in 1850, that a man was "morally bound to marry."[36] Yet these questions involved men's expected gender roles, not women's.

Indeed, explicit questions about women were few and far between. Between the two societies, students debated questions about women only thirty times from 1795 to 1860, or a few times per decade. Not only were women excluded physically from debates, but they were also excluded discursively, underscoring young men's conception of public life as entirely masculine.[37] They held fast, in other words, to the doctrine of separate spheres. Separate spheres reflected a belief in sex roles rooted in innate biological differences and affirmed through divine revelation in Scriptures.[38] Students relied on these ideas in debates about women's education and political rights. In 1809, John Briggs Mebane explained this doctrine to his fellow members of the Dialectic Society: "It is evident then from reason from the uniform course of nature from experiment and from the word of God that females are destined for different persuits and employments from men, and that the sphere of their activity should be different."[39] Moreover, young men demonstrated a developing consciousness of their own paternalistic duties to women that, in many ways, resembled their racial and cultural consciousness in debates about slaves, free blacks, and Native Americans. As one student put it in a composition delivered before the Dialectic Society in 1816, men had a duty "to defend an amiable, and helpless part of Creation."[40] Yet the discourse of separate spheres was quite powerful, and young men relied on this ideology in their formal and informal university education.

Questions involving women fit into three major categories. First, students probed theoretical questions about whether or not women and men possessed the same intellectual and moral qualities, whether, in the words of one Philanthropic Society question, "the female sex [is] inferior in intellectual faculties to the male sex." Sometimes, however, students argued from an a priori assumption that women's intellectual faculties were inferior; the task in such a case was to identify the root of "mental differences between the sexes" in nature or nurture. Second, these questions about women's mental capacities were related to the most prevalent question appearing in the records about women: whether women ought to have liberal educations. Third, they debated whether women ought, in any circumstance, to hold political office. Elsewhere in the United States, collegians debated similar questions with similarly varying and unpredictable resolutions. For example, in 1820 the Ohio University Athenian Society debated whether females were "capable of receiving & retaining knowledge as males, and is their faculty of judging as correct" and decided the question in the negative. Three years later, in a close 8–6 vote, the Athenians reversed their position. In 1856, Harvard College's Institute of 1770 debated the question "Are women equally gifted with men?" and decided that they were not. While the spirit of many of these questions about women and society echoed a commitment to reform found in other current affairs debates, the nuance of student resolutions reflected a resistance to democratic views regarding the equality of women and men in citizenship.[41]

Even though these questions did not immediately influence women's lives, students addressed similar topics in broader community discourse and women participated. In 1852, a series of essays about women's rights was published in the *North Carolina University Magazine*, causing quite the ruckus among students and the magazine's female readers. The hullabaloo began with the anonymous publication of a short essay entitled "A Glance into the Social Circle," which declared women's intrinsic inferiority. "We make no appeals to revelation or statute for evidence of her [woman's] natural inferiority to man," the author began, "since it seems to us that Nature grants the fact without interrogation." In the author's estimation, young women grew up with "no appreciation of man and no concern about worth of virtue or greatness." Moreover, excessive interest in fashion and polite society made women degenerate and certainly unworthy of the rights and independence for which they clamored. "Woman's Rights," the author continued, "must not be left to the determination of her own silly caprices. The glittering allurements of pomp and Fashion are too enticing for her weakness. Rather reinstate her in the bounds of her past seclusion." The author's solution, in other words, was the doctrine of separate spheres: "Task her [woman] with stern lessons of obedience, and conquer the will which refuses to know its duty, and she will bless and adorn the paths of virtue. But leave her in this age to the false training of Fashion, subject her yielding intellect to the guidance of modern customs and schools, and you form a tawdry instrument to dam the currents of social life, and finally fret out its own short existence beneath the tortures of artificial restraint."[42]

This perspective did not go uncontested. In the same issue, the editors included another article, "Mind—Masculine and Feminine," refuting the premise of woman's natural inferiority. Writing under the pseudonym

Prexsus, the author argues that women, like men, share the ultimate destiny for salvation under God and cannot be deemed inferior to man. Yet the author did not undermine the doctrine of separate spheres. Women were "weaker intellectually, as physically," he argued, "and therefore calculated for a subordinate and dependent station." And contrary to the claims of women who gathered in "conventions," the author mocked, women were naturally unfit to claim the mantle of author. Any woman who ever possessed authority in literature or government were only exceptions to that norm, for "Providence," concludes the author, "surely intended such women to be only the exceptions."[43]

"A Glance into the Social Circle" generated more attention from female readers perhaps than any other publication in the *Magazine*. "Messrs. Editors," one female reader wrote, "you cannot imagine what a very gratifying circumstance it is to your lady-readers, to see the marked interest in their improvement manifested by certain of your correspondents. A crowd of us have just had a conference over the April number of your Magazine, and we agreed, unanimously, that it spoke well for the N. C. U. M., that so large a portion of its early pages should be devoted to furthering the progress of the world's 'better half.'" Speaking for a united front of female readers, the author took issue with the haphazard dismissal of women as inferior, suggesting, "If the Marys and Elizabeths of our day were to set up a magazine," she wrote, perhaps the conversation "might be pointed out in another direction." And in what direction would that conversation go? Yes, she argued, women "are the great social agents," and yes, "their educations are incomplete, and their schools mere nurseries for the respective churches," but this is not the whole story. She asked the authors to provide evidence for women's caprices and silly "chit chat"; she defied them to "point out to us, any young *man* of reasonable years of discretion, who has, to his knowledge, either directly or indirectly made an attempt to raise the general tone of social chit chat, by the introduction or suggestion of higher topics." "Our caprices are not so very 'silly,'" she concluded. "At all events, don't think of such a thing as 'tasking *all* of us with stern lessons of obedience, to conquer the wills that refuse to know their duty.' (We should like to see you try it, by the way.)"[44] Although women could not participate in society debates, when young men introduced the topic in public forums, women voiced opinions.

This volley between male authors and female readers not only demonstrates intellectual exchange outside of an all-male collegiate context but also reveals women's willingness and power to challenge social boundaries. In reality, separate spheres were not so tidy as young men expressed in their ideological invectives against women's rights. Historians have demonstrated that boundaries between women's "domestic sphere" and men's "public sphere" were fluid; women found ways to participate in public life and men often participated in domestic life.[45] Not surprisingly, then, women entered the discussion about their own rights and social position that young men introduced in the *North Carolina University Magazine*.

Debating Native Americans

Public policy questions concerning Native Americans were among the greatest facing educated men in the Old South. After the War of 1812, the U.S. economy and infrastructure developed at an unprecedented rate, and the South's cotton economy expanded to meet new industrial demands. Southerners increasingly looked to the territory of the Old Southwest for land to plant cotton, and Indian lands became highly coveted. In the 1820s and 30s, states pressured Native Americans to sell lands in Georgia, Mississippi, and Tennessee, and members of Congress, including some North Carolina graduates, considered measures for forcefully removing Indians. In 1830, Congress passed the Indian Removal Act, which President Jackson promptly signed into law, beginning years of forced migration westward to Oklahoma. By the decade's end approximately 100,000 Indians were removed.[46]

Young men did not shy away from debating Indian removal policy. In the Dialectic and Philanthropic Societies, students debated many questions relevant to broader discourse about Native Americans and their place in the U.S. South: whether Europeans justifiably took possession of Indian lands, whether the United States had any rights to those lands, and whether white citizens had a moral obligation to protect Indians from their supposed impending extinction.[47]

Students' outlook rested squarely on Enlightenment philosophies about civilization, savagery, and the perfectibility of mankind. They often debated whether or not civilization or savagery produced more social happiness.[48] These questions about civilization and savagery in the abstract had a bearing on students' more practical debates about the place of Indians in the contemporary United States. Antebellum students clung to prevailing assumptions that Indians lived in a state of nature and, as a result, faced extinction as white civilization progressed materially and technologically. Yet their humanity was certain. Echoing Jefferson's profession to the Marquis de Chastellux that Indians were "in body and mind equal to the whiteman," young North Carolinians believed that Indians possessed a "natural disposition" to civilization but were so "long clouded and obscured by barbarism" that they did not know how to civilize themselves.[49] One student put it this way in 1825: "Did Rome—did England produce her specimens of great talents, whilst in a state even as much better [than] that of the American Indians? But sir they [Indians] do possess talents, which were the[y] cultivated would shine as bright as those of the proud Americans."[50] Indians, in other words, were culturally, but not racially, inferior to whites. Student debates on the place of Indians in the South and United States reflected these assumptions.

Between 1800 and 1825, students debated whether or not the federal government should attend to civilizing American Indians. Students in each society voted, in every instance, in favor of establishing religious missions for civilizing Indians and for a federal civilization policy. In August 1818, members of the Dialectic Society debated—and supported—Congress's recent Civilization Bill. According to students, the bill allowed the federal government to take "measures to civilize the Indians within their Territories," providing subsidies to churches to establish missions in Indian country. And, in 1823, the society agreed that missionaries should be "encouraged in Christianizing the Indians." When the question of whether to continue late eighteenth- and early nineteenth-century civilization policy emerged in national politics in the early 1820s, both the Dialectic and the Philanthropic Societies voted for its continuation, arguing that civilization was "practicable," and that Congress should not repeal the annual grant for civilization.[51]

In the midst of heated national and state debates about removal, the Dialectic and Philanthropic Societies took interest in federal removal policy but tended to vote against it. On 8 June 1825, students in the Dialectic Society debated the question "Should the U.S. remove the Indians now within her territory beyond the Mississippi and would it be of advantage to them?"[52] Henry B. Elliott, a junior from Randolph County, North Carolina, opened the debate in support of the affirmative position, appealing to his classmates' interest in civilization. The "State of the Indians . . . requires that we collect the scattered tribes of Indians now with[in] our territory, establish them in a permanent home, strip them of their barbarism—enlighten their clouded reason—& arrest the hand of death which is gradually thinning their numbers." Removal promised to promote "justice to ourselves" and "justice to the Indians." He offered five reasons for removal. First, removal guaranteed that miscegenation would "be greatly checked by the removal of the Indians beyond the Mississippi." Second, whites had a paternalistic duty to protect Indians. "It is the duty of the United States to protect the Indians to act in the manner of guardians over them," Elliott explained, "to point out for them the way of life which would be most conducive to their general happiness, and to the endeavour to persuade them to follow that way." Third, removal promised to promote more peaceful relations among whites and Indians. Otherwise, whites and Indians would continue to fight among themselves until Indians were completely extinct. Fourth, removal would excite "national pride and emulation" among Indians. Finally, Elliott argued that Indians "would be under less temptations to vice on the other side of the Mississippi than on this."[53] Elliott betrayed a host of assumptions about Indians as childlike and intemperate.

Those who opposed removal played into many of the stereotypes underscored in the affirmative argument. In an "able" and "elegant manner," they depicted "the miseries of the Indians in . . . glowing language." First, they argued that Indians would not have the strength or power to "maintain continual peace with the neighboring nations" if removed from white society. Second, Indians did not "wish to be removed," and whites "should let them remain in the situation they are at present." Third, removal would "only *delay* their final destruction." Western lands, they argued, would never be exclusively for Indians, for whites' manifest destiny was to expand the republic westward. So those opposed to removal concluded that any hope for Indians' survival rested not on exclusion from, but integration within, white civilization. "They [Indians] are rapidly advancing towards a state of comparative refinement, but their removal will have a tendency to give them an increased relish for their former [barbaric] pursuits" and "cause them to forget the sweets of civilized of life; and prefer to pass their lives in their favourite forests, following the pleasures of hunting and the chase, rather than be compelled to obtain their subsistence by the cultivation of the soil."[54]

In the end, the Dialectic Society voted that the United States should not remove the Indians beyond the Mississippi. Yet this resolution is not as significant as the shared assumptions contained in each side's argument. Those who participated in this 1825 debate only differed over the questions of whether Indians should be civilized while mixed in society with whites or in their own territory. Each side based its arguments on three shared assumptions. First, Indians could not be happy unless they were civilized (and they could be civilized). Second, virtuous republican citizens had to mediate civilization building among Indians. Each citizen's responsibility was to promote the general welfare—"happiness," to use their language—of their fellow man, white or Indian. Finally, Indians' cultural, rather than racial, otherness was a common thread holding together North Carolina students' debates about Indians. Students based their historical and contemporary arguments on claims about American Indians' aptitude, especially whether they could be civilized. Students learned to combine the languages of civilization, civic virtue, and cultural difference to argue for and against public policy.

Debating Slavery

The issues that young men debated regarding improvement and reform, women's rights, and Indian removal were all a variation of the question of progress in a slave society that nagged southern intellectuals during the antebellum period. Like other educated southerners, slavery provided a formidable conundrum for young men who believed in advancement of human freedom through material and moral progress and, at the same time, rejected the rights of freedom of others. In other words, what Eugene Genovese has termed "the slaveholder's dilemma" echoes in literary society debates, as young men took on the issue of slavery head-on.[55]

A significant portion of U.S. current affairs debates held in the Dialectic and Philanthropic Societies in every decade of the University of North Carolina's antebellum history comprised questions about slavery.[56] Between 1795 and 1799, 14 percent of twenty-nine questions about U.S. current affairs addressed slavery (48 percent dealt with Franco- and Anglo-U.S. relations and the French Revolution). In the first decade of the nineteenth century, 11 percent of the forty-three questions about U.S. current affairs addressed slavery. Between 1810 and 1819, 18 percent of the thirty-six U.S. current affairs questions addressed slavery; between 1820 and 1829, 20 percent of seventy-eight questions in the category addressed slavery; and between 1830 and 1839, 26 percent of fifty-three questions addressed slavery. In other words, the numbers rose in the period leading up to the Missouri Compromise and dropped to 14 percent by the time of the Mexican War. In the final two decades before the Civil War, questions about slavery returned to approximately 12 percent of the total questions about U.S. current affairs, and none appears in the records between 1860 and 1861.[57]

Early debates in each society indicate that antislavery sentiment had been strong among the first generations of students who attended the University of North Carolina. In 1799, for example, one student from a slaveholding family explained his antislavery position in these terms: "Is it not to be expected that slavery will, ere long, be abolished in our state, as it already has in several others? I presume it will. Justice & humanity urges its necessity, while example corroborates its certainty. We anticipate the time when justice shall prevail over tyranny, and liberty shall triumph among the Africans, as it once did among the Americans. I confess I see no way by which we can restore tranquility among them without difficulty or danger, or some disquietude among ourselves: but we must suppose these will be surmounted, and some plan fallen on to restore them their liberty." This student could see no other way by which the United States could promote happiness among whites or restore peace among slaves than by "restor[ing] them [slaves] their liberty."[58]

Between 1795 and 1820, students tended to debate whether slavery was disadvantageous to state and national development and to the stability of a republican government. In 1800, for example, one year after New York passed a gradual emancipation statute, and when Gabriel Prosser's rebellion was revealed in Virginia, members of the Dialectic Society debated whether North Carolina should adopt a plan for immediate emancipation and determined that it would be proper. Similarly, in 1804, when New Jersey passed a statute for gradual emancipation of slaves, North Carolina students debated—and supported—the proposition that the United States should stop importing slaves. Indeed, as the 1808 end of the transatlantic slave trade approached, students took interest in debates about abolishing slavery nationally and in their own state.[59]

In the early national period, whether a student argued for or against the abolition of slavery, his argument tended to address the relationship between slavery and republican government rather than racialist positions that would emerge later. In 1807, John D. Jones offered a defense of slavery in which he appealed only to republicanism and patriotism. The slavery question, he argued, did not require addressing human nature, claims to black inferiority, or natural rights' of humans to enslave one another.[60] "What rights a man may have to retain the Africans in servitude," in Jones's opinion, was not as important a question as "whether the manumission of slaves is compatible with the interest of the United States." Jones insisted that civil society requires men "to consult the good of the whole aggregate." In ways that anticipated Senator John C. Calhoun's famous speech in which he declared slavery to be "positive good," Jones concluded that slavery advanced the material progress of the republic and, therefore, promoted the common good. Yet Jones's appeal to civic virtue and patriotism did not win the day. The affirmative side won the debate, arguing that slavery ought to be abolished based, presumably, on that which Jones opposed: an argument resting on moral philosophy and the natural rights of man.

Early national students' attitudes about race may explain much of this discourse between arguing for slavery based on compatibility with free institutions rather than based on human nature claims. Students in the early national period were, intellectually at least, coming to terms with the meaning of physiological differences between human beings. As early as 1799, students were curious about the origins of human difference. Students questioned human origins, including whether different "races" of man were, in fact, different species. In 1799 and 1801, for example, the Dialectic Society debated the theory of polygenesis or, in their words, whether "all mankind [were] descended from one pair," as opposed to if there were multiple creations. While eighteenth-century philosophers had solved this problem, the early nineteenth-century witnessed increased scientific scrutiny of the idea of the unity of a human species, and the theory of polygenesis emerged, suggesting that multiple creations accounted for visible racial difference. Polygenesis was almost categorically untenable among southern whites, including slaveholders, who were unwilling to reject biblical explanations of human unity.[61] Students at North Carolina were no different from the vast majority of southern intellectuals who spurned the theory of polygenesis for the less-risky Christian theory of monogenesis. They resolved every debate about human origins in favor of monogenesis.[62] Students did not argue for the innate inferiority of the enslaved (or "savage" Indians), but instead resolved that blacks could be educated and that Indians could be civilized.

If students could allow for the innate equality of races and the improvability of all humans through education and civilization, then they had to deal with the potential of a multi-racial republic. After the War of 1812, this began to bother students, especially as they imagined the expansion of American civilization into western territories. Perhaps the best way to ensure a monoracial republic was by removing blacks altogether, if not through emancipation then through colonization. Students expressed interest in prevailing discourse about the removal of free blacks from the United States through colonization. In 1818, students debated colonizing freed slaves in the Pacific Northwest, and determined that establishing the colony would not be "politic." Likewise, they resolved in 1822 that it would not be "expedient in the U. States to appropriate 500 million acres of land" to emancipated slaves in Africa. Yet, in 1826, the Dis agreed that the American Colonization Society was "worthy of individual and national patronage." In 1827, they resolved that freed slaves should not be moved anywhere west of the Rocky Mountains, though in 1832 a different group of students decided that Liberia should be protected by the U.S. flag. These debates suggest that students, ideologically at least, were eager to see slaves withdrawn from white society, but did not wish to colonize them in the United States.[63]

A marked antislavery sentiment pervaded the University of North Carolina well into the antebellum period, but for reasons other than the racial equality of all people. A major argument against slavery among North Carolina students was that it impeded state development and the progress of civilization. In 1832, a year before he was appointed justice to North Carolina's Supreme Court, William Gaston delivered before the Dialectic and Philanthropic Societies at Chapel Hill a speech on advice to young men. In discussing students' responsibilities as adults, he identified slavery as the "worst evil that afflicts the South": "It stifles industry and represses enterprise—it is fatal to economy and providence—it discourages skill—impairs our strength as a community, and poisons morals at the fountain head. How this evil is to be encountered, how subdued, is indeed a difficult and delicate enquiry, which this is not the time to examine, nor the occasion to discuss. I felt, however, that I could not discharge my duty, without referring to this subject, as one which ought to engage the prudence moderation and firmness of those who, sooner or later, must act decisively upon it."[64]

Thousands of copies of Gaston's speech had been published after he first delivered it and it went through two publications in other states, including Alabama.[65] At North Carolina, David Swain frequently recommended that students read his address, and in 1844 students published Gaston's address in the first volume of the *North Carolina University Magazine*.[66] While the speech circulated widely for its advice to young men, it is significant too that Gaston's stance on slavery did not undermine its popularity.

Like Gaston, young men included in their critiques of slavery the institution's negative effect on North Carolina's material advancement. For instance, on 20 June 1832, the members of the Dialectic Society debated whether the United States, were it to be divided one day, would become a republic or a monarchy. The society resolved that republican forms of government would be established, but in the process of debating this point, William Hayes Owen argued that slavery was an institution that "paralyzes the energies of freemen."[67] This line of thought was typical among southern antislavery writers and found its most contentious application in Hinton Rowan Helper's scathing attack against slavery in his *Impending Crisis of the South* (1857).

The emergence of northern abolition in the 1830s did much to wear away the antislavery sentiment at the university, though it never did completely. When Congress adopted a "gag rule" in 1835 to prevent the House of Representatives from reading antislavery petitions on the House Floor, North Carolina students debated the issue also. In 1836, members of the Dialectic Society argued that Congress was *not* "justifiable in not receiving the petitions praying for the abolition of slavery in the District of Columbia." In 1838, however, they reversed the decision, arguing that Congress *should* "reject the petitions of citizens praying for the abolition of slavery in the District of Columbia."[68] In the 1840s, expansion of slavery again became an issue of debate among students, not surprisingly, as they contemplated the Mexican War and the annexation of Texas. And in 1850, students debated the politics of slavery as they relate to the Compromise of 1850. As with debates about abolitionist petitions in Congress, students' resolutions on these issues varied, suggesting a formidable lack of consensus among literary society members on the issue of slavery. By the 1850s, then, students continued to argue both sides of the issue, but they typically resolved slavery debates in favor of the proslavery argument that earlier generations had wrestled with and had attempted to reconcile with compromise.[69] Moreover, after 1850, debates on slavery were less frequent. These findings, in turn, suggest that students found less cause to debate slavery, as the ranks of the proslavery argument began to close in on southern intellectual life, but were not hostile to debate when there was a consensus among members to take up the topic.

Student debates about slavery throughout the antebellum period serve as one important example of how the intellectual culture of higher education facilitated spaces where young men could remain flexible on ideas about slavery. Significantly, these debates attest to young men's place within the transition from boyhood to manhood. Indeed, youthful ideal-ism—which many young men viewed as innate—might have encouraged students to speak more freely. Some evidence for this conclusion exists in comparing collegiate and academy debates and resolutions. Boys in Greens-boro's Philomathean Society, for example, were more willing to stake claims in moral arguments against slavery. On 10 July 1848 the Philomathean so-ciety debated the question "Which have the greatest reason to complain of the white people the Indian or slave," and they resolved the debate in favor of the slaves. The next year, the society took up the question again and decided by a margin of one vote that blacks, rather than Indians, had "the greatest reason to complain of the whites." The votes for these debates were close, suggesting that boys already held strong beliefs on this issue. But when it came to assessing whether "free negroes or slaves" were "in the wors[t] condition" in the South, these students resolved that free blacks were worse off than enslaved blacks. Moreover, in 1850 the Philomatheans resolved that slavery was a moral evil. Students seemed amenable, at least in the abstract, to moral critiques of southern slavery at the same time as they held onto notions of southern paternalism. Perhaps it is not surpris-ing, then, that on 10 August 1849, when students debated whether aboli-tionism or Catholicism presented "the greatest danger" to the republic, they decided that Catholics were far more dangerous than abolitionists.[70]

Or perhaps young men's societies were simply safe spaces to entertain ideas they normally would not entertain in other venues. One reason for this flexibility might have been the secrecy of their meetings. Not open to the public, or even the faculty, student debates could have engendered a greater degree of free expression than otherwise might have existed on campus. Indeed, the case of Benjamin S. Hedrick, a North Carolina alum-nus who became a science professor, demonstrates that student culture may have been unique in its open questioning of slavery. Hedrick became Professor of Chemistry at North Carolina in 1854. He was opposed to the extension of slavery into the western territories. In August 1856 rumors be-gan to circulate that, if he could, Hedrick would have voted for John C. Frémont, the Republican presidential candidate, who opposed extending slavery in the territories. The Raleigh *Standard* printed a scathing article, and, according to Hedrick, "the mandate went forth from that represen-tative of sham Democracy 'if there are Black Republicans amongst us let them be driven out." Even after Hedrick wrote a piece for the *Standard* in his own defense, the students taunted him and even burned him in effigy, yet not one of them refused to attend Hedrick's class. By October, however, Hedrick was dismissed for having voiced his political views.[71] Even in this climate, students did not shy away from debating slavery or its westward expansion. Yet the breakdown of free discourse in the Hedrick affair does point to the gradual emergence of sectionalism in the late antebellum period. Sectionalism, however, was not a foregone conclusion, as student debates on disunion suggest.

The Gradual Emergence of Sectionalism

Not surprisingly, students who attended North Carolina during the Missouri Compromise, the Nullification Crisis, and the Compromise of 1850 debated whether or not republicanism was a stable form of government, whether the Union was permanent, and whether secession was right. According to Lorri Glover, this question preoccupied young men in the early national South who feared "they would be not just the first but tragically the last generation of American sons."[72] if they did not learn good citizenship. Yet every generation of students at North Carolina seemed to fear that they would be the last, and they addressed these issues about the stability of republican government and the federal Union.

The nullification controversy instilled fear that the republican experiment might fail. On 15 February 1828, the Philanthropic Society debated the question "Is it probable that the jealousies which now exist between the different members of the American confederacy will finally prove fatal to their union?" They decided that nothing good could come out of sectional strife. On 18 August of that same year, they debated whether "the course which S. Carolina has been pursuing with respect to disunion [was] a justifiable and expedient one," and they determined that it was not. And on 20 June 1832—just months before South Carolina called a convention to nullify the Tariffs of 1828 and 1832—the members of the Dialectic Society debated the following question: "If a dissolution of the Union should take place, is it probable that monarchy would be established in any part of the country?" Arguing for a perpetual republic, William Owen, then a junior, said to his classmates in the heat of debate, "The soul of the American patriot sinks within him when he contemplates even the possibility of disunion. What! he exclaims, shall this noble fabrick of republicanism whose foundations are so broad and ample and whose superstructure was raised by Architects that cemented it with their blood be prostrated in the dust [?]"[73]

In his inaugural address as president of the Dialectic Society, eighteen-year-old John Hargrave from Lexington, North Carolina, offered a scathing attack against the "violent parties" threatening republican stability. "It is evident from past observation that a crisis is near at hand in the affairs of Government," he explained. "N. Carolina has always been distinguished for a zealous devotion to the constitution—that Constitution has been violated, and the rights of the States invaded—Now then is the time for us to arise and as vigilant sentinels of the watch-tower of Liberty to make one united Stand for the preservation of 'Liberty—The Constitution—Union.'" Hargrave continued to commend his students to viewing the current crisis as an opportunity to serve North Carolina. "Here then is a wide field opened to us for arriving at distinction. And the call which the present comparatively degraded condition of our native state awaits us, will, I feel assured meet with a responsive throb in the breast of every person now within the reach of my voice."[74] Hargrave's encouragement to strengthen the Union by strengthening North Carolina is significant, for it underscores the importance of that state to young men's discourse in literary society debates.

Other debates on disunion prove that students were willing to uphold the Union. In 1851, when the Di and Phi Societies debated whether a state had the right to secede, each society decided the debate against secession. Sectionalism began to trump nationalism in student debates only after 1856, but even then not completely. The result is that the state produced proslavery progressives, torn between national, state, and regional loyalties, who in great measure would find it rather difficult to support the Confederacy until after the war.

BY CREATING A LIVING CURRICULUM of debate in their literary societies, students tackled big issues that fit the adult roles they imagined and idealized in formal education and informal self-culture. Students believed that weekly literary society debating was an important part of the broader cultural process of mental and moral improvement occurring during college. Moreover, they believed it was an effective way to find meaning for their emerging mental maturity, or intellectual manhood: to use their education for the betterment of their families, society, state, and nation. Antebellum students tended to favor questions relating to practical ethics and practical politics, especially regarding current affairs. They debated questions that consistently emphasized the duty of educated men to promote progress and greater democracy (albeit for free white persons), but also used debates to articulate established power boundaries between themselves and others, including women, Indians, and slaves. Although these weekly debates did not have immediate consequences in the lives of these groups, they certainly contributed to the emerging worldviews on which men would rely when they assumed positions of authority as North Carolina's leading lawyers, doctors, clergy, and statesmen.

Regionalism, however, was not the primary reason for students' attitudes about race and gender, though it did play a role. This was most pronounced in terms of students' attitudes about slavery. Debates on slavery reveal that late antebellum students espoused a stronger, though by no means unanimous, proslavery ideology than students of earlier generations. Students' proslavery stances did not entirely replace the antislavery leanings of the first three decades of the university's history, but it did challenge them. By the late 1850s, political strife began to wear away any hope for compromise. Students began to think, not surprisingly, in terms of region more than nation. Sectionalism, however, was not a foregone conclusion, and neither was its influence on young men's emerging adult identities.

Conclusion

On Thursday, 2 June 1842, James Dusenbery, William Mullins, Joseph Summerell, and Ruffin Tomlinson, along with twenty-four of their classmates,
were graduated from the University of North Carolina. As was customary,
the whole week had been devoted to commencement exercises for which
students had spent months preparing and advertising.[1] On Monday and
Tuesday evenings, freshmen and sophomores declaimed before a public
audience, and on Wednesday, a prominent speaker addressed the two literary societies. This year, the speaker canceled at the last minute, and Elisha
Mitchell, the chemistry professor, conducted "electro-magnetic" experiments in lieu of the annual address. The big day was Thursday, however,
which began at nine o'clock in the morning with a procession across campus.
Musicians, usually free and enslaved blacks, led the procession, followed by
students, alumni, local citizens, parents and guardians, clergy, faculty, university trustees, and finally the state governor and university president. As
they passed the monument to Joseph Caldwell, all members of the procession removed their hats to honor the university's first president. Graduation marshals directed procession members to their appropriate seats in
Gerrard Hall, ensuring that the university community sat apart from visi-
tors and that "the ladies" sat in a reserved area. Following an opening prayer
and salutatory address (sometimes given in Latin and English), Joseph Summerell delivered an oration, "Obligations of Educated Men." Later that afternoon, just before degrees were conferred, William Mullins, in keeping
with his love of history, biography, and personal introspection, delivered an
oration entitled "Reverence for the Past."[2] Local newspapers reported that
students' "orations were distinguished by manly good sense and graceful
elocution."[3] President Swain then conferred degrees and, for the first time
in the university's history, gave each graduating student a Bible bearing his
autograph. Thomas J. Morrisey delivered the valedictory address, a final

prayer was offered, and participants left to prepare for the commencement ball, held later that evening at Nancy Hilliard's Eagle Hotel.

Not only was commencement an important rite of passage for young men, marking their departure from boyhood and entry into the public life of men, but it also reinforced important aspects of the intellectual culture of antebellum higher education and the power of intellectual manhood—its exclusivity, its public import, and its exaltation of mind over temperament, restraint over impulse, and independence over dependence. In taking to the stage to declaim and deliver orations, young men performed leadership roles before the community. Not all graduates spoke at commencement, however; only those students who, by virtue of ambition and hard work, earned distinction were appointed to speak. Thus, commencement exercises suggested that antebellum higher education was as much about becoming a laureled leader as it was a conscientious citizen. This was further emphasized by faculty when the annual report of student performance was read just before the conferral of degrees. Young men's strengths as thinkers and leaders were on display for all to see. Each year, newspaper reports confirmed the appeal of intellectual manhood on display. In 1845, the *Weekly Raleigh Register* noted that "a more imposing and brilliant occasion has never been witnessed in the Republic of Letters in North Carolina," as at least 1,500 people attended commencement exercises. Graduates' original orations "left on the auditory not only a deep impression of their own intellectual acquirements but of reflected honor worthy of distinguished literary reputation, zeal, and industry of the heads of College."[4]

For many young men, the community of listeners that sat before them on commencement day anticipated numerous other communities whose attention they would command as adults. North Carolina graduates went on to become leaders in their families, communities, state, nation, and intellectual culture. The vast majority of North Carolina alumni pursued occupations that required intellectual manhood and relied on the curriculum's emphasis on rhetoric, science, and moral philosophy. Most University of North Carolina alumni became lawyers and physicians. Many students continued education in these fields elsewhere. Alumni who became physicians, for instance, typically attended northern colleges such as the University of Pennsylvania. These lawyers and physicians maintained close ties with the region's agricultural community, as they simultaneously occupied positions as planters or farmers. Seventeen percent of alumni became planters; many planters either simultaneously or later in life also became lawyers, physicians, educators, manufacturers, merchants, and engineers. While lawyers, doctors, and planters were the three most prominent professions, many alumni found leadership roles in education as teachers, professors, and principals, and in Christian ministry. Perhaps most significantly, many alumni also became statesmen at the local, state, and federal level, reaching the stature of the great men whose portraits literary societies collected and whom students emulated. Thus, alumni professions demonstrate how antebellum education served North Carolina and the South's middle class, as well as its gentry.

Even for those who did not reach the heights of fame (and there were many), higher education endowed them with the ability to lead their own small worlds. According to Kemp P. Battle, a college diploma might not always "prove scholarship" but nevertheless "gave him an advantage over his neighbors not blessed as he was." By virtue of education, an alumnus "had learned human nature and how to manage men. He had learned to a considerable extent polished manners. He could think and speak on his feet. In county meetings he knew rules of order and how to conduct business. He had confidence in himself, and realized that he secures the fruit who has boldness to seize it and to hold it with tenacious grasp."[5] The trajectories of University of North Carolina alumni, therefore, allow for several suggestions about the role of university in shaping self and society not just in antebellum North Carolina but in the South generally.

The first of these suggestions is that the professional paths of college alumni underscore just how inaccurate the relentless emphasis on collegians as "elites" has been. In this book, I have relied on a cultural understanding of the middle class—what I sometimes describe as bourgeois or Victorian. Student writing has allowed me to reconstruct an intellectual culture on campus in which bourgeois worldviews and practices common in the United States and Britain, especially self-fashioning, framed identity formation for many of these students.

The social dimensions of this emerging bourgeoisie are also evident. Many students, as we have seen, were sons of shopkeepers, merchants, and farmers, including the earnest son of a Fayetteville shopkeeper, William Sidney Mullins. Alumni professions and individual life journeys also confirm the extent to which the university served a growing middle class. A comparison of University of North Carolina alumni professions to Jennifer

Green's research on southern military academies and middle-class formation reveals that these seemingly disparate alumni groups shared professional trajectories. Green finds, for instance, that approximately 61 percent of military alumni with single occupations pursued professional careers as ministers, doctors, engineers, lawyers, judges, and teachers, and approximately 21 percent of these alumni entered an agricultural profession as planters or farmers.[6] The data from the University of North Carolina reveal similar trends. Among students who were graduated between 1840 and 1859, at the height of student enrollment, 71 percent of alumni with single occupations pursued professional careers and approximately 23 percent of them pursued agricultural professions (see Appendix 1). Fewer North Carolina graduates pursued engineering than military academy graduates, though the expansion of science would be a major pursuit of education reformers who had attended the university in the late antebellum period. Indeed, after the Civil War, many of the antebellum leaders of educational reform, with the exception of a few from large planter families such as Kemp Battle, fit solidly with the New South's middle class.[7] Although this book has largely focused on intellectual culture, these data provide important insight into the ways in which intellectual culture and social class were related and expanded together in the antebellum South. The growth of the University of North Carolina's student body and intellectual culture by the late antebellum period allowed for an expansion of its class base and, therefore, its role in building a strong middle class in North Carolina and the South.

This is not to suggest that higher education did not also serve North Carolina's elites, for many college students came from planter families. Jane Turner Censer's research on planter families, for instance, shows that a vast majority of planters, great and small, sent children to college. Families such as the Camerons, who were the state's biggest slaveholders and the university's staunchest supporters, as well as the Hawkins and Pettigrew families with long North Carolina ancestry, sent sons to North Carolina in the antebellum period and afterward.[8] Students from families like these certainly brought the values of southern elites with them, including traditions of honor, reputation, and gentility. This book has shown, however, that these values existed alongside pervasive bourgeois values in the antebellum period. In students' experiences of higher education, middle-class values infused the South's upper class, creating a shared intellectual culture for a southern educated class.

In terms of their private lives, students typically waited until they entered professions and established themselves before they married, suggesting the significant power they would wield as patriarchs of their households as well as of their communities. Some of the students highlighted in the preceding pages help to paint this picture of students' professional and personal lives after college. Consider James Dusenbery, who continued his studies at the University of Pennsylvania as a medical student. He first practiced medicine in 1845 in his hometown of Lexington, but soon thereafter moved to Statesville, North Carolina, to continue his career. He corresponded with "Miss Mary S." through 1848. They became engaged for a short time that year, but Mary ultimately broke off the engagement. We cannot know for sure what her reason was, though correspondence suggests she thought that Dusenbery's father might have opposed their marriage.[9] After the engagement ended, Dusenbery copied some of his correspondence with her into the final pages of his journal, including this final statement from Mary: "I hope you do not think I have forgotten you—no I love you the same as ever but we can do nothing but love; I am compelled to send your notes back, but *will you permit me to keep the ring*—you may have mine & keep it while you live. Look at it often and *think of Mary*."[10] During the Civil War, Dusenbery was a surgeon in the 14th Battalion, Lexington Home Guard. After surviving the war, he practiced medicine in Lexington, North Carolina, and served as a member of the board of trustees for the University of North Carolina.[11] He died on 28 January 1886, never having found his "fair incognita," and was buried in Lexington City Cemetery. We have no record of whether he returned the ring, or thought of Mary at all, but he never married. Some evidence suggests that he may have fathered two children with a black woman.[12]

Others followed more conventional paths. Dusenbery's classmate, Joseph Summerell, received a master's degree from North Carolina in 1842 and a medical degree from the University of Pennsylvania in 1845. Ultimately, he married Ellen Mitchell, Professor Mitchell's daughter. William Mullins likewise went on to earn a master's degree from North Carolina, eventually becoming a railroad president and member of the South Carolina General Assembly. He married Sarah Hodges of Cumberland County in 1847, and they had four children—William, Edward, Mary, and Charles. Ruffin Tomlinson served as a clerk and master in equity for Johnson County, North Carolina, a position he acquired by appointment of a North Carolina alumnus, Richmond M. Pearson, who operated a successful law school and served as a state superior court justice.[13] Tomlinson died, however, in

1844, just two years after commencement.[14] Students who were graduated later pursued similar paths. George Thompson, who was graduated in 1853, for instance, became a planter, physician, and lawyer. In the last two years of his life, he served on the board of trustees for the university. He married three times and had several children. We have no evidence that one of those wives was Susan Lindsay whom he had courted while at college (see chapter 6), though census data show that he was married to Berta N. Thompson in 1880.

For each of these young men, and countless others, the Civil War had a profound influence on life after college, but it certainly was not something that their education at college anticipated. In May 1861, North Carolina reluctantly joined the Confederacy. Few alumni from the antebellum period escaped the crises of disunion, the Civil War, and Reconstruction. Fifty-seven percent of students who attended the university between 1850 and 1862 fought in the war.[15] Many alumni who had become doctors served as surgeons for the Confederacy; many ministers served as chaplains. But it is important to note that few students anticipated the conflict, nor did they view their education in any way as preparatory for it. Consider Walter Lenoir, for example. According to the historian William L. Barney, Lenoir reluctantly joined the Confederacy out of a sense of family duty.[16] Countless other young "reluctant Confederates" found themselves thrown into the conflict only to emerge from it with more rabid sectional perspectives than when the conflict began.

Early in the war, little at the university seemed to have changed for students. They continued to study Latin, Greek, science, mathematics, and moral philosophy. Wayland's *Elements of Moral Science*, with its antislavery tract, however, was no longer taught to seniors, and literary societies seemed far more interested in historical questions than current affairs. The realities of disunion and war only heightened as the war raged on. By 1862, enrollments dropped from nearly four hundred to fifty, as students decided to take up arms or were forced into service by conscription. By 1865, one soldier passing through Chapel Hill remarked that the university was "attended by 25 students mostly small boys."[17] Meanwhile, the few students who remained on campus found college a "very dull and lonesome place," expensive due to poor enrollment, and scarcely able to provide students with food.[18] Yet the university never closed its doors during the war and is the only southern university able to make this claim.

During Reconstruction, the university, as with the state and region generally, came under Republican control.[19] These Republicans installed a new Republican faculty, administration, and board of trustees. President Swain was widely criticized for collaborating with Republicans (including allowing his daughter to marry General Smith D. Atkins, who commanded the Union troops occupying Chapel Hill).[20] As a result, enrollments plummeted, and the trustees were forced to close the university in 1871. The university reopened in 1875 with the help of federal land-grant funds. The university's leaders after Reconstruction, many of whom had been students during the antebellum period, including Kemp Battle, wanted to point the university in a new direction. They advocated abandoning the classics and replacing them with mathematics, science, and engineering; this would be the surest way to create a practical and useful new form of schooling for a New South.[21]

Although young men's adult lives help to explain why their education mattered in terms of social power and the transformation of North Carolina in the antebellum period, their education is in itself an important cultural process to understand because it illuminates the power of education in the construction of identity, age, manhood, region, and intellectual culture. In particular, the transition from boyhood to manhood occurring at college reveals the extent to which young men viewed manhood as defined by the child-adult dichotomy, which touched all aspects of their formal and informal education. Indeed, the transition from boyhood to manhood was the most important and pervasive feature of education for young men, not the development of regionalism as some scholars have argued. While southern males took various routes to become men, those who chose to attend college sought more than what we consider manliness or masculinity; they sought mental maturity, or what contemporaries called intellectual manhood.

Intellectual manhood offers a new and unique perspective on southern manhood for its connection to the emerging American bourgeoisie but also to antebellum intellectual culture more broadly. This was an ideal of restrained manhood that required deep commitment to self-improvement, particularly when it came to mitigating nagging tensions associated with youth: mind versus temperament, restraint versus impulse, and dependence versus independence. College life, especially in the literary societies, pedagogy, and curriculum, catered to this spirit of self-improvement. In the process, an intellectual culture developed on campus that promoted popular bourgeois values of American selfhood: industry, self-restraint, self-mastery, sobriety, and chastity. This culture demanded, moreover, that young men appropriate these values into daily exercises of self-fashioning, which took distinctively literary forms as young men read, wrote, and spoke their way through college.

These findings have broader implications for our understanding of manhood in the nineteenth century, particularly its intellectual and cultural construction. Here an important contribution is linking what Stephen Berry has written about southern manhood and ambition to the broader literature of self-improvement in nineteenth-century America. Like the great poet of Rome's golden age, Horace, students wished to create monuments for themselves more enduring than bronze.[22] In this way, perhaps they differed little from the young men featured in Berry's work, who believed men lived, in part, for immortal fame.[23] This book has attempted to show, however, that ambition was not an innate feature of boyhood, youth, or manhood. Instead, it was an intellectual construction that required a lot of hard work in many overlapping areas, including mind, morals, speech, and friendship. Not unlike other young people throughout the early republic—in and out of formal educational settings—North Carolina students created a vibrant self-culture, which made these exercises of self-improvement seem urgent and heroic. Young men defined, understood, and articulated the self and its heroic potential in the many acts of reading, writing, and speaking that enlivened their world of intentional intellectualism.

Given the intellectual work of honing ambition and cultivating one's heroic potential, one of the most important things about the cultural processes of antebellum higher education was the role it played in bolstering existing systems of social power. Whether among men, between men and women, or masters and slaves, the power of intellectual manhood was incontrovertible. Significantly, young men were not silent about this exclusivity, nor did they understate its broader social significance. They sought to master the self in order to distinguish themselves from uneducated others, who might emulate but never attain intellectual manhood. That each individual possessed heroic potential enhanced the already explicit spirit of gendered and racial exclusivity that higher education cultivated in the antebellum period. Learning to set boundaries and create communities of listeners and followers shaped the education they created for themselves in informal rituals, especially debate. Thus, in practice, "intellectual manhood" becomes, for modern readers, a synthesis of the man of reason, judgment, and propriety, and the man of social performance, eloquence, and leadership often discussed in the literature on "southern manhood." Of course rowdiness, dissipation, alcohol, and sex got in the way of these serious pursuits; this was common among male youth throughout the country when they left home to seek independence, and not symptomatic of a particular regional disposition.

Just as this more nuanced understanding of education and maturation redresses long-held assumptions about southern students and higher education, it also suggests the need for broader reassessment of the Old South's intellectual culture. Historians such as Michael O'Brien, Elizabeth Fox-Genovese, and Eugene Genovese have convincingly demonstrated how southern intellectual life drew from and reflected broad, transatlantic trends, underscoring in particular what some might call high intellectual culture. Yet in the region's rich and growing intellectual history, *young* southerners have not been taken seriously as thinkers. Fortunately, antebellum collegians wrote extensively about their intellectual developments in a variety of sources—letters, diaries, speeches, class essays, literary magazines, and debates. The examples of college youth such as James Dusenbery, William Mullins, Edmund Covington, Thomas Miles Garrett, and their classmates, whose thoughts remain for historical analysis only by virtue of their status as students, show how ordinary men engaged with high (and low) intellectual culture. Here, the case of reading is most instructive, for students derived their attitudes about university, self, and society from a variety of literature. Their engagement with classroom texts, their collection, treatment, and reading of books in literary society libraries, and their reader responses not only prove that young men incorporated ideas and values in their daily lives but also reveal that the process of doing so had special meaning to them as they attempted to fashion adult lives. Even in the most unpredictable situations—as James Dusenbery, for example, wrote about visiting prostitutes in the woods and about his sexual desires—we see that students drew from texts and literature in moments of reflection. Dusenbery's literary world was rooted in biblical language, English poetry, and chivalric fiction just as much as in youth culture at college. Moreover, his commonplace book—and those of his classmates, too—demonstrates that Horace, Cicero, Sir Walter Scott, and Byron existed alongside popular American ballads and folk songs in students' literary imaginations. Students' social world of friendship and ritual, in other words, was also distinctively literary.

Understanding how young men read, wrote, spoke, and imagined their way to adulthood at antebellum North Carolina contributes significantly to our evolving understanding of a South that was connected to the nation intellectually and culturally. North Carolina students' intellectual culture is discernible elsewhere in the United States, in both formal and informal educational settings where young women and men sought to create adult lives. The idea that the self was malleable, improvable—even perfectible—was a defining feature of a national and transatlantic bourgeois culture. Within the South, dozens of colleges and universities provided opportunities for self-formation through intellectual means on a daily basis. Daniel Walker Howe, Scott Casper, and Thomas Augst, for instance, have suggested that self-improvement was one of the most prevalent ideas shaping cultural life in antebellum America and occurred almost always in moments of education—among clerks, poor farmers, and literate elites. Moreover, Mary Kelley, Anya Jabour, and others have also shown that girls and young women created meaningful opportunities for self-culture and cultivated a sense of ambition that helped them resist patriarchy and contribute to public life.[24] Significantly, these efforts occurred in gendered ways, reflecting the pervasive influence of separate spheres in antebellum subjects' understanding of intellectual life.

If this book is any indication, education remains a rich area for understanding cultural patterns in the South as they related to national and transatlantic intellectual life. In particular, the book has shown the fruitfulness of employing strategies of reader-response criticism to the texts of education and of everyday life. This interpretation has uncovered a vision of educational culture that was meaningful and rich for the students who lived it, even in the face of the juvenile fun that has colored so much of the preceding scholarship. While this is the first study to take seriously young southern men's educational culture, it also suggests direction for further research. The tools from literary studies have not yet been used, for instance, in studies of pre-collegiate education or young people's intellectual lives in families and in institutions of public intellectual life (other than schools), such as libraries, debating and literary societies, and churches. The consumption of intellectual life should also continue to present opportunities for scholars of gender, family, and culture, as well as the Civil War. Persistent research into the consumption of ideas among disparate groups of southerners will allow historians to understand more fully the South's diverse patterns of thought and expression.

Although this book has served as a historical corrective to a one-dimensional perception of students of a particular place and time—the antebellum South—ultimately there is much to gain by understanding the relationships among university, self, and society in our time. One thing we gain is a sense of how little things have changed. Students remain self-focused, and they constantly question what ends education serves. Too, tensions between mind and temperament, impulse and restraint, and childhood and adulthood still color experiences of teaching and learning, behavior and misbehavior. Thus, higher education must always be viewed as a process occurring alongside personal development. When curriculum and pedagogy are divorced from self and society—when education becomes a set of targeted goals and teaches college students there is only one, timed and tested path to learning and success—then it ceases to be educational in any true sense of the word. Indeed, we run a great risk of entirely separating the individual from education when we allow public policy concerns with metrics and goals, enrollment and retention, to trump the lived process of higher education.

Thus in looking to the past, we also gain a sense of profound difference, allowing us to examine more critically how we measure education in self and society in the twenty-first century. What and whom does higher education now serve? Since the mid-twentieth century, higher education has increasingly focused on over-specification of majors, vocational training, and making money. Consequently, the humanities that figured so prominently in antebellum students' self-culture are under attack more than ever, as state legislatures throughout the country seek to eliminate the very courses that teach mental and moral improvement such as history, literature, the classics, philosophy, art, and writing. Many state universities that were once the epicenters of liberal education have been divorced from their histories in the name of practicality and expediency. Moreover, generations of students who have come of age in an era of testing and standardization seem to have little patience for exploration when it does not prepare them for a test. My hope is that this book joins scholars across many disciplines who are engaged in understanding how and why students learn in this new culture of higher education that favors completion over process, careers over self-fashioning. Important research is being done in the fields of anthropology and education policy, for example, to understand the unique experiences of college students today and the weight and effect of expectations for a rising educated class in America.[25] Yet we must also look into the past to arrive at creative solutions to contemporary problems; there, we can imagine a world in which current indices of knowledge, talent, and learning never existed. Indeed, persistent exploration of the past will help us to think more creatively and productively about the present and future roles of education and educated citizenship in the American republic.

Appendix
Alumni Occupations and Denominational Affiliations of Alumni Ministers

TABLE I. Alumni Occupations: Single Profession (1840–1859)

Occupation	Number of Alumni	Percentage
Professional	395	71
Lawyer	174	
Physician	112	
Teacher	54	
Engineer	9	
Railroad Employee	3	
Clergy	41	
Dentist	1	
Jurist	1	
*Agricultural**	125	23
Planter	102	
Farmer	23	
Proprietors	30	<1
Merchant	23	
Banker	5	
Manufacturer	2	
White-collar Employees	5	<1
Journalist	4	
Accountant	1	

N =555 individuals

Note: The 161 alumni with at least two occupations (see Table 2) are not included in the number of alumni.

Source: Daniel Lindsey Grant, ed., *Alumni History of the University of North Carolina*, Durham, N.C.: Printed by Christian & King Printing Co., 1924), http://docsouth.unc.edu/true/grant/grant.html.

*I have maintained Grant's language when it comes to describing professions. He does not explain the distinction between planter and farmer. This is likely a result from inconsistent data reporting in the original research.

TABLE 2. Alumni Occupations: Two Professions (1840–1859)

Occupation	Number of Alumni
Lawyers	*60*
Lawyer & Planter	20
Lawyer & Educator	10
Lawyer & Merchant	5
Lawyer & Farmer	5
Lawyer & Banker	4
Lawyer & Journalist	3
Lawyer & Jurist	2
Lawyer & Minister	2
Lawyer & Railroad Employee	2
Lawyer & Author	2
Lawyer & Hotel Manager	1
Lawyer & Sherriff	1
Lawyer & Mayor	1
Lawyer & Manufacturer	1
Lawyer & Engineer	1
Physicians	*21*
Physician & Planter	10
Physician & Lawyer	1
Physician & Educator	2
Physician & Manufacturer	1
Physician & Merchant	4
Physician & Farmer	1
Physician & Druggist	1
Physician & Journalist	1
Planters	*21*
Planter & Manufacturer	5
Planter & Lawyer	4
Planter & Physician	4
Planter & Educator	4
Planter & Merchant	2
Planter & Engineer	1
Planter & Professional Military	1
Farmers	*8*
Farmer & Educator	2
Farmer & Merchant	2
Farmer & Lawyer	1
Farmer & Engineer	1
Farmer & Miller	1
Farmer & Surveyor	1

Occupation	Number of Alumni
Educators	*17*
Educator & Lawyer	5
Educator & Merchant	3
Educator & Planter	2
Educator & Farmer	2
Educator & Physician	1
Educator & Minister	1
Educator & Journalist	1
Educator & Railroad Employee	1
Educator & Accountant	1
Ministers	*7*
Minister & Educator	6
Minister & Lawyer	1
Merchants	*7*
Merchant & Lawyer	1
Merchant & Planter	3
Merchant & Farmer	1
Merchant & Insurance Broker	1
Merchant & Surveyor	1
Banker	*7*
Banker & Planter	4
Banker & Journalist	1
Banker & Merchant	1
Banker & Accountant	1
Manufacturer	*5*
Manufacturer & Merchant	2
Manufacturer & Banker	1
Manufacturer & Farmer	1
Manufacturer & Railroad Employee	1
Journalist	*3*
Journalist & Lawyer	1
Journalist & Planter	1
Journalist & Physician	1
Engineer	*2*
Engineer & Lawyer	1
Engineer & Railroad Employee	1

TABLE 2. (continued)

Occupation	Number of Alumni
Jurist	3
Jurist & Lawyer	2
Jurist & Educator	1
Druggist	4
Druggist & Physician	2
Druggist & Educator	1
Druggist & Farmer	1
Author	1
Author & Educator	1
N=168	

Source: Daniel Lindsey Grant, ed., *Alumni History of the University of North Carolina* (Durham, N.C.: Printed by Christian & King Printing Co., 1924), http://docsouth.unc.edu/true/grant/grant.html.

Note: Grant does not explicitly state when alumni held professions simultaneously or in succession. He does indicate that he attempted to provide "a complete chronological statement of the career including professional, business or civil activities, military service, writings, etc." Thus, "Jurist & Lawyer" represent different individuals than "Lawyer & Jurist" and I have represented them as such.

TABLE 3. Denominational Affiliations of Alumni Ministers, 1840–1859

Denomination	Number of Alumni
Presbyterian	20
Episcopalian	13
Methodist	7
Baptist	4
Not Reported	4
N= 48	

Source: Daniel Lindsey Grant, ed., *Alumni History of the University of North Carolina* (Durham, N.C.: Printed by Christian & King Printing Co., 1924), http://docsouth.unc.edu/true/grant/grant.html.

Notes

Abbreviations

DAS   Documenting the American South, University of North Carolina at Chapel Hill, Chapel Hill, North Carolina, http://docsouth.unc.edu.

DSR   Dialectic Society Records, University Archives, Wilson Library, University of North Carolina at Chapel Hill, Chapel Hill, North Carolina

NCC   North Carolina Collection, Wilson Library, University of North Carolina at Chapel Hill, Chapel Hill, North Carolina.

NCDAH   North Carolina Department of Archives and History, Raleigh, North Carolina.

NCUM   *North Carolina University Magazine*

PSR   Philanthropic Society Records, University Archives, Wilson Library, University of North Carolina at Chapel Hill, Chapel Hill, North Carolina.

SHC   Southern Historical Collection, Wilson Library, University of North Carolina, Chapel Hill, North Carolina.

UA   University Archives, Wilson Library, University of North Carolina, Chapel Hill, North Carolina

USC   South Caroliniana Library, University of South Carolina, Columbia, South Carolina

WFU   University Archives, Z. Smith Reynolds Library, Wake Forest University, Winston-Salem, North Carolina

Introduction

1. Adams, *The Education of Henry Adams*, 57–58.

2. The scholarship on American higher education has generally marginalized southern schooling outside the broader context of American intellectual life. See, for instance, Cremin, *American Education*; Rudolph, *Curriculum*; Kaestle, *Pillars of the Republic*. The dismissal of intellectualism at southern universities is also perpetuated in works with a regional focus, including Faust, *A Sacred Circle*, 8–9 and Glover, *Southern Sons*. In many ways, this tradition can be traced to the first histories of southern colleges, which were institutional histories written by alumni. In his *History of the University of North Carolina*, for example, UNC alumnus Kemp P. Battle disparages the antebellum university's intellectual life under the leadership of David Swain. See esp. *History*, 780–82. While Battle's *History* is the most thorough history of the university, it is problematic insofar as it also serves as memoir, filled with anecdotes from Battle's own time at UNC. For this reason, I use this work as both a secondary and a primary source. E. Merton Coulter's *College Life in the Old South* is the first academic history of southern higher education and focuses on the University of Georgia. Specific arguments for the exceptionalism of southern higher education can be found in Eaton, *Freedom of Thought in the Old South*, 196–217; Ezell,

"A Southern Education for Southrons"; Durrill, "The Power of Ancient Words," 497–98; Sugrue, "'We Desired Our Future Rulers to Be Educated Men'"; Glover, *Southern Sons*, 37–82. Many interpretations focus on college men and honor: Pace, *Halls of Honor*; Drinkwater, "Honor and Student Misconduct in Southern Antebellum Colleges"; Wagoner, "Honor and Dishonor at Mr. Jefferson's University"; Wall, "Students and Student Life at the University of Virginia"; Tomlinson and Windham, "Northern Piety and Southern Honor"; Wakelyn, "Antebellum College Life and the Relations between Fathers and Sons." Important efforts to redress the neglect of southern schooling and its superficiality include Farnham, *The Education of the Southern Belle*; Green *Military Education*, 3–4; Kilbride, "Southern Medical Students in Philadelphia, 1800–1861"; Stowe, *Doctoring the South*, chap. 1.

3. On collegians and southern society, see Carmichael, *The Last Generation*, 6; Glover, *Southern Sons*. Prominent works using collegians to understand manhood in a more national context include Syrett, *The Company He Keeps*; Townsend, *Manhood at Harvard*; Clark, *Creating the College Man*.

4. Notable exceptions include Green, *Military Education*, esp. chaps. 2–5, and Mayfield, *Counterfeit Gentlemen*. More typically, however, men's intellectual lives have been the provenance of biography; their college experiences are usually discussed anecdotally. Some examples include Faust, *James Henry Hammond and the Old South*, esp. chap. 1; Fellman, *The Making of Robert E. Lee*; Isaac, *Landon Carter's Uneasy Kingdom*, esp. chap. 5.

5. In contrast, Lorri Glover argues that southern colleges were "seldom havens of intellectualism or contemplation." See *Southern Sons*, 83.

6. Rotundo, *American Manhood*, 55. See also Syrett, *The Company He Keeps*, 4.

7. On differences between youth and adult culture, see Rotundo, *American Manhood*, chap. 3. On youth culture in the United States, see Kett, *Rites of Passage*, 11–61, and "Adolescence and Youth in Nineteenth-Century America," 283–98; Rotundo, *American Manhood*, 56; Reinier, *From Virtue to Character*; Hemphill, "Isaac and 'Isabella,'" and *Bowing to Necessities*; Mintz, *Huck's Raft*; Frisch, "Youth Culture in America, 1790–1865," 94–114. Anya Jabour has focused on these tensions associated with youth in her work on the Wirt family. See her "Masculinity and Adolescence in Antebellum America," 393–416.

8. Hessinger, *Seduced, Abandoned, and Reborn*, 2.

9. A full listing of university graduates is available in Battle, *History*, 787–820. The geographic origins of the 1,683 University of North Carolina graduates between 1795 and 1861 are as follows: Alabama (61); Arkansas (3); Connecticut (1); Florida (13); Georgia (15); Iowa (3); Kentucky (7); Louisiana (24); Maryland (1); Missouri (1); Mississippi (44); North Carolina (1,322); New York (1); South Carolina (32); Tennessee (70); Texas (10); and Virginia (75). These numbers do not include the many students who matriculated at Carolina but never graduated.

10. Censer, *North Carolina Planters and Their Children*, 43. Censer's study verifies the importance of education to planters, showing that that 68 percent of North Carolina planters sent at least one son to college, and approximately 33 percent of planters sent two or more sons. According to Colin Burke, 30 percent of students attending the University of North Carolina in the antebellum period came from families with fathers within professional or business-oriented occupations. See his *American Collegiate Populations*, 49, 119, 121, 124–25.

11. Censer, *North Carolina Planters and Their Children*, 48.

12. Although historians generally agree that a southern middle class existed in the

antebellum period, they disagree as to whether this was a developed or developing class of white southerners. See Frank Byrne's overview of this debate in *Becoming Bourgeois*, 1–12. See also the introduction to Delfino, Gillespie, and Kyriakoudes, *Southern Society and Its Transformations*.

13. Wells, *The Origins of the Southern Middle Class*, 10–13, 42.

14. Green, *Military Education*, 1–13, and "Networks of Military Educators," 41, 45–46.

15. Censer, *North Carolina Planters and Their Children*, 48; Scarborough, *Masters of the Big House*, 426.

16. Carmichael, *The Last Generation*, 10.

17. Berry, *All That Makes a Man*.

18. For biographical information about these individuals see the following: Lindemann, "Introduction," The James Lawrence Dusenbery Journal, unpublished essay, 2007, and "Verses & Fragments: The James Lawrence Dusenbery Journal (1841–1842)," DAS. Ishkanian, "Religion and Honor at Chapel Hill," 57–58; Barney, *The Making of a Confederate*; Hamilton, "Diary of Thomas Miles Garrett at the University of North Carolina," 63–65; Sanders, "The Journal of Ruffin Wirt Tomlinson," 86–115, 233–59.

19. Greenberg, *Manifest Manhood*, 11–14. According to Greenberg, the opposite of "restrained manhood" was "martial manhood." Most collegians did not aspire to the unrestrained models of manhood explored in the wider literature on American manhood: Stott, *Jolly Fellows*; Johnson, *Roaring Camp*; Horowitz, *Rereading Sex*, 125–43; Gorn, "Gouge and Bite, Pull Hair and Scratch."

20. On honor and restraint, see Stowe, *Intimacy and Power*, 6–15. Restrained manhood in the South has also been discussed in terms of religion. See Heyrman, *Southern Cross*; Lindman, "Acting the Manly Christian"; Carney, *Ministers and Masters*.

21. On going to college to become men, see Glover, *Southern Sons*; Carmichael, *The Last Generation*; Stowe, *Doctoring the South*, 16–17. See also the introduction to Leloudis, *Schooling the New South*.

22. Winslow, *Elements of Intellectual Philosophy*, 231–32.

23. Peck, *Formation of a Manly Character*, chaps. 2–3. This philosophy derived from the Scottish Enlightenment's "faculty psychology," which characterized the human mind as comprised of mental powers, or "faculties," such as reason, emotion, or will, which had to be exercised and disciplined through education. On faculty psychology and higher education, see Meyer, *The Instructed Conscience*, 66–67. Yale Report quoted in Pak, "The Yale Report of 1828," 50.

24. Keen, *An Address*, 23

25. Simms, *Charlemont*, 160, and *Beauchampe*, 355.

26. Henry Craft, 20 August 1848, in Berry, *Princes of Cotton*, 465.

27. The phrase "boundaries of power" is Stephanie McCurry's. See her *Masters of Small Worlds*, chap. 1

28. Cashin, *A Family Venture*, 55.

29. "Women," *The Atheneum* II (April–October 1822): 107; "Mind—Masculine and Feminine, *NCUM* I (April 1852): 120.

30. Stringfellow, *Slavery*, 10.

31. William Bagley to Margaret Bagby, 18 November 1841, Folder 1, Volume 1, William Bagley Papers, SHC.

32. Watson, "The Man with the Dirty Black Beard," 2–4.

33. Charles Wilson Harris Alexander, 14 March 1827, Address, DSR.

34. On honor, see Cash, *The Mind of the South*; Wyatt-Brown, *Southern Honor*; Greenberg, *Honor and Slavery*. On mastery, see McCurry, *Masters of Small Worlds*; Bleser, *Secret and Sacred*; Stowe, "The Rhetoric of Authority"; Carney, *Ministers and Masters*. No synthetic work on southern manhood yet exists. Stephen Berry offers the most concise state of the field in *Princes of Cotton*, ix–xiv. For another overview of scholarship on southern manhood, particularly the relationships among honor, mastery, and manhood, see Friend and Glover, *Southern Manhood*, vii–xvii. We rely, however, on several strong monographs on manhood. On young manhood and the southern frontier, see Cashin, *A Family Venture*; Baptist, *Creating an Old South*. On the Revolutionary and early national eras, see Glover, *Southern Sons*; Jabour, "Male Friendship and Masculinity in the Early National South" and "Masculinity and Adolescence in Antebellum America." Two exceptional works on the antebellum period are Mayfield, *Counterfeit Gentlemen*, and Pflugrad-Jackisch, *Brothers of a Vow*. On the Civil War era, see Berry, *All That Makes a Man* and *Princes of Cotton*; Taylor, *The Divided Family in Civil War America*; Carmichael, *The Last Generation*. Important works on southern manhood that fall outside of this study's chronological parameters include Ownby, *Subduing Satan*, and Wise, *William Alexander Percy*.

35. Baptist, "Me and Southern Honor," 14. I share Baptist's perspective that critiques of men's history as not focused on gendered power miss an important quality of antebellum men's history, which was that gendered power flowed among men, particularly in all-male settings. Bryce Traister, for instance, has called on historians to consider the effects of heterosexual male subjectivity on women. See his "Academic Viagra." Also see Allen, "Men Interminably in Crisis?"; Dierks, "Men's History, Gender History, or Cultural History?"

36. Pflugrad-Jackish, *Brothers of a Vow*, 2.

37. Symbolic presence is one of Toby L. Ditz's solutions to incorporating gendered power in men's history, and it is most fitting for this study. Although this book focuses on the cultural and intellectual processes of becoming men and, thus, the intellectual construction of male subjectivity, viewing their "uses of the symbolic woman" reveals assumptions of power in students' understanding of their maturation and education. See Ditz, "The New Men's History and the Peculiar Absence of Gendered Power," 17, 27.

38. Stowe, *Intimacy and Power*, 6–15.

39. Wyatt-Brown, *Southern Honor*, 164. Wyatt-Brown overemphasizes this point about the regionalism of male youth culture. Joseph Kett and E. Anthony Rotundo make similar arguments. See *Rites of Passage* and *American Manhood*, respectively.

40. Pace, *Halls of Honor*.

41. Jabour, "Male Friendship and Masculinity in the Early National South," 83–87, 106–11.

42. Berry, *All That Makes a Man*, 18.

43. More than forty years ago, Bernard Bailyn urged scholars to examine books, libraries, and readers in the context of education, yet male student writing remains surprisingly unexplored as artifacts of intellectual life in southern cultural and intellectual history. See *Education in the Forming of an American Society*, 85–86.

44. The model study of women's intellectual life to which I am most indebted is Kelley, *Learning to Stand and Speak*, 16. I have also relied on Cohen, "Making Hero Strong"; Kerrison, *Claiming the Pen*; Winterer, *The Mirror of Antiquity*, and "Victorian Antigone: Classicism and Women's Education in America"; Farnham, *Education of the Southern Belle*.

45. I have relied on many important histories of the book and reading: Roger Chartier, "Texts, Printing, Readings"; Darnton, *The Great Cat Massacre*; Davidson, *Revolution and*

the Word; Ginzburg, *The Cheese and the Worms*; Hall, *Cultures of Print*; Isaac, *Landon Carter's Uneasy Kingdom*, chap. 5; Machor, "Fiction and Informed Reading in Early Nineteenth-Century America"; Pawley, *Reading on the Middle Border*; Radway, *Reading the Romance*, and *A Feeling for Books*; Rose, *The Intellectual Life of the British Working Classes*; Ryan, *Reading Acts*; Sicherman, "Reading and Ambition"; Zboray, *A Fictive People*; Zboray and Zboray, *Everyday Ideas*. Two model approaches to young men's interactions with literature are August, *The Clerk's Tale*, and Casper, *Constructing American Lives*. Two volumes from the University of North Carolina Press's "History of the Book in America" series have been invaluable: Gross and Kelley, *An Extensive Republic*, and Casper et al., *A History of the Book in America, Volume 3: The Industrial Book*. In the field of southern history, Stephen Berry's *All That Makes a Man* and *Princes of Cotton* and John Mayfield's *Counterfeit Gentlemen* have most successfully integrated literary history within men's history.

46. On "interpretive communities," see Chartier, "Texts, Printing, Readings," 156–57; Fish, *Is There a Text in This Class?*, 317–18. On "literary socialization," see Zboray and Zboray, *Everyday Ideas*, 151–74.

47. On moral practice of writing among young men, see August, *The Clerk's Tale*.

48. Certeau, *The Practice of Everyday Life*, xiv.

49. Marginalia presents a bit of a conundrum, however, and I have only studied it when I was able to determine certainly that marginalia belonged to an antebellum student (usually by means of date or signature). Some books that students read have been preserved in the Old Library of the North Carolina Collection at the University of North Carolina, making marginalia analysis easier and more reliable than those books that have continued to circulate in the main library at the University of North Carolina.

50. The only other study to analyze college literary society debate questions is Harding, *College Literary Societies*. Other studies have also been helpful: Westbrook, "Debating Both Sides"; Ray, "The Permeable Public"; Woods, "Women Debating Society."

51. On this term, see especially Sellers, *The Market Revolution*; Larson, *The Market Revolution in America*. There has been much debate over the character of this era. My analysis favors Howe, *What Hath God Wrought*. Though distant from the epicenters of these so-called market, transportation, and communication revolutions, southern men were deeply affected by the transformations it wrought. See Pflugrad-Jackish, *Brothers of a Vow*.

52. Kagle, *Early Nineteenth-Century American Diary Literature*, 1–5. On young men and diary practices in particular, see August, *The Clerk's Tale*, 28. Also see O'Brien, *Conjectures of Order*, 456–57.

53. Stowe, *Intimacy and Power*, chap. 2, esp. 67.

54. In this regard, students most resembled the young men in August, *The Clerk's Tale*, who found journalizing to be a moral enterprise of the self.

55. On the continuity of intellectual life in the antebellum period, I have relied on Zboray, *A Fictive People*; Zboray and Zboray, *Everyday Ideas*; Stowe, *Intimacy and Power*, xvi.

56. For an explanation of how these cultural phenomena related to antebellum self-improvement, I have relied primarily on Howe, *Making the American Self*, and Casper, *Constructing American Lives*.

57. Houghton, *The Victorian Frame of Mind*, xv. Queen Victoria reigned from 1837 until 1901. Like Houghton, I take 1830 as a general marker for the consolidation of a particular cultural consciousness that can be defined as "Victorian" based on attitudes about the self and heroism in particular. Indeed, this study's richest sources are from the 1830s onward, so the use of the term Victorian is fitting here. The term highlights significant cultural

connections not only between the North and the South but also between the United States and Great Britain.

58. I have found Deborah Lowenberg Ball and Francesca M. Forzani's thinking about education research helpful in formulating these questions. See their "What Makes Educational Research 'Educational'?"

59. Burke, *American Collegiate Populations*, 48; *Catalogue of the Trustees* (1841).

60. "The University of North Carolina, By Judge Williamson, of Maine," *NCUM* 1 (November 1852): 382.

61. Battle, *History*, 647 (Baptist church); 479–80 (Episcopal church); 290, 519 (Presbyterian church); 619–20 (Methodist church).

62. The literature on evangelicalism is vast. I have relied principally on Mathews, *Religion in the Old South*; Heyrman, *Southern Cross*, chaps. 1–2; Hatch, *The Democratization of American Christianity*. Also see Carney, *Ministers and Masters*.

63. See, for example, Paschal, *History of Wake Forest College;* Young, "Religious Coming of Age." For a perspective outside of the South, see Findlay, "Agency, Denominations, and the Western Colleges."

64. On the early history of American collegiate literary societies, see Horowitz, *Campus Life*, 25; Potter, "The Literary Society," 238–40; Robson, *Educating Republicans*, 186. For a general history of the literary societies at UNC see Battle, *History*, 72–85; Lindemann, "The Debating Societies," in "True and Candid Compositions," DAS; Leloudis, "What Should a University Be?," 4–5. On the core values of the Dialectic and Philanthropic Societies, see membership pledge of the Dialectic Society, Dialectic Society Minutes, vol. 3, DSR.

65. Fraternities at UNC were forbidden in the early 1840s, though Battle notes that they began to be founded at UNC in 1851. See Battle, *History*, 476, 620–21. On the rise of fraternities in American colleges and universities, see Syrett, *The Company He Keeps*, 13–79. Correspondence from UNC's Alpha Sigma of Chi Psi Fraternity with Alphas across the country reveals the networks Syrett describes elsewhere. Records of Chi Psi, Alpha Sigma Chapter, University Archives. See also Autographs, NCC, and various autograph books held in University of North Carolina Miscellaneous Personal Papers, 1802–1976, SHC. This book does not focus on fraternities because of their limited reach at antebellum North Carolina and because of the excellent treatment they already receive in the work of Nicholas Syrett. For a list of other social organizations that appeared in the antebellum period, see Snider, *Light on the Hill*, 60.

66. I rely on Richard Storr's definition of "informal education" as anything that "can sensibly be described as educational." See his "The Education of History: Some Impressions," 124; Warren, "The Wonderful Worlds of the Education of History," 108–15.

67. Lefler and Wagner, *Orange County*, 96.

68. Battle, *History*, 602. Also see Lindemann, "Slaves and Servants," *True and Candid Compositions*, DAS. Slavery at antebellum colleges has recently received some attention from historians as well as education researchers, who have created websites to educate the general public on slavery's legacy at southern colleges. The University of North Carolina's Manuscripts Department offers an accessible website about slavery, which includes digital access to documents regarding slavery. See "Slavery and the Making of the University," <http://www2.lib.unc.edu/mss/exhibits/slavery/intro.html>. Also see Meyers, "Thinking about Slavery at the College of William and Mary."

Part 1

1. Battle, *History*, 2.

2. Robson, *Educating Republicans*, esp. 186–215. Also see Miller, *The Revolutionary College*; Pangle and Pangle, *The Learning of Liberty*.

3. I have relied on several histories of the University of North Carolina in this study. The principal work is Kemp P. Battle's *History of the University of North Carolina*. Others include Smith, *The History of Education in North Carolina*; Connor, Wilson, and Lefler, *A Documentary History of the University of North Carolina*; Vickers, Scism, and Qualls, *Chapel Hill: An Illustrated History*; Snider, *Light on the Hill*; Peterkin, "Lux, Libertas, and Learning." In addition, two online resources are very thorough: "The First Century of the First State University," DAS; and "True and Candid Compositions," DAS.

4. Burke, *American Collegiate Populations*, 14.

5. Snider, *Light on the Hill*, chap. 2.

6. On state escheats, see *Battle*, History, 150–52, 621–24.

7. Zboray and Zboray, *Literary Dollars and Social Sense*, 325. See also Zboray, *A Fictive People*.

8. Greenblatt, *Renaissance Self-Fashioning*, 1. On the emergence of the self in the South's romantic culture, see Fox-Genovese and Genovese, *The Mind of the Master Class*, 546.

Chapter 1

1. "Musings of a Student," *NCUM* 2 (February 1853): 30.

2. Berry, *Princes of Cotton*, 46.

3. Glover, *Southern Sons*, 3.

4. Censer, *North Carolina Planters and Their Children*, 42–64.

5. On common schools in the antebellum North Carolina, see Watson, "The Man with the Dirty Black Beard"; Lockley, *Welfare and Charity in the Antebellum South*, 180–84; Coon, *The Beginnings of Public Education in North Carolina*.

6. Knight, *Public School Education in North Carolina*, 48–54.

7. Harry St. John Dixon in Berry, *Princes of Cotton*, 42–43.

8. *Acts of the General Assembly and Ordinances of the Trustees*, 10.

9. William Bagley to William Grimes, 28 May 1842, William Bagley Papers, SHC.

10. William Bagley to Edward C. Yellowley, 28 February 1843, William Bagley Papers, SHC.

11. William Bagley to D. W. Bagley, 2 June 1843, William Bagley Papers, SHC.

12. Harry St. John Dixon, 9 March 1860 in Berry, *Princes of Cotton*, 45.

13. Ezell, "A Southern Education for Southrons," 303–27. An excellent study on southern students in the North is Kilbride, "Southern Medical Students in Philadelphia."

14. D. Wilkins to Thomas Williamson Jones, 2 April 1820, Folder 2, Thomas Williamson Jones Papers, SHC.

15. Burke, *American Collegiate Populations*, 40. According to Burke, South Carolina College's tuition was the highest.

16. I have used a basic online inflation calculator to determine these values: <http://www.westegg.com/inflation/> (accessed 8 October 2012).

17. *Catalogue*, 18.

18. Henry A. London, Diary, Henry Armand London Papers, SHC; Powell, ed., *Dictionary of North Carolina Biography*, vol. 4, 85–86.

19. William Bagley to his father, 1 July 1843, Folder 1, Volume 1, William Bagley Papers, SHC. See also letters from an earlier period: Moses John DeRosset, 12 October 1815, in Tolbert, *Two Hundred Years*, 77; Iveson Brookes to his father, 5 July 1817, Iveson L. Brookes Papers, SHC.

20. Glover, *Southern Sons*, 45–46; Censer, *North Carolina Planters and Their Children*, 50–51.

21. Rotundo, *American Manhood*; Kett, *Rites of Passage*.

22. Walter Lenoir to Thomas Lenoir, 6 January 1843, Box 7, Folder 86, Lenoir Family Papers, SHC.

23. Walter W. Lenoir and Thomas Lenoir, 3 May 1843, Box, 7, Folder 87, SHC.

24. *Acts of the General Assembly and Ordinances of the Trustees*, 10.

25. On the important role of extended family among southern planters, see Cashin, *A Family Venture*, 9–20. A contemporary example can be found in Lenoir Family Papers, SHC.

26. Garrett, 12–14 July 1849, Diary, Typed Transcript, 56–60, Thomas Miles Garrett Diary, SHC. On kinship and community, see Glover, *Southern Sons*, 48.

27. "Musings of a Student," *NCUM* 2 (February 1853): 30.

28. Preston Sessoms to Penelope White, 27 September 1861, University of North Carolina Miscellaneous Papers, SHC.

29. For additional examples of the difficulty of travel to Chapel Hill, see T. R. Caldwell to John Caldwell, 2 August 1837, Box 1, Folder 8, John Caldwell Papers, SHC. See also Pace, *Halls of Honor*, 34–35. On transportation in antebellum North Carolina, see Lefler and Newsome, *North Carolina*, 316–17.

30. Henry R. Bryan, 19 January 1853, in Tolbert, *Two Hundred Years*, 28.

31. William R. Burk, "The University of North Carolina Campus," *The First Century of the First State University*, DAS.

32. "The Campus," *NCUM* 4 (1856): 378–79.

33. Slaves' contributions to the construction and life of the university were often undocumented and not included in institutional histories. The most extensive discussion of this topic can be found on the University of North Carolina's online exhibit, "Slavery and the Making of the University" < http://www2.1ib.unc.edu/mss/exhibits/slavery/buildings. html>.

34. Henderson, *The Campus of the First State University*, 355–56. See also "Buildings," *The First Century of the First State University*, DAS.

35. Lindemann, "The School Day and the School Year," *True and Candid Compositions*, DAS.

36. Thomas Brown to his sister, 26 July 1855; Henry R. Bryan, 19 January 1853, in Tolbert, *Two Hundred Years*, 28–29.

37. Dusenbery, 29 August 1841, Diary, Folder, 1, James Lawrence Dusenbery Diary and Clipping, SHC.

38. Charles Pettigrew, 19 August 1833, in Tolbert, *Two Hundred Years*, 23–24.

39. *NCUM* 2 (May 1853): 207–8.

40. Battle, *History*, 273–74.

41. William D. Lowther to his sister, 7 April 1814, in Tolbert, *Two Hundred Years*, 21. On Steward's Hall, see Battle, *History*, 224–26.

42. Nathan Neal, 2 September 1857, in Tolbert, *Two Hundred Years*, 29–30.

43. William A. Wooster, "Home and College Life Contrasted," 31 October 1857, Wooster Family Papers, SHC. The nature of parent-child relations in the South is contested. Bertram Wyatt-Brown has argued that southern fathers imposed total authority over their sons, even at college. See his "Ideal Typology," 5–28. Others take a more complicated view. See Stowe, "The Rhetoric of Authority"; Wakelyn, "Antebellum College Life and the Relations between Fathers and Sons"; Rotundo, *American Manhood*, chaps. 2–3; Censer, *North Carolina Planters and Their Children*, 54–64. Censer's view is most accurate, arguing that parents preferred to emphasize affection instead of obedience, and entrusted to children a degree of autonomy during youth.

44. Bledstein, *The Culture of Professionalism*, 208.

45. Battle, *History*, 787–815; Burke, *American Collegiate Populations*, 119–20.

46. *NCUM* 1 (1852): 107–10.

47. "Diversity of Individual Character," *NCUM* 1 (October 1852): 335–36.

48. In the antebellum period, the bell was located atop South building. It was "rung by a long rope and when it rings you can hear it a mile off." See Preston H. Sessoms to Penelope E. White, 27 September 1861, University of North Carolina Miscellaneous Papers, SHC. Some students awoke earlier to read or study. See Mullins, 20 January 1841, William Sidney Mullins Diary, SHC.

49. Snider, *Light on the Hill*, 62. Also see "Fall Fashions," *NCUM* 1 (November 1852): 416.

50. Thomas W. Mason, "The Journal of a Day," 1856, Sally Long Jarman Papers, SHC.

51. *Acts of the General Assembly and Ordinances of the Trustees*, 11–12. Lindemann, "The School Day and the School Year," *True and Candid Compositions*, DAS; Mason, "Journal of a Day," 1856, Sally Long Jarman Papers, SHC.

52. D. Wilkins to Thomas Williamson Jones, 2 April 1820, Folder 2, Thomas Williamson Jones Papers, SHC. See also John Cagrill Jones to Thomas Williamson Jones, Folder 2, 28 May 1812, SHC; Walter W. Lenoir to Thomas Lenoir, 1 February 1840, Folder 78, Lenoir Family Papers, SHC; William Bagley to Samuel Watts, 14 October 1844, Folder 2, Volume 2, William Bagley Papers, SHC.

53. John T. Jones, 16 April 1836, Box 1, Folder 3, James Gwyn Papers, SHC. Emphasis in original.

54. Hugh Torrence to William Latta, 4 September 1828, Box 1, Folder 5, UNC Personal Papers, Misc., SHC.

55. Dusenbery, 24 April 1842, Diary, Folder, 1, James Lawrence Dusenbery Diary and Clipping, SHC.

56. Kett, *Rites of Passage*; Novak, *The Rights of Youth*; Jackson, "The Rights of Man and the Rites of Youth"; McLachlan, "The Choice of Hercules," 474.

57. Bartholomew Fuller, "The 'Danger of a College Life,'" 1848, Folder 1, Bartholomew Fuller Papers, SHC. For additional reports of rowdiness and dissipation in student writing, see Tolbert, *Two Hundred Years*, 59–75.

58. James Johnston Pettigrew to his father, 21 February 1847, Pettigrew Family Papers, SHC. See also Walter W. Lenoir to Thomas Lenoir, 17 February 1841, Folder 81, Lenoir Family Papers, SHC.

59. Faculty records are replete with instances of rowdiness and misbehavior, especially fights, absences, drinking in town, and vandalism of college property. Faculty Minutes, vols. 1:1–6, Faculty Records, UA.

60. Allmendinger, "The Dangers of Ante-Bellum Student Life," 75–85, and *Paupers and*

Scholars; Horowitz, *Campus Life*, 23–55; Mullins, "Honorable Violence," 161–79; Hessinger, "'The Most Powerful Instrument of College Discipline,'" 237–62; Syrett, *The Company He Keeps*, chap. 1.

61. Swearing was not exclusively an antebellum concern, for papers from the early national period are replete with complaints about offensive language. See, for example, John Pettigrew to Charles Pettigrew, 27 June 1797, Pettigrew Family Papers, SHC.

62. Minutes, 25 August 1805, vol. 1:1, General Faculty and Faculty Council of the University of North Carolina at Chapel Hill Records, UA.

63. "Conversation Enriches the Mind," *NCUM* 3 (April 1854): 138–39. Emphasis in original.

64. *NCUM* 1 (April 1852): 127.

65. Henry Armand London Jr., Diary, Folder 2, Volume 1, Henry Armand London, SHC, 65. See also Fuller, *Sea-Gift*, 191–94.

66. Battle, *History*, 465. See also Mullins, 20 October 1840, William Sidney Mullins Diary, SHC; Ishkanian, "Religion and Honor," 120–28.

67. On college students and alcohol, see Hevel, "'Betwixt brewings,'" 43.

68. Minutes, 14 September 1818, vol. 1:2, General Faculty and Faculty Council of the University of North Carolina at Chapel Hill Records, UA.

69. Garrett, 12 September 1849, Diary, Typed Transcript, 125–27. Another vivid example of collegiate spreeing can be found in William Bagley to Clementina Bagley and Marietta Bagley, 15 February 1845, Folder 2, Volume 2, William Bagley Papers, SHC. Students also drank excessively between terms, when many students remained at college because of the difficulty and expenses of traveling. See James Johnston Pettigrew to his father, 13 January 1844, Pettigrew Family Papers, SHC.

70. Dusenbery, 29 August and 5 September 1841, Diary, Folder, 1, James Lawrence Dusenbery Diary and Clipping, SHC.

71. Adams, *Education of Henry Adams*, 95.

72. Bledstein, *The Culture of Professionalism*, 236.

73. *Acts of the General Assembly and Ordinances of the Trustees*, 14–17.

74. Battle, *History*, 357, 359. On tutors and American colleges, see Jackson, "The Rights of Man," 55; Bledstein, *Culture of Professionalism*, 237; Syrett, *The Company He Keeps*, 19–20.

75. Battle, *History*, 275–76.

76. See, for example, Mitchell, *Statistics, Facts, and Dates*.

77. Battle, *History*, 417, 462.

78. Ibid., 54–55.

79. Dusenbery, 7 August 1841, Diary, Folder, 1, James Lawrence Dusenbery Diary and Clipping, SHC.

80. Mullins, 1 August 1841, William Sidney Mullins Diary, SHC.

81. Lindman, "Acting the Manly Christian"; Causey, "The Character of a Gentleman"; Heyrman, *Southern Cross*; Carney, *Ministers and Masters*.

82. On fanaticism and revivals, see Samuel B. Stephens to William Gaston, 11 July 1831, Box 3, Folder 49, William Gaston Papers, SHC. See also Solomon Lea, 14 September 1832, Box 1, Folder 1, Lea Family Papers, SHC.

83. Dusenbery, 22 August 1841, Diary, Folder, 1, James Lawrence Dusenbery Diary and Clipping, SHC.

84. Hooper, *The Discipline of the Heart*, 1, 8, 12–13, 19–20.

85. See Hessinger, *Seduced, Abandoned, and Reborn*, 127.

86. Glover, *Southern Sons*, 81.

87. McLachlan, "The Choice of Hercules," 472.

88. Battle, *History*, 72–76; Leloudis, "What Should a University Be?," 4–5.

89. Potter, "The Literary Society," 238–40; Horowitz, *Campus Life*, 25; Robson, *Educating Republicans*, 186.

90. Battle, *History*, 476.

91. William Gaston Lewis, Inaugural Address, 9 March 1855, DSR.

92. Syrett, *The Company He Keeps*, 13–79. Correspondence from UNC's Alpha Sigma of Chi Psi Fraternity with Alphas across the country reveals the networks Syrett describes elsewhere. Records of Chi Psi, Alpha Sigma Chapter, University Archives. See also Autographs, NCC, and various autograph books held in University of North Carolina Miscellaneous Personal Papers, SHC.

93. Virginius Henry Ivy, Inaugural Address, 18 October 1844, DSR.

94. McLachlan, "The Choice of Hercules," 474.

95. Robert John Donnell, Composition, 3 August 1805, DSR.

96. Julius Alexander Caldwell, Inaugural Address, 6 April 1850, DSR.

97. Manly, Inaugural Address, 28 August 1813, DSR.

98. Junius Cullen Battle, Inaugural Address, 16 September 1859, DSR.

99. William James Cowan, Inaugural Address, 1808, DSR.

100. Student advice against swearing on campus also can be found in Elias Hawes to Thomas Williamson Jones, 19 March 1810, Folder 1, Thomas Williamson Jones Papers, SHC; formal complains about swearing in the Dialectic and Philanthropic Society minutes books; "Conversation Enriches the Mind," *NCUM* 3 (April 1854): 138–39. On swearing and southern elites in the early national era, see also Glover, *Southern Sons*, 85, 101–2.

101. James Hooper Colton, Inaugural Address, 18 August 1854, DSR. On these bourgeois values, also see William Polk Boylan, Inaugural Address, 20 October 1824; William Martin Crenshaw, Inaugural Address, 23 February 1833, DSR.

102. Joseph John Jackson, Inaugural Address, 6 February 1838, DSR.

103. Jabour, "Male Friendship and Masculinity in the Early National South." On women's learning and friendship, see Kelley, *Learning to Stand and Speak*, 16.

104. John Wilder Cameron, Composition, 1848, DSR. "Dialectic Society Minutes," 1798–1804, vol. 3, Dialectic Records, UA. Also see Jeremiah Battle, Address, 1799, DSR.

105. Lucius Frierson, "Retributive Dreams," 5 March 1859, DSR.

106. George Shonnard Bettner, Inaugural Address, September 1822, DSR. See also Samuel Thomas Hauser, Inaugural Address, 1 April 1817; Hector H. McAlister, Address, 1841; Charles L. Manly, Valedictory Address, 23 June 1814; Robert Williams Henry, Inaugural Address, 1835, all in DSR.

107. John Davis Hawkins, Inaugural Address, 4 September 1800, DSR.

108. Green, *Military Education*, 98.

109. Mullins, 12 July 1841, William Sidney Mullins Diary, SHC. Ishkanian, "Religion and Honor at Chapel Hill," 57–66. Ishkanian has speculated that William Mullins's father may have had a drinking problem and that his youngest brother may have had a physical disability that caused the family grief, though Mullins did not explicitly say so in his diary.

110. Mullins, 15 November 1840, William Sidney Mullins Diary, SHC. See also Ishkanian, "Religion and Honor at Chapel Hill," 73-4. Despite his dissipation at college, Lucius Johnson went on to become a lawyer.

111. For a fictional account of a very similar story as Mullins's, see "John Bright's Three Years in College," *NCUM* 1 (August 1852): 230-34.

112. Mullins, 15 November 1840, William Sidney Mullins Diary, SHC.. Additional discussions of the "sham duel" can be found in Ishkanian, "Religion and Honor at Chapel Hill," 72-76; Robert F. Pace, *Halls of Honor*, 96; Pace and Bjornsen, "Adolescent Honor," 21-24.

113. Mullins, 28 October 1840, William Sidney Mullins Diary, SHC. Emphasis in original.

114. Greenberg,*Honor & Slavery*, 8, 25, 49, 135.

115. Mullins, 4 July 1841; 7 February 1841; 20 June 1841; 10 July 1841, William Sidney Mullins Diary, SHC.

116. William Seawell, 30 March 1825, Address, DSR.

Chapter 2

1. Sanders, "The Journal of Ruffin Wirt Tomlinson," 108.

2. The best book on the history of classical learning and its American tradition is Kimball, *Orators and Philosophers*, esp. 138-56.

3. Drake, *Higher Education in North Carolina before 1860*, 156-57. For a contemporary summary, see Iveson L. Brookes, Inaugural Address, September 1818, DSR.

4. Lorri Glover makes this claim about ornamentalism in *Southern Sons*, 57. Also see Causey, "The Character of a Gentleman," 74; Green, *Military Education*.

5. Censer, *North Carolina Planters and Their Children*, 43-44.

6. Winterer, *The Culture of Classicism*, 2, 6.

7. The literature on classicism is vast, and I have relied on significant works, including Richard, *The Founders and the Classics*; Winterer, *The Culture of Classicism*; Durrill, "The Power of Ancient Words," 469-98; Fox-Genovese and Genovese, *The Mind of the Master Class*, 249-304; Farnham, *The Education of the Southern Belle*, 73. See also Gimbert, "The Purpose and Effects of Classical Education in the Antebellum South."

8. Science is not usually a focus in studies on southern higher education, though it was central to the overall curriculum. See Miller, *The Revolutionary College*, 18. Important works on this topic include Guralnick, *Science and the Ante-Bellum American College*, 159; Hornberger, *Scientific Thought in the American College*, 48; Dyer, "Science in the Antebellum College," 36-54.

9. Both professors' lecture notes and assigned textbooks included guiding questions in the marginalia, which provide insight into how this pedagogy worked. For lecture marginalia, see James Phillips's lecture notes in Cornelia Phillips Spencer Papers, SHC. For guiding questions in textbooks, see Abercrombie, *Inquiries Concerning the Intellectual Powers and the Investigation of Truth*, 23.

10. Battle, *History*, 464.

11. Thomas W. Mason, "The Journal of a Day," Sally Long Jarman Papers, SHC; Lindemann, "The School Day and the School Year," DAS.

12. Henry Francis Jones, 6 October 1857, Diary, Folder 1, Henry Francis Jones Diary, SHC.

13. Archibald McLauchlin to Sarah McLauchlin, 17 August 1853, Folder 1, Archibald McLauchlin Correspondence, SHC.

14. George N. Thompson, 17 January 1851, Diary, George N. Thompson Diary, SHC.

15. Thomas W. Mason, "The Journal of a Day," Sally Long Jarman Papers, SHC.

16. "William Hooper's Critique of Instruction at the University of North Carolina, December 19, 1833," University of North Carolina Papers, UA.

17. Baker, *Affairs of Party*, 88. Baker argues that mid-nineteenth-century classrooms in the North conveyed a democratic political culture in the same way as didactic, biographical, and historical literature.

18. Pace, *Halls of Honor*, 11, 21, 28. On revealing ignorance, see Greenberg, *Honor & Slavery*.

19. Henry Francis Jones, 14 September 1857, Diary, Folder 1, Henry Francis Jones Diary, SHC.

20. James Phillips, "Natural Philosophy Lecture 2d. History completed, Its importance Shewn," undated, Folder 203, Volume 47, Cornelia Phillips Spencer Papers, SHC. On science lectures, see Brubacher and Rudy, *Higher Education in Transition*, 89.

21. Dusenbery, 10 October 1841, Diary, Folder, 1, James Lawrence Dusenbery Diary and Clipping, SHC. See also Sanders, "The Journal of Ruffin Wirt Tomlinson," 241.

22. Mullins, 20 January 1841, 21 July 1841, William Sidney Mullins Diary, SHC.

23. Joseph Hubbard Saunders, undated, Notebook, Box 1, Folder 4, Miscellaneous Students' Notebooks, SHC. Emphasis in original. Olmstead, *Outlines of the Lectures on Chemistry*, 8.

24. James Henderson Dickson, Inaugural Address, 23 August 1822, DSR.

25. Thomas Miles Garrett, 20 December 1849, Diary, Typed Transcript, 252, SHC.

26. On social life and study, see George Shonnard Bettner, Inaugural Address, September 1822, DSR. Sometimes students discussed the importance of study in letters to younger siblings. See, for example, Kenelm H. Lewis to Emma Lewis, 8 September 1834, Box 1, Folder 6, John Francis Speight Papers, SHC

27. James Hilliard Polk, 22 July 1859, Diary, Folder 1, James Hilliard Polk Diary, SHC, 9.

28. Edward C. Easterling to Rebecca Easterling, 26 August 1858, Rebecca Easterling Papers, USC.

29. Garrett, 13 September 1849, Diary, Typed Transcript, 127, SHC.

30. Jones, Diary, 30 October 1857, Folder 1, Henry Francis Jones Diary, SHC.

31. Fuller, *Sea-Gift*, 168–69.

32. Charles L. Pettigrew, 11 October 1835, Pettigrew Family Papers, SHC.

33. Charles L. Pettigrew, 7 November 1835, Pettigrew Family Papers, SHC. On other students' reactions to grading, see James Lawrence Dusenbery, 3 October 1841, Diary, Folder, 1, James Lawrence Dusenbery Diary and Clipping, SHC; William S. Grandy, 31 July 1842, Willis G. Briggs Papers, SHC.

34. "A grade report for Tod Caldwell to John Caldwell," Circular, 15 April 1837, Box 1, Folder 8, John Caldwell Papers, SHC. Some faculty kept ledgers in which they noted whether students' recitations were "very good," "good," "respectable," or "tolerable." See Battle, *History*, 553.

35. Nationally, awarding distinctions began in the 1830s. See David F. Allmendinger, *Paupers and Scholars*. On distinctions and bourgeois values, see Hessinger, *Seduced, Abandoned, and Reborn*, 94–95.

36. Richmond Nicholas Pearson, [Junior] Oration [ca. 1840], Senior and Junior Orations, NCC. See also Robert Duncan Dickson, [Junior] Oration [ca. 1840]; Charles Phillips, "[On College Distinctions]" [ca. 1840], Senior and Junior Orations, NCC.

37. Edmund Covington, 6 October 1842, Diary, SHC.

38. Kenelm H. Lewis to William F. Lewis, 16 May 1835, K. H. Lewis Papers, NCDAH. See also Walter W. Lenoir to Rufus T. Lenoir, 5 February 1842, Lenoir Family Papers, SHC.

39. Greenblatt, *Renaissance Self-Fashioning*; Bowen, "Education, Ideology and the Ruling Class," 161–86; Ong, "Latin Language Study as a Renaissance Puberty Rite," 121, 123.

40. Fox-Genovese and Genovese, *Mind of the Master Class*, 257. This is the conventional interpretation of classics study and southern elites found, for instance, in Durrill, "The Power of Ancient Words," 471, and Glover, *Southern Sons*, 57. While female academies offered Latin and Greek, it was not to the extent that male academies, colleges, and universities did. See Farnham, *The Education of the Southern Belle*, 73; Tolley, "Science for Ladies, Classics for Gentlemen," 143.

41. Caldwell, "Address to the Senior Class," 7.

42. Drake, *Higher Education in North Carolina before 1860*, 178; Winterer, *The Culture of Classicism*, 32–33. Major texts include John Mair's *Introduction to Latin Syntax* (1820) and John Popkin's American edition of *Collectanea Graeca Majora* (1809); Neilson's *Greek Exercises* (1810); and Fisk's *Greek Grammar* and *Greek Exercises* (1831).

43. Durrill, "The Power of Ancient Words," 473.

44. Drake, *Higher Education in North Carolina before 1860*, 177–78. I have selected titles that have appeared most consistently in the University of North Carolina's college catalogues for the antebellum period. See the online collection of catalogs at *North Carolina College and University Yearbooks*.

45. George N. Thompson, 13 January 1851, George N. Thompson Diary, SHC.

46. William Bagley to D. W. Bagley, 10 August 1844, Folder 1, Volume 1, William Bagley Papers, SHC. See also James Hilliard Polk, 7 September 1859, Diary, Folder 1, James Hilliard Polk Diary, SHC.

47. "The Freshman's Friend," 1846, Box 3, Folder 17, UNC Personal Papers, Misc., SHC.

48. Walter W. Lenoir to Thomas Lenoir, 5 October 1842, Box 6, Folder 85, Lenoir Family Papers, SHC.

49. Wilbur Fisk Foster, "Speech of W. F. Foster of Ala[bama], Junior Debate for 1858," DSR. For a similar critique of antebellum science instruction, see David Alexander Barnes, Diary, 10 February 1840, 15 February 1840, David Alexander Barnes Papers, SHC.

50. Durrill, "The Power of Ancient Words," 497–98; Fox-Genovese and Genovese, *Mind of the Master Class*, 250–52, 262. Elizabeth Fox-Genovese and Eugene Genovese have demonstrated that North Carolina was unique in the South for maintaining its heavy emphasis on antiquity while at the same time expanding its scientific curriculum.

51. Xenophon, *Memorabilia* 2.1.7, *Perseus Digital Library*.

52. Ibid., 2.1.21–34.

53. Cicero, *De Officiis* 3.5.25, quoted in McLachlan, "The Choice of Hercules," 449.

54. James Alfred Patton, Inaugural Address, 24 July 1850, DSR.

55. Elam Alexander, Address, February 1825, DSR.

56. Powell, *Cicero: Cato Maior De Senectute*, 1–3.

57. An exemplary student response to *De Amicitia* is Robert Williams Henry, Inaugural Address, 1835, DSR.

58. Garrett, 21 August 1849, Diary, Typed Transcript, 98.

59. Houghton, *The Victorian Frame of Mind*, 265–67.

60. Berry, *All That Makes a Man*, 26–27.

61. Thomas Clark Hooper, Address, 1812, DSR.

62. Rufus M. Rosebrough, Address, February 1832, DSR.

63. Harry St. John Dixon, 19 June 1860 and 7 July 1860, in Berry, *Princes of Cotton*, 125, 138.

64. Dialectic Society Minutes, 2 August 1810, DSR.

65. Winterer, *The Culture of Classicism*, 26.

66. Fox-Genovese and Genovese, *Mind of the Master Class*, 252.

67. Drake, *Higher Education in North Carolina before 1860*, 171.

68. Brookes, Inaugural Address, September 1818, DSR. See also Iveson L. Brookes to Jonathan Brookes, 13 February 1818, Iveson Lewis Brookes Papers, SHC.

69. Drake, *Higher Education in North Carolina before 1860*, 171–72. According to Drake, these textbooks included Thomas Simpson, *A Treatise of Algebra* (1809), and John Radford Young, *An Elementary Treatise on Algebra* (1832). Simpson's text was simpler than Young's and the switch to the latter suggests an increased interest in advanced mathematics by the late antebellum period.

70. Davies, *Elements of Geometry and Trigonometry*. Walter Lenoir studied "Davies' Legendre." See Walter W. Lenoir to Thomas Lenoir, 20 January 1840, Lenoir Family Papers, SHC.

71. Joseph Caldwell, "A New System of Geometry by the Reverend Joseph Caldwell, Professor of Mathematics and President of the University of North Carolina," 1806, Folder 4, Volume 2, Joseph Caldwell Papers, SHC, 14–15.

72. Caldwell, *A Compendious System of Elementary Geometry*, 291. Board of Trustees Minutes, 19 December 1818, DAS. For mathematical problems, see James Phillips, "Mathematical Questions," undated, Folder 174, Volume 17, Cornelia Phillips Spencer Papers, SHC.

73. The development of the curriculum is most evident in the college catalogs for this period, but also in records of student final examinations. See Faculty Records, vols. 1:2–4 (1814–1846), Faculty Records, UA. For student commentary, see Frederick William Harrison to Thomas Williamson Jones, 3 March 1834, Folder 2, Thomas Williamson Jones Papers, SHC.

74. Faculty Records, vol. 1:4, 319, Faculty Records, UA.

75. James Phillips, "The Elements of Plane and Spherical Trigonometry. Compiled for the use of the Students of the University of N. Carolina by James Phillips Prof. of Math. & Nat. Phil.," undated, Folder 172, Volume 16, Cornelia Phillips Spencer Papers, SHC.

76. Carmichael, *The Last Generation*, 60.

77. Foster, "Speech of W. F. Foster of Ala[bama], Junior Debate for 1858," DSR.

78. Guralnick, *Science and the Ante-Bellum American College*, 154.

79. Miller, *The Life of the Mind in America*, 275.

80. James Phillips, Natural Philosophy lectures, undated, Folders 202–8, Volumes 46–52, Cornelia Phillips Spencer Papers, SHC. Phillips's lectures included topics such as the properties of matter, Newton's laws of motion, gravity, the theories and measurement of time, "experiments on the mechanic powers," and the nature of bodies, fluids, and liquids, as well as their properties and relationships. It culminated in lectures about air

pressure, theories of winds, hurricanes, waterspouts, and the media and transmission of sound.

81. James Phillips, "Astronomy. Lecture 1st. Its attractions, its uses, history, cultivators &c.," undated, Folder 175, Volume 19, Cornelia Phillips Spencer Papers, SHC.

82. Phillips, James Phillips Volumes, vol. 24, Cornelia Phillips Spencer Papers, SHC.

83. Phillips, "On the Sun, & zodiacal light," James Phillips Volumes, vol. 25, Cornelia Phillips Spencer Papers. James Thomson, "Summer" (1727), in Samuel Johnson, *The Works of the English Poets, From Chaucer to Cowper. . . .*, Volume 41 (London, 1810), 422. Phillips wrote, "May I talk of thee," while Thomson wrote, "May I sing of thee."

84. Phillips, "Astronomy. Lecture 9th. The 'Cui bono'? question noticed; the Milky way; figments of the ancients respecting it; its real constitution explained; distance of some of its stars; its superior magnificence in southern latitudes. . . . ," undated, Folder 183, Volume 28, Cornelia Phillips Spencer, SHC.

85. Phillips, "Astronomy. Lecture 2nd. Discoveries of Halley, Bradley, Herschel. . . . ," undated, Folder 176, Volume 20, Cornelia Phillips Spencer Papers, SHC.

86. Garrett, 25 October 1849, Diary, Typed Transcript, 182, SHC.

87. Phillips, "Introductory Lecture to Natural Philosophy," undated, Folder 202, Volume 46, Cornelia Phillips Spencer Papers, SHC.

88. Cicero Stephens Croom, "Motion Universal," 15 March 1859, DSR. Croom's grandfather held the same views. See also Hardy Bryan Croom, Address, 5 March 1817, DSR.

89. James Phillips, "Natural Philosophy Lecture 2d. History completed, Its Importance Shewn," undated lecture, Folder 203, Volume 47, Cornelia Phillips Spencer Papers, SHC.

90. Rudolph, *Curriculum*, 40, 90. These were the driving questions of eighteenth- and nineteenth-century moral philosophy. See Goetzmann, *Beyond the Revolution*, 56. In general, the history of moral philosophy in American higher education has gone largely unstudied and only two historians have dealt substantively with the philosophers and texts studied: Meyer, *The Instructed Conscience*, and Howe, *The Unitarian Conscience*. Like these works, this section relies largely on eighteenth- and nineteenth-century moral philosophy texts more than on manuscript sources because primary sources for this part of the educational experience at North Carolina are rare. For example, I have been unable to locate David L. Swain's lectures on the subject or any detailed engagement with readings in student writing. Uncovering marginalia in texts was also difficult for this subject because the texts that students would have read for class continue to circulate in the University of North Carolina's main library, removing any reliability. The primary means by which students seemed to have engaged with the lessons of moral philosophy, however, are more evident in student literary society debates. As I argue in chapter 7, students regularly engaged the ethical concerns of moral philosophy in weekly debates. Their debate questions reflected the major ethical concerns of Paley, Wayland, and others. Moreover, the questions closely resembled the questions that Yale College president Timothy Dwight Jr. asked his moral philosophy students in the early nineteenth century, suggesting a certain correlation between moral and ethical thought in and outside of the classroom. See Dwight, *President Dwight's Decisions*.

91. Rudolph, *Curriculum*, 90. Between 1795 and 1835, North Carolina students studied William Paley's *Principles of Moral and Political Philosophy* (1785) and Montesquieu's *On the Spirit of Laws* (1748). After 1835, students read the Bible, John Abercrombie's *Inquiries Concerning the Intellectual Powers and the Investigation of Truth* (1830), and Francis Way-

land's *Elements of Moral Science* (1835), *Elements of Political Economy* (1837), and *Elements of Intellectual Philosophy* (1854). In addition, they read the first volume of James Kent's *Commentaries on American Law* (1826) and Joseph Story's *Familiar Exposition of the Constitution* (1833). In tandem with these works, Swain delivered lectures on the history of constitutional law. The catalog states that these works were used "with constant reference" to Thomas Brown, *Lectures on the Philosophy* (1824), and Thomas C. Upham, *Elements of Mental Philosophy* (1840). See *Catalogue of the Trustees, Faculty, and Students, of the University of N. Carolina*, 1846.

92. Julian E. Leach, "On Moral & Intellectual Philosophy," 25 May 1835, DSR.

93. Dusenbery, 12 October 1841, Diary, Folder, 1, James Lawrence Dusenbery Diary and Clipping, SHC. Dusenbery's diary report also suggests that Swain may have used John Witherspoon's famous Princeton lectures on moral philosophy. Witherspoon said at Princeton that the study of morals began with the study of man. He explained, "It seems a point agreed upon that the principles of duty and obligation must be drawn from the nature of man. That is to say, if we can discover how his Maker formed him, or for what he intended him, that certainly is what he ought to be." Witherspoon quoted in Meyer, *The Instructed Conscience*, 35.

94. Goetzmann, *Beyond the Revolution*, 56–58.

95. Dugald Reid quoted in Meyer, *The Instructed Conscience*, 39.

96. Meyer, *The Instructed Conscience*, 24–25, 54–55, 66.

97. Abercrombie, *Inquiries Concerning the Intellectual Powers and the Investigation of Truth*, 267.

98. Ibid., 277.

99. Julian E. Leach, "On Moral & Intellectual Philosophy," 25 May 1835, DSR.

100. Hooper, *The Discipline of the Heart*, 8–9. Meyer, *The Instructed Conscience*, 63.

101. D. L. Le Mahieu, in foreword to Paley, *The Principles of Moral and Political Philosophy*, xii–xiv. Joseph L. Blau, in foreword to Wayland, *The Elements of Moral Science*, xli–xlii.

102. Wayland, *The Elements of Moral Science*, 137, 150.

103. Ibid., 271.

104. Ibid., 275.

105. Gabrielse, "Making Men, Colleges and the Midwest," 134–51.

106. Dew, "Dissertation on the Characteristic Differences Between the Sexes," 495.

107. Hugh T. Brown, 26 September 1857, "Journal," Box 6, Folder 110, Volume 23, Hamilton Brown Papers, SHC.

108. Wayland, *The Elements of Moral Science*, 277–305.

109. Sugrue, "'We Desired Our Future Rulers to Be Educated Men'"; Durrill, "The Power of Ancient Words."

110. Pangle and Pangle, *The Learning of Liberty*, 36–37.

111. Wayland, *Elements of Moral Science*, 182–83, 188. Emphasis in original.

112. Ibid., 191. Emphasis in original.

113. Ibid., 196.

114. Ibid., xliii–xlix.

115. The University of North Carolina was the only southern college to assign Wayland's book, as Elizabeth Fox-Genovese and Eugene Genovese have explained in their comprehensive *The Mind of the Master Class*. Higher schools, including girls' academies, however, did assign the book. See Farnham, *Education of the Southern Belle*, 86. On southerners'

diverse and unpredictable attitudes about slavery, see Freehling, *The Road to Disunion, Volume II*, and Ford, *Deliver Us from Evil*, esp. chaps. 12–14.

116. Smith, *The History of Education in North Carolina*, 79–80.

117. Mitchell, *The Other Leaf of the Book of Nature*, 21, 63–64. The field of proslavery writing in North Carolina remains fertile ground for scholars. Mitchell's published sermons are rarely, if ever, included in works on proslavery writers in the South.

118. Brophy, "The Republics of Liberty and Letters," 1957–1960. Also see Battle, *History*, 667n80.

119. Sugrue, "'We Desired Our Future Rulers to Be Educated Men'," 105.

120. *Catalogue of the Trustees, Faculty, and Students of the University of N. Carolina, 1846–47*, 25.

121. Kimball, *Orators and Philosophers*, 138–56.

122. "The Rewards of Educated Men, and Their Indebtedness to the World," *NCUM* I (September 1852): 276. See also Alfred Gowan Merritt, "The Man of Superior Intellect alone gains admiration," Composition, 6 October 1852, DSR.

Chapter 3

1. James Knox Polk, "James K. Polk's Inaugural Address Delivered in the Dialectic Hall May 20th 1818," DSR.

2. *Dictionary of North Carolina Biography*, vol. 5, 107–9.

3. Reynolds, *Walt Whitman's America*, 167. Eastman, *A Nation of Speechifiers*, esp. chap. 4.

4. The term "community of listeners" is my adaptation of Joseph L. Featherstone's phrase "community of hearers" in his foreword to Kimball, *Orators and Philosophers*, xix. Young men wanted a community to do more than hear them; they wanted the community to listen to them.

5. Hatch, *The Democratization of American Christianity*.

6. On the antebellum South's many venues for public speech, see Wells, *The Origins of the Southern Middle Class*, 90–93; O'Brien, *Conjectures of Order*, 421. On honor, reputation, and speech, see Greenberg, *Masters and Statesmen*, 12–13.

7. Walt Whitman, "Song of Joys," quoted in Reynolds, *Walt Whitman's America*, 174.

8. Judson, "Eloquence," 536.

9. "Ancient and Modern Eloquence," 169.

10. *Johnson's Dictionary, Improved by Todd, Abridged for the Use of Schools; with the Addition of Walker's Pronunciation; an Abstract of His Principles of English Pronunciation, with Questions; a Vocabulary of Greek, Latin, and Scripture Proper Names; and an Appendix of Americanisms* (Boston: Charles J. Hendee, 1836), 116. See also House, "What Is Eloquence?," 139; Howard, "Ancient Eloquence," 703.

11. Judson, "Eloquence," 536–37.

12. Howard, "Ancient Eloquence," 703. Emphasis in original.

13. House, "What Is Eloquence," 138.

14. Christophersen, "The Anti-Nullifiers," 74–76.

15. Eastman, "The Female Cicero," 260–61; Curtis, "The Bingham School and Classical Education in North Carolina," 328–77. For an amusing scene of boys declaiming in a private North Carolina academy, see Fuller, *Sea-Gift*, 51–53.

16. Christopherson, "The Anti-Nullifiers," 74–75.

17. Kimball, *Orators and Philosophers*; Frederick Rudolph, *Curriculum*.

18. Winterer, *The Culture of Classicism*, chap. 1; Longaker, *Rhetoric and the Republic*, 36, 42.

19. Caspari, *Humanism and the Social Order in Tudor England*, 15; Gustafson, *Eloquence Is Power*, 13; Robson, *Educating Republicans*, 60-70.

20. Glover, *Southern Sons*, 102.

21. Winterer, *The Culture of Classicism*, esp.11-12, 25-26.

22. Longaker, *Rhetoric and the Republic*, 186.

23. Alexander Pope quoted in Howard, "Ancient Eloquence," 705. Robert Fagels's modern translation is more accurate. Its comparison to Pope's translation is noteworthy: "Now, when they mingled with our Trojans in assembly, / standing side-by-side, Menelaus' shoulders / mounted over his friend's in height and spread, / when both were seated Odysseus looked more lordly. / But when they spun their appeals before us all, / Menelaus spoke out quickly—his words racing,/ few but clear as a bell, nothing long-winded / or off the mark, though in fact the man was younger. / But when Odysseus sprang up, the framed tactician / would just stand there, staring down, hard, / his eyes fixed on the ground, / never shifting his scepter back and forth, / clutching it stiff and like a mindless man. / You'd think him a sullen fellow or just plain fool. / But when *he* let loose that great voice from his chest / and the words came piling on like a driving winter blizzard— / we no longer gazed in wonder at his looks." Fagels, trans., *The Iliad*, 135-36.

24. Howard, "Ancient Eloquence," 705.

25. See, for example, Durrill, "The Power of Ancient Words."

26. Gleason, *Making Men*, 107.

27. "Eloquence," *SLM*, 165-66.

28. Ibid., 166. Cf. treatment of Cicero in Stiles, *An Address Delivered before the Phi Kappa and Demosthenian Societies of Franklin College*, 17-19.

29. Winterer, *The Culture of Classicism*, 26. See also Carr, Carr, and Schultz, *Archives of Instruction*, 33-43. On the South specifically, see O'Brien, *Conjectures of Order*, 683-84. Other texts used at UNC included Thomas Sheridan's *Lectures on Elocution* (1762) and Charles Rollins, *Traité des études* (*The Method of Teaching and Studying the Belles Lettres*, 1758). On these, see Connor, *A Documentary History of the University of North Carolina*, 1:451-55.

30. O'Brien, *Conjectures of Order*, 689.

31. Garrett, 4 August 1849, Diary, Typed Transcript, 81-82. Garrett's references are to Quintilian's *Institutio Oratoria* (ca. A.D. 95) and George Campbell's *The Philosophy of Rhetoric* (1776).

32. Mullins, Diary, 25 October 1840, William Sidney Mullins Diary, SHC.

33. Mullins, 1 November 1840, William Sidney Mullins Diary, SHC. Also see his entry for 11 November 1840. On a similar topic, see Thompson, 12 January 1851, George N. Thompson Diary, SHC.

34. Thompson, 7 February 1851, George N. Thompson Diary, SHC.

35. Pace, *Halls of Honor*, 28-33.

36. Battle, *History*, vol. 2, 128. Battle explains, "Those who were in the first class, at one time as many as eight, cast lots for the Salutatory and Valedictory orations. The memory of former precedence made the latter the most prized, while the drawer of the other frequently exchanged it with one entitled to an English speech. Rarely a student was so preëminent that the Valedictory was conceded to him by the Faculty."

37. Lindemann, "The School Day and the School Year," *True and Candid Compositions*,

DAS. Between 1795 and 1836 students who ranked among the top three seniors delivered orations on topics they selected, but after 1836 the debating societies were responsible for electing three speakers for commencement.

38. William Lafayette Scott, "Presidential Address of Will. Lafayette Scott," 23 July 1853, DSR.

39. Robert Williams Henry, "Address," 1835, DSR.

40. Oliver Pendleton Meares, "Address by O. P. Meares," November 1847, DSR.

41. James Martin, Inaugural Address, 7 February 1820, and Angus McNeil, Inaugural Address, 20 September 1838, DSR.

42. William Bonner Jr., Inaugural Address, 1858, DSR.

43. Henry Branson Elliott, Inaugural Address, 4 May 1826, DSR.

44. Ibid. Emphasis in original.

45. Longaker, *Rhetoric and the Republic*, 75

46. Connor, *A Documentary History of the University of North Carolina, Volume 2*, 147–48.

47. Ibid., 267.

48. The Dialectic Society held in its library a number of oratorical collections, including Thomas Brown's *British Cicero*, containing speeches by British orators; John Wetherall's *Sixteen Orations on Various Subjects* (1803), which contains mostly selections of religious sermons; and William Hazlitt's *Eloquence of the British Senate* (1810), containing historical legal and political speeches. On use and appropriation, see students' marginalia and underscoring in Hazlitt, *Eloquence of the British Senate*, which is housed in the North Carolina Collection's Old Library, Wilson Library, University of North Carolina at Chapel Hill.

49. Welles, *The Orator's Guide*, 34.

50. Bingham, *The Columbian Orator*, 34. Also see Daniel Walker Howe, *What Hath God Wrought*, 646.

51. Adams, *Lectures on Rhetoric and Oratory*, 30–31, 65.

52. Ibid., 61–62.

53. Ibid., 20.

54. Ibid., 190.

55. Ibid., 103.

56. Ibid., 356.

57. Henry Chambers, Inaugural Address, 1805, DSR.

58. William Hill, Address, 25 October 1843, DSR.

59. Alfred Gowan Merritt, "The Man of Superior Intellect alone gains admiration," 6 October 1852, DSR. See also Alfred M. Burton, Composition, April 1805; Robert John Donnell, Composition, 3 August 1805; Henry Branson Elliott, Inaugural Address, 5 May 1826; Bedford Brown, Inaugural Address, 27 June 1839, DSR; William Hooper Haigh, "Eloquence," Junior Oration, Chapel Hill, 19 November 1840, NCC; Henry Armand London Jr., Diary, Folder 2, Volume 1, Henry Armand London Papers, SHC.

60. William Polk Boylan, Inaugural Address, 20 October 1824, DSR.

61. Winterer, *The Culture of Classicism*, 72–73, 76. On Demosthenes, also see Robson, *Educating Republicans*, 63; Durrill, "Power of Ancient Words," 472; Eastman, *A Nation of Speechifiers*, chap. 1.

62. Coulter, *College Life in the Old South*, 103.

63. William Bonner Jr., Inaugural Address, 4 February 1858, DSR. On freshmen and speaking, also see Garrett, 14 September 1849, Diary, Typed Transcript, 128, SHC.

64. Daniel Moreau Barringer, Inaugural Address, 23 November 1825, DSR.

65. Philemon Hawkins, Inaugural Address, 25 April 1809, DSR.

66. Correctors Records, 14 November 1851; 17 October 1851; 13 May 1853, DSR.

67. Thomas Bog Slade, Address, 10 September 1819, DSR.

68. Elliott, Inaugural Address, 4 May 1826, DSR. Emphasis in original.

69. Thomas Pleasant Hall, Oration [ca. 1825–1827], DSR.

70. Eastman, "The Female Cicero," 268.

71. Daniel Forney, Inaugural Address [ca.1804 and 1805], DSR.

72. John Briggs Mebane, Address, 24 May 1809, DSR.

73. Greenberg, *Masters and Statesmen*, 13.

PART II

1. Reynolds, *Walt Whitman's America*, 309, 80.

2. Augst and Carpenter, eds., *Institutions of Reading*.

3. American intellectual history abounds with studies of the influence of these market developments on everyday readers, especially in the urban northeast among middle-class men and women. Davidson, *Revolution and the Word*; Reynolds, *Walt Whitman's America* and *Beneath the American Renaissance*; Zboray, *A Fictive People*; Zboray and Zboray, *Everyday Ideas*; Hessinger, *Seduced, Abandoned, and Reborn*, esp. 151–65. Less is known about the influence of new forms of books and reading on young southern men.

Chapter 4

1. Garrett, Diary, Typed Transcript, 134-35, SHC. Garrett's original essay has not survived.

2. Hamilton, "Diary of Thomas Miles Garrett," 63–65.

3. In the nineteenth century, three different modes of engagement with literature constituted what we today call "reading": study, desultory reading, and perusal. Students "studied" texts such as Homer's *Iliad* or the Bible and then recited them in class, but they "read" letters and newspapers and "perused" novels, biographies, histories, among other literary genres. Zboray and Zboray, *Everyday Ideas*, 165.

4. Thomas Jefferson Pitchford, Address, 11 November 1830, DSR. See also William Andrew Shaw, Inaugural Address, 4 April 1821, DSR. On gentility, male respectability, and education among southern elites see Glover, *Southern Sons*, 83–111; Causey, "The Character of a Gentleman," 6, 52–53.

5. Curricular texts emphasized these reading ideals, especially James Beattie's *Dissertations Moral and Critical* (1783), Hugh Blair's *Lectures on Rhetoric and Belles Lettres* (1793), and Francis Wayland's *Elements of Moral Science*.

6. Zboray and Zboray, *Everyday Ideas*, 151–74.

7. On "interpretive communities," see Chartier, "Texts, Printing, Readings," 156–57, and Fish, *Is There a Text in This Class?*, 317–18.

8. "View and Review of the University Catalogue," *NCUM* 2 (October 1853): 364.

9. John Cagrill Jones to Thomas Williamson Jones, 28 May 1812, Folder 2, Thomas Williamson Jones Papers, SHC; Walter W. Lenoir to Thomas Lenoir, 20 September 1841, Box 6, Folder 82, Lenoir Family Papers, SHC; Sanders, "The Journal of Ruffin Wirt Tomlinson," 96.

10. Montezuma Jones to Calvin Jones, 31 December 1841, Box 2, Folder 18, Calvin Jones Papers, SHC.

11. William Little to George Little, 27 March 1858, Little-Mordecai Collection, NCDAH.

12. On transfer of literature, see Hugh T. Brown to Carrie L. Gordon, 14 August 1857, Box 2, Folder 14, Gordon-Hackett Papers, SHC. Examples of literary excerpts in letters abound in antebellum correspondence. See especially James Boylan to Kate Boylan, September 1839, Box 1, Folder 5, John Haywood Papers, SHC.

13. Walter W. Lenoir and Thomas I. Lenoir, 12 May 1840, Folder 79, Lenoir Family Papers, SHC.

14. Jesse Goodwyn Ross to mother, 1 September 1860, Box 1, Folder 5, UNC Personal Papers, Misc., SHC.

15. William Bagley to Clementina Bagley, 7 August 1843, Folder 1, Volume 1, William Bagley Papers, SHC.

16. John Dudley Tatum to Anna Tatum, 14 February 1857, Folder 1, John Dudley Tatum Papers, SHC.

17. John Dudley Tatum to Anna Tatum, 18 September 1857, Folder 1, John Dudley Tatum Papers, SHC.

18. Augst, *The Clerk's Tale*, 74. On southern families, see Stowe, *Intimacy and Power*.

19. Sanders, "The Journal of Ruffin Wirt Tomlinson," 112.

20. Henry Armand London Jr., Diary, Folder 2, Volume 1, Henry Armand London Papers, SHC.

21. Edmund Covington, undated entry, Edmund De Berry Covington Diary, SHC.

22. Covington, "Catalogue of Books read by ED Covington Commencing Jany 1st 1842," Edmund De Berry Covington Diary, SHC.

23. Covington, "Dissertation on Shakespeare's Hamlet," undated entry, Edmund De Berry Covington Diary, SHC. Covington likely wrote this essay in June 1841, when the play was performed in Chapel Hill. See Mullins, 8 June 1841, William Sidney Mullins Diary, SHC.

24. On the long history of this genre, see Moss, *Printed Commonplace Books*.

25. Zboray and Zboray, *Everyday Ideas*, 52.

26. Mullins, 2 March 1841, William Sidney Mullins Diary, SHC; Barnes, David Alexander Barnes Diary, Folder 16, David Alexander Barnes Papers, SHC. William Mullins's inspiration was John Locke, *A new commonplace book . . .* , 2nd ed. (London, 1799), *Eighteenth Century Collections Online*.

27. Summerell, 25 January 1842, Joseph John Summerell Diary, SHC.

28. Augst, *The Clerk's Tale*, chap. 4, esp. 159.

29. See "Library & Librarian Regulations," Faculty Minutes, Volume 1:2, General Faculty and Faculty Council of the University of North Carolina at Chapel Hill Records, UA.

30. Battle, *History*, 404-11; "The Libraries of Our Institutions," *NCUM* 3 (March 1854): 63.

31. Garrett, 8 September 1849, Diary, Typed Transcript, 120.

32. Fordyce M. Hubbard, quoted in Battle, *History*, 407. On Hubbard, see Battle, *History*, 518.

33. O'Brien, *Conjectures of Order*, 523.

34. "Catalogue of Books Belonging to the Dialectic Society," vol. 3, DSR. The manuscript catalog for 1852 lists the following works as "prohibited": "Walker's Dictionary"; "Chalmers British Poets"; "Hume's History of England"; "Hinton's United States";

"Hogarth's Works"; "Oriental Field Sports"; "Cunningham's Cabinet Gallery"; "Flora's Dictionary"; "British Essayists"; "Marryatt's Works"; "Bulwer's Works"; "Hone's Everyday Book"; "Scott's Family Bible"; "Poets of America Illustrated"; "Moor's Works"; "Coleridge's Works"; "Pictorial Bible"; "Encyclopedias, Except Chambers Encyclopedia of English"; "Coleridge Shelley & Keats 9 vol."; "Encyclopedia Metropolitana"; "Constitution of the U. States"; "Millmans Horrace"; "All Folios"; "Waverly Novels (Illustrated)"; "Punch."

35. Murphy, "The Growth of the Library of the Philanthropic Society," 3. See also Harding, *College Literary Societies*, 115.

36. Coates and Coates, *The Story of Student Government*, 45–48.

37. Harding, *College Literary Societies*, 107, 205. According to Harding, Yale's two society libraries held 15,000 volumes, Dartmouth's 8,500, Union College's 8,450, and Dickinson College's 7,300 in 1839. North Carolina's holdings approached—but did not quite reach—these numbers in 1839 at 7,000 volumes. Nevertheless, North Carolina's holdings in 1839 far exceeded those elsewhere in the South: the University of Georgia held 3,000, for example, and Hampden-Sydney College in Virginia reported 2,200 holdings in 1834. In 1840, the society libraries at the University of Alabama and at the University of South Carolina had 1,000 volumes each; the University of Virginia had 350. By 1860, the combined holdings in the Dialectic and Philanthropic Societies at UNC doubled to nearly 14,000 volumes. See also Murphy, "The Growth of the Library of the Philanthropic Society at the University of North Carolina," 46.

38. "The Libraries of Our Institutions," *NCUM* 3 (March 1854): 64–65.

39. Murphy, "The Growth of the Library of the Philanthropic Society at the University of North Carolina, Chapel Hill, 1797–1822," 19. See Philanthropic Society Minutes, vol. S-7, PSR, and *Catalogue of Books Belonging to the Philanthropic Society at Chapel-Hill* (1822).

40. Harding, *College Literary Societies*. Harding does not show many regional differences in society libraries. Cf. other elite southerners in Cantrell, "The Reading Habits of Ante-Bellum Southerners," ix–xii, 1–23.

41. Bushman, *The Refinement of America*, 85–86, 287–89.

42. "Academic and College Compositions," *NCUM* 1 (April 1852): 95.

43. "Libraries of Our Institutions," *NCUM* 3 (March 1854): 63.

44. Zboray, *A Fictive People*, xxi, 136–37.

45. Thomas L. Spragins to Melchizedek Spragins, 22 September 1808, Box 1, Folder 5, UNC Personal Papers, Misc., SHC.

46. Walter W. Lenoir to Sarah J. Lenoir, 4 April 1843, Box 7, Folder 87, Lenoir Family Papers, SHC.

47. Circulation Records, 1832–1840, vol. S-2, DSR.

48. Battle, *History*, 565; Lindemann, "The Debating Societies," *True and Candid Compositions*, DAS.

49. Henry Armand London, 30 January 1863, Diary, Folder 2, Volume 1, Henry Armand London, SHC; Battle, *History*, 574; Fuller, *Sea-Gift*, 189–91.

50. Lindemann, "The Debating Societies," *True and Candid Compositions*, DAS. See also Dialectic Society Minutes, vol. 1, DSR.

51. Garrett, 22 September 1849, Diary, Typed Transcript, 140, SHC.

52. "The Libraries of Our Institutions," *NCUM* 3 (March 1854): 64.

53. See, for example, Thomas Jefferson Robinson, Address, 21 July 1848, DSR.

54. Robert Graham Barrett, Inaugural Address, 29 March 1856, DSR.

55. Iveson L. Brookes, Inaugural Address, September 1818, DSR.

56. John Madison Stedman, Inaugural Address, 25 February 1830, DSR.

57. Erasmus Darwin North, 3 August 1825, Address, DSR. Emphasis in original. See also William Hayes Owen, Inaugural Address, 17 April 1833, DSR. Some students took a harder line against extracurricular reading. See William Hill, Address, 25 October 1843, DSR.

58. Beattie quoted in "David Alexander Barnes Diary," Folder 16, David Alexander Barnes Papers, SHC. Barnes's citation is "Beattie. Lib. 1st p. 23." Barnes likely read the first volume of the ten-volume *Works of James Beattie* (1809). On Beattie, see O'Brien, *Conjectures of Order*, 999, 1001, 1007, 1017, 1029.

59. Mullins, 23 January 1841, William Sidney Mullins Diary, SHC. Emphasis in original. Also see Garrett, Diary, Typed Transcript, 240.

60. *Catalogue of Books Belonging to the Dialectic Society* (1835), 3; "Catalogue of Books in the Library of the Dialectic Society, January 1849," Manuscript Catalog, Library Records, Catalog of Books, Folder 812, DSR.

61. "The Banks of the Epac Reef," *NCUM* 1 (March 1852): 59; "Indian legend," *NCUM* 1 (April 1852): 116–19; "A visit to the Cartooge-Chage Indians," *NCUM* 1 (June 1852): 116–18; "Junaluskee—The Last of the Cherokees," *NCUM* 1 (June 1852): 216–20.

62. Parker, *Literary Magazines and British Romanticism*. An excellent contemporary response to *Harper's New Monthly Magazine* can be found in Hugh T. Brown, "Journal, kept by H. T. Brown, of his Thoughts and reflections from Sept. the 11th 1857," Diary, Box 6, Folder 110, Volume 23, Hamilton Brown Papers, SHC.

63. *Catalogue of Books Belonging to the Dialectic Society*, 1821 and 1849. There were 187 volumes of "novels and tales" in 1821 and 684 volumes in 1849.

64. Thomas Turner Slade, Inaugural Address, 18 March 1845, DSR.

65. "The Libraries of Our Institutions," *NCUM* 3 (March 1854): 64.

66. Student debated these questions about novel reading in their literary societies. See Philanthropic Society Minutes, 28 March 1815; 22 April 1843; 1 August 1851; 25 September 1857, vols. S-7, 10, S-12, 14, PSR; Dialectic Society Minutes, 27 April 1809; 8 February 1810; 1 October 1811; 9 October 1822; 11 September 1833; 3 April 1841; 9 August 1850; 30 January 1852; 9 March 1860, vols. 4, 6, 8, 9, S-10, S-11, DSR. Academy students also debated these issues. See Philomathean Society Minutes [Greensboro, N.C.], 25 August 1849, Records of the Philomathean Society, SHC.

67. O'Brien, *Conjectures of Order*, 742–48; Horlick, *Country Boys and Merchant Princes*, 178; Hessinger, *Seduced, Abandoned, and Reborn*, 151–65. Many female academies prohibited novel reading, though young women did not typically heed that advice either. See Farnham, *The Education of the Southern Belle*, 132–33. For one contemporary example of advice about novel reading, see a review of "The Mysteries of Paris, A Novel. By Eugene Sue. Translated from the French by Charles H. Toune, Esq. New-York: Harper & Brothers. 1843," *SQR* 5 (April 1844): 497–516.

68. Wayland, *The Elements of Moral Science*, 261.

69. Sanders, "The Journal of Ruffin Wirt Tomlinson," 234. The Dialectic and Philanthropic Society libraries each contained at least one copy of *The Student's Manual*.

70. Todd, *The Student's Manual*, 144–47.

71. Alfred Osborne Nicholson, Address, 14 September 1826, DSR.

72. Owen, Inaugural Address, 17 April 1833, DSR.

73. Slade, Inaugural Address, 18 March 1845, DSR.

74. Garrett, 24 July 1849, Diary, Typed Transcript, 70, SHC.

75. *NCUM* 2 (April 1853): 137. Emphasis in original. See also "John Bright's Three Years in College," *NCUM* 1 (August 1852): 234; *NCUM* 1 (December 1852): 419.

76. William Nelson Mebane, Inaugural Address, 3 October 1832, DSR.

77. William Hayes Owen, Inaugural Address, 17 April 1833, DSR.

78. See library records for Walter L. Steele, William Long, William Owen, William H. Hill, Circulation Records, vol. S-2, 40, 12, 239, 288, 336, 361, 397, 491, DSR. For southerner novel reading, see O'Brien, *Conjectures of Order*, 747; Cantrell, "The Reading Habits of Ante-Bellum Southerners," 112–18.

79. O'Brien, *Conjectures of Order*, 745. Summerell, 9 January 1842, Joseph John Summerell Diary, SHC.

80. Hessinger, *Seduced, Abandoned, and Reborn*, 151–65; Horowitz, *Rereading Sex*, 125–43.

81. Nichols, "Female Readers and Printed Authority in the Early Republic," 6.

82. "Ik. Marvel," *NCUM* 1 (February 1852): 8. Emphasis in original.

83. Garrett, 3 February 1850, Diary, Typed Transcript, 268–69.

84. *NCUM* 2 (April 1854): 126–27.

85. An excellent resource, outlining Dusenbery's diary and the books he read, is Sarah H. Ficke's discussion of literature on Erika Lindemann's internet cite for Dusenbery's diary, *Verses and Fragments*, DAS; Also see Lindemann, "About the Journal," *Verses and Fragments*, DAS.

86. Dusenbery, 12 September 1841, Diary, Folder 1, James Lawrence Dusenbery Diary and Clipping, SHC.

87. Dusenbery, 28 March and 6 March 1842, Diary, Folder 1, James Lawrence Dusenbery Diary and Clipping, SHC.

88. Cantrell, "The Reading Habits of Ante-Bellum Southerners," 112–18. On Scott's broad appeal, see Houghton, *The Victorian Frame of Mind*, chap. 12.

89. Shepard, "James B. Shepard's Address: Delivered before the Two Literary Societies of the University of North Carolina, June 5, 1844," *NCUM* 1 (August–September 1844): 258.

90. Polk, 4 and 7 September 1859, Diary, Folder 1, James Hilliard Polk Diary, SHC.

91. Borrowing Record for William Sidney Mullins, vol. 8, 1838–1841, Library Records, Circulation Records, PSR.

92. Dusenbery, 26 September 1841, Diary, Folder 1, James Lawrence Dusenbery Diary and Clipping, SHC. For a young woman's response to *Redgauntlet*, see Carrie L. Gordon to Hugh T. Brown, 7 February 1857, Box 2, Folder 14, Gordon-Hackett Papers, SHC.

93. Farnham, *The Education of the Southern Belle*, 30–31.

94. Garrett, 16 July 1849, Diary, Typed Transcript, 60–62, SHC. For a similar assessment of novel reading's benefits among students at South Carolina College, see E. J. Avery, "Monthly Address Delivered by E. J. Avery before the Euphradian Society April 1847," Euphradian Literary Society Records, 1806-1925, vol. 6, microfilm roll #7, USC.

95. Summerell, 9 January 1842, 12 January 1842, Diary, SHC.

96. See library records for Walter L. Steele, William Long, William Owen, William H. Hill, Circulation Records, 1832, vol. S-2, 40, 12, 239, 288, 336, 361, 397, 491, DSR.

97. Covington, Diary, 1–6.

98. Theodore Bryant Kingsbury, "Our Literature," September 1848, DSR. See also Samuel Hall, "Influence of adversity upon literary character," 2 March 1839, DSR. For a response to Cooper's naval history, see Mullins, 14 July 1841, William Sidney Mullins Diary, SHC.

99. On reading and national identity, see Scott, "'This Cultivated Mind,'" 48.

100. See Douglas Cronk's introduction to Richardson, *Wacousta*, xvii–xviii.

101. Mullins, 25 February 1841, William Sidney Mullins Diary, SHC.

102. "New Books," *NCUM* 1 (November 1852): 414.

Chapter 5

1. Channing, "Self-Culture," 354, 357.

2. Cicero Croom, Inaugural Address, 4 February 1859, DSR.

3. Longfellow, "A Psalm of Life." For contemporary use of the battle metaphor, see James Hilliard Polk, 16 October 1859, James Hilliard Polk Diary, SHC.

4. Walter W. Lenoir to Thomas Lenoir, 21 November 1841, Box 6, Folder 83, Lenoir Family Papers, SHC.

5. "The Voyage of Life," in *Harrison's British Classicks: Dr. Johnson's Rambler. Lord Lyttleton's [i.e. Lyttelton's] Persian letters*, vol. 2, no. 102 (9 March 1751): 231–33.

6. Kasson, "The Voyage of Life," 42–56.

7. William Sidney Mullins, Valedictory Oration, June 1842, Folder 1, PSR.

8. The most comprehensive treatment of addresses to students is Brophy, "'The Law of the Descent of Thought.'" See also Causey, "The Character of a Gentleman."

9. Stowe, *Intimacy and Power*, 164–67, 179–82.

10. Gaston, *Address*, 12.

11. Brown, *An Address Delivered before the Two Literary Societies*, 21. On Brown, see Grant, *Alumni History*, 76.

12. Inventories of the libraries of the Dialectic and Philanthropic Societies indicate that students had access to a sizeable and diverse collection of sermons and advice manuals for young men.

13. Sanders, "The Journal of Ruffin Wirt Tomlinson," 234.

14. Wise, *The Young Man's Counsellor*, 19. See also Horlick, *Country Boys and Merchant Princes*, 160.

15. Samuel Holms, 4 April 1851, DSR.

16. Houghton, *The Victorian Frame of Mind*, 316.

17. This interpretation of Childe Harold is from Walter Houghton's *Victorian Frame of Mind*, 308. For Childe Harold in student writing see Samuel Hall, "Influence of adversity upon literary character," Composition, 2 March 1839, DSR; Beatty, *Journal of a Southern Student*, 48.

18. Watson, *Liberty and Power*, esp. chap. 6.

19. John Lindsay Morehead, "Presidential Address of John L. Morehead. Blandwood N.C. Dec. 1852," DSR.

20. Reckford, "The Dialectic and Philanthropic Society Portraits," 20, 52, 61–63, 79, 100, 105.

21. Longfellow quoted in Evander J. McIver, Inaugural Address, July 1854, DSR. Strike in original.

22. Leroy Magnum McAfee, Inaugural Address, 18 September 1857, DSR. On famous alumni as inspiration, see also John Lindsay Morehead, "Presidential Address of John L. Morehead. Blandwood N.C. Dec. 1852," DSR, 1–2; James Turner Morehead Jr., Inaugural Address, 16 October 1857, DSR.

23. On collegiate portrait collections, including those at William and Mary and Bowdoin, see Reckford, "The Dialectic and Philanthropic Society Portraits," 7–10. Also see Burroughs, *Harvard Portraits*, and Egbert, *Princeton Portraits*. On similar collections in England, see Cust, *Eton College Portraits*.

24. Philanthropic Society Minutes, 18 April 1821, PSR. See also Philanthropic Society Minutes, 3 April 1822, PSR.

25. Reckford, "The Dialectic and Philanthropic Societies Portraits," 15–25.

26. Casper, *Constructing American Lives*, esp. chap. 1. Howe explores Franklin's influence in particular in *Making the American Self*, esp. chap. 1.

27. William Wirt, undated letter, William Wirt and Elizabeth Washington Papers, Rare Book, Manuscript, and Special Collections Library, Perkins Library, Duke University, Durham, North Carolina. See also Kennedy, *Memoirs of the Life of William Wirt*, 416.

28. Greenberg, *Honor & Slavery*, 29, 49.

29. Bushman, *The Refinement of America*. On the social challenges of this culture see Halttunen, *Confidence Men and Painted Women*; Kasson, *Rudeness & Civility*; Hemphill, *Bowing to Necessities*. For a compelling example of "reading" art, see Lovell, "Reading Eighteenth-Century American Family Portraits."

30. Reckford, "The Dialectic and Philanthropic Societies Portraits," 113–15.

31. "David Lowry Swain," *Dictionary of North Carolina Biography*, DAS.

32. William Edward Hill, Inaugural Address, February 1849, DSR.

33. James K. Polk to a committee of the Dialectic Society, 15 March 1847, DSR.

34. "Characteristics; Or, Who Is the True Hero?" *NCUM* 2 (August 1852): 235. Also see Jesse Hargrave, Composition, 23 August 1856, DSR.

35. "Biography," 282–83.

36. Ransom Hinton, Composition, 7 May 1805, DSR. On biography and character formation see Alexander Franklin Brevard, Inaugural Address, 1846, and Jesse Hargrave, Composition, 23 August 1856, DSR.

37. Yale Literary Magazine, June 1845, quoted in Casper, *Constructing American Lives*, 1. On biography in the South, see Fox-Genovese and Genovese, *The Mind of the Master Class*; O'Brien, *Conjectures of Order*, 653–71. A sample from the 1840s reveals a wide range of biographical interests in the *Southern Quarterly Review*, which students at North Carolina held in their literary society libraries: "Lives of the Queens of England," *SQR* 1 (April 1842): 330–76; "Lives of Literary and Scientific Men of Italy," SQR 1 (April 1842): 527–53; "Life of John C. Calhoun," *SQR* 3 (April 1843): 496–531; "Sketch of the Hon. Hugh S. Legare," *SQR* 4 (October 1843): 347–62; "Life and Character of M. de Malesherbes, The First Chancellor of Louis XVI. London: 1843," *SQR* 5 (April 1844); "Life and Writings of Rabelais," *SQR* 7 (January 1845); "Life, Character and Speeches of the Late Robert Y. Hayne," *SQR* 8 (October 1845): 496–512; "Life of Emanuel Swedenborg," Reviewed, *SQR* 10 (October 1846): 306–28; "The Life and Correspondence of John Foster, by John Sheppard, reviewed," *SQR* 11 (April 1847): 321–45; "The Auto-Biography of Goethe," *SQR* 11 (April 1847): 441–67. Similar reviews and biographical sketches can be found in issues of both the *Southern Literary Messenger* and *DeBow's Review*. For one example, see "Dabney Carr," *SLM* 4 (February 1838): 9. Occasionally, editors included criticism of the genre more specifically. See "Biography," 282–88. Students engaged these ideas in literary societies and in the literary magazine. For example, see "Biographical Notices," *NCUM* 1 (October 1844): 354–60.

38. One hundred and eighteen volumes of biographical works were listed in the 1821 catalog of books belonging to the Dialectic Society; 302 were listed in 1849. Likewise, 364 volumes of historical works were listed in 1821 and 615 were listed in 1849.

39. *Catalogue of Books Belonging to the Dialectic Society* (1835), 19–22.

40. Entry for William H. Owen, 1832, vol. S-2, Circulation Records, DSR.

41. William White Harris, Untitled Junior Oration, Chapel Hill, undated, Senior and Junior Orations, NCC, 3. See also William Andrew Shaw, Inaugural Address, 4 April 1821, DSR; Andrew Polk to Sarah Polk, 18 March 1841, Box 2, Folder 28, Polk and Yeatman Papers, SHC.

42. Philanthropic Society Minutes, 16 February 1808, vol. 4, PSR.

43. Alexander Franklin Brevard, Inaugural Address, 1846, DSR.

44. Jesse Hargrave, Composition, 23 August 1856, DSR. Bedford Brown spoke a similar message in his 1839 address to the two literary societies. See Brown, "Address," 1839.

45. Casper, *Constructing American Lives*, chap. 1.

46. Theodore Bryant Kingsbury, "Our Literature," September 1848, DSR.

47. Harding, *College Literary Societies*, esp. appendices.

48. Philanthropic Society Minutes, 13 October 1807 [Columbus]; 21 February 1809 [Columbus]; 31 July 1810 [Washington]; 31 March 1812 [Columbus]; 19 March 1828 [Washington]; 7 February 1840 [Washington]; 2 October 1841 [Resolution Not Given]; 21 August 1857 [Washington], PSR.

49. Alexander Justice, "Napoleon," 12 March 1844, Composition Book, Box 1, Folder 12, Alexander Justice Papers, SHC.

50. Erasmus Decatur Scales, "What Is Glory?," Senior Oration, 15 October 1859, DSR.

51. Channing, *The Works of William E. Channing*, 166. On Napoleon in North Carolina student discourse, see "Diversity of Success—On What Does It Depend," *NCUM* 1 (April 1852): 88; "Characteristics—Or Who is the True Hero," *NCUM* 1 (August 1852):238. Also see Walker Brookes's note about Napoleon in his letter to his aunt, Olivia Oliver, 15 June 1850, Folder 13, Iveson L. Brookes Papers, USC.

52. "Women," *The Atheneum* 11 (April–October 1822): 107.

53. William White Harris, Untitled Junior Oration, Chapel Hill, undated, Senior and Junior Orations, NCC.

54. "Female Heroism," *NCUM* 2 (September 1853): 340–42. On republican motherhood, see Kerber, *Women of the Republic*. Rosemarie Zagarri explains this ideology's origins in the Scottish Enlightenment, which was foundational to American intellectual culture (through higher education). See her "Morals, Manners, and the Republican Mother," 193–97.

55. William Campbell Lord, Senior Oration, 6 March 1858, DSR.

56. Mullins, 27 October 1840, William Sidney Mullins Diary, SHC.

57. Beatty, *Journal of a Southern Student*, 27. Other UNC examples include Covington, Diary, 25 September 1841, SHC; Dusenbery, 12 September 1841, Diary, Folder 1, James Lawrence Dusenbery Diary and Clipping, SHC; Barnes, 8 February 1840, Diary, Folder 16, David Alexander Barnes Papers, SHC; Sanders, "The Journal of Ruffin Wirt Tomlinson," 90. North Carolina students' reasons for journalizing are consistent among other elite young men in antebellum America. See Cole, Diary, 18 September 1852, MS 269, Benson Field Cole Papers, WFU; Friend, "Belles, Benefactors, and the Blacksmith's Son," in Friend and Glover, *Southern Manhood*, 92–112. On adult advice to write in journals, see Thomas

Miles Garrett, 13 June 1849, Diary, Thomas Miles Garrett Diary, SHC. On youth advising other youth to write in journals, see Harry St. John Dixon's Diary in Berry, ed., *Princes of Cotton*, 49. On diaries and age, see O'Brien, *Conjectures of Order*, 458, 468–71. On northern diarists, see Augst, *The Clerks Tale*, chap. 1; Frisch, "Youth Culture," 309.

58. Edmund Covington, undated entry, Edmund De Berry Covington Diary, SHC.

59. Sanders, "The Journal of Ruffin Wirt Tomlinson," 97.

60. Mullins, 14 June 1841, William Sidney Mullins Diary, SHC. Emphasis in original.

61. Mullins, 26 August 1841, ibid.

62. Edmund Covington, undated, Edmund De Berry Covington Diary, SHC.

63. Entry for William Sidney Mullins, 1838–41, vol. 8, Library Records, Circulation Records, PSR.

64. Mullins, 26 January 1841, William Sidney Mullins Diary, SHC.

65. Mullins, 11 February 1841, ibid.

66. Garrett, 4 September 1849, Diary, Typed Transcript, 114, SHC.

67. Garrett, 15 October 1849, ibid.

68. Mullins, 13 June, 8 August, and 2 September 1841, William Sidney Mullins Diary, SHC. Mullins's language fits the language of "self-pollution," or masturbation. See Laqueur, *Solitary Sex*, 222. On masturbation in men's diaries from an earlier period see Carroll, "'I indulged my desire too freely,'" 158.

69. Mullins, 8 August 1841, William Sidney Mullins Diary, SHC.

70. Dusenbery, 7 August 1841, Diary, Folder 1, James Lawrence Dusenbery Diary and Clipping, SHC. Also see Thompson, 1851, George N. Thompson Diary, SHC.

71. Benson Field Cole, Diary, 1852–56, MS 269, Benson Field Cole Papers, WFU. On young southern evangelicals, see Causey, "The Character of a Gentleman"; Young, "Religious Coming of Age among Students at Antebellum Georgia's Evangelical Colleges."

72. Mullins, 7 March and 14 February 1841, William Sidney Mullins Diary, SHC.

73. Mullins, 8 January 1841, ibid.

74. For the Pauline discourse on Christian soldiers, see Eph. 6:10–17. See also Is. 11:5 and 59:16–18; Wis. 5:17–23; Phil. 3:14; 1 Tm. 6:12; Heb. 12:1; Cor. 9:24. On martial Christianity in the Early Republic, see Heyrman, *Southern Cross*, 234–35, 245, 317–18n45.

75. Mullins, 7 February, 21 February, 18 July 1841, William Sidney Mullins Diary, SHC.

76. Casper, *Constructing American Lives*, 14–15.

Chapter 6

1. Summerell, 19 January 1842, Joseph John Summerell Diary, SHC.

2. Lystra, *Searching the Heart*, 7–10.

3. On mothers, young women, and feminine ideals see Kennedy, *Born Southern*, 10–11; Censer, *North Carolina Planters and Their Children*, 34–38, 54; young men and male collegians in both northern and English families shared these views. See Rotundo, *American Manhood*, 122; Deslandes, *Oxbridge Men*, 172–73.

4. Richard Don Wilson, "On the influence of woman," 1841, Senior and Junior Orations, NCC.

5. Berry, *All That Makes a Man*, 85.

6. Ibid., 118.

7. In regard to sex and intimacy, North Carolina students are representative of national,

middle-class youth culture as well as southern campus culture. Analogs can be found in Glover, *Southern Sons*; Berry, *All That Makes a Man*; Kett, *Rites of Passage*; Rotundo, *American Manhood*; Hemphill, "Isaac and 'Isabella'"; Frisch, "Youth Culture in America."

8. On courting and courtship, see Kett, *Rites of Passage*, 42; Lystra, *Searching the Heart*, 190–91; Rothman, *Hands and Hearts*; Wright, *Revolutionary Generation*, 72–75. Putting off courtship was common among males in antebellum youth culture. See Hemphill, "Isaac and 'Isabella,'" 412–18 and esp. 434. Little work has been done on bachelors in nineteenth-century America. For an excellent foundational study for the Revolutionary and early national period, see McCurdy, *Citizen Bachelors*.

9. Edward C. Easterling to Rebecca Easterling, 26 August 1858, Rebecca Easterling Papers, USC. Some students expected to wait up to three years after graduation to entertain serious courtship and marriage. See Sanders, "The Journal of Ruffin Wirt Tomlinson," 113. See also William Bagley to Edward C. Yellowley, 18 June 1841 and 13 August 1842, Folder 1, Volume 1, William Bagley, SHC.

10. Jabour, *Scarlett's Sisters*, 129.

11. Young men's reliance on family networks to meet and court young women in the antebellum period is consistent with Lorri Glover's findings for the early national period. See *Southern Sons*, 142.

12. Lystra, *Searching the Heart*, chap. 6.

13. *NCUM* 2 (September 1853): 344.

14. Thompson, 2–4 January 1851, George N. Thompson Diary, SHC. Emphasis in original.

15. Thompson, 8 January 1851, ibid. Emphasis in original.

16. Thompson, 20 January 1851, ibid.

17. Battle, *History*, 311.

18. Summerell, 23 October 1841, Diary; Mullins, 3 June 1841, William Sidney Mullins Diary; Covington, 12 October 1841, Diary, SHC.

19. Douglas Pearson Beatty to Gustavus Adolphus Bingham, 12 February 1849, Box 1, Folder 5, UNC Personal Papers, Misc., SHC.

20. Walter Lenoir to Mary A. Gwynn, 18 October 1842, Box 6, Folder 85, Lenoir Family Papers, SHC.

21. Mullins, 29 September 1841, William Sidney Mullins Diary, SHC.

22. Battle, *History*, 595–97.

23. Sanders, "The Journal of Ruffin Wirt Tomlinson," 249.

24. Jabour, *Scarlett's Sisters*, 83–149.

25. Summerell, 21 January 1842, Joseph John Summerell Diary, SHC; Battle, *History*, 566, 597, 311.

26. Battle, *History*, 584. Seranades were so prevalent that the university implemented in 1856 a law requiring permission for serenading a week in advance. See Battle, *History*, 645. For a contemporary description of student serenades, see Elisha Mitchell to Maria North, 11 February 1818, DAS; *NCUM* 1 (December 1852): 418.

27. *NCUM* 1 (March 1852): 61, 6; 1 (September 1852): 305; 2 (August 1853): 295; 2 (September 1853): 337.

28. *NCUM* 1 (February 1852): 13.

29. *NCUM* 1 (August 1852): 245.

30. Thompson, 4 February 1851, George N. Thompson Diary, SHC.

31. Battle, *History*, 603.

32. William Bagley to Clementina Bagley, 24 February 1844, Folder 1, Volume 1, William Bagley Papers, SHC.

33. Sherman, ed., *The Black Bard of North Carolina*, 1–3. On learning to read among young slaves, see Williams, *Self-Taught*, esp. chap. 1. Surprisingly little scholarship exists on slave manhood *as manhood*, and the relationships between white and black males *as males* in the Old South has not received adequate treatment in the literature on American masculinity. Notable exceptions include Baptist, "The Absent Subject: African American Masculinity and Forced Migration to the Antebellum Plantation Frontier," in Friend and Glover, *Southern Manhood*, 136–73; Lussana, "To See Who Was Best on the Plantation."

34. Polk, 26 July 1859, James Hilliard Polk Diary, SHC.

35. John T. Jones, letter, 16 April 1836, Box 1, Folder 3, James Gwyn Papers, SHC.

36. Sanders, "The Journal of Ruffin Wirt Tomlinson," 254–55. For another example of caution, see Covington, 20 October 1841, Diary. See also Glover, *Southern Sons*, and Jabour, *Scarlett's Sisters*.

37. James Boylan to Kate Boylan, September 1839, Box 1, Folder 5, John Haywood Papers, SHC.

38. Montezuma Jones to Calvin Jones, 8 March 1842, Box 2, Folder 18, Calvin Jones Papers, SHC.

39. William Bagley to Moses G. Pierce, 15 February 1845, Folder 2, Volume 2, William Bagley Papers, SHC.

40. Sanders, "The Journal of Ruffin Wirt Tomlinson," 96–97.

41. Iveson Brookes to Walker Brookes, 7 August 1846; "G" from New Market S.C. to Walker Brookes, 13 April 1845, Iveson Brookes Papers, USC.

42. Mullins, 3 June 1841, William Sidney Mullins Diary, SHC.

43. Covington, 12 October 1841, Diary, SHC. Emphasis in original.

44. Dusenbery, 17 July 1841, Diary, Folder 1, James Lawrence Dusenbery Diary and Clipping, SHC.

45. Dusenbery, 24 July 1841, ibid. John Milton, *L'Allegro, John Milton: Complete Shorter Poems*, ed. John Carey (New York: Longman, 2007), 143–44; Thomas Moore, "Fanny of Timmol: A Mail-Coach Adventure," *The Poetical Works of Thomas Moore* (1812).

46. Dusenbery, 24 July 1841, Diary, Folder 1, James Lawrence Dusenbery Diary and Clipping, SHC.

47. Dusenbery, undated, ibid.

48. See, for instance, Thomas, "Reading the Silences," 131–32, and Zboray and Zboray, *Everyday Ideas*, 52.

49. Dusenbery, undated, Diary, Folder 1, James Lawrence Dusenbery Diary and Clipping, SHC.

50. Dusenbery, 24 October 1841, ibid.

51. Dusenbery, 14 August 1841, ibid.

52. Battle, *Memories of an Old-Time Tar Heel*, 86. See also Vickers et al., *Chapel Hill*, 29.

53. *Acts of the General Assembly and Ordinances of the Trustees*, 14–17.

54. Dusenbery, 7 August, 10 October, 21 November 1841, 13 March, 3 April 1842, Diary, Folder, 1, James Lawrence Dusenbery Diary and Clipping, SHC.

55. The Wilderness of Sin is not mentioned in either the first or second book of Chronicles, as Dusenbery's title would suggest, but those books follow the same style and tradition as Numbers, Kings, and Deuteronomy. See Ralph W. Klein, "1 Chronicles:

Introduction," *The Harper Collins Study Bible* (NRSV), ed. Wayne A. Meeks (New York: HarperCollins, 1993), 605–7.

56. Sanders, "The Journal of Ruffin Wirt Tomlinson," III, 239, 244; Mullins, 12 October 1841, William Sidney Mullins Diary, SHC. On Mullins, also see Ishkanian, "Religion and Honor at Chapel Hill," 260–65.

57. Faculty Meeting Minutes, 14 March 1803, 2 June 1829, 16 April 1839, 4 September 1854, 8 March 1856, General Faculty and Faculty Council of the University of North Carolina at Chapel Hill Records, UA; Minutes of the Board of Trustees of the University of North Carolina, 24 March 1810.

58. Sanders, "The Journal of Ruffin Wirt Tomlinson," 253.

59. Faculty Minutes, 22 January 1855, General Faculty and Faculty Council of the University of North Carolina at Chapel Hill Records, UA.

60. Battle, *History*, 560.

61. Dusenbery, 13 and 20 March 1842, Diary, Folder 1, James Lawrence Dusenbery Diary and Clipping, SHC.

62. Dusenbery, 1 August 1841, ibid. On Dusenbery's friends, see Lindemann, "Introduction," James Lawrence Dusenbery Journal, unpublished essay, 2007.

63. Dusenbery, 12 September 1841, Diary, Folder 1, James Lawrence Dusenbery Diary and Clipping, SHC. One of Dusenbery's companions was Rufus Clay Barringer (1821–1895) of Cabarrus County, N.C., but "Gabriel" remains unidentifiable in the manuscript as well as in student records.

64. Mullins, 30 October 1840 and 1 November 1840, William Sidney Mullins Diary, SHC. Emphasis in original.

65. Hemphill, "Isaac and 'Isabella,'" 416.

66. Cohen, *The Murder of Helen Jewett*, 95. On the position that prostitution was uncommon, see Wyatt-Brown, *Southern Honor*, 262–324, esp. 297; Glover, *Southern Sons*, 126–31. The reach of sexual commerce in the North and in the South expanded from cities into more rural locations in the nineteenth century, and Chapel Hill was no exception. See D'Emilio and Freedman, *Intimate Matters*, 50–52, 130–38, esp. 133. In terms of prostitution, Dusenbery and his classmates more closely resemble the middle-class northern youth described in Frisch, "Youth Culture in America," 211–37, and in Cohen, *The Murder of Helen Jewett*, 117. Most prostitutes in southern towns were white. See Lebsock, *The Free Women of Petersburg*, 179.

67. Cott, "Passionlessness."

68. Cohen, *The Murder of Helen Jewett*, 202.

69. On young men away from home, see Cohen, *The Murder of Helen Jewett*; Horowitz, *Rereading Sex*; Hemphill, "Isaac and 'Isabella'"; Dorsey, *Reforming Men and Women*; Hessinger, *Seduced, Abandoned, and Reborn*; Frisch, "Youth Culture in America."

Chapter 7

1. Shepard, "James B. Shepard's Address: Delivered before the Two Literary Societies of the University of North Carolina, June 5, 1844," *NCUM* 1 (August–September 1844): 258.

2. College debates have been viewed as extensions of the formal curriculum, affairs of honor, and as an intellectual outgrowth of a broader, competitive American "boy culture." On debate and informal curriculum, see McLachlan, "The Choice of Hercules," 485; Hard-

ing, *College Literary Societies*. On debating as an exercise of southern honor, see Pace, *Halls of Honor*, 68. On debating and boy culture, especially among male siblings, see Taylor, *The Divided Family in Civil War America*, 64–66.

3. William John Long, Inaugural Address, 1838, DSR.

4. Battle, *History*, 781.

5. McCurry, *Masters of Small Worlds*, 5–36.

6. Genovese, *The Slaveholders' Dilemma*, 10–45.

7. Potter, "The Literary Society," 238–58; *College Literary Societies*; McLachlan, "The Choice of Hercules," 485–86. Debate procedures did not change between 1795 and 1861. See Dialectic Society Minutes, 1795–1798, vol. 1, DSR.

8. Battle, *History*, 79–84.

9. Rarely, students might alter a question's original wording or even abandon a question altogether. Philanthropic Society Minutes, 13 March 1798 and 8 May 1798, vol. 2; 14 August 1800, vol. 3; 12 April 1820, vol. S-7, PSR.

10. Dialectic Society Minutes, 5 June 1855, vol. S-11 and 19 November 1858, vol. S-12, DSR. Minutes for both the Dialectic and Philanthropic Societies are contained in twenty-seven bound volumes (twelve for the Dialectic and fifteen for the Philanthropic).

11. Potter, "The Literary Society," 243–45.

12. Lindemann, "The Debating Societies," *True and Candid Compositions*, DAS.

13. Thompson, Diary, 24 January 1851, George N. Thompson Diary, SHC. See also Johnson Pinkston, Inaugural Address, 15 April 1842, DSR.

14. Polk, Diary, 67, Folder 1, James Hilliard Polk Diary, SHC.

15. The minutes of the Dialectic and Philanthropic Societies are replete with reports of students who had to pay fines for not being prepared to participate in composition, declamation, and debate. On fines, see Virginius Henry Ivy, Inaugural Address, 18 October 1844, DSR.

16. These categories of analysis are mine; students did not categorize their debates. I have based them on nearly 4, 000 questions debated in both the Dialectic and Philanthropic Society. As much as possible, I have chosen my categories of analysis based on nineteenth-century epistemology.

17. Dialectic Society Minutes, 12 November 1795, vol. 1, DSR; Dialectic Society Minutes, 11 May 1815, vol. 5, DSR. This was true among young men throughout the South. See O'Brien, *Conjectures of Order*, 424.

18. Dialectic Society Minutes, 14 August 1812, 6 September 1815, vol. 5, DSR.

19. When students posed questions about specific governmental policies and practices related to the United States or North Carolina specifically, or used the term "at present," I assigned the question to the current affairs category.

20. Regarding national comparisons, several works have been indispensable: Harding, *College Literary Societies*; McLachlan, "The Choice of Hercules"; Ray, "The Permeable Public," 1–16; Westbrook, "Debating Both Sides," 339–56. For transatlantic similarities, I have relied on research that I conducted on the Oxford Union Debating Society: Oxford Union Society, Record Book, vol. 1, 5 December 1825–3 February 1831, Oxfordshire Record Office, Cowley Road, Oxford, UK. See also Walter, *The Oxford Union*; Hollis, *The Oxford Union*, 11–64. Useful for my work and also read by students at North Carolina was Bristed, *Five Years in an English University*.

21. Between 1840 and 1849, the Philomatheans held sixty-eight debates. Current affairs

questions made up 37 percent of these debates (n=25) and historical questions were 29 percent (n=20). Records, 1847–50, Philomathean Society Records, SHC.

22. Euzelian Constitution, Euzelian Records, 1835, WFU; Philomathesian Constitution, Philomathesian Records, 1836, WFU. Paschal, *History of Wake Forest College*, vol. 1, 539. See also Williams, "Literary Societies at Wake Forest College."

23. "Should political questions be discussed in debating societies?" [Decided in the Negative.] Dialectic Society Minutes, 27 August 1852, vol. S-11, DSR. Also see John Washington Graham, Inaugural Address, 16 October 1856, DSR.

24. Parrish, "Books Read by Members of the Philanthropic Society," 14–15, 27.

25. Elliott, *The Raleigh Register*.

26. Olmstead, *A Journey in the Seaboard Slave States*, 366.

27. Jonathan Lindsay Hargrave, 30 April 1832, Address, DSR. Several other student addresses discuss the importance of reform in antebellum North Carolina: James W. Osborne, 26 June 1839, Address; Robert H. Cowan, c. 1843–44, address; William E. Hill, February 1849, Inaugural Address; John R. Hutchin, 1852, address; Cicero Croom, 1858, composition, DSR. Faculty delivered addresses that often touched on reform as well. See Brophy, "The Republics of Liberty and Letters."

28. Lefler and Newsome, *North Carolina*, 371. For one southern argument against capital punishment elsewhere in the South, see Porter, *Address Delivered before the Philomathic Society of the University of Alabama*. Agitation for ending capital punishment and reforming penal codes was also a national endeavor. Walt Whitman's New York literary society, for example, engaged in debates about abolishing capital punishment in the 1830s. See Reynolds, *Walt Whitman's America*, 59.

29. The Dialectic Society debated penal reform and the establishment of a penitentiary fifty times between 1795 and 1835, and continued at this rate throughout the antebellum period. See Dialectic Society Minutes 15 June 1797, 16 May 1799, 21 August 1800, 6 March 1800, 8 October 1801, 18 March 1802, 21 April 1802, 7 June 1804, 1 March 1805, 8 August 1805, 23 January 1806, 17 April 1806, 10 July 1806, 16 October 1806, 21 July 1808, 28 July 1808, 29 September 1808, 1 February 1810, 18 July 1810, 13 September 1810, 27 September 1810, 2 April 1812, 25 March 1813, 7 October 1813, 14 April 1814, 17 March 1815, 28 June 1815, 30 August 1815, 31 July 1816, 9 October 1816, 29 January 1817, 12 August 1818, 26 August 1818, 19 October 1819, 23 February 1820, 21 March 1821, 6 February 1822, 5 February 1823, 29 September 1824, 1 February 1826, 1 March 1826, 17 October 1828, 4 May 1831, 31 March 1832, 4 April 1832, 1 October 1833, 22 January 1834, 4 February 1835, 9 September 1835, vols. 1–8, DSR.

30. Lefler and Newsome, *North Carolina*, 334–35.

31. Dialectic Society Minutes, 25 October 1820 [favored calling a constitutional convention], 27 February 1822 [the state legislature should not have repealed resolutions to assemble a constitutional convention], 27 April 1826 [the state constitution should be reformed to allow Roman Catholics rights to holding public office], 14 April 1830 [Buncome and Burke Counties should be split for greater representation], 3 February 1831 and 16 April 1834 [a convention ought to be convened], vols. 6–8, DSR. The one exception to this desire for a more democratic constitution was that members of the Dialectic Society believed that sheriffs should not be elected by popular vote. Cf. Philanthropic Society Minutes, 22 September 1819 and 14 January 1822 [against calling a convention], 17 March 1824 [voting should not be confined to freeholders alone], 20 April 1825 and 5 October 1825 [it's fine to exclude non-Christians from the legislature], 27 September 1826, 16 April

1828, 19 February 1829 [sheriffs should not be elected by the people], 4 November 1829 [governor should not be elected by the people], 10 February 1830 [against calling a convention], 27 January 1831 [against calling a convention], 2 February 1831 [governor should be elected by the legislature], vols. S-7 and S-8, PSR.

32. Philanthropic Society Minutes, 27 January 1831.

33. Dialectic Society Minutes, 14 April 1830 [splitting Buncombe and Burke Counties]; 3 February 1831 [calling a convention]; 5 October 1831 [moving the capital out of Raleigh].

34. Lefler and Newsome, *North Carolina*, 362.

35. The Phis supported Internal Improvements once on 24 August 1825. They supported common schools in debates on 17 September 1830 and 19 October 1831. See Philanthropic Society Minutes, vol. S-8, PSR. The Dis voted against common schools on 13 April 1811, but supported it in every debate after that point, viz. on 2 September 1818, 6 March 1822, 8 November 1826, and 5 November 1828. See Dialectic Society Minutes, vols. 5, S-7, S-8, S-9, DSR.

36. Dialectic Society Minutes, 3 April 1800, 7 May 1800, vol. 3; 15 May 1807, vol. 4; 11 November 1835, vol. 8; 27 October 1824, vol. 6; 26 April 1850, vol. 10, DSR.

37. Ray, "The Permeable Public," 1–16. Debating women rarely occurred in most men's debating societies in the antebellum United States.

38. On the use of this term, see Kerber, "Separate Spheres, Female Worlds, Woman's Place."

39. John Briggs Mebane, Address, 24 May 1809, DSR.

40. Lawson Henderson Alexander, Composition, 13 March 1816, DSR.

41. Harding, *College Literary Societies*, 369, 392.

42. "A Glance into the Social Circle," *NCUM* 1 (April 1852): 106–7.

43. "Mind—Masculine and Feminine," *NCUM* 1 (April 1852): 121.

44. *NCUM* 1 (May 1852): 146. Emphasis in original.

45. Some important works include, Kelley, *Learning to Stand and Speak*; Varon, *We Mean to Be Counted*; Stansell, *City of Women*.

46. On federal Indian policy, including removal, see Prucha, *The Great Father*; Sheehan, *Seeds of Extinction*. Thomas Jefferson flirted with colonizing Indians in the Louisiana territory in 1803 and again in the Arkansas territory in 1808. For early attitudes about colonization, see Wallace, *Jefferson and the Indians*; DuVal, *The Native Ground*, 199. On race, see Horsman, *Race and Manifest Destiny*. See also Guyatt, "'The Outskirts of Our Happiness,'" 987. On changing perceptions of Indians from culturally to racially different from whites, see Berkhofer, *The White Man's Indian*.

47. Dialectic Society Minutes, 18 May 1800 [Negative], 9 September 1802 [Affirmative], 8 July 1805 [Affirmative], 7 February 1806 [Affirmative], 28 March 1811 [Affirmative, viz. Indians had right to land], 19 March 1817 [Affirmative], 24 April 1820 [Affirmative], and 16 April 1841, vols. 3–6, 9, DSR. Philanthropic Society Minutes, 13 June 1797 [Negative, viz., not "consistant with Justice to drive the Indians from their territories"], 12 February 1799 [Negative], 25 October 1815 [Negative, viz., Indians "had the greatest right to the continent of America"], 3 October 1816 [Negative], 12 September 1832 [Affirmative], 2 April 1834 [Negative], vols. 2, S-7, S-9, PSR.

48. Dialectic Society Minutes, 17 May 1798, 7 August 1800, 15 August 1801, 26 January 1804, 4 October 1804, 13 March 1806, 8 May 1807, 11 February 1813, 13 April 1815, 23 August 1816, 30 June 1817, 21 August 1822, 12 March 1829, 8 October 1834, vols. 2–8, DSR. Philanthropic Society Minutes, 22 September 1801, 10 August 1802, 16 August 1808, 14 January

1812, 18 October 1814, 14 March 1815, 18 October 1820, 24 April 1824, vols. 3–4, 5, S-7, S-8, PSR.

49. Thomas Jefferson to the marquis de Chastellux, 7 June 1785, quoted in Waldstreicher, *Notes on the State of Virginia*, 69. Dialectic Society Minutes, 3 February 1819, vol. 6, DSR; Alexander M. Rogers, "Was it just & equitable that the Europeans should take possession of those lands in America formerly held by the aborigines?" 9 August 1804, DSR.

50. Henry Elliott, "Debate," 9 June 1825, DSR

51. Philanthropic Society Minutes, 15 September 1818, 27 April 1822, 11 February 1824, 13 September 1826, 5 March 1828, vols. S-7, S-8, PSR. Dialectic Society Minutes, 13 February 1822, 23 October 1823, vol. 6, DSR.

52. Dialectic Society Minutes, 8 June 1825, vol. 6, DSR.

53. Ibid.

54. Oliver Wolcott Treadwell, Speech, 8 June 1825, DSR. Emphasis in original. Treadwell was actually assigned to support the affirmative position, that the United States *should* remove the Indians. There are no extant debate speeches from the negative side, but because Treadwell diligently quoted and paraphrased the negative position in his own rebuttal, it serves as a reliable summary of the main points argued in support of each position.

55. Eugene D. Genovese, *The Slaveholders' Dilemma*, 10–45. See also Faust, *A Sacred Circle*.

56. Here I consider only questions that explicitly addressed slavery. Sometimes slavery also appeared in debates on other topics not about slavery per se.

57. These numbers are based on debates held in the Dialectic Society only, though they are representative of the overall trends in both societies.

58. Jeremiah Battle, literary society composition, 17 April 1799, DSR.

59. Dialectic Society Minutes, 2 October 1800, 11 March 1802, 8 September 1803, 2 February 1804, 6 June 1807, 15 May 1806, 9 July 1807, vols. 3–4, DSR.

60. John D. Jones, "A Speech delivered in the Dialectic Society at the annual meeting July 9th 1807 advocating the negative of this question. Ought slavery to be abolished in the United States," 9 July 1807, DSR. This is the only extant debate speech on the topic of slavery from this period.

61. Saunt, *Black, White, and Indian*, 59.

62. Dialectic Society Minutes, 6 March 1799, September 1801, 22 July 1858, vols. 2, 3, S-12, DSR. By the early antebellum period, however, students tended to develop more nuanced racial attitudes. By 1834, for example, the Philanthropic Society was, by a comfortable majority of eight votes to five, willing to concede that "negroes [were] black by nature," rather than by climate. Philanthropic Society Minutes, 7 May 1834, vol. S-9, PSR.

63. Dialectic Society Minutes, 14 January 1818; 30 January 1822; 22 June 1826; 4 April 1827; 29 February 1832, vols. 6–7, DSR.

64. Gaston, "Address Delivered before the Philanthropic and Dialectic Societies at Chapel-Hill," 14. On Gaston and his advice to his own son, see Stowe, *Intimacy and Power*, chap. 4, esp. 179–82.

65. "Hon. William Gaston's Address," *NCUM* 1 (August–September 1844): 297–316.

66. Sanders, "The Journal of Ruffin Wirt Tomlinson," 95. Also see Mullins, 19 July 1841, William Sidney Mullins Diary, SHC.

67. William Hayes Owen, "William H. Owen's Debate on the 20th of June 1832 on the

negative of the question, 'If a separation of the union were to take place, is it probable that a monarchical form of government would be established?'" 20 June 1832, DSR.

68. Dialectic Society Minutes, 10 February 1836, 3 February 1838, vol. 8, DSR.

69. These findings affirm what Amy Murrell Taylor has identified as "an ideological congruence on the issue of slavery" among young men and their fathers'—and even grandfathers'—generations. See *The Divided Family in Civil War America*, 25.

70. Records, 1847–50, Philomathean Society Records, SHC. In addition to age, religion might also have factored into the Philomatheans' debates, for Greensboro was heavily influenced by the Quakers, who tended to critique slavery.

71. Benjamin S. Hedrick to Hinton Rowan Helper, 27 October 1856, Benjamin Sherwood Hedrick Papers, SHC. For a complete account of the Hedrick affair, see Smith, *A Traitor and a Scoundrel*.

72. Glover, *Southern Sons*, 3.

73. William Hayes Owen, "William H. Owen's Debate on the 20th of June 1832 on the negative of the question, 'If a separation of the union were to take place, is it probable that a monarchical form of government would be established'"? 20 June 1832, DSR.

74. John Lindsay Hargrave, 19 October 1831, Inaugural Address, DSR.

Conclusion

1. For details regarding preparations for commencement week and student examinations, see Drake, *Higher Education in North Carolina before 1860*, 216. For an example of advertising commencement, see *The Register*, 17 May 1842 (Raleigh, N.C.).

2. Sanders, "The Journal of Ruffin Wirt Tomlinson," 258. Graduating seniors who won first or second "distinctions" delivered orations at commencement.

3. Battle, *History*, 477. On commencement proceedings in general, also see Lindemann, "The School Day and the School Year," *True and Candid Compositions*, DAS.

4. "University of North Carolina—Annual Commencement, &c.," *The Weekly Raleigh Register, and North Carolina Gazette*, 13 June 1845. Other examples of similar newspaper reports can be found in *The Observer* (Fayetteville, N.C.), 9 June 1851, 17 June 1851, and 11 June 1860; "Our University," *The Register* (Raleigh, N.C.), 13 June 1849.

5. Battle, *History*, 781–82.

6. Green, *Military Education*, 269.

7. Snider, *Light on the Hill*, chaps. 5–9, esp. 99; Leloudis, *Schooling the New South*, 60. The Confederacy provided a moment to begin this reform. See Bernath, *Confederate Minds*, and Frost, *Thinking Confederates*. The antebellum foundation for postwar intellectual developments is implicit, albeit understated, in each of these works. They do, however, open the field to future study of how individuals experienced changing intellectual climate in everyday life.

8. For a complete listing of the state's "great planters" who sent sons to college (including but not limited to UNC), see Censer, *North Carolina Planters and Their Children*, 155–60.

9. "Mary S." to James Dusenbery, undated, Diary, Folder 1, James Lawrence Dusenbery Diary and Clipping, SHC.

10. "Mary S." to James Dusenbery, 25 April 1848, ibid. Emphasis in original.

11. Lindemann, "Introduction to the James Lawrence Dusenbery Journal Site," *Verses and Fragments*, DAS.

12. This is inconclusive evidence based on genealogical research conducted by Sandra Beane-Milton. Her genealogical work suggests that Dusenbery may have fathered two African American daughters, Alice and Mollie, by a woman named Helen Trexler (1844–1903). Marriage licenses for both Alice and Mollie suggest this possibility. See Marriage License for Simon Adams and Alice Dusenbery, License Number 512, State of North Carolina, Register of Deeds, Davidson County, 7 February 1887. Alice Dusenbery married Simon Adams on 7 February 1887; her marriage license states that Alice was the "colored daughter of James Dusenbery and Helen Trexler, the father dead, the mother living. . . ." These dates correspond with Dusenbery's date of death (28 January 1886). The second daughter, Mollie Dusenbery, married George W. Albright on 7 November 1900. Her marriage license contains the following information: "Mollie Dusenbery of Davidson Co., aged 34 years, color Black, daughter of not known and Helen Dusenbery, the father—, the mother Living." If the James Dusenbery on these marriage licenses is the same James Dusenbery who attended the University of North Carolina, he and Helen Trexler may have been the parents of these two children.

13. *Dictionary of North Carolina Biography*, vol. 5, 49–51.

14. Sanders, "The Journal of Ruffin Wirt Tomlinson," 89.

15. In all, North Carolina contributed more soldiers to the Confederate Army than any other southern state, including nearly one-fifth of all war conscripts. See James Leloudis, "Civil War and Reconstruction," *The First Century of the First State University*, DAS. On North Carolina and the secession crisis, see Escott, *Many Excellent People*, chaps. 2–3.

16. Barney, *The Making of a Confederate*, chaps. 1–2.

17. R. Y. Woodlief, 17 April 1865, R. Y. Woodlief Diary, USC.

18. Preston H. Sessoms to Penelope E. White, 28 August 1862, Jonathan Jacocks Papers, SHC. For another account of the wartime university, see Henry Armand London Jr., Diary, Folder 2, Volume 1, Henry Armand London Papers, SHC.

19. On the university during Reconstruction, including its low enrollment numbers, see Battle, *History*, 774–80.

20. Powell, *Dictionary of North Carolina Biography*, vol. 5, 486.

21. Battle, *History*, vol. 2, 71–73.

22. "The love of distinction is the gentle gale which first sets in motion the mental ship & then wafts it continually onwards to glory & renown. Such incentives [cause] the student to exert himself, his mind is enlarged & strengthened, he gradually with his 'blushing honours thick upon him,' & may exclaim with justice 'Exegi monumentum aere perennius [I have erected a monument more lasting than bronze]." Samuel H. Walkup, Oration, 30 April 1840, Senior and Junior Orations, NCC. Horace *Odes* III, 30: 1.

23. Berry, *All That Makes a Man*, 12–13.

24. For the transatlantic scope of these attitudes and practices, especially how they related to education, see Rogers, *From the Salon to the Schoolroom*; De Bellaigue, *Educating Women*; Deslandes, *Oxbridge Men*. On the intellectual and moral efforts for self-improvement in the United States, see especially Howe, *Making the American Self*, and Casper, *Constructing American Lives*. On young women, education, and ambition, see Kelley, *Learning to Stand and Speak*; Jabour, *Scarlett's Sisters*; Winterer, "Victorian Antigone"; Sicherman, "Reading and Ambition."

25. Some prominent examples include Nathan, *My Freshman Year*; Arum and Roksa, *Academically Adrift*; Bain, *What the Best College Students Do*.

Bibliography

Primary Sources

Manuscript and Archive Collections

Chapel Hill, North Carolina
    Southern Historical Collection, Manuscripts Department, Wilson Library,
        University of North Carolina at Chapel Hill
        William Bagley Papers
        David Alexander Barnes Papers
        Daniel Moreau Barringer Papers
        Alexander Davis Betts Papers
        Willis G. Briggs Papers
        Iveson Lewis Brookes Papers
        Hamilton Brown Papers
        Brownrigg Family Papers
        Joseph Caldwell Papers
        John Caldwell Papers
        David Carter Papers
        Edmund De Berry Covington Diary
        James Lawrence Dusenbery Diary and Clipping
        Bartholomew Fuller Papers
        Thomas Miles Garrett Diary
        William Gaston Papers
        Gordon-Hackett Papers
        Bryan Grimes Papers
        James Gwyn Papers
        William Mercer Green Papers
        William Hooper Haigh Papers
        Edward Joseph Hale Papers
        Hawkins Family Papers
        John Haywood Papers
        Heartt-Wilson Papers
        Benjamin Sherwood Hedrick Papers
        Gustavus A. Henry Papers
        John DeBerniere Hooper Papers
        Edward Vernon Howell Papers
        Leander Hughes Papers
        Jonathan Jacocks Papers
        Calvin Jones Papers
        Isaac Jarratt Papers
        Sarah A. Jarret Papers

Sally Long Jarman Papers
Henry Francis Jones Diary
Thomas Williamson Jones Papers
Alexander Justice Papers
Kenan Family Papers
Theodore Bryant Kingsbury Papers
Lea Family Papers
Lenoir Family Papers
Lewis Family Papers
Henry Armand London Papers
Archibald McLauchlin Correspondence
William H. McLaurin Papers
Hector James McNeill Letters
Miscellaneous Student Notebooks
Elisha Mitchell Papers
William Sidney Mullins Diary
Adlai Osborne Papers
Charles Phillips Papers
Records of the Philomathean Society
James Hilliard Polk Diary
Polk and Yeatman Papers
Rufus Reid Papers
John Francis Speight Papers
Cornelia Phillips Spencer Papers
Joseph John Summerell Diary
John Dudley Tatum Papers
George Nicholas Thompson Diary and Notebooks
UNC Personal Papers, Misc.
Nathan Wilson Walker Papers
Wilson and Hairston Family Papers
Wooster Family Papers
University Archives, Manuscripts Department, Wilson Library, University of North
    Carolina at Chapel Hill
    General Faculty and Faculty Council of the University of North Carolina at Chapel
        Hill Records
    Records of the Board of Trustees of the University of North Carolina
    Records of Chi Psi, Alpha Sigma Chapter (UNC-Chapel Hill)
    Records of the Dialectic Society
    Records of the Philanthropic Society Records
North Carolina Collection, Wilson Library, University of North Carolina at Chapel
    Hill
    Autographs
    Senior and Junior Orations
Columbia, South Carolina
    South Caroliniana Library, University of South Carolina
        Iveson L. Brookes Papers
        Rebecca Easterling Papers

Euphradian Literary Society Records
Henri Harrisse Papers
Sullivan Family Papers
R. Y. Woodlief Diary
Durham, North Carolina
Rare Book, Manuscript, and Special Collections Library, Duke University
George C. Dromgoole and Richard B. Robinson Papers
William Slade Papers
Melchizedek Spragins Papers
William Wirt and Elizabeth Washington Papers
Raleigh, North Carolina
North Carolina State Archives
Julius F. Allison Papers
K. H. Lewis Papers
Little-Mordecai Collection
Nicholas Long Papers
Randolph Webb Papers
Winston-Salem, North Carolina
University Archives, Z. Smith Reynolds Library, Wake Forest University
Benson Field Cole Diary
Euzelian Society Records
Philomathesian Society Records

Newspapers and Magazines

DeBow's Review
North Carolina University Magazine
Southern Literary Messenger
Southern Quarterly Messenger
Yale University Magazine

Internet Archival Collections

Documenting the American South, University Library, University of North Carolina at
Chapel Hill
The First Century of the First State University (http://docsouth.unc.edu/unc/)
*True and Candid Compositions: The Lives and Writings of Antebellum Students at the
University of North Carolina* (http://docsouth.unc.edu/true/)
Verses and Fragments: The James L. Dusenbery Journal (1841–42) (http://docsouth.unc.
edu/dusenbery/)
Manuscripts Department, University of North Carolina at Chapel Hill
Slavery and the Making of the University (http://www2.lib.unc.edu/mss/exhibits/
slavery/)

Published Diaries and Manuscript Collections

Beatty, Richmond Groom, ed. *Journal of a Southern Student, 1846–1848, with Letters of a
Later Period*. Nashville: Vanderbilt University Press, 1944.
Berry, Stephen W., ed. *Princes of Cotton: Four Diaries of Young Men in the South, 1848–1860*.
Athens: University of Georgia Press, 2007.

Connor, R. D. *A Documentary History of the University of North Carolina, 1776–1799.* 2 vols. Chapel Hill: University of North Carolina Press, 1953.

Hamilton, John Bowen, ed. "Diary of Thomas Miles Garrett at the University of North Carolina, 1849." Parts 1–4. *North Carolina Historical Review* 38 (1961): 68–93, 241–62, 380–410, 534–63.

O'Brien, Michael, ed. *An Evening When Alone: Four Journals of Single Women in the South, 1827–67.* Charlottesville: University of Virginia Press, 1993.

Sanders, John L., ed. "The Journal of Ruffin Wirt Tomlinson, the University of North Carolina, 1841–1842." *North Carolina Historical Review* 30 (January 1953): 86–115, 233–59.

Tolbert, Lisa, ed. *Two Hundred Years of Student Life at Chapel Hill: Selected Letters and Diaries.* Southern Research Report #4. Chapel Hill, N.C.: Center for the Study of the American South, IRSS Faculty Working Group in Southern Studies, 1993.

Published Primary Sources

Abercrombie, John. *Inquiries Concerning the Intellectual Powers, and the Investigation of Truth.* Boston: John Allen & Co., 1835.

Acts of the General Assembly and Ordinances of the Trustees, for the Organization and Government of the University of North-Carolina. Raleigh, N.C.: Printed at the Office of the Raleigh Register, 1838.

Adams, John Quincy. *Lectures on Rhetoric and Oratory: Delivered to the Classes of Senior and Junior Sophisters in Harvard University.* Cambridge, Mass.: Printed by Hilliard and Metcalf, 1810.

Adams, Henry. *The Education of Henry Adams.* Edited by Ernest Samuels. Boston: Houghton Mifflin, 1973.

"Ancient and Modern Eloquence." *Southern Literary Messenger* 8 (March 1842): 169–85.

Battle, Kemp P. *Memories of an Old-Time Tar Heel.* Chapel Hill: University of North Carolina Press, 1945.

Bingham, Caleb. *The Columbian orator: containing a variety of original and selected pieces; together with rules; calculated to improve youth and others in the ornamental and useful art of eloquence. By Caleb Bingham, a.m. author of The American preceptor, Young lady's accidence, &c. [Three lines from Rollin] Published according to act of Congress.* 2nd ed. Boston: May, 1799. Eighteenth Century Collections Online.

"Biography." *Southern Literary Messenger* 23 (October 1856): 282–88.

Bristed, Charles Astor. *Five Years in an English University.* 2nd ed. New York: G. P. Putnam & Co., 1852.

Brown, Bedford. *An Address Delivered before the Two Literary Societies of the University of North Carolina: In Gerard Hall: On the Day Preceding the Annual Commencement, in June 1839, Under the Appointment of the Dialectic Society. By Hon. Bedford Brown.* Raleigh, N.C.: T. Loring, Office of the North Carolina Standard, 1839.

Brown, Thomas. *Lectures on the Philosophy of the Human Mind.* Philadelphia: J. Grigg; Charleston, S.C.: W. P. Bason, 1824.

Caldwell, Joseph A. *A Compendious System of Elementary Geometry, in Seven Books: To Which an Eighth Is Annexed, Containing Such Other Propositions As Are Elementary, Among Which Are a Few That Are Necessary, Beyond Those of the System, To the More Advanced Parts of the Mathematics.* Philadelphia: Printed by William Fry, 1822.

————. *Address to the Senior Class and Before the Audience Assembled at the Annual Commencement on the 28th of June, 1827.* Raleigh: Printed by J. Gales & Son, 1827.

Campbell, George. *The Philosophy of Rhetoric. By George Campbell . . . In two volumes.* London: Printed for W. Strahan and T. Cadell, 1776.

Catalogue of the Trustees, Faculty, and Students, of the University of N. Carolina. Raleigh, N.C.: W. R. Gales, Printer, Register Office, 1799–1861.

A Catalogue of Books Belonging to the Philanthropic Society at Chapel-Hill. Taken 6th May, 1822. Raleigh, N.C.: Printed by J. Gales & Son, 1822.

A Catalogue of Books Belonging to the Dialectic Society, Chapel Hill, February, 1821. Hillsborough, N.C.: Printed by D. Heartt, 1821.

A Catalogue of Books Belonging to the Dialectic Society at Chapel Hill, May 1835. Raleigh, N.C.: Printed by J. Gales & Son, 1835.

Channing, William E. "Self-Culture. An Address Introductory to the Franklin Lectures, Delivered at Boston, Sept., 1838." In *The Works of William E. Channing, D.D. First Complete American Edition, with an Introduction,* 349–411. Boston: James Munroe and Company, 1841.

Clapp, J. W. *An Address Delivered before the Calliopean Society of Emory & Henry College, on the Day of This Annual Commencement of the College, and the First Anniversary of the Society. August 6th, 1840: By J. W. Clapp, A.M.* Abingdon, Va., 1840.

Cooper, Thomas. *Address to the Graduates of the South-Carolina College, 3rd December, 1821, By Thomas Cooper, M.D., President, S.C. College.* Columbia, S.C.: Published by D. Faust, 1821.

Davies, Charles. *Elements of Geometry and Trigonometry from the works of a.m. Legendre: revised and adapted to the course of mathematical instruction in the United States.* New York: A. S. Barnes, 1836.

Dew, Thomas R. "Dissertation on the Characteristic Differences Between the Sexes, and on the Position and Influence of Women in Society, No. I." *Southern Literary Messenger* 1 (May 1835): 493–512.

Doggett, David S. *The Destiny of Educated Young Men. An Address Delivered Before the Literary Societies of Emory and Henry College, by the Rev. David S. Doggett, D.D., On Wednesday, June 21st, 1848.* Richmond: Methodist Office—C. H. Wynne, 1848.

Dwight, Timothy Jr. *President Dwight's Decisions of Questions Discussed by the Senior Class in Yale College in 1813 and 1814.* New York: Leavitt, 1833.

"Eloquence." *Southern Literary Messenger* 1 (December 1834): 165–66.

"Eloquence." *Southern Literary Messenger* 17 (January 1851): 24.

Fuller, Edwin W. *Sea-Gift: A Novel.* New York: E. J. Hale & Son, Publishers, 1873.

Gaston, William. *Address Delivered Before the Philanthropic and Dialectic Societies at Chapel-Hill, June 20, 1832. By the Hon. William Gaston.* Raleigh, N.C.: J. Gales & Son, 1832.

Hazlitt, William. *The Eloquence of the British Senate: Being a Selection of the Best Speeches of the Most Distinguished English, Irish, and Scotch Parliamentary Speakers, from the Beginning of the Reign of Charles I to the Present Time: With Notes Biographical, Critical, and Explanatory.* Brooklyn: Printed by Thomas Kirk, 1810.

Hooper, William. *The Discipline of the Heart, To Be Connected with the Culture of the Mind; a Discourse on Education, Delivered to the Students of the College, at Chapel Hill, North Carolina, August 22, 1830, and Published by Their Request.* New York: Sleight and Robinson, Printers, 1830.

House, Erwin. "What Is Eloquence?" *Ladies Repository* 12 (April 1852): 138–39.

Howard, W. G. "Ancient Eloquence." *Southern Literary Messenger* 6 (September 1840): 703–6.

———. "Ancient Eloquence." *Southern Literary Messenger* 7 (January 1841): 68–72.

Johnson, Samuel. *Johnson's Dictionary, Improved by Todd, Abridged For the Use of Schools; with the Addition of Walker's Pronunciation; an Abstract of His Principles of English Pronunciation, with Questions; a Vocabulary of Greek, Latin, and Scripture Proper Names; and an Appendix of Americanisms.* Boston: Charles J. Hendee, 1836.

Judson, A. M. "Eloquence." *Southern Literary Messenger* 20 (September 1854): 535–39.

Keen, T. G. *An Address, Delivered before the Franklin & Adelphi Societies of Howard College, at their Anniversary, Held at Marion, Alabama, July 24, 1850.* Tuscaloosa: Printed by M. D. Slade, 1850.

Kennedy, John P. *Memoirs of the Life of William Wirt, Attorney General of the United States,* Vol. 2. Philadelphia: Lea and Blanchard, 1849.

Miller, Henry Watkins. *Address Delivered before the Philanthropic and Dialectic Societies of the University of North-Carolina, June 2, 1857 by Henry W. Miller, Esq.* Raleigh, N.C.: Holden & Wilson, Standard Office, 1857.

Mitchell, Elisha. *Statistics, Facts, and Dates, for the Sunday Recitations of the Junior Class in the University.* New York: R. Craighead, Printer, 1850.

———. *The Other Leaf of the Book of Nature and the Word of God.* 1848.

Norton, William A. *An Elementary Treatise on Astronomy, in Four Parts, Containing a Systematic and Comprehensive Exposition of the Theory, and the More Important Practical Problems: with Solar, Lunar, and other Astronomical Tables, Designed for Use as a Text-book in Colleges and Academies.* New York: Wiley & Putnam, 1839.

Olmstead, Denison. *Outlines of the Lectures on Chemistry, Mineralogy, & Geology Delivered at the University of North-Carolina, for the Use of the Students.* Raleigh, N.C.: J. Gales, 1819.

Olmstead, Frederick Law. *A Journey in the Seaboard Slave States, with Remarks on Their Economy.* New York: Dix & Edwards, 1856.

Paley, William. *The Principles of Moral and Political Philosophy.* Edited by D. L. Le Mahieu. Indianapolis: Liberty Fund, 2002.

Peck, George. *Formation of a Manly Character: A Series of Lectures to Young Men.* New York: Carlton & Phillips, 1854.

Porter, B. F. *Address Delivered Before the Philomathic Society of the University of Alabama, on the Occasion of Its Fourth Anniversary, by B. F. Porter, an Honorary Member.* Tuskaloosa: Printed by M.D. J. Slade, 1836.

Powell, J. G. F., ed. *Cicero: Cato Maior De Senectute.* Cambridge: Cambridge University Press, 1988.

Richardson, Major (John). *Wacousta, or, The Prophecy : a Tale of the Canadas.* Edited by Douglas Cronk. Ottawa: Carleton University Press, 1987.

Shepard, William B. *An Address Delivered Before the Two Literary Societies of the University of North Carolina by Hon. William B. Shepard, June 27, 1838.* Raleigh, N.C.: Printed at the Office of the Raleigh Register, 1838.

Simms, William Gilmore. *Charlemont; or the Pride of the Village, a Tale of Kentucky,* 1856; New York: AMS Press, 1970.

———. *Beauchampe, or the Kentucky Tragedy: A Sequel to Charlemont.* 1842. Chicago: Belford, Clarke & Co., 1888.

Simpson, Thomas. *A Treatise of Algebra: wherein the principles are demonstrated and applied in many useful and interesting inquiries, and in the resolution of a great variety of problems of different kinds: to which is added, the geometrical construction of a great number of linear and plane problems with the method of resolving the same numerically*. Philadelphia: Printed for Mathew Carey, 1809.

Stiles, William H. *An Address Delivered Before the Phi Kappa and Demosthenian Societies of Franklin College, (University of Georgia,) at The Annual Commencement, August 4th, 1852*. Augusta: F. H. Singer, Georgia Home Gazette Office, 1852.

Stringfellow, Thornton. *Slavery: Its Origin, Nature, and History, Considered in the Light of Bible Teachings, Moral Justice, and Political Wisdom*. New York: John F. Trow, Printer, 1861.

Todd, John. *The Student's Manual; Designed, by Specific Directions, to Aid in Forming and Strengthening the Intellectual and Moral Character and Habits of the Student*. 1840. Reprint, Northampton [Mass.]: Bridgman and Childs, 1876.

Upham, Thomas C. *Elements of Mental Philosophy, Embracing the Two Departments of the Intellect and Sensibilities*. New York: Harper & Brothers, 1840.

Waldstreicher, David, ed. *Notes on the State of Virginia by Thomas Jefferson with Related Documents*. Boston and New York: Bedford/St. Martin's Press, 2010.

Wayland, Francis. *The Elements of Moral Science*. Boston: Gould, Kendall, and Lincoln, 1843.
——. *The Elements of Moral Science*. Edited by Joseph L. Blau. Cambridge, Mass.: Belknap Press of Harvard University Press, 1963.

Welles, E. G. *The Orator's Guide, Or, Rules for Speaking and Composing: From the Best Authorities*. Philadelphia: Printed for the compiler G. L. Austin printer, 1822.

Winslow, Hubbard. *Elements of Intellectual Philosophy Designed for a Textbook and for Private Reading*. Boston: Jenks, Hickling, & Swan, 1853.

Xenophon. *Xenophon: Apology and Memorabilia I*. Edited by M.D. Macleod. Oxford: Aris & Phillips, 2008.

Young, John Radford. *An Elementary Treatise on Algebra, Theoretical and Practical; with attempts to simplify some of the more difficult parts of the science . . . Intended for the use of students*. Philadelphia: Carey & Lea, 1832.

Secondary Sources

Books

Abzug, Robert H. *Cosmos Crumbling: American Reform and the Religious Imagination*. New York: Oxford University Press, 1994.

Allmendinger, David F. *Paupers and Scholars: The Transformation of Student Life in Nineteenth-Century New England*. New York: St. Martin's Press, 1975.

Arum, Richard, and Josipa Roksa. *Academically Adrift: Limited Learning on College Campuses*. Chicago: University of Chicago Press, 2011.

Augst, Thomas. *The Clerk's Tale: Young Men and Moral Life in Nineteenth-Century America*. Chicago: University of Chicago Press, 2003.

Augst, Thomas, and Kenneth Carpenter, eds. *Institutions of Reading: The Social Life of Libraries in the United States*. Amherst: University of Massachusetts Press, 2007.

Augst, Thomas, and Wayne Wiegand, eds. *Libraries as Agencies of Culture: Print Culture History in Modern America*. Lawrence, Kans.: American Studies, 2001.

Bailyn, Bernard. *Education in the Forming of American Society: Needs and Opportunities for Study*. Chapel Hill: University of North Carolina Press, 1960.

Bain, Ken. *What the Best College Students Do*. Cambridge, Mass.: Belknap Press of Harvard University Press, 2012.

Baker, Jean H. *Affairs of Party: The Political Culture of Northern Democrats in the Mid-Nineteenth Century*. New York: Fordham University Press, 1998.

Baptist, Edward E. *Creating an Old South: Middle Florida's Plantation Frontier before the Civil War*. Chapel Hill: University of North Carolina Press, 2002.

Barney, William L. *The Making of a Confederate: Walter Lenoir's Civil War*. Oxford: Oxford University Press, 2008.

Battle, Kemp P. *History of the University of North Carolina from Its Beginning to the Death of President Swain, 1789–1868*. Raleigh, N.C.: Edwards & Broughton Printing Company, 1907.

———. *History of the University of North Carolina, Volume Two: From 1868 to 1912*. Raleigh, N.C.: Edwards & Broughton Printing Company, 1912.

Bender, Thomas. *New York Intellect: A History of Intellectual Life in New York City, from 1750 to the Beginnings of Our Own Time*. Baltimore: Johns Hopkins University Press, 1987.

Benfield, G. J. Barker. *The Horrors of the Half-Known Life: Male Attitudes toward Women and Sexuality in Nineteenth-Century America*. New York: Harper & Row, 2000.

Berkhofer, Robert F. *The White Man's Indian: Images of the American Indian from Columbus to the Present*. New York: Alfred A. Knopf, 1978.

Bernath, Michael T. *Confederate Minds: The Struggle for Intellectual Independence in the Civil War South*. Chapel Hill: University of North Carolina Press, 2010.

Berry, Stephen W. II. *All That Makes a Man: Love and Ambition in the Civil War South*. New York: Oxford University Press, 2003.

Bledstein, Burton J. *The Culture of Professionalism: The Middle Class and the Development of Higher Education in America*. New York: W. W. Norton & Company, 1978.

Bleser, Carol, ed. *Secret and Sacred: The Diaries of James Henry Hammond, a Southern Slaveholder*. Oxford: Oxford University Press, 1989.

Braden, Waldo W. *Oratory in the Old South, 1828–1860*. Baton Rouge: Louisiana State University Press, 1970.

Brodhead, Richard H. *Cultures of Letters: Scenes of Reading and Writing in Nineteenth-Century America*. Chicago: University of Chicago Press, 1993.

Broughton, Trev Lynn. *Men of Letters, Writing Lives: Masculinity and Literary Auto/Biography in the Late Victorian Period*. London: Routledge, 1999.

Brown, Richard D. *The Strength of a People: The Idea of an Informed Citizenry in America, 1650–1870*. Chapel Hill: University of North Carolina Press, 1996.

Brubacher, John S., and Willis Rudy. *Higher Education in Transition: A History of American Colleges and Universities*. New Brunswick, N.J.: Transaction Publishers, 1997.

Bunkers, Suzanne L., and Cynthia A. Huff, eds. *Inscribing the Daily: Critical Essays on Women's Diaries*. Amherst: University of Massachusetts Press, 1996.

Burke, Colin. *American Collegiate Populations: A Test of the Traditional View*. New York: New York University Press, 1982.

Burroughs, Alan E. *Harvard Portraits*. Cambridge, Mass.: Harvard University Press, 1976.

Bushman, Richard L. *The Refinement of America: Persons, Houses, Cities*. New York: Alfred A. Knopf, 1992.

Baym, Nina. *Novels, Readers, and Reviewers: Responses to Fiction in Antebellum America*. Ithaca, N.Y.: Cornell University Press, 1984.

Byrne, Frank J. *Becoming Bourgeois: Merchant Culture in the South, 1820–1865*. Lexington: University Press of Kentucky, 2006.

Carmichael, Peter S. *The Last Generation: Young Virginians in Peace, War, and Reunion*. Chapel Hill: University of North Carolina Press, 2005.

Carney, Charity R. *Ministers and Masters: Methodism, Manhood, and Honor in the Old South*. Baton Rouge: Louisiana State University Press, 2011.

Carr, Jean Ferguson, Stephen L. Carr, and Lucille M. Schultz. *Archives of Instruction: Nineteenth-Century Rhetorics, Readers, and Composition Books in the United States*. Carbondale: Southern Illinois University Press, 2005.

Cash, W. J. *The Mind of the South*. 1941. New York: Vintage Books, 1991.

Cashin, Joan E. *A Family Venture: Men and Women on the Southern Frontier*. Oxford: Oxford University Press, 1991.

Caspari, Fritz. *Humanism and the Social Order in Tudor England*. Chicago: University of Chicago Press, 1954.

Casper, Scott. *Constructing American Lives: Biography and Culture in Nineteenth-Century America*. Chapel Hill: University of North Carolina Press, 1999.

Casper, Scott, et al., eds. *A History of the Book in America, Volume 3: The Industrial Book, 1840–1880*. Chapel Hill: University of North Carolina Press, 2007.

Censer, Jane Turner. *North Carolina Planters and Their Children, 1800–1860*. Baton Rouge: Louisiana State University Press, 1984.

Certeau, Michel de. *The Practice of Everyday Life*. Berkeley: University of California Press, 1984.

Clark, Daniel A. *Creating the College Man: American Mass Magazines and Middle-Class Manhood, 1890–1915*. Madison: University of Wisconsin Press, 2010.

Clark, Gregory, and S. Michael Halloran, eds. *Oratorical Culture in Nineteenth-Century America: Transformations in the Theory and Practice of Rhetoric*. Carbondale: Southern Illinois University Press, 1993.

Clarke, G. W., ed. *Rediscovering Hellenism: The Hellenic Inheritance and the English Imagination*. Cambridge: Cambridge University Press, 1989.

Cmiel, Kenneth. *Democratic Eloquence: The Fight over Popular Speech in Nineteenth-Century America*. New York: William Morrow, 1990.

Coates, Albert, and Gladys Hall Coates. *The Story of Student Government in the University of North Carolina at Chapel Hill*. Chapel Hill, N.C.: Professor Emeritus Fund, 1985.

Cohen, Patricia Cline. *The Murder of Helen Jewett: The Life and Death of a Prostitute in Nineteenth-Century New York*. New York: Alfred A. Knopf, 1998.

Cole, Thomas. *Thomas Cole: Landscape into History*. Edited by William H. Truettner and Alan Wallach. New Haven, Conn.: Yale University Press, 1994.

Coon, Charles L. *The Beginnings of Public Education in North Carolina: A Documentary History, 1790–1840*. Raleigh: Edwards & Broughton Print. Co, 1908.

———. *North Carolina Schools and Academies (1790–1840)*. Raleigh, N.C.: Edwards & Broughton Printing Company, 1915.

Coulter, E. Merton. *College Life in the Old South*. New York: Macmillan Company, 1928.

Crain, Caleb. *American Sympathy: Men, Friendship, and Literature in the New Nation*. New Haven, Conn.: Yale University Press, 2001.

Cremin, Lawrence A. *American Education: The National Experience, 1783–1876*. New York: Harper & Row, 1980.

Cust, Lionel. *Eton College Portraits*. London: Spottiswoode & Co., 1910.

Daniels, George H. *American Science in the Age of Jackson*. New York: Columbia University Press, 1968.

Darnton, Robert. *The Great Cat Massacre and Other Episodes in French Cultural History*. New York: Vintage Books, 1984.

Davidson, Cathy N. *Revolution and the Word: The Rise of the Novel in America*. New York: Oxford University Press, 1986.

Dawidoff, Robert. *The Education of John Randolph*. New York: W.W. Norton & Company, 1979.

De Bellaigue, Christina. *Educating Women: Schooling and Identity in England and France, 1800–1867*. Oxford: Oxford University Press, 2007.

Delfino, Susanna, Michele Gillespie, and Louis M. Kyriakoudes. *Southern Society and Its Transformations, 1790–1860*. Columbia: University of Missouri Press, 2011.

D'Emilio, John, and Estelle B. Freedman. *Intimate Matters: A History of Sexuality in America*. Chicago: University of Chicago Press, 1997.

Deslandes, Paul R. *Oxbridge Men: British Masculinity and the Undergraduate Experience, 1850–1920*. Bloomington: Indiana University Press, 2005.

Dorsey, Bruce. *Reforming Men and Women: Gender in the Antebellum City*. Ithaca, N.Y.: Cornell University Press, 2002.

Drake, William Earle. *Higher Education in North Carolina before 1860*. New York: Carlton Press, 1964.

DuVal, Kathleen. *The Native Ground: Indians and Colonists in the Heart of the Continent*. Philadelphia: University of Pennsylvania Press, 2006.

Eastman, Carolyn. *A Nation of Speechifiers: Making an American Public after the Revolution*. Chicago: University of Chicago Press, 2010.

Eaton, Clement. *Freedom of Thought in the Old South*. Durham, N.C.: Duke University Press, 1940.

Egbert, Donald Drew. *Princeton Portraits*. Princeton, N.J.: Princeton University Press, 1947.

Elliott, Robert Neal Jr. *The Raleigh Register, 1799–1863*. Chapel Hill: University of North Carolina Press, 1955.

Escott, Paul D. *Many Excellent People: Power and Privilege in North Carolina, 1850–1900*. Chapel Hill: University of North Carolina Press, 1985.

Farnham, Christie Anne. *The Education of the Southern Belle: Higher Education and Student Socialization in the Antebellum South*. New York: New York University Press, 1994.

Faust, Drew Gilpin. *James Henry Hammond and the Old South: A Design for Mastery*. Baton Rouge: Louisiana State University Press, 1982.

———. *A Sacred Circle: The Dilemma of the Intellectual in the Old South, 1840–1860*. Baltimore: Johns Hopkins University Press, 1977.

Fellman, Michael. *The Making of Robert E. Lee*. New York: Random House, 2000.

Fish, Stanley E. *Is There a Text in This Class? The Authority of Interpretive Communities*. Cambridge, Mass.: Harvard University Press, 1980.

Ford, Lacy K. *Deliver Us from Evil: The Slavery Question in the Old South*. Oxford: Oxford University Press, 2009.

Fox-Genovese, Elizabeth, and Eugene D. Genovese. *The Mind of the Master Class: History and Faith in the Southern Slaveholders' Worldview*. Cambridge: Cambridge University Press, 2005.

Fraser, Walter J. Jr., et al. *The Web of Southern Social Relations: Women, Family, & Education*. Athens: University of Georgia Press, 1985.

Freehling, William W. *The Road to Disunion, Volume II: Secessionists Triumphant, 1854–1861*. New York: Oxford University Press, 2007.

Friend, Craig Thompson, and Lorri Glover, eds. *Southern Manhood: Perspectives on Masculinity in the Old South*. Athens: University of Georgia Press, 2004.

Fronsman, Bill Cecil. *Common Whites: Class and Culture in Antebellum North Carolina*. Lexington: University Press of Kentucky, 1992.

Frost, Dan R. *Thinking Confederates: Academia and the Idea of Progress in the New South*. Knoxville: University of Tennessee Press, 2000.

Garland, Martha McMackin. *Cambridge before Darwin: The Ideal of a Liberal Arts Education, 1800–1860*. Cambridge: Cambridge University Press, 1980.

Gay, Peter. *Schnitzler's Century: The Making of Middle-Class Culture, 1815–1914*. New York: W. W. Norton & Company, 2002.

Geiger, Roger L., ed. *The American College in the Nineteenth Century*. Nashville: Vanderbilt University Press, 2000.

Genovese, Eugene D. *The Slaveholders' Dilemma: Freedom and Progress in Southern Conservative Thought, 1820–1860*. Columbia: University of South Carolina Press, 1992.

Gilmore, William J. *Reading Becomes a Necessity of Life: Material and Cultural Life in Rural New England, 1780–1835*. Knoxville: University of Tennessee Press, 1989.

Gilpatrick, Delbert Harold. *Jeffersonian Democracy in North Carolina, 1789–1816*. New York: Columbia University Press, 1931.

Ginzburg, Carlo. *The Cheese and the Worms: The Cosmos of a Sixteenth-Century Miller*. New York: Penguin Books, 1982.

Gleason, Maud W. *Making Men: Sophists and Self-Presentation in Ancient Rome*. Princeton, N.J.: Princeton University Press, 1995.

Glover, Lorri. *Southern Sons: Becoming Men in the New Nation*. Baltimore: Johns Hopkins University Press, 2007.

Goetzmann, William H. *Beyond the Revolution: A History of American Thought from Paine to Pragmatism*. New York: Basic Books, 2009.

Graff, Harvey. *Conflicting Paths: Growing Up in America*. Cambridge, Mass.: Harvard University Press, 1995.

Grant, Daniel Lindsey, ed. *Alumni History of the University of North Carolina*. 2nd ed. Durham, N.C.: Christian and King Printing Company, 1924.

Grasso, Christopher. *A Speaking Aristocracy: Transforming Public Discourse in Eighteenth-Century Connecticut*. Chapel Hill: University of North Carolina Press, 1999.

Green, Jennifer R. *Military Education and the Emerging Middle Class in the Old South*. Cambridge: Cambridge University Press, 2008.

Greenberg, Amy S. *Manifest Manhood and the Antebellum American Empire*. Cambridge: Cambridge University Press, 2005.

Greenberg, Kenneth S. *Honor & Slavery: Lies, Duels, Noses, Masks, Dressing as a Woman, Gifts, Strangers, Humanitarianism, Death, Slave Rebellions, the Proslavery Argument, Baseball, Hunting, and Gambling in the Old South*. Princeton, N.J.: Princeton University Press, 1996.

——. *Masters and Statesmen: The Political Culture of American Slavery*. Baltimore: Johns Hopkins University Press, 1985.

Greenblatt, Stephen. *Renaissance Self-Fashioning: From More to Shakespeare*. Chicago: University of Chicago Press, 1980.

Gross, Robert A., and Mary Kelley. *The History of the Book in America, Volume 4: An Extensive Republic: Print, Culture, and Society in the New Nation, 1790–1840*. Chapel Hill: University of North Carolina Press, 2010.

Guralnick, Stanley M. *Science and the Ante-Bellum American College*. Philadelphia: American Philosophical Society, 1975.

Gustafson, Sandra M. *Eloquence Is Power: Oratory & Performance in Early America*. Chapel Hill: University of North Carolina Press, 2000.

Hall, David D. *Cultures of Print: Essays in the History of the Book*. Amherst: University of Massachusetts Press, 1996.

Halttunen, Karen. *Confidence Men and Painted Women: A Study of Middle-Class Culture in America, 1830–1870*. New Haven, Conn.: Yale University Press, 1982.

Harding, Thomas S. *College Literary Societies: Their Contribution to Higher Education in the United States, 1815–1876*. New York: Pageant Press International Corp., 1971.

Hatch, Nathan O. *The Democratization of American Christianity*. New Haven, Conn.: Yale University Press, 1989.

Hemphill, C. Dallett. *Bowing to Necessities: A History of Manners in America, 1620–1860*. New York: Oxford University Press, 1999.

Henderson, Archibald. *The Campus of the First State University*. Chapel Hill: University of North Carolina Press, 1949.

Hessinger, Rodney. *Seduced, Abandoned, and Reborn: Visions of Youth in Middle-Class America, 1780–1850*. Philadelphia: University of Pennsylvania Press, 2005.

Heyrman, Christine Leigh. *Southern Cross: The Beginnings of the Bible Belt*. Chapel Hill: University of North Carolina Press, 1988.

Hoeveler, J. David. *Creating the American Mind: Intellect and Politics in the Colonial Colleges*. New York: Rowman & Littlefield, 2003.

Hollis, Christopher. *The Oxford Union*. London: Evans Brothers Ltd., 1965.

Horlick, Allan Stanley. *Country Boys and Merchant Princes: The Social Control of Young Men in New York*. Lewisburg, Pa.: Bucknell University Press, 1975.

Hornberger, Theodore. *Scientific Thought in the American College, 1638–1800*. Austin: University of Texas Press, 1945.

Horowitz, Helen Lefkowitz. *Campus Life: Undergraduate Cultures from the End of the Eighteenth Century to the Present*. New York: Alfred A. Knopf, 1987.

——. *Rereading Sex: Battles over Sexual Knowledge and Suppression in Nineteenth-Century America*. New York: Vintage Books, 2003.

Horsman, Reginald. *Race and Manifest Destiny: The Origins of American Racial Anglo-Saxonism*. Cambridge, Mass.: Harvard University Press, 1981.

Houghton, Walter E. *The Victorian Frame of Mind, 1830–1870*. New Haven, Conn.: Yale University Press, 1957.

Howe, Daniel Walker. *Making the American Self: Jonathan Edwards to Abraham Lincoln*. Oxford: Oxford University Press, 1997.

——. *The Political Culture of the American Whigs*. Chicago: University of Chicago Press, 1979.

——. *The Unitarian Conscience: Harvard Moral Philosophy, 1805–1861.* Cambridge, Mass.: Harvard University Press, 1970.

——. *What Hath God Wrought: The Transformation of America, 1815–1848.* Oxford: Oxford University Press, 2007.

Hunt, Lynn, ed. *The New Cultural History.* Berkeley: University of California Press, 1989.

Isaac, Rhys. *Landon Carter's Uneasy Kingdom: Revolution and Rebellion on a Virginia Plantation.* Oxford: Oxford University Press, 2004.

Jabour, Anya. *Scarlett's Sisters: Young Women in the Old South.* Chapel Hill: University of North Carolina Press, 2007.

Johnson, Paul E. *A Shopkeeper's Millennium: Society and Revivals in Rochester, New York, 1815–1837.* New York: Hill & Wang, 1978.

Johnson, Susan Lee. *Roaring Camp: The Social World of the California Gold Rush.* New York: W. W. Norton, 2000.

Kaestle, Carl F. *Pillars of the Republic: Common Schools and American Society, 1780–1860.* New York: Hill & Wang, 1983.

Kagle, Steven. *Early Nineteenth-Century American Diary Literature.* Boston: Twayne Publishers, 1986.

Kaplan, Catherine O'Donnell. *Men of Letters in the Early Republic: Cultivating Forums of Citizenship.* Chapel Hill: University of North Carolina Press, 2008.

Kasson, John F. *Rudeness & Civility: Manners in Nineteenth-Century Urban America.* New York: Hill and Wang, 1990.

——. *Houdini, Tarzan, and the Perfect Man.* New York: Hill & Wang, 2001.

Kelley, Mary. *Learning to Stand and Speak: Women, Education, and Public Life in America's Republic.* Chapel Hill: University of North Carolina Press, 2006.

Kerber, Linda K. *Women of the Republic: Intellect and Ideology in Revolutionary America.* Chapel Hill: Published for the Institute of Early American History and Culture by the University of North Carolina Press, 1980.

Kerrison, Catherine. *Claiming the Pen: Women and Intellectual Life in the Early American South.* Ithaca, N.Y.: Cornell University Press, 2006.

Kett, Joseph F. *The Pursuit of Knowledge under Difficulties: From Self-Improvement to Adult Education in America, 1750–1990.* Stanford, Calif.: Stanford University Press, 1994.

——. *Rites of Passage: Adolescence in America, 1790 to the Present.* New York: Basic Books, 1977.

Kimball, Bruce A. *Orators and Philosophers: A History of the Idea of Liberal Education.* New York: Columbia University Press, 1986.

Knight, Edgar W. *Public Education in the South.* New York: Ginn and Company, 1922.

Koschnik, Albrecht. *"Let a Common Interest Bind Us Together": Associations, Partisanship, and Culture in Philadelphia, 1775–1840.* Charlottesville: University of Virginia Press, 2007.

Laqueur, Thomas Walter. *Solitary Sex: A Cultural History of Masturbation.* New York: Zone Books, 2003.

Larson, John Lauritz. *The Market Revolution in America: Liberty, Ambition, and the Eclipse of the Common Good.* Cambridge: Cambridge University Press, 2010.

Lebsock, Suzanne. *The Free Women of Petersburg: Status and Culture in a Southern Town, 1784–1860.* New York: Norton, 1984.

Lefler, Hugh Talmage, and Albert Ray Newsome. *North Carolina: The History of a Southern State.* Chapel Hill: University of North Carolina Press, 1954.

Lefler, Hugh Talmage, and Paul W. Wager. *Orange County, 1752–1952*. Chapel Hill: Orange Print Shop, 1953.

Leloudis, James L. *Schooling the New South: Pedagogy, Self, and Society in North Carolina, 1880–1920*. Chapel Hill: University of North Carolina Press, 1996.

Lieber, Todd M. *Endless Experiments: Essays on the Heroic Experience in American Romanticism*. Columbus: Ohio State University Press, 1973.

Lockley, Timothy James. *Welfare and Charity in the Antebellum South*. Gainesville: University Press of Florida, 2007.

Longaker, Mark Garrett. *Rhetoric and the Republic: Politics, Civic Discourse, and Education in Early America*. Tuscaloosa: University of Alabama Press, 2007.

Loughran, Trish. *The Republic in Print: Print Culture in the Age of U.S. Nation Building, 1770–1870*. New York: Columbia University Press, 2007.

Lystra, Karen. *Searching the Heart: Women, Men, and Romantic Love in Nineteenth-Century America*. New York: Oxford University Press, 1989.

Machor, James L., ed. *Readers in History: Nineteenth-Century American Literature and the Contexts of Response*. Baltimore: Johns Hopkins University Press, 1993.

MacMillan, Dougald. *English at Chapel Hill, 1795–1969*. Chapel Hill: Department of English, University of North Carolina at Chapel Hill, 1970.

Marcus, Steven. *The Other Victorians: A Study of Sexuality and Pornography in Mid-Nineteenth-Century England*. New York: Basic Books, 1966.

Mathews, Donald G. *Religion in the Old South*. Chicago: University of Chicago Press, 1977.

Mayfield, John. *Counterfeit Gentlemen: Manhood and Humor in the Old South*. Gainesville: University Press of Florida, 2009.

Mazon, Patricia M. *Gender and the Modern Research University: The Admission of Women to German Higher Education, 1865–1914*. Stanford, Calif.: Stanford University Press, 2003.

McCall, Laura, and Donald Yacovone, eds. *A Shared Experience: Men, Women, and the History of Gender*. New York: New York University Press, 1998.

McCoy, Drew. *The Elusive Republic: Political Economy in Jeffersonian America*. Chapel Hill: University of North Carolina Press, 1980.

McCurdy, John Gilbert. *Citizen Bachelors: Manhood and the Creation of the United States*. Ithaca: Cornell University Press, 2009.

McCurry, Stephanie. *Masters of Small Worlds: Yeomen Households, Gender Relations, and the Political Culture of the Antebellum South Carolina Low Country*. New York: Oxford University Press, 1997.

McGill, Meredith L. *American Literature and the Culture of Reprinting, 1834–1853*. Philadelphia: University of Pennsylvania Press, 2003.

Mellor, Anne K. *Romanticism & Gender*. New York: Routledge, 1993.

Meyer, Donald H. *The Instructed Conscience: The Shaping of the American National Ethic*. Philadelphia: University of Pennsylvania Press, 1972.

Miller, Howard. *The Revolutionary College: American Presbyterian Higher Education, 1707–1837*. New York: New York University Press, 1976.

Miller, Perry. *The Life of the Mind in America from the Revolution to the Civil War*. New York: Harcourt, Brace & World, 1965.

Mintz, Steven. *Huck's Raft: A History of American Childhood*. Cambridge, Mass: Belknap Press of Harvard University Press, 2004.

Morison, Samuel Eliot. *Harvard College in the Seventeenth Century*. Cambridge, Mass.: Harvard University Press, 1936.

Moss, Ann. *Printed Commonplace Books and the Structuring of Renaissance Thought.* Oxford: Clarendon Press, 1996.

Nathan, Rebekah. *My Freshman Year: What a Professor Learned by Becoming a Student.* New York: Penguin Books, 2005.

Noble, Louis Legrand. *The Life and Works of Thomas Cole.* Edited by Elliot S. Vesell. Cambridge, Mass.: Belknap Press of Harvard University Press, 1964.

Noll, Mark A. *Princeton and the Republic, 1768–1822: The Search for a Christian Enlightenment in the Era of Samuel Stanhope Smith.* Princeton, N.J.: Princeton University Press, 1989.

Nord, David Paul. *Faith in Reading: Religious Publishing and the Birth of Mass Media in America.* Oxford: Oxford University Press, 2004.

Novak, Steven J. *The Rights of Youth: American Colleges and Student Revolt, 1798–1815.* Cambridge, Mass.: Harvard University Press, 1977.

Numbers, Ronald L., and Todd L. Savitt, eds. *Medicine in the Old South.* Baton Rouge: Louisiana State University Press, 1989.

O'Brien, Michael. *Conjectures of Order: Intellectual Life and the American South, 1810–1860.* Chapel Hill: University of North Carolina Press, 2004.

———. *Henry Adams & the Southern Question.* Athens: University of Georgia Press, 2007.

Opal, J. M. *Beyond the Farm: National Ambitions in Rural New England.* Philadelphia: University of Pennsylvania Press, 2008.

Osterweis, Rollin G. *Romanticism and Nationalism in the Old South.* New Haven, Conn.: Yale University Press, 1949.

Ostrander, Gilman M. *Republic of Letters: The American Intellectual Community, 1775–1865.* Madison, Wisc.: Madison House, 1998.

Ownby, Ted. *Subduing Satan: Religion, Recreation, & Manhood in the Rural South, 1865–1920.* Chapel Hill: University of North Carolina Press, 1990.

Pace, Robert F. *Halls of Honor: College Men in the Old South.* Baton Rouge: Louisiana State University Press, 2004.

Pangle, Lorraine Smith, and Thomas L. Pangle. *The Learning of Liberty: The Educational Ideas of the American Founders.* Lawrence: University of Kansas Press, 1993.

Parker, Mark. *Literary Magazines and British Romanticism.* Cambridge: Cambridge University Press, 2000.

Paschal, George Washington. *History of Wake Forest College*, vol. 1. Raleigh, N.C.: Edwards and Broughton, 1935.

Pawley, Christine. *Reading on the Middle Border: The Culture of Print in Late Nineteenth-Century Osage, Iowa.* Amherst: University of Massachusetts Press, 2001.

Pflugrad-Jackisch, Ami. *Brothers of a Vow: Secret Fraternal Orders and the Transformation of White Male Culture in Antebellum Virginia.* Athens: University of Georgia Press, 2010.

Pinkney, David H. *Decisive Years in France, 1840–1847.* Princeton, N.J.: Princeton University Press, 1986.

Powell, William S. *Dictionary of North Carolina Biography*, vol. 5. Chapel Hill: University of North Carolina Press, 1994.

Prucha, Francis Paul. *The Great Father: The United States Government and the American Indians.* Lincoln: University of Nebraska Press, 1995.

Radway, Janice A. *A Feeling for Books: The Book-of-the-Month Club, Literary Taste, and Middle-class Desire.* Chapel Hill: University of North Carolina Press, 1997.

———. *Reading the Romance: Women, Patriarchy, and Popular Literature*. Chapel Hill: University of North Carolina Press, 1991.

Ray, Angela G. *The Lyceum and Public Culture in the Nineteenth-Century United States*. East Lansing: Michigan State University Press, 2005.

Ready, Milton. *The Tar Heel State: A History of North Carolina*. Columbia: University of South Carolina Press, 2005.

Reese, William J., and John L. Rury, eds. *Rethinking the History of American Education*. New York: Palgrave Macmillan, 2008.

Reingold, Nathan, ed. *Science in America since 1820*. New York: Science History Publications, 1976.

Reinhold, Meyer. *Classica Americana: The Greek and Roman Heritage in the United States*. Detroit: Wayne State University Press, 1984.

Reinier, Jacqueline S. *From Virtue to Character: American Childhood, 1775–1850*. New York: Twayne Publishers, 1996.

Reynolds, David. *Beneath the American Renaissance: The Subversive Imagination in the Age of Emerson and Melville*. New York: Alfred A. Knopf, 1988.

———. *Walt Whitman's America: A Cultural Biography*. New York: Alfred A. Knopf, 1995.

Richard, Carl. *The Founders and the Classics: Greece, Rome, and the American Enlightenment*. Cambridge, Mass.: Harvard University Press, 1994.

Robson, David W. *Educating Republicans: The College in the Era of the American Revolution, 1750–1800*. Westport, Conn.: Greenwood Press, 1985.

Rogers, Rebecca. *From the Salon to the Schoolroom: Educating Bourgeois Girls in Nineteenth-Century France*. University Park: Pennsylvania State University Press, 2005.

Rose, Jonathan. *The Intellectual Life of the British Working Classes*. New Haven, Conn.: Yale University Press, 2001.

Rothman, Ellen K. *Hands and Hearts: A History of Courtship in America*. New York: Basic Books, Inc, 1984.

Rotundo, E. Anthony. *American Manhood: Transformations in Masculinity from the Revolution to the Modern Era*. New York: Basic Books, 1993.

Rudolph, Frederick. *Curriculum: A History of the American Undergraduate Course of Study since 1636*. San Francisco: Jossey-Bass, 1977.

Russell, Gillian, and Clara Tuite, eds. *Romantic Sociability: Social Networks and Literary Culture in Britain, 1770–1840*. New York: Cambridge University Press, 2002.

Ryan, Barbara, ed. *Reading Acts: U.S. Readers' Interactions with Literature, 1800–1950*. Knoxville: University of Tennessee Press, 2002.

Saunt, Claudio. *Black, White, and Indian: Race and the Unmaking of an American Family*. Oxford: Oxford University Press, 2005.

Scarborough, William Kauffman. *Masters of the Big House: Elite Slaveholders of the Mid-Nineteenth-Century South*. Baton Rouge: Louisiana State University Press, 2003.

Sellers, Charles Grier. *The Market Revolution: Jacksonian America, 1815–1846*. Oxford: Oxford University Press, 1991.

Sellers, M. N. S. *American Republicanism: Roman Ideology in the United States Constitution*. New York: New York University Press, 1994.

Sheehan, Bernard W. *Seeds of Extinction: Jeffersonian Philanthropy and the American Indian*. Published for the Institute of Early American History and Culture at Williamsburg, Va. Chapel Hill: University of North Carolina Press, 1973.

Shields, David S. *Civil Tongues and Polite Letters in British America*. Chapel Hill: University of North Carolina Press, 1997.

Sherman, Joan R., ed. *The Black Bard of North Carolina: George Moses Horton and His Poetry*. Chapel Hill: University of North Carolina Press, 1997.

Simpson, David. *The Politics of American English, 1776–1850*. New York: Oxford University Press, 1986.

Smith, Charles Lee. *The History of Education in North Carolina*. Washington, D.C.: Government Printing Office, 1888.

Smith, Michael Thomas. *A Traitor and a Scoundrel: Benjamin Hedrick and the Cost of Dissent*. Newark: University of Delaware Press, 2003.

Snider, William D. *Light on the Hill: A History of the University of North Carolina at Chapel Hill*. Chapel Hill: University of North Carolina Press, 1992.

Stansell, Christine. *City of Women: Sex and Class in New York, 1789–1860*. New York: Alfred A. Knopf, 1986.

Stone, Lawrence, ed. *The University in Society*. Princeton, N.J.: Princeton University Press, 1974.

Stott, Richard. *Jolly Fellows: Male Milieus in Nineteenth-Century America*. Baltimore: Johns Hopkins University Press, 2009.

Story, Ronald. *The Forging of an Aristocracy: Harvard and the Boston Upper Class, 1800–1870*. Middletown: Wesleyan University Press, 1980.

Stowe, Steven M. *Intimacy and Power in the Old South: Ritual in the Lives of the Planters*. Baltimore: Johns Hopkins University Press, 1987.

———. *Doctoring the South: Southern Physicians and Everyday Medicine in the Mid-Nineteenth Century*. Chapel Hill: University of North Carolina Press, 2004.

Syrett, Nicholas L. *The Company He Keeps: A History of White College Fraternities*. Chapel Hill: University of North Carolina Press, 2009.

Taylor, Amy Murrell. *The Divided Family in Civil War America*. Chapel Hill: University of North Carolina Press, 2005.

Taylor, William R. *Cavalier and Yankee*. Oxford: Oxford University Press, 1993.

Tewksbury, Donald G. *The Founding of American Colleges and Universities before the Civil War, With Particular Reference to the Religious Influences Bearing upon the College Movement*. New York: Archon Books, 1965.

Tolley, Kim. *The Science Education of American Girls: A Historical Perspective*. New York: RoutledgeFalmer, 2003.

Tompkins, Jane P., ed. *Reader-Response Criticism: From Formalism to Poststructuralism*. Baltimore: Johns Hopkins University Press, 1980.

Townsend, Kim. *Manhood at Harvard: William James and Others*. New York: W.W. Norton, 1996.

Turner, James. *The Liberal Education of Charles Eliot Norton*. Baltimore: Johns Hopkins University Press, 1999.

Vance, William. *America's Rome. Vol. 1: Classical Rome*. New Haven, Conn.: Yale University Press, 1989.

Varon, Elizabeth R. *We Mean to Be Counted: White Women & Politics in Antebellum Virginia*. Chapel Hill: University of North Carolina Press, 1998.

Veysey, Laurence. *The Emergence of the American University*. Chicago: University of Chicago Press, 1965.

Vickers, James, Thomas Scism, and Dixon Qualls. *Chapel Hill: An Illustrated History.* Chapel Hill: Barclay Publishers, 1985.

Wallace, Anthony F. C. *Jefferson and the Indians: The Tragic Fate of the First Americans.* Cambridge, Mass.: Belknap Press of Harvard University Press, 1999.

Walter, David. *The Oxford Union: Playground of Power.* London: MacDonald & Co., 1984.

Watson, Harry L. *Jacksonian Politics and Community Conflict: The Emergence of the Second American Party System in Cumberland County, North Carolina.* Baton Rouge: Louisiana State University Press, 1981.

———. *Liberty and Power: The Politics of Jacksonian America.* 2nd ed. New York: Hill & Wang, 2006.

Wells, Jonathan Daniel. *The Origins of the Southern Middle Class, 1800–1861.* Chapel Hill: University of North Carolina Press, 2004.

Welter, Rush. *The Mind of America, 1820–1860.* New York: Columbia University Press, 1975.

Wilentz, Sean. *The Rise of American Democracy.* New York: W. W. Norton & Company, 2005.

Winterer, Caroline. *The Culture of Classicism: Ancient Greece and Rome in American Intellectual Life, 1780–1910.* Baltimore: Johns Hopkins University Press, 2002.

———. *The Mirror of Antiquity: American Women and the Classical Tradition, 1750–1900.* Ithaca, N.Y.: Cornell University Press, 2007.

Wise, Benjamin E. *William Alexander Percy: The Curious Life of a Mississippi Planter & Sexual Freethinker.* Chapel Hill: University of North Carolina Press, 2012.

Wright, Conrad Edick. *Revolutionary Generation: Harvard Men and the Consequences of Independence.* Amherst: University of Massachusetts Press, 2005.

Wyatt-Brown, Bertram. *Southern Honor: Ethics & Behavior in the Old South.* Oxford: Oxford University Press, 2007.

Zboray, Ronald J. *A Fictive People: Antebellum Economic Development and the American Reading Public.* Oxford: Oxford University Press, 1993.

Zboray, Ronald J., and Mary Saracino Zboray. *Everyday Ideas: Socioliterary Experience among Antebellum New Englanders.* Knoxville: University of Tennessee Press, 2006.

———. *Literary Dollars and Social Sense: A People's History of the Mass Market Book.* New York: Routledge, 2005.

Articles, Book Chapters, Dissertations, and Theses

Allen, Judith A. "Men Interminably in Crisis? Historians on Masculinity, Sexual Boundaries, and Manhood." *Radical History Review* 82 (Winter 2002): 191–207.

Allmendinger, David F. "The Dangers of Ante-Bellum Student Life." *Journal of Social History* 7 (Autumn 1973): 75–85.

Ball, Deborah Lowenberg, and Francesca M. Forzani. "What Makes Educational Research 'Educational'?" *Educational Researcher* 36 (2009): 529–40.

Baptist, Edward E. "Me and Southern Honor." *Historically Speaking* 9 (August 2008): 13–14.

Blue, Frederick J. "The Poet and the Reformer: Longfellow, Sumner, and the Bonds of Male Friendship, 1837–1874." *Journal of the Early Republic* 15 (Summer 1995): 273–97.

Bowen, James. "Education, Ideology and the Ruling Class: Hellenism and English Public Schools in the Nineteenth Century." In *Rediscovering Hellenism: The Hellenic Inheritance and the English Imagination*, edited by G. W. Clarke, 161–86. Cambridge: Cambridge University Press, 1989.

Brooke, John L. "Cultures of Nationalism, Movements of Reform, and the Composite-Federal Polity: From Revolutionary Settlement to Antebellum Crisis." *Journal of the Early Republic* 29 (Spring 2009): 1-33.

Brophy, Alfred L. "'The Law of the Descent of Thought': Law, History, and Civilization in Antebellum Literary Addresses." *Law & Literature* 20 (2008): 343-402.

———. "The Republics of Liberty and Letters: Progress, Union, and Constitutionalism in Graduation Addresses at the Antebellum University of North Carolina." *North Carolina Law Review* 89 (2011): 1881-1964.

Calvert, Karin. "Children in American Family Portraiture, 1670-1810." *William and Mary Quarterly* 39 (January 1982): 87-113.

Cantrell, Clyde. "The Reading Habits of Ante-Bellum Southerners." Ph.D. diss., University of Illinois, 1960.

Carroll, Brian D. "'I indulged my desire too freely': Sexuality, Spirituality, and the Sin of Self-Pollution in the Diary of Joseph Moody, 1720-1724." *William and Mary Quarterly* 60 (January 2003): 155-70.

Causey, Evelyn D. "The Character of a Gentleman: Deportment, Piety, and Morality in Southern Colleges and Universities, 1820-1860." Ph.D. diss., University of Delaware, 2006.

Chartier, Roger. "Texts, Printing, Readings." In *The New Cultural History*, edited by Lynn Hunt, 154-75. Berkeley: University of California Press, 1989.

Cohen, Daniel A. "Making Hero Strong: Teenage Ambition, Story-Paper Fiction, and the Generational Recasting of American Women's Authorship." *Journal of the Early Republic* 30 (Spring 2010): 85-136.

Come, Donald Robert. "The Influence of Princeton on Higher Education in the South before 1825." *William and Mary Quarterly* 2 (October 1945): 359-96.

Cott, Nancy F. "Passionlessness: An Interpretation of Victorian Sexual Ideology, 1790-1850." *Signs* 4 (Winter 1978): 219-36.

Curtis, Robert. "The Bingham School and Classical Education in North Carolina, 1793-1873." *North Carolina Historical Review* 73 (July 1996): 328-77.

Dierks, Konstantin. "Men's History, Gender History, or Cultural History?" *Gender & History* 14 (April 2002): 147-51.

Ditz, Toby L. "The New Men's History and the Peculiar Absence of Gendered Power: Some Remedies from Early American History." *Gender & History* 16 (April 2004): 1-35.

Drinkwater, L. Ray. "Honor and Student Misconduct in Southern Antebellum Colleges." *Southern Humanities Review* 27 (Fall 1993): 323-44.

Durrill, Wayne K. "The Power of Ancient Words: Classical Teaching and Social Change at South Carolina College, 1804-1860." *Journal of Southern History* 65 (August 1999): 469-98.

Dyer, Thomas G. "Science in the Antebellum College: The University of Georgia, 1801-1860." In *Medicine in the Old South*, edited by Ronald L. Numbers and Todd L. Savitt, 36-54. Baton Rouge: Louisiana State University Press, 1989.

Eastman, Carolyn. "The Female Cicero: Young Women's Oratory and Gendered Public Participation in the Early American Republic." *Gender & History* 19 (August 2007): 260-83.

Ezell, John S. "A Southern Education for Southrons." *Journal of Southern History* 17 (August 1951): 303-27.

Findlay, James. "Agency, Denominations, and the Western Colleges, 1830–1860: Some Connections between Evangelicalism and American Higher Education." In *The American College in the Nineteenth-Century*, edited by Roger L. Geiger, 115–26. Nashville: Vanderbilt University Press, 2000.

Fish, Stanley E. "Interpreting the Variorium." In *Reader-Response Criticism: From Formalism to Poststructuralism*, edited by Jane P. Tompkins, 164–83. Baltimore: Johns Hopkins University Press, 1980.

Frisch, John R. "Youth Culture in America, 1790–1865." Ph.D. diss., University of Missouri-Columbia, 1970.

Gabrielse, David Randall. "Making Men, Colleges and the Midwest: The Building and Writing of Indiana Colleges, 1802–1860." Ph.D. diss., Michigan State University, 2002.

Gimbert, Aliana. "The Purpose and Effects of Classical Education in the Antebellum South." Honors thesis, University of North Carolina at Chapel Hill, 1996.

Glover, Lorri. "An Education in Southern Masculinity: The Ball Family of South Carolina in the New Republic." *Journal of Southern History* 69 (February 2003): 39–70.

Gorn, Elliot J. "'Gouge and Bite, Pull Hair and Scratch': The Social Significance of Fighting in the Southern Backcountry." *American Historical Review* 90 (February 1985): 18–43.

Green, Jennifer R. "Networks of Military Educators: Middle-Class Stability and Professionalization in the Late Antebellum South." *Journal of Southern History* 73 (February 2007): 39–74.

Guyatt, Nicholas. "'The Outskirts of Our Happiness': Race and the Lure of Colonization in the Early Republic." *Journal of American History* 95 (March 2009): 986–1011.

Hansen, Karen V. "'Our Eyes Behold Each Other': Masculinity and Intimate Friendship in Antebellum New England." In *Men's Friendships*, 35–58. London: Sage Publications, 1992.

Hemphill, C. Dallett. "'Isaac and 'Isabella': Courtship and Conflict in an Antebellum Circle of Youth." *Early American Studies* 2 (2004): 398–434.

Hessinger, Rodney. "'The Most Powerful Instrument of College Discipline': Student Disorder and the Growth of Meritocracy in the Colleges of the Early Republic." *History of Education Quarterly* 39 (1999): 237–62.

Hevel, Michael Stephen. "'Betwixt brewings': A History of College Students and Alcohol, 1820–1933." Ph.D. diss., University of Iowa, 2011.

Ishkanian, Judith Mitchell. "Religion and Honor at Chapel Hill: The College Odyssey of William Sidney Mullins, 1840–42." Ph.D. diss., University of California, Santa Barbara, 1993.

Jabour, Anya. "'Grown Girls, Highly Cultivated': Female Education in an Antebellum Southern Family." *Journal of Southern History* 64 (February 1998): 23–64.

———. "Male Friendship and Masculinity in the Early National South: William Wirt and His Friends." *Journal of the Early Republic* 20 (Spring 2000): 83–111.

———. "Masculinity and Adolescence in Antebellum America: Robert Wirt at West Point, 1820–1821." *Journal of Family History* 23 (October 1998): 393–416.

Jackson, Leon. "The Reader Retailored: Thomas Carlyle, His American Audiences, and the Politics of Evidence." In *Reading Acts: U.S. Readers' Interactions with Literature, 1800–1950*, edited by Barbara Ryan and Amy M. Thomas, 79–106. Knoxville: University of Tennessee Press, 2002.

————. "The Rights of Man and the Rites of Youth: Fraternity and Riot at Eighteenth-Century Harvard." In *The American College in the Nineteenth Century*, edited by Roger L. Geiger, 46–79. Nashville: Vanderbilt University Press, 2000.

Kamensky, Jane. "Talk Like a Man: Speech, Power, and Masculinity in Early New England." In *A Shared Experience: Men, Women, and the History of Gender*, edited by Laura McCall and Donald Yacovone, 19–50. New York: New York University Press, 1998.

Kasson, Joy S. "The Voyage of Life: Thomas Cole and Romantic Disillusionment." *American Quarterly* 27 (March 1975): 42–56.

Kelley, Mary. "Reading Women/Women Reading: The Making of Learned Women in Antebellum America." In *Reading Acts: U.S. Readers' Interactions with Literature, 1800–1950*, edited by Barbara Ryan and Amy M. Thomas, 53–78. Knoxville: University of Tennessee Press, 2002.

Kerber, Linda K. "Separate Spheres, Female Worlds, Woman's Place: The Rhetoric of Women's History." *Journal of American History* 75 (June 1988): 9–39.

Kett, Joseph F. "Adolescence and Youth in Nineteenth-Century America." *Journal of Interdisciplinary History* 2 (Autumn 1971): 283–98.

Kett, Joseph F., and Patricia A. McClung. "Book Culture in Post-Revolutionary Virginia." *Proceedings of the American Antiquarian Society* 94 (1984): 97–148.

Kilbride, Daniel. "Southern Medical Students in Philadelphia, 1800–1861: Science and Sociability in the 'Republic of Medicine.'" *Journal of Southern History* 65 (November 1999): 697–732.

Leloudis, James L. "What Should a University Be? Students, Curriculum, and Campus Life at the University of North Carolina." In *Two Hundred Years of Student Life at Chapel Hill: Selected Letters and Diaries*, edited by Lisa Tolbert, 1–14. Chapel Hill, N.C.: Center for the Study of the American South, IRSS Faculty Working Group in Southern Studies, 1993.

Lindman, Janet Moore. "Acting the Manly Christian: White Evangelical Masculinity in Revolutionary Virginia." *William and Mary Quarterly* 57 (April 2000): 393–416.

Lovell, Margaretta M. "Reading Eighteenth-Century American Family Portraits: Social Images and Self-Images." *Winterthur Portfolio* 22 (Winter 1987): 243–64.

Lussana, Sergio. "To See Who Was Best on the Plantation: Enslaved Fighting Contests and Masculinity in the Antebellum Plantation South." *Journal of Southern History* 76 (November 2010): 901–22.

Machor, James L. "Fiction and Informed Reading in Early Nineteenth-Century America." *Nineteenth-Century Literature* 47 (December 1992): 320–48.

McInvaill, Dwight Emlyn Huger. "The Georgetown Library Society of South Carolina and the Book-Borrowing Habits of Ten of Its Antebellum Members." M.S.L.S. thesis, University of North Carolina at Chapel Hill, 1978.

McLachlan, James. "The Choice of Hercules: American Student Societies in the Early 19th Century." In *The University in Society*, edited by Lawrence Stone, 449–94. Princeton, N.J.: Princeton University Press, 1974.

Miles, Edwin. "The Old South and the Classical World." *North Carolina Historical Review* 48 (1971): 258–75.

Morgan, Edmund S. "Ezra Stiles and Timothy Dwight." *Proceedings of the Massachusetts Historical Society* 72 (1963): 101–17.

Mullins, Jeffrey A. "Honorable Violence: Youth Culture, Masculinity, and Contested Authority in Liberal Education in the Early Republic." *American Transcendental Quarterly* 17 (2003): 161–79.

Murphy, Evangeline Burbank. "The Growth of the Library of the Philanthropic Society at the University of North Carolina, Chapel Hill, 1797–1822." M.S.L.S. thesis, University of North Carolina at Chapel Hill, 1979.

Myers, Terry L. "Thinking about Slavery at William and Mary." *William and Mary Bill of Rights Journal* 21, no. 4 (2013): 1215–57. http://scholarship.law.wm.edu/wmborj/vol21/iss4/6

Nichols, Elisabeth B. "Female Readers and Printed Authority in the Early Republic." In *Reading Acts: U.S. Readers' Interactions with Literature, 1800–1950*, edited by Barbara Ryan and Amy M. Thomas, 1–28. Knoxville: University of Tennessee Press, 2002.

Ong, Walter. "Latin Language Study as a Renaissance Puberty Rite." *Studies in Philology* 56 (April 1959): 103–24.

Opal, J. M. "The Making of the Victorian Campus: Teacher and Student at Amherst College, 1850–1880." *History of Education Quarterly* 42 (Autumn 2002): 342–67.

Owen, Mary Catherine. "The Education of Distinguished Southerners as Revealed in Biographies." Ph.D. diss., George Peabody College, 1942.

Pace, Robert F., and Christopher A. Bjornsen. "Adolescent Honor and College Student Behavior in the Old South." *Southern Cultures* 6 (Fall 200): 9–28.

Pak, Michael S., "The Yale Report of 1828: A New Reading and New Implications." *History of Education Quarterly* 48 (February 2008): 30–57.

Parrish, Laura Frances. "Books Read by Members of the Philanthropic Society and Their Correlation with Debate Topics, 1828–1832." M.S.L.S. thesis, University of North Carolina at Chapel Hill, 1979.

Peterkin, Darryl Lynn. "'Lux, Libertas, and Learning': The First State University and the Transformation of North Carolina, 1789–1816." Ph.D. diss., Princeton University, 1995.

Potter, David. "The Literary Society." In *History of Speech Education in America,* edited by Karl R. Wallace, 238–58. New York: Appleton-Century-Crofts, 1954.

Ray, Angela G. "The Permeable Public: Rituals of Citizenship in Antebellum Men's Debating Clubs." *Argumentation & Advocacy* 41 (Summer 2004): 1–16.

Reckford, Joseph K. L. "The Dialectic and Philanthropic Societies Portraits, 1795–1868." Honors thesis, University of North Carolina, 1981.

Rudolph, Frederick. "Neglect of Students as a Historical Tradition." In *The College and the Student: An Assessment of Relationships and Responsibilities in Undergraduate Education by Administrators, Faculty Members, and Public Officials,* edited by Lawrence E. Dennis and Joseph F. Kauffman, 47–58. Washington, D.C.: American Council on Education, 1966.

Scott, Alison M. "'This Cultivated Mind': Reading and Identity in a Nineteenth-Century Reader." In *Reading Acts: U.S. Readers' Interactions with Literature, 1800–1950,* edited by Barbara Ryan and Amy M. Thomas, 29–52. Knoxville: University of Tennessee Press, 2002.

Sicherman, Barbara. "Reading and Ambition: M. Carey Thomas and Female Heroism." *American Quarterly* 45 (March 1993): 73–103.

———. "Reading and Middle-Class Identity in Victorian America: Cultural Consumption, Conspicuous and Otherwise." In *Reading Acts: U.S. Readers' Interactions with*

Literature, 1800–1950, edited by Barbara Ryan and Amy M. Thomas, 137–60. Knoxville: University of Tennessee Press, 2002.

Storr, Richard. "The Education of History: Some Impressions." *Harvard Educational Review* 31 (Spring 1961): 124–35.

Stowe, Steven M. "The Rhetoric of Authority: The Making of Social Values in Planter Family Correspondence." *Journal of American History* 73 (March 1987): 916–33.

Sugrue, Michael. "'We Desired Our Future Rulers to Be Educated Men': South Carolina College, the Defense of Slavery, and the Development of Secessionist Politics." In *The American College in the Nineteenth Century*, edited by Roger L. Geiger, 91–114. Nashville: Vanderbilt University Press, 2000.

Thomas, Amy M. "Reading the Silences: Documenting the History of the American Tract Society Readers in the Antebellum South." In *Reading Acts: U.S. Readers' Interactions with Literature, 1800–1950*, edited by Barbara Ryan and Amy M. Thomas, 107–36. Knoxville: University of Tennessee Press, 2002.

Tolley, Kim. "Science for Ladies, Classics for Gentlemen: A Comparative Analysis of Scientific Subjects in the Curricula of Boys' and Girls' Secondary Schools in the United States, 1794–1850." *History of Education Quarterly* 36 (Summer 1996): 129–53.

Tomlinson, Stephen, and Kevin Windham. "Northern Piety and Southern Honor: Alva Woods and the Problem of Discipline at the University of Alabama, 1831–1837." *Perspectives on the History of Higher Education* 25 (2006): 1–42.

Traister, Bryce. "Academic Viagra: The Rise of American Masculinity Studies." *American Quarterly* 52 (June 2000): 274–304.

Valentine, Patrick M. "Libraries and Print Culture in Early North Carolina." *North Carolina Historical Review* 82 (July 2005): 293–325.

Wagoner, Jennings. "Honor and Dishonor at Mr. Jefferson's University: The Antebellum Years." *History of Education Quarterly* 26 (Summer 1986): 155–79.

Wakelyn, Jon L. "Antebellum College Life and the Relations between Fathers and Sons." In *The Web of Southern Social Relations: Women, Family, & Education*, edited by Walter J. Fraser Jr. et al., 107–26. Athens: University of Georgia Press, 1985.

Wall, Charles Coleman Jr. "Students and Student Life at the University of Virginia, 1825 to 1861." Ph.D. diss., University of Virginia, 1978.

Warren, Donald. "The Wonderful Worlds of the Education of History." *American Educational History Journal* 32 (March 2005): 108–14.

Watson, Harry L. "The Man with the Dirty Black Beard: Race, Class, and Schools in the Antebellum South." *Journal of the Early Republic* 32 (Spring 2012): 1–26.

Westbrook, Evelyn. "Debating Both Sides: What Nineteenth-Century College Literary Societies Can Teach Us about Critical Pedagogies." *Rhetoric Review* 21 (2002): 339–56.

Williams, Timothy J. "Confronting a 'Wilderness of Sin': Student Writing, Sex, and Manhood in the Antebellum South." *Perspectives on the History of Higher Education* 27 (2008): 1–31.

———. "Literary Societies at Wake Forest College." Honors thesis, Wake Forest University, 2002.

Winterer, Caroline. "Victorian Antigone: Classicism and Women's Education in America, 1840–1900." *American Quarterly* 53 (March 2001): 70–93.

Woods, Carly Sarah. "Women Debating Society: Negotiating Difference in Historical Argument Cultures." Ph.D. diss., University of Pittsburgh, 2010.

Yacovone, Donald. "'Surpassing the Love of Women': Victorian Manhood and the Language of Fraternal Love." In *A Shared Experience: Men, Women, and the History of Gender*, edited by Laura McCall and Donald Yacovone, 195–221. New York: New York University Press, 1998.

Young, Pearl J. "Religious Coming of Age among Students at Antebellum Georgia's Evangelical Colleges." M.A. thesis, Emory University, 2010.

Zagarri, Rosemarie. "Morals, Manners, and the Republican Mother." *American Quarterly* 44 (June 1992): 192–215.

Index

student, 28, 32, 34, 199; venality of, 111, 160–67, 207, 246 (n. 66), 252 (n. 12)
Dwight, Timothy, Jr., 230 (n. 90)

Eastman, Carolyn, 74
Edgeworth, Maria, 106, 114
Education: academies, 22, 77; classical education, 19, 48, 56, 59, 70, 73; among peers, 41, 46, 82, 88, 108; and upward mobility, 26, 140
Elizabeth I, 136, 138
Elliott, Henry, 83–84, 88–89, 188, 189
Eloquence, 76–77, 78–79, 85–86, 87, 173
Emancipation, 156, 191, 193
Entrance examinations, 22
Erskine, Thomas, 85
Evangelicalism, 36, 75–76, 123, 144

Family relationships, 22, 24
Farnham, Christie Anne, 116, 215–16 (n. 2)
Faust, Drew Gilpin, 215 (n. 2)
Fetter (Mr.), 49
Fielding, Henry, 114, 117
Flirtation, 151, 154, 159
Forney, Daniel, 89, 90
Foster, A. G., 142
Foster, Wilbur, 56, 62
Fox-Genovese, Elizabeth, 54, 207, 228 (n. 50), 231–32 (n. 115)
Franklin, Benjamin, 85, 129, 136
Franklin College. See University of Georgia
Franklin Street (Chapel Hill), 27
Frémont, John C., 195
Frugality, 25, 53, 71
Fuller, Edwin W., 52

Garrett, Thomas Miles, 5, 34, 145, 207; readings of, 58, 97, 103, 107, 111–13, 116, 143–44; as UNC student, 26, 51, 52, 63, 80
Gaston, William, 125, 193
Gender roles, 54, 69, 70, 74, 76, 78, 140, 168, 208. See also Manliness; Moral philosophy: sex and gender; Patriarchy; Women
Genovese, Eugene D., 54, 207, 228 (n. 50), 231–32 (n. 115)

Gerrard Hall, 28, 199
Gleason, Maud W., 79
Glover, Lorri, 9, 25, 39, 78, 85, 196, 216 (n. 5), 244 (n. 11)
Goldsmith, Oliver, 122
Goodrich, S. G., 99
Gracchi, 59
Graham, Sylvester, 159
Grant, Daniel Lindsey, 214
Green, Jennifer R., 3, 42, 202
Green, William Mercer, 36, 45, 81, 146
Greenberg, Amy S., 5
Greenberg, Kenneth S., 45, 90, 129, 217 (n. 19)
Greenblatt, Stephen, 19

Haigh, William H., 43
Hall, James, 84
Hall, Thomas, 89
Hamlin, Richard, 56
Hannibal, 59
Harding, Thomas S., 219 (n. 50), 237 (nn. 37, 40)
Hargrave, Jesse, 137, 197
Hargrave, Jonathan Lindsay, 180
Harris, William White, 139
Harvard College, 17, 23, 32, 128
Hawkins, John Davis, 142
Hawkins, Philemon, 142
Hazing, 33
Hazlitt, William, 234 (n. 48)
Hedrick, Benjamin S., 195, 196
Helper, Hinton Rowan, 194
Hemphill, C. Dallett, 166
Henry, Patrick, 83
Henry, William Roberts, 83
Henry VIII, 138, 143
Hercules, 56–57, 65, 68, 127
Herodotus, 55
Heroism, 7, 15, 19, 58–59, 91, 113–14, 132, 136–37, 169, 219–20 (n. 57); as aspiration, 46, 56, 59–60, 67, 69, 121–22, 125–27, 147, 171; and manhood, 76, 78–79, 117, 134–35, 138–40, 206; potential for, 10, 11, 63, 75, 83, 113, 120, 141, 143, 146, 206; worship of, 19, 93–94, 114, 127–28
Hessiger, Rodney, 3

Hill, William, 87
Hodges, Sarah, 203
Holley, Augustus, 26
Holt, Eliza, 115
Homer, 52, 55, 78, 79, 142
Homesickness, 32
Honor, 32, 43–44, 50, 53, 115–16, 158–59, 162, 202
Hooper, William, 36, 38, 68, 127, 129
Horace, 55, 57, 101, 206, 207
Horton, George Moses, 155, 156
Houghton, Walter E., 12, 58, 126, 219–20 (n. 57)
Howe, Daniel Walker, 208
Hubbard, Fordyce, 103
Hume, David, 97, 142, 143–44
Humility, 81, 89, 90
Hunt, William C., 47
Hutcheson, Francis, 66

Indian Removal Act (1830), 187
Institute of 1770 (Harvard College), 185
Intellectual culture, 1, 2, 123, 208
Intellectual manhood, 6–15, 74, 79, 90–91, 200, 205; and college curricula, 6, 15, 20, 48, 50, 56, 60, 67, 73, 83–84, 169; and debate societies, 89, 107, 169–70, 173, 175–76; and emulation, 93, 171; icons of, 87, 134, 139; and mental and moral improvement, 40, 93, 111, 136; and mental maturity, 107, 197, 205; and peer influences, 41–42, 45–46, 88; and racial hierarchy, 120, 170, 206; and reading, 110, 136; and restraint, 18, 37, 39, 93, 98, 111, 169, 171; and self-discipline, 93, 111; societal role of, 15, 21, 49. See also Heroism: and manhood; Novels: as educational impediment
Intentional intellectualism, 1, 91, 93, 120, 122, 147, 206
Irving, Washington, 99, 114, 117, 137
Ivy, Virginius H., 89

Jabour, Anya, 9–10, 151, 154, 208, 216 (n. 7)
Jackson, Andrew, 126, 139, 140, 187
Jackson, Joseph John, 41
James, George Payne Rainsford, 114, 117
James, Hinton, 84
Jefferson, Thomas, 188

Jewett, Helen, 166
Johnson, Andrew, 85
Johnson, Lucious J., 43, 44, 226 (n. 110)
Johnson, Martha, 153
Johnson, Samuel, 76
Jones, Henry Francis, 49, 50, 52
Jones, John, 157
Jones, John D., 191, 192
Jones, Montezuma, 98, 158
Justice, Alexander, 138
Juvenal, 55

Keen, T. G., 6
Kelley, Mary, 208, 218 (n. 44)
Kennedy, John Pendleton, 119
Kett, Joseph F., 218 (n. 39)
Kingsbury, Theodore, 99, 137

Lafayette, Marquis de, 136
Language studies, 22, 23, 47, 54–60, 75, 77, 204, 228 (n. 40)
Lardner, Dionysius, 143
Leach, Julian, 65–66, 67
Lectures, 51–52, 58, 61, 64, 72, 81, 85, 94, 109, 226; on constitutional law, 72, 230–31 (n. 91); on mathematics and sciences, 61, 62, 63, 148, 229–30 (n. 80); as model of intellectual manhood, 50, 73
Lee, Rooney, 35
Legaré, Hugh, 87
Lenoir, Walter, 5, 25, 38, 55, 99, 106, 122, 153, 204
Leo X (pope), 136
Library catalogs, 104
Lindsay, Susan, 151, 152, 155, 204
Literary societies, 18, 39, 41–42, 46, 59, 93, 94, 181; and literary socialization, 10, 97, 98, 103, 107, 120; and literary taste, 10, 97, 101, 110. See also Dialectic Society; Philanthropic Society
Little, William, 98
Locke, John, 101, 127
London, Henry A., 24, 100
Longfellow, Henry Wadsworth, 122, 126, 128
Longstreet, Augustus Baldwin, 119
Lord, William, 140
Louis XVI, 138

Love letters, 94, 152, 157–58, 166
Love poetry, 154–55, 156
Lucretius, 101
Lystra, Karen, 149

Mackintosh, James, 142
Manhood. *See* Intellectual manhood;
    Manliness; Southern manhood
Manliness, 12, 59, 62, 78, 116, 205
Market Revolution, 93, 174
Marriage, 14, 94, 149–50, 160–61, 166,
    183–84, 244 (n. 9)
Marshall, John, 136, 137
Mary Queen of Scots, 136, 138, 139
Mason, Jonathan, 85
Mason, Thomas, 49
Masturbation, 144, 146, 159
Mayhs, Suky, 166
McAffee, Leroy, 128
McCurry, Stephanie, 173
McIver, Evander, 127, 128, 129
McLachlan, James, 39, 40, 57
Mental philosophy, 65–66, 67
Merritt, Alfred, 87
Middle class, 216–17 (n. 12), 235 (n. 3), 243–
    44 (n. 7), 246 (n. 66); education of, 3, 18;
    professions of, 2, 103, 201–2; values of,
    57, 91, 110, 149, 166–67
Miller, Henry Watkins, 129
Miller, Perry, 62
Miller, William, 130, 134
Milton, John, 85, 161
Miscegenation, 167, 189, 203, 252 (n. 12)
Missouri Compromise, 196
Mitchell, Donald Grant, 112
Mitchell, Elisha, 36, 47, 71–72, 154, 199,
    203, 232 (n. 117)
Mitchell, Ellen, 203
Monogenesis/polygenesis, 192
Moore, Thomas, 114, 161
Moral philosophy: curriculum of, 14,
    48, 65–66, 72, 130, 132, 176, 183, 200,
    204, 230 (n. 90), 231 (n. 93); and sex
    and gender, 68, 69; and slavery, 70, 71,
    192; textbooks on, 68, 71
More, Thomas, 143
Morehead, John Lindsay, 127
Morrisey, Thomas J., 199
Mossop, James, 84

Motier, Gilbert du. *See* Lafayette,
    Marquis de
Mullins, William Sidney, 5, 36, 203, 225
    (n. 109); honor of, 43, 45; oratory of,
    123, 199; readings of, 118–19, 142–43,
    144; relations of with women, 153, 159,
    164; religion of, 144–46; self-fashioning
    of, 140–42, 146, 147; as UNC student,
    43–45, 50, 81, 105, 118, 199
Murphey, Archibald Debow, 180, 181
Murray, Charles Augustus, 117, 152

Nancy Hilliard's Eagle Hotel, 29, 34, 153,
    200
Nash, Shepard K., 43, 44
Nationalism, 85, 118, 137, 178, 197. *See also*
    Didactic nationalism
Native Americans, 118, 140, 174, 179, 187–
    90, 195, 198, 250 (n. 54). *See also* Indian
    Removal Act (1830)
Neal, Nathan, 29
Nelms, Joseph, 165
New East, 28
Newton, Isaac, 127
New West, 28
Nichols, Elisabeth, 112
Nicholson, Alfred, 110
North, Erasmus, 108
North Carolina General Assembly, 25
Nott, Eliphalet, 85
Novels, 104, 109, 118, 160, 235 (n. 3), 238
    (n. 67); as educational impediment,
    109, 110–13, 136; as educational tool,
    112, 113, 114–17, 120, 122, 136; as pastime,
    32, 98, 106; popularity of, 109, 111, 113,
    119, 136, 142, 152
Nullification Crisis, 19

O'Brien, Michael, 111, 207
Odysseus, 127, 233 (n. 23)
Old East, 28
Olmstead, Denison, 51
Olmstead, Frederick Law, 179
Oratory, 74, 76, 78–81, 85; debating
    societies, 22, 87; and manhood, 83, 90,
    170, 173, 175; oratorical ideal, 75, 76, 77
Osborne, Edwin, 84
Ovid, 55
Owen, John, 127

Owen, William H., 110, 111, 136, 194, 196
Ownby, Ted, 218 (n. 34)

Pace, Robert F., 9
Paintings, 122, 123, 166. *See also*
    Dialectic Society: portrait collection
    of; Philanthropic Society: portrait
    collection of
Paley, William, 68, 230 (n. 90), 230-31
    (n. 91)
Parley, Peter, 99
Paternalism, 184, 189, 195
Patriarchy, 203, 208
Patriotism, 79, 87, 138, 191, 192
Patterson, Giles, 141
Patton, James, 57
Pearson, Richard, 153
Pearson, Richmond M., 53, 203
Pedagogy, 9, 14, 18, 20, 54, 108, 209, 226
    (n. 9); and deference to authority,
    50, 51; and memorization, 49, 55; and
    morality, 70, 74; and recitation, 48, 50,
    77; and self-improvement, 19, 49, 205.
    See also Lectures; Recitation
Periodical literature, 11, 76, 98, 100, 109,
    120, 142, 178
Person Hall, 28, 31
Peter the Great, 136, 138
Pettigrew, Charles, 53
Pettigrew, John, 84
Pflugrad-Jackisch, Ami, 8
Philanthropic Society, 28, 39, 43, 46, 106,
    181-82; biography collection of, 136,
    147; debates of, 180, 184, 187-88, 196;
    library of, 55, 80, 97, 103-4, 113-14, 142;
    portrait collection of, 128-29, 130; and
    public speaking, 82-90
Phillips, Cornelia, 157
Phillips, James, 50, 61, 62, 63, 64, 157,
    229-30 (n. 80)
Philomathean Society (Greensboro), 177,
    195, 247-48 (n. 21), 251 (n. 70)
Pinckney, Thomas, 87
Pitt, William, 83, 85
Planters: community approval of, 21,
    54, 167; culture of, 26, 56, 173, 202;
    education of, 2, 3, 22, 48, 216 (n. 10);
    political power of, 181, 200

Pliny, 101
Pocahontas, 140
Polk, James Hilliard, 52, 156, 175-76
Polk, James Knox, 74, 77, 127, 132-34
Polygamy, 183
Pope, Alexander, 66, 233 (n. 23)
Pornography, 35
Princeton College, 23
Private writings, 8, 94, 100
Proslavery sentiment, 71, 72, 127, 174, 194,
    198
Prosser, Gabriel, 191
Prostitution, 115, 150, 162, 163-68, 207, 246
    (n. 66)
Puberty, 31
Public speaking, 81-82, 89, 139. *See also*
    Oratory

Quintilian, 78, 80

Racial mixing, 37
Radcliffe, Ann, 106
Railroads, 27
Randolph Macon College, 26
Rape, 150, 166, 168
Reading, 11, 47, 67, 77, 94, 108, 143-45,
    147, 207, 235 (n. 3); of biographies,
    136-37, 142, 147; and coursework,
    50, 52, 65, 80-81, 86-87, 103, 207; as
    cultural practice of manhood, 10, 93,
    97-101, 108, 113, 121; literary societies,
    106, 107; self-imagining, 113, 114; social
    culture, 51, 69, 99. *See also* Novels;
    Periodical literature
Recitation, 31-32, 36, 49-50, 55, 75, 77;
    and bourgeois values, 50, 73; and
    intellectual manhood, 48; pedagogical
    value of, 31-32, 36, 49-50, 75, 77; and
    student reactions, 52-53, 55, 61
Reconstruction, 204, 205
Reform: educational, 64, 68, 202, 251
    (n. 7); penal, 180, 181, 248 (nn. 28, 29);
    political, 174, 179-83, 248-49 (n. 31)
Regionalism, 171, 174. *See also*
    Sectionalism
Reid, Thomas, 66, 67
Religious life, 35, 36, 37, 45. *See also*
    Christianity

Republicans, 205
Restrained manhood, 5, 45, 48, 69, 109, 217 (n. 19); as intellectual expression, 8, 18, 52, 54, 205; and morality, 36–37, 56, 65, 149–50
Reynolds, David, 94
Rice, William D., 34
Richardson, John, 118, 119
Robertson, Mary, 158
Romanticism, 58, 123, 132
Romantic love, 94, 114, 149, 152, 154, 157–58, 160, 166, 168
Room and board, 24, 25
Ross, Jesse Goodwin, 99
Rotundo, E. Anthony, 218 (n. 39)
Rudolph, Frederick, 65
Ruffin, Thomas, 127

Saunders, Joseph Hubbard, 51
Scales, Erasmus, 138
Scott, Walter, 114, 115, 126, 136, 139, 207
Scottish realism, 66, 217 (n. 23)
Seawell, William, 46
Secessionism, 72, 197
Second Party System, 76, 178
Sectionalism, 119, 174, 196–98. See also Regionalism
Self, 23, 66, 89, 93, 121, 127; fashioning of, 93, 129, 140–41, 146; improvement of, 19, 93, 125–26
Seneca, 122
Sessoms, John, 27
Sessoms, Preston H., 27
Sex, 68–69, 95, 115, 146, 150, 160–61, 207, 243–44 (n. 7). See also Masturbation; Prostitution
Sexually transmitted disease, 164
Shakespeare, William, 97, 100
Sheppard, James Biddle, 173
Sheridan, Richard Brinsley, 83
Sherrod, Benjamin, 84
Simms, William Gilmore, 6, 114, 117–18, 119
Simpson, Thomas, 229 (n. 79)
Sims, Alexander, 183
Skepticism, 63, 64
Slavery, 190–96, 198, 245 (n. 33); at colleges/universities, 220 (n. 68), 222 (n. 33); and westward expansion, 195, 196. See also African Americans: enslaved blacks; Antislavery sentiment; Proslavery sentiment
Sledstein, Burton, 31
Smith, John, 140
Smith, John B., 106
Smith Hall, 28, 103
Smoking (cigar or pipe), 32
Social class, 19, 111, 167, 202
Socrates, 127
Sons of Temperance, 34
Sophocles, 55
South Building, 28, 31, 106
South Carolina College, 17, 70, 72, 141
Southern manhood, 19, 112, 120, 130, 146, 150, 205–7, 218 (n. 34)
Southrons, 23
Speech education, 74–75, 77–82, 87
Stedman, John Madison, 108
Steele, W. L., 142
Steward Hall, 29
Stewart, Dugald, 66, 67
Storr, Richard, 220 (n. 66)
Stowe, Harriet Beecher, 119
Stowe, Steven M., 11, 125
Stringfellow, Thornton, 7
Student life, 23, 32; carousing, 34, 111; dormitories, 28, 29; drinking, 32–33, 35, 38, 43, 144, 146, 176, 207, 223 (n. 59); dueling, 35, 44, 45; fighting, 32, 34, 35, 40, 111, 146, 223 (n. 59); fraternities, 8, 13, 39, 40, 220 (n. 65), 225 (n. 92); gambling, 32, 38, 43, 111; pranking, 32–33, 44, 166; serenading, 154, 244 (n. 26); sprees, 34, 164, 166, 224 (n. 69); swearing, 32, 35, 36, 41, 43, 144, 224 (n. 61). See also Courtship; Flirtation; Religious life
Study habits, 52, 54
Sue, Eugene, 97, 114, 117
Suffrage, 179, 181–82
Sugrue, Michael, 72
Summerell, Joseph John, 5, 101, 111, 117, 148–49, 154, 199, 203
Swain, David Lowry, 25, 34, 36, 38, 47, 66, 71, 72, 127, 130, 131, 132, 134, 180, 193, 199

CPSIA information can be obtained at www.ICGtesting.com
Printed in the USA
LVOW07s1706070916

503623LV00003B/172/P

9 781469 618395